AF505881

The Art of Walking

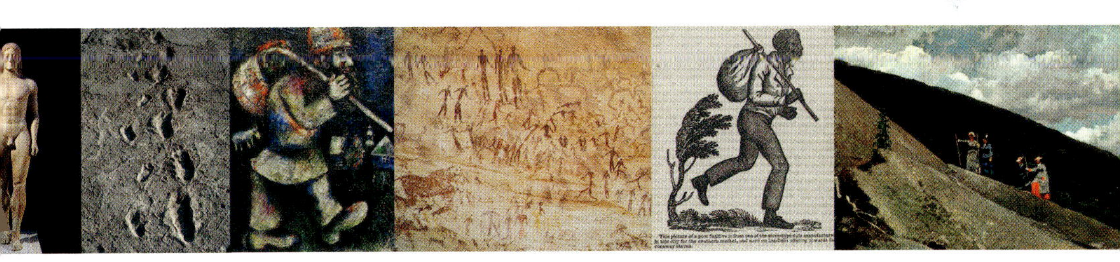

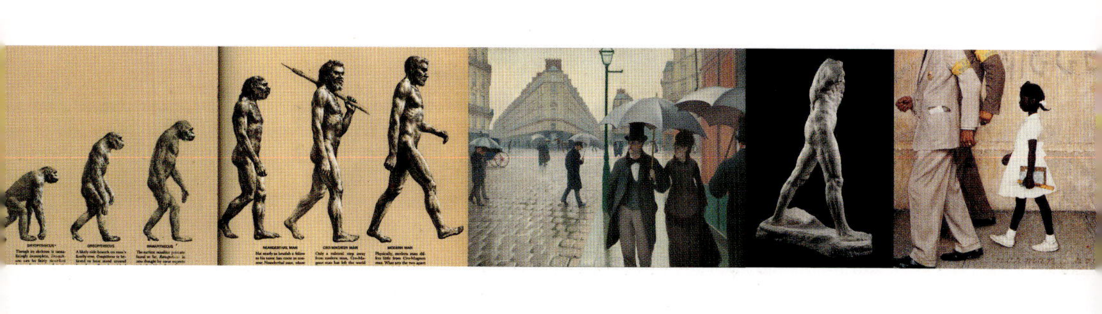

The Art of Walking A History in 100 Images

William Chapman Sharpe

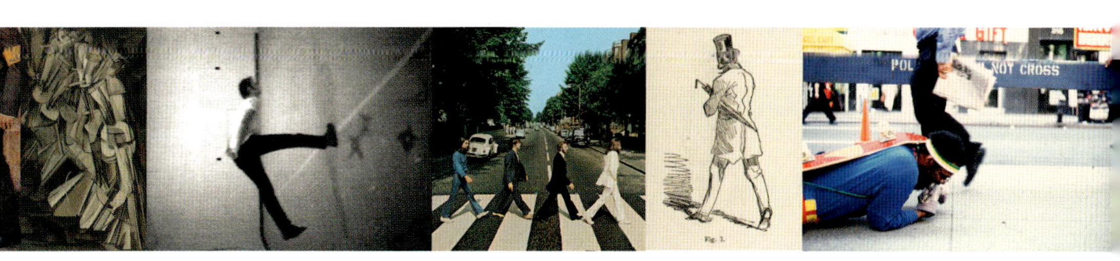

Yale University Press
New Haven and London

Published with support from the Fund established in memory of Oliver Baty Cunningham, a distinguished graduate of the Class of 1917, Yale College, Captain, 15th United States Field Artillery, born in Chicago September 17, 1894, and killed while on active duty near Thiaucourt, France, September 17, 1918, the twenty-fourth anniversary of his birth.

Library of Congress Control Number: 2022946526
ISBN 978-0-300-26684-9

A catalogue record for this book is available from the British Library.
This paper meets the requirements of ANSI/NISO z39.48-1992 (Permanence of Paper).

10 9 8 7 6 5 4 3 2 1

yalebooks.com/art

Designed by Jeff Wincapaw
Set in Sentinel type
Printed in China through Asia Pacific Offset

Jacket illustrations: *(front top)* Jeremy Wood, *My Ghost (Sixteen Years of Mapping My Life in London with GPS)*, 2016 (see pp. 207, 251); *(details, image strip, left to right)* Vincent van Gogh, *Shoes*, 1886 (see pp. 121, 236); Claude Monet, *Woman with a Parasol: Madame Monet and Her Son*, 1875 (see pp. 106, 234); Charles Chaplin in *The Tramp*, 1915 (see pp. 143, 239); Masaccio, *Expulsion from the Garden of Eden*, 1425 (see pp. 33, 223); John Cleese, "The Ministry of Silly Walks," *Monty Python's Flying Circus*, 1970 (see pp. 183, 246); F. O. C. Darley, "Walker Drawn from Stereoscopic View," in Oliver Wendell Holmes, "The Physiology of Walking," 1859 (see pp. 98, 233); Gustave Caillebotte, *Paris Street; Rainy Day*, 1877 (see pp. 109, 235); Raphael, *The School of Athens*, 1509–11 (see pp. 42, 43, 225); Giuseppe Pellizza da Volpedo, *The Fourth Estate/The Path of Workers*, 1899–1901 (see pp. 133, 238); Eugène Delacroix, *Liberty Leading the People*, 1830 (see pp. 118, 236); Louis-Léopold Boilly, *Pay to Pass (Passez-Payez)*, c. 1803 (see pp. 77, 230).

To My Walking Companions,
Past, Present, and Yet to Come

By tracking our foot-prints in the sand,

we track our own nature in its wayward course,

and steal a glance upon it, when it never dreams

of being so observed.

—Nathaniel Hawthorne, 1842

Contents

Acknowledgments

I begin by thanking my friend and colleague Nathalie Cochoy of the University of Toulouse, who first showed me that walking is indeed a field of study. Little did I know then how far out of sight that field stretches, or how thoroughly our joint love of cities is bound up in the topic. I hope she enjoys this excursion! Next I would like to recognize my Barnard and Columbia students, who have made BC3146, "Walk This Way," into a highlight of my teaching career. I salute you for the energy, ideas, and wide range of experiences you have brought to our discussions. Also in the Barnard context, no walk in my life has been a more honored ritual than the almost annual pilgrimage to the urn of an Amiable Child, taken in the treasured company of Emily Elliot and Caroline Ranald, BC '87.

In Great Britain, I benefited from participating in two memorable events, the Deveron Projects Slow Marathon of 2018 and the "Walking's New Movements" conference at the University of Plymouth in 2019. I thank Phil Smith for the invitation to the latter, and for the opportunity to be involved in the ensuing publication, *Walking Bodies*.

At the start of my journey as an apprentice walking scholar, I learned much about art walking from strolls with Moira Williams, Elisabetta Rattolino, Valerie Mendelson, Bibi Calderaro, and Leonie Dunlop. On jaunts in Britain, Blake Morris generously shared his walking knowledge and artistic perspective, along with a few jolly pints. His good cheer and helpful analysis have carried over into our correspondence.

My formal research was made possible by two fellowships that brought me valuable opportunities to study, lecture, and learn from illustrious colleagues. First, I thank the Fulbright Commission and the University of Edinburgh for enabling me to work in one of the cradles of Romantic walking, Scotland, and while there to enjoy the wonderful hospitality of the Institute for Advanced Study in the Humanities in its cozy building on the Meadows in Edinburgh. On the other side of the Channel, I am deeply grateful to the Paris-based Columbia University Institute for Ideas and Imagination, which made it possible for me to haunt the legendary streets of Lutèce and retrace the steps of so many artists and writers who have found their way into this book. Special thanks to Mark Mazower, Marie d'Origny, James Allen, and Eve Grinstead for making the institute the best possible place to stroll out from and saunter back to. Thanks also to my fellow Fellows, whose insights enriched my understanding each step of the way, in particular Fiona Sze-Lorrain, Ralph Ghoche, and James Graham.

These paragraphs would not be complete without mention of the good friends in whose company I have walked through landscapes both spectacular and sodden:

Martin Bradshaw and Pilar Socarras, David and Mary Kidd, Stephanie and Peter Rae, Jean-Louis Lacordaire, Adeline Lacordaire, Francois Bernardeau, Barbara Peers, and Thierry Niau.

On the writing journey itself, my sister Elizabeth Sharpe improved the manuscript with her eagle historical eye. Chris Baswell shared his medieval lore and valuable perspectives. Mark Getlein brought his immense art-historical knowledge to bear on my pictorial insufficiencies. And Peter Platt again proved that I can't write a book without him.

In the home stretch, the two anonymous readers for Yale University Press provided many helpful suggestions, as did my editor Amy Canonico, who deftly poked and prodded the essays into their final shape. Patrick Hazlewood Sharpe secured the images with resourcefulness and good cheer. The production team at Yale University Press put all the stepping stones in just the right place.

Finally, deepest gratitude to my closest, most essential walking companions, whether on a hike through a forest full of trolls or up to a glacier lake, whether tromping around a chateau in France or rushing across the Columbia campus in New York. For suggestions, ideas, visual expertise, and making it all better, merci Alexander, William, Patrick, and Heather.

Introduction

What does a walk look like? Artists have asked themselves this question for thousands of years, photographers and filmmakers for less than two hundred. But no matter the moment or the medium, they have sought to capture something special: how the human race, each member of it possessing a unique way of moving, makes its way on two feet. Ever since humans began to draw pictures of their own bodies, about ten thousand years ago, walking has been one of their most fundamental subjects. The history of walking is woven into Western visual culture, which has in turn been continuously responsive to walking's changing conditions. Collectively, ambulatory images reveal that the history of art and the history of walking are intertwined, in more ways than one might think, shaping each other over the course of centuries.

A new way of walking generally means a new way of representing it, which in turn has influenced how viewers regard subsequent acts of walking. The dual purpose of this book is to offer a visual history of walking that is also a history of how walking has permeated Western visual culture from its very beginnings. Whether decorating a cave wall or a papal apartment, whether filming pedestrians or photographing protest marchers, those who represent walking translate fleeting shapes and sensations into images that measure a double imprint. They map the impact of the world on the walker no less than the impact of the walker on the world.

For walking is not only one of the most natural things humans do. It is also one of the most culturally determined. Bipedal motion may be biologically programmed in our species, but the ways and places in which people walk are deeply conditioned by an array of social forces. This makes walking a representational form par excellence; a walk taken is never just about itself. From gait, dress, and footwear to path chosen, obstacles met, and destination sought, every aspect of walking is shaped by environmental conditions and social practices.

For centuries, artists have explored the symbolically freighted roles that a walk can play—in Adam and Eve's expulsion from the Garden of Eden, for example, or Jesus's carrying of his cross, or a pilgrim's progress toward a distant shrine. As artistic expression evolves, a walk may dazzle with its gloriously framed complexity—Raphael's *School of Athens*—or it may look like "an explosion in a shingle factory"—Marcel Duchamp's *Nude Descending a Staircase*—or it may turn into a tangle of light, an itinerary tracked by GPS on a computer screen—Jeremy Wood's *My Ghost*.

Many walking scenes artistically frame historically significant events, such as the Women's March on Versailles that altered the course of the French Revolution, or the choreographed goose steps that Nazis took through Nuremberg in

1934. Sometimes the artistic medium is itself historic, as in Eadweard Muybridge's Edenic stop-motion photographs of naked walkers, or the Lumière brothers' first films of crowds on city streets. Some walking images record new styles of locomotion, such as teetering on high heels, or strolling in the first public parks, or responding to the command of a traffic light, or even gingerly stepping toward the untrodden surface of the moon. Some images can inspire admiration and emulation, such as those capturing the spirited steps of civil rights activists. And some evoke emotions beyond the reach of words, such as the photographs documenting the death marches of Native Americans and European Jews.

The Art of Walking: A History in 100 Images follows a path that winds between images of walking history and the history of walking images. Those presented here tell the story of Western walking in chronological order, from the first hominin footsteps on our planet to the first human footsteps on the moon. And then beyond, into subsequent social and technological turbulence and the pandemic walking of the present moment. The images bear witness to a social and aesthetic history that shaped medieval pilgrimages and royal processions, city parks and country estates, performance art and fashion shows. They evoke the larger social forces that have shaped walking behavior, from the etiquette of nobles to the rise of the shopping mall and the ubiquity of the mobile phone. Who planned out walking tours at Versailles? Where was the first self-guided nature trail? How did jaywalking become a crime? Why do Britons have a "right to roam"? The answers to these questions emerge in the course of exploring how societies respond to people who walk not only because they have to, but because they want to.

Why focus on walking? There is widespread agreement among scientists that, evolutionarily speaking, bipedal motion—walking upright—is what makes humans human. About 3.8 million years ago, a bipedal hominin took its first steps, setting off a chain reaction that increased cranial capacity and brain power while freeing the hands for carrying, killing, and creating. Capitalizing on the energy efficiency of upright locomotion, protohumans began the migrations that would eventually make humans the farthest-flung of all species. About three hundred thousand years ago, anatomically modern people, *Homo sapiens*, began to spread across the globe from Africa, in the process developing "behavioral modernity," the bundle of essential human traits that includes cooking, complex language, and the ability to make tools and images. The capacity of humans to depict themselves in ritual moments, or going about their daily lives, leads inevitably to the representation of walking.

Walking is so central to humanity's sense of itself that we use footsteps to describe our development as individuals and as a species. Since the nineteenth century, the peopling of Planet Earth has been pictured as not only a geographical walk out of Africa but a chronological walk forward into anatomical modernity. In 1863 "Darwin's bulldog," Thomas Henry Huxley, explained Charles Darwin's

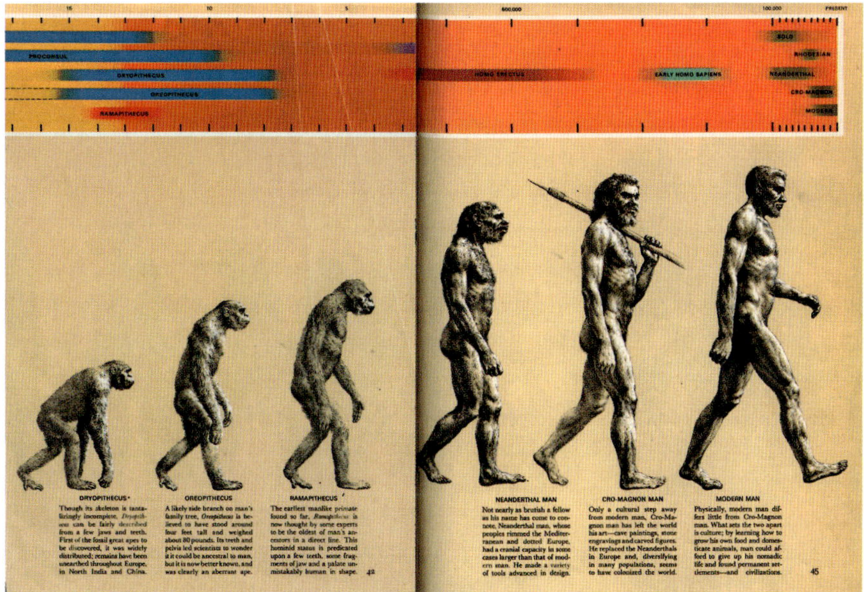

Rudolph Franz Zallinger, "The Road to Homo Sapiens," 1965

theory of evolution to the general public by depicting a range of primate skeletons as if they were walking, left to right, in an evolutionary progression toward the modern human.

In 1965 Rudolph Franz Zallinger made the evolutionary walk even more explicit. His foldout illustration "The Road to Homo Sapiens" showed smaller, stooping primates succeeded by taller, more erect hominids taking ever longer steps. Reaching a popular audience of millions in the Time-Life book *Early Man*, Zallinger's frieze became perhaps the most famous scientific illustration ever made.

Why a picture book? The relatively new field of walking studies involves scholars in every domain, from anthropology to urban studies, as they pursue a holistic understanding of the ways people navigate physical and social space. But much of the attention remains focused on what might be called "worded walking"—the poems, novels, travelogues, essays, scriptures, and rules of behavior that have shaped the contours of walking since ancient times. This is due in large part to the literary legacy of the Romantic walker. Since the late eighteenth century, writers have assigned to this usually masculine figure a rich interiority, a restless self-consciousness. A solitary wanderer who came to prominence in the works of Jean-Jacques Rousseau and William Wordsworth, the Romantic walker goes forth into the natural world to learn as much about himself as about the terrain he crosses.

The emphasis on the interior life of Romantic walkers and their successors, the urban strollers known as flâneurs, has been so strong that we risk losing sight of the expressiveness of the walking body itself. Critics have noted the role of walking as a social phenomenon and a creative form of personal self-expression, and how walking has become a vibrant part of contemporary artistic practice. But few have traveled across the broader historical terrain to consider what visual media can add to our understanding of how people walk, and why.

This book attempts to loosen the hold that words have on walking. It is time to give the visual record its due. Too often, images of walkers have been treated as illustrations of texts rather than expressive statements in their own right. We not only learn from images basic information—the walker's gender, health, class, age, race, and occupation—but also gather clues about the physical and cultural land-scape where this walk takes place, what it signifies for its artist and audience, and where it may take them on a social or spiritual plane. Paying attention to the visual walker shifts the emphasis from verbalized imagination to the dynamic interaction of body and world. It reveals the ways in which artists have confronted an ongoing challenge: how to represent a body and mind in motion. The walking image is not a mere illustration of social and artistic history but an active part of that history, which is incomplete without it.

Why one hundred images? I found I could embark on this long journey only in short steps. Not only is the distance daunting, but there is no clear path to take. There is as yet no consensus about great walking painters as there is about the lead-ing writers on walking, nor is there a recognized body of great walking moments, iconic images that instantly define the high points in human locomotion. While current literary histories of walking move confidently through a range of times, practices, and influential personalities, from pilgrims and poets to flâneurs and psychogeographers, the visual record unfolds in a less predictable way.

The challenge lies in walking's variousness. Because it is fundamental to human life and culture, the act of walking contains all the contradictions therein. Walking is a matter of processions and protests, dogged labor and poetic self-discovery, the nature hike and the street crossing. It can be a liberating force that is nonetheless tightly bound to social conventions. Walking images show us virtue and transgres-sion, liberation and punishment, the soldiers' march toward destruction and the lovers' promenade toward the birth of future generations. Walking spells both free-dom and constraint, solitude and solidarity. Some people walk to join with others, others walk to flee them.

Since no one road can take us through the history of walking, I have chosen to present its visual history as a limited series of images that are still numerous enough to capture the larger motions of walking's cultural and artistic impact. Each essay foregrounds the visual elements that makes the image a milestone in itself, a valuable step toward our understanding of walking's evolution as a socially complex and aesthetically compelling activity. Roman footwear, landscaped gardens, shopping arcades, and the invention of hiking trails and crosswalks and walkathons—all have their own surprising narratives that lend depth to classic scenes of rural ramblers and protest marchers, urban crowds and isolated wanderers.

The images that appear here have been selected on the basis of their visual energy, the way they show the maker grappling with new ways of walking and new means of representation, at the same time that they reveal the central concerns about walking in their era. They are presented in the order of their making, so that the reader can see how evolving changes in technology, artistic technique, and social attitudes may influence each other. When in the later 1870s, for example, Winslow Homer, Claude Monet, and Gustave Caillebotte were painting memorable pictures of women walking, competitive walking was the world's most popular spectator sport, and a woman, Ada Anderson, had just equaled the male record of walking fifteen hundred miles in a thousand hours.

Any individual walk, from a step around the garden to a great feat of endurance, participates in the larger march of humanity toward its ever-elusive goal. The next few paragraphs sketch out a map of where the trail has twisted and turned so far, offering some orientation points for the visual journey that lies ahead.

The earliest paved or wooden pathways date from six thousand years ago, about the time of the invention of the wheel. Shortly after that, detailed walking figures, apparently engaged in hunting or sacred rites, appear in various places worldwide, molded, drawn, or carved in stone. And with them comes hierarchy. The Egyptian bas-relief the Narmer Palette (circa 3000 BCE) shows by figure size that in a procession, some walkers are more important than others.

Influenced by the bas-reliefs of the pharaohs, ancient Greeks created three-dimensional kouroi from about 600 BCE, each statue representing a young man taking a decisive step forward. Making no distinction between the bodies of gods and humans, the Greeks rapidly developed the skill to carve and cast figures that demonstrated the physical beauty they admired. By the classical period in the fifth century BCE, these figures celebrated human movement to the point that they lent it an almost divine aspect.

Judeo-Christian scripture gives travel on foot a central place. Starting with Adam and Eve's expulsion from Eden, the Hebrew Bible is preoccupied by migration, especially the incessant travels of Abraham, the crossing of the Red Sea by Moses and his followers, and the forty years wandering in the desert on the way to the Promised Land. The Christian gospels recenter the journey of a walking people around the travels of just one individual. They stress the peripatetic preaching of Jesus, his carrying of the cross, and his post-resurrection journey to Emmaus, elements that make every walk into a potential imitation of Christ. These devotional acts can be local (stations of the cross) or long-distance (pilgrimages to Rome or Santiago or any shrine whose holiness beckons). Using this peripatetic framework, art from the Middle Ages onward depicts Christianity as a religion in motion.

If medieval walkers saw their time on earth as a lifelong journey to another world, less humble Renaissance walkers promenaded in this world to display their social status. As emphasis shifted from the spiritual to the worldly, monarchs, aristocrats, courtiers, and the wealthy populated images of gardens and galleries, performing elaborate rituals designed to confirm their own importance. With their sorties came rules for how to dress, how to turn a corner in company, how to progress in a stately manner, and above all, how not to look like a servant by rushing, slouching, dragging along, or carrying anything practical.

When landscape art emerged during the seventeenth and eighteenth centuries, trudging peasants filled genre scenes while landowners stood proudly for their portraits amid their gardens and fields. But by the early nineteenth century both groups gave way to more dynamic images of middle-class explorers of wilder places. The figure who has come to be called the Romantic walker, a person who walks by choice, is shown reveling not only in natural scenery but also in the corresponding spiritual and psychological elevation that a vigorous walk can bring.

It is hard to overstate the importance of the cultural shift that allowed recreational walking, walking "for its own sake," to emerge as a highly valued practice. If earlier eras had seen walks taken by nonlaborers as displays of devotion or social status, henceforth the deliberate decision to walk, when one might ride or rest, became indicative of a quest for personal fulfillment. As the Industrial Revolution made speed and efficiency central to profit, rebellious walkers created their own subversive form of manufacture. They slowed down.

Instead of producing from the land, Romantic walkers became worksites in themselves, internalizing the growth that hitherto had been the duty of crops and herds. Their physical labor did not cultivate the soil but generated healthy bodies. They did not obtain raw materials and organic goods from the earth, but extracted spiritual nourishment from the mere sight of the countryside. And they used their brains not for better methods of farming but for writing or painting or composing works that would transmit their sensations to a larger market of potential landscape consumers. The increasing presence of walkers on the hills and in the valleys, thanks to expanding networks of railway lines, became the outward sign of an idea-based economy that gathered strength over the course of the nineteenth century. Hikers found value in leisure, precious commodities in vistas, and inner sustenance in fresh air and vigorous exercise.

Meanwhile, in cities, strolling spectators and parading dandies joined other bourgeois explorers of urban modernity to take a similarly self-conscious course. They enlarged the adventure of leisure-time walking, making a walk in the park or the crossing of a street into a noteworthy experience. Like it or not, they began to rub elbows with working-class pedestrians, merging into the democratizing tide that filled city streets and weekend retreats. They lost themselves in the crowd and their own thoughts, stimulated by the myriad manifestations of modern capitalism. Observers and shoppers in the marketplace of ideas and images, the idle but alert strollers called flâneurs created an urban parallel to Romantic walkers. Both types of walker enjoyed the same possibility for self-discovery, and through their dedication to wandering both told onlookers that their ambulation was more than a pastime; it was a way of life.

Aided by photography and drawn to crowds and family groups, artists focused on what Karl Marx called "the march of modern history." They depicted ordinary people in motion, going about their daily lives, strolling for recreation or marching for social change. Artistically, the fascination with everyday walking expressed itself across styles and genres, from realism to Impressionism to Post-Impressionism and Futurism. The first film made by the Lumière brothers, in 1895, simply showed workers opening factory gates and flooding toward the viewer, liberated from their jobs at the end of the day.

In the twentieth century, working people, especially urbanites, joined with Romantic walkers to create outing clubs that had a profound social impact, enlarging access to and protecting natural resources in Europe and North America. Faced with a steady erosion of the places where they could travel freely, activists fought against car-dominant planning, ultrarich landowners, and antipedestrian engineering of the built environment. They fought for safe walkways, disability accommodations, rights of way, and rights to roam. They shared with progressive organizations everywhere an appreciation of protest marching as a political and economic tool.

Recognizing that in a political context, walking is speech, marchers vocally reminded their societies where they had failed their citizens. Starting with the women's suffrage movement before World War I, the march for social justice became a vital tool for those impatient with governments and institutions. Applied to great effect in India by Gandhi and in the United States by civil rights activists, protest marches have spread across the globe as prodemocracy demonstrators denounce tyranny, racism, and violence against women.

Beginning in the 1960s, a small number of artists mixed insights from conceptual art, performance art, land art, and political activism to declare that certain walks, enacted with certain intentions, were works of art themselves. Others sought to implicate the viewer's body in the consumption of their works, requiring audiences to enter, circumambulate, or navigate a work. The "art" of the piece often depended more on the visceral responses of a physically engaged public than on their visual evaluation of a static object. Acknowledging that the decision to walk has always had a performative aspect, artists opened up the range of potential meanings that real-world steps could take. They explored personal psychology, social issues, gender roles, and state power, as well as human ecology and the obstacles faced by women and minority groups as they move.

As walking art and political walking borrowed from each other, awareness developed that not all people were free to experience walks in the idealized, universalist terms in which white male proponents such as Jean-Jacques Rousseau or Henry David Thoreau had presented them. In the twenty-first century, ever fewer disciples of Romantic walking or *flânerie* still pretend that the mere act of walking liberates *all* individuals from the constraints of society, or that "in walking one escapes even the idea of identity." While walking has emerged as a vital tool in fighting inequality, the harrowing, sometimes fatal experiences of individual walkers continue to show just how unequal is the access to a safe and rewarding stroll.

Today, modern walkers take on many different roles, almost all of them ambitious, alternating between consumption and production, social engagement and personal fulfillment. Depending on the moment, a walker can be a hiker, a refugee, a shopper, a commuter, a protester, a fundraiser, a pursuer of sexual adventure, or a purported outsider whose seeming otherness draws hostile attention. When it is not a matter of survival, contemporary walking is partly a citizen's march of solidarity toward social goals, and partly a consumer's saunter toward a better quality of life.

In 2020 a new, symbolically fraught type of walker emerged. Harried, defiant, desperate, furtive, imperiled by disease, police, and sometimes fellow citizens, the pandemic walker debuted on the world stage. Limited in many parts of the planet to short outings close to home, and sometimes unable even to go outside at all, people of all nationalities rapidly realized how precious walking is—for health, for sanity, for solving and coping with problems, for simple self-assertion as a human being. The ease with which authorities were able to declare and enforce walking bans troubled even those who agreed with the reasoning behind them.

Lockdowns and quarantines revealed how thoroughly the new millennium had already been marked by a further evolution of walking, one that is likely to shape pedestrian behavior for decades or centuries to come. We are witnessing the advent of what I call the "watched walker," the pedestrian who because of surveillance technology is tracked twenty-four hours a day, from home to work or school, on errands or during a leisure activity. Watched walkers move continually under and among surveillance cameras, even as they carry tracking devices, in the guise of smartphones, that convey their whereabouts to governments and commercial interests. The web they use has caught them in its toils. Seemingly more mobile than ever, consumer-citizens weave Ariadne's thread ever tighter around themselves in the labyrinth of modern life.

It's the task of the one hundred images presented here, along with their accompanying essays, to tell this story in more detail. Since walking and its accessories have been represented in every medium, readers will find a wide variety of sources and evidence to ponder: paintings, photos, films, sculpture, and stained glass, but also more ephemeral forms such as posters, advertisements, illustrations, and street signs. Alas, there could easily been a thousand steps chosen to describe this journey. Books, like walking images themselves, are inevitably incomplete, unable to capture the fullness of an itinerary, the sights, sounds, and smells, the feeling of each step. In view of what's inevitably missing here, the author hopes that readers will be inspired to create their own galleries of walks and walkers. Similarly, this geographical trail has its limits. It sticks close to the main corridors of the Western world, tracing developments in Europe and North America, because that is what the author knows best. Since fascinating images of walking know no boundaries, readers will want to consider how the art of other continents might complement or complicate this story.

Individually, the images assembled here can be pondered and their essays read in any order. You are invited to regard this book as a promenade and yourself as a flâneur. Go where your interest leads you. After all, as Balzac said, "Flâner, c'est vivre"—"To stroll is to live." Yet followed in sequence, these pages offer what I hope will be an informative, entertaining itinerary, a journey worth taking for the views alone. They tell the story of walking's restless energy, its revelatory and revolutionary potential to change not only the world but also the walker. Walking made us human. If we pay attention to the lessons that the art of walking has traced for us, it can make us more human still.

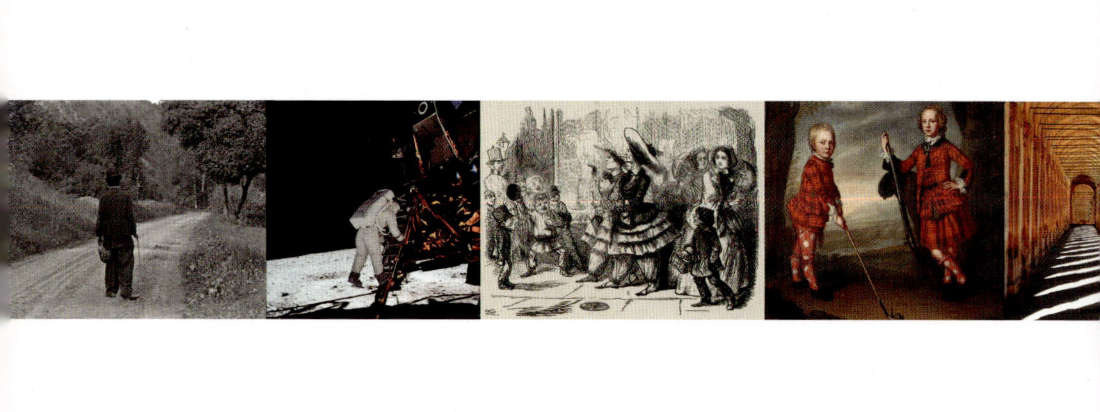

The Art of Walking

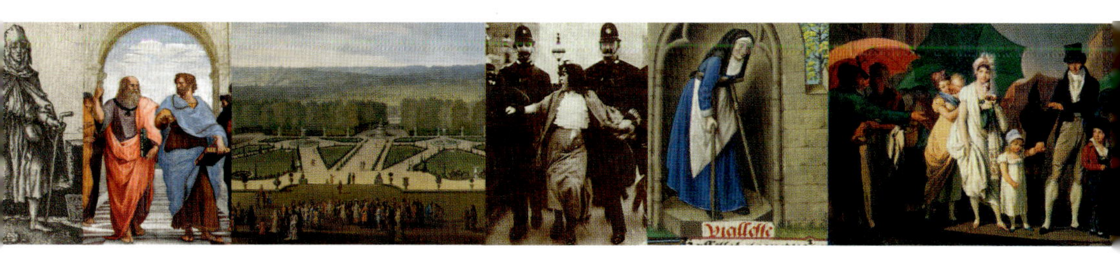

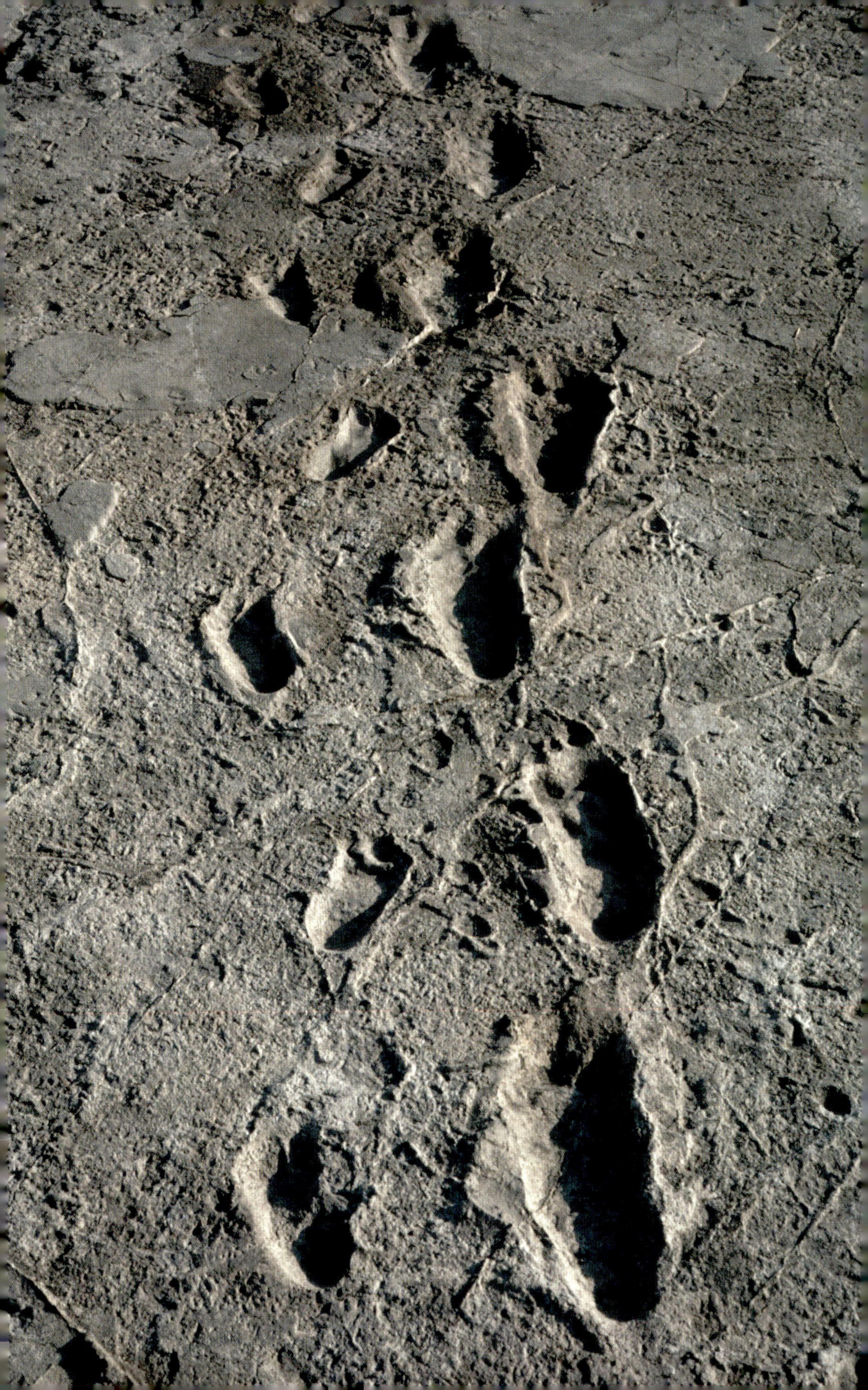

First Steps

Where does a walk go, once it is taken? At the very least, into the mind, the body, the air, the earth. And then, into the past. Most footprints vanish almost as soon as they come into being. And yet against all odds, some endure, like the startlingly crisp impressions pictured here. They look as if they were made yesterday, but these tracks enable us to travel through eons, back to a decisive moment when our distant ancestors took some of the first literal steps in our evolutionary direction.

About 3.6 million years ago, in what is now Laetoli, Tanzania, two hominins (ancient protohumans now categorized as *Australopithecus afarensis*) walked side by side through wet volcanic ash, likely heading toward a water hole. A smaller female took the left and a larger male the right. It was possibly a nuclear family; another male trailed behind them, stepping in the prints of the larger individual. The footprints trace only a few seconds of an actual passage that enabled their makers to survive another day. But, hauntingly, they represent the start of a physiological journey that has crossed millennia and the globe to arrive at . . . us. To see these footprints is to witness the strides of our ancestors at a time when, as the poet Milton said of Adam and Eve leaving Eden, "the world was all before them."

The three walkers would have been less than five feet tall, and, having short legs and long arms, they probably moved more slowly than the humans of today. But their gait was decidedly more human than apelike. Already at this early stage of hominin development, the splayed big toes that enable apes to grasp tree branches had disappeared, reducing the flat-footed, side-to-side rolling gait of walking primates. The increased size of the big toe and its repositioning close to the smaller ones has created a stable platform and a shock-absorbing arch that can generate energy for the next step.

As this summary suggests, footprints can encode an astonishing amount of information about those who have passed before us. Modern science reads in them not only basic facts about the walker—height, weight, sex, age, infirmity, style of motion—but also telling details: Was the person right or left-handed? pregnant? hunting? And most particularly in terms of human evolution, when were these tracks made, and by what species of humanlike creatures?

In the case of the Laetoli prints, the fact that these protohumans walked upright is of huge importance, as paleoanthropologist Mary Leakey and her team realized when they made the discovery in the 1970s. The fifty-four Laetoli footprints established that bipedalism preceded the enlarged brains that distinguish the human species, thereby marking two-footed locomotion as perhaps the single most important evolutionary advantage. The footprints provide key evidence that walking upright triggered a series of evolutionary advances, from thinking to talking to making. As Leakey remarked, "one cannot overemphasize the role of bipedalism in hominid development."

Why stand up in the first place? Most theories cite the advantages of having the hands free to use tools, carry infants, or reach for food and bring it to share in social groups. Bipedal locomotion also permitted further, more energy-efficient travel across the open savannah as leafy habitats thinned out due to climate change. This in turn generated endurance-running capabilities that enabled humans to move faster than both prey and predators over distance. Standing upright gave humans a better view over tall grasses to spot dangers. It also reduced the amount of the body exposed to the sun, significantly increasing energy efficiency. And the reduction of pressure on the neck, chest, and shoulders made it possible for humans to emit a more nuanced variety of sounds that, with hand signals, would lead to spoken languages.

Two further discoveries offer tantalizing glimpses into the long dawn of human walking. About 1.5 million years ago, several individuals skirted the edge of a lake near Ileret in northern Kenya. Their tracks indicate that *Homo erectus*, probably the first human ancestor to have short arms and long legs like *Homo sapiens*, had by then developed the foot structure and walking gait characteristic of modern humans. The heels, arches, and uniformly aligned toes of the walkers closely resemble those of people today. Capable of long-distance walking and running, they moved in a familiar manner, each step transferring weight from the heel to the ball of the foot and pushing off with the big toe, which stabilized the whole foot.

A third set of footprints belongs to us. *Homo sapiens*, the species to which all the world's current population belongs, emerged about 300,000 years ago, although the oldest known footprints of an anatomically modern human date back only to 117,000 years ago. They appear to have been made by a young woman heading downhill on a sand dune during a rainstorm at Langebaan Lagoon near the Atlantic coast of South Africa. Dry sand blew over the wet footprints, and later sedimentation preserved them. Known as "Eve's footprints," they provide evidence that their maker was about five foot four, and would, if alive today, wear an American size 7½ woman's shoe. Not waiting for Adam, Eve had places to go.

Walking on the Wall

When the first human figures appear in art, they are busy. About ten thousand years ago, at several European, North African, and Middle Eastern locations, silhouette-style forms began to populate cave walls by the hundreds or even thousands. Some are simple naked stick figures, while others have headdresses, clothing, and weapons. Importantly, they are depicted in motion: they walk, run, dance, and hunt. They also confront beasts both real and mythic, ranging from antelopes and giraffes to headless bull- or lion-like creatures ready to devour people. The scenes may conflate memories of actual events with ritual rewards and punishments, dreamlike imaginings of the artists' hopes and fears.

Ancient as they are, the pictures were a long time in coming. Our species was biologically human before we were "human" in a cultural sense. What archaeologists call behavioral modernity begins sometime in the last 200,000 years, picking up speed 80,000 to 50,000 years ago, by which time our ancestors could cook, fish, sew, make tools and ornaments, and use complex language.

As part of that advance, humans started making art. Forms ranged from geometric patterns to carefully rendered images of local animals—mammoths, rhinos, horses, and bears. Despite their skill, the artists were apparently in no hurry to represent themselves. An exception may be "therianthropes": part human, part animal creatures such as those found in the 40,000-year-old cave paintings of Sulawesi in Indonesia. Apart from scattered handprints, or rare totemic figurines like the female statuette found in the Hohle Fels cave, human forms are strikingly absent from cave walls and domestic sites.

But with the end of the last glacial period, human depictions began to emerge, eventually dominating the scenes they animate. Ten thousand years ago, at the Cave of Swimmers and the nearby Cave of Beasts in the then-fertile Libyan desert in southern Egypt, artists covered the rock walls with thousands of figures. In the Cave of Swimmers, humans painted in red ochre move in friezelike groups in a line around the cave interior. The artists have paid close attention to how joints and gestures communicate motion and purpose. Flexed legs, bent knees, long strides, raised heels, outstretched arms, even joined hands: all these sinuous positions show people engaged in an apparent combination of aggressive and ritual actions. At the Cave of Beasts, pictured here, the helter-skelter stick-figure humans far outnumber the much larger animals—bulls, giraffes, gazelles, an elephant—they move among. The superpositions of human and beast make it difficult to tell where scenes begin and end, and who is predator or prey. What is clear is that the artists now valued the individual and collective action of human locomotion highly enough to study and re-create it, to show humans spreading out, in art, life, or dream, to occupy the space available to them.

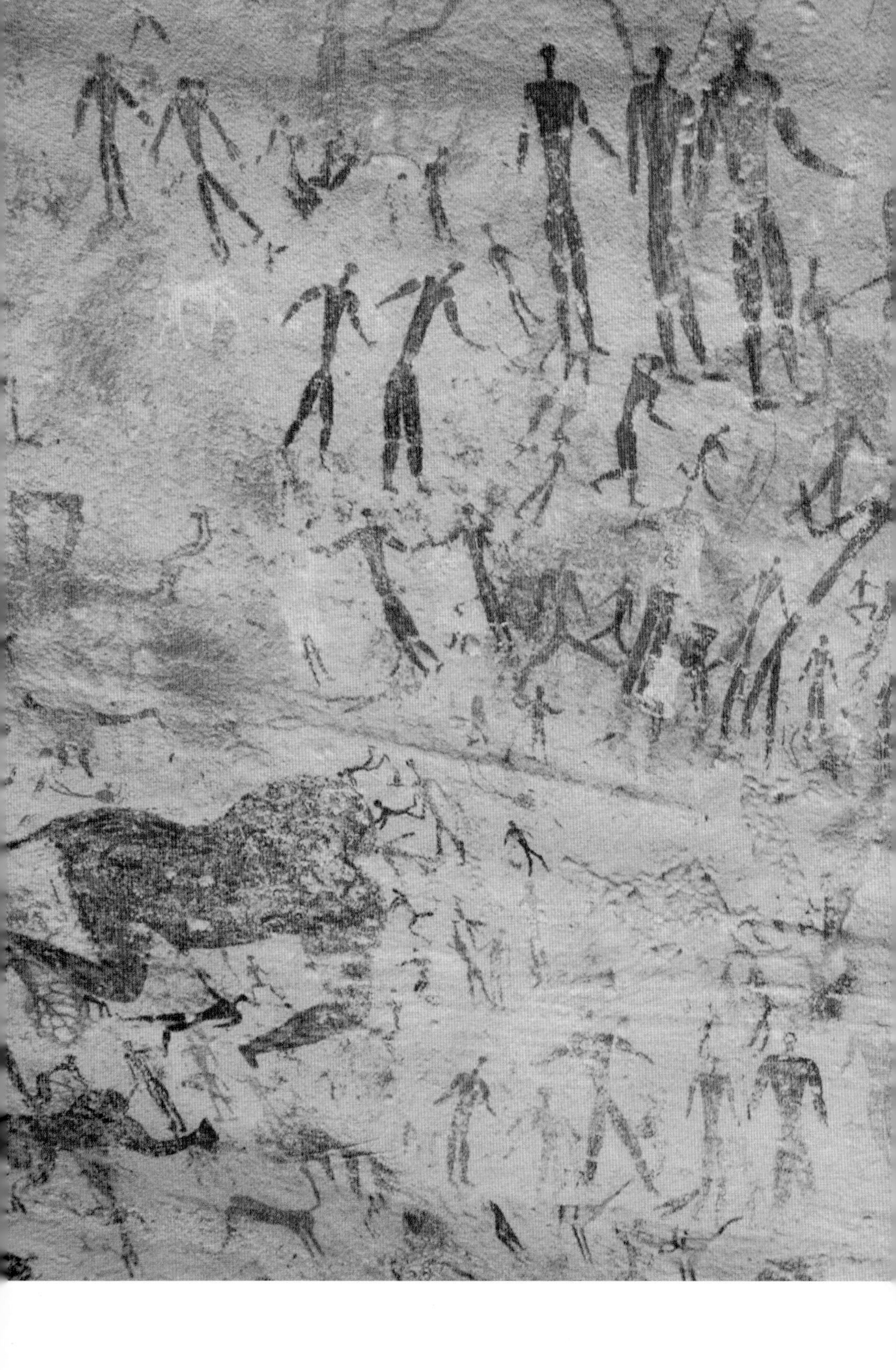

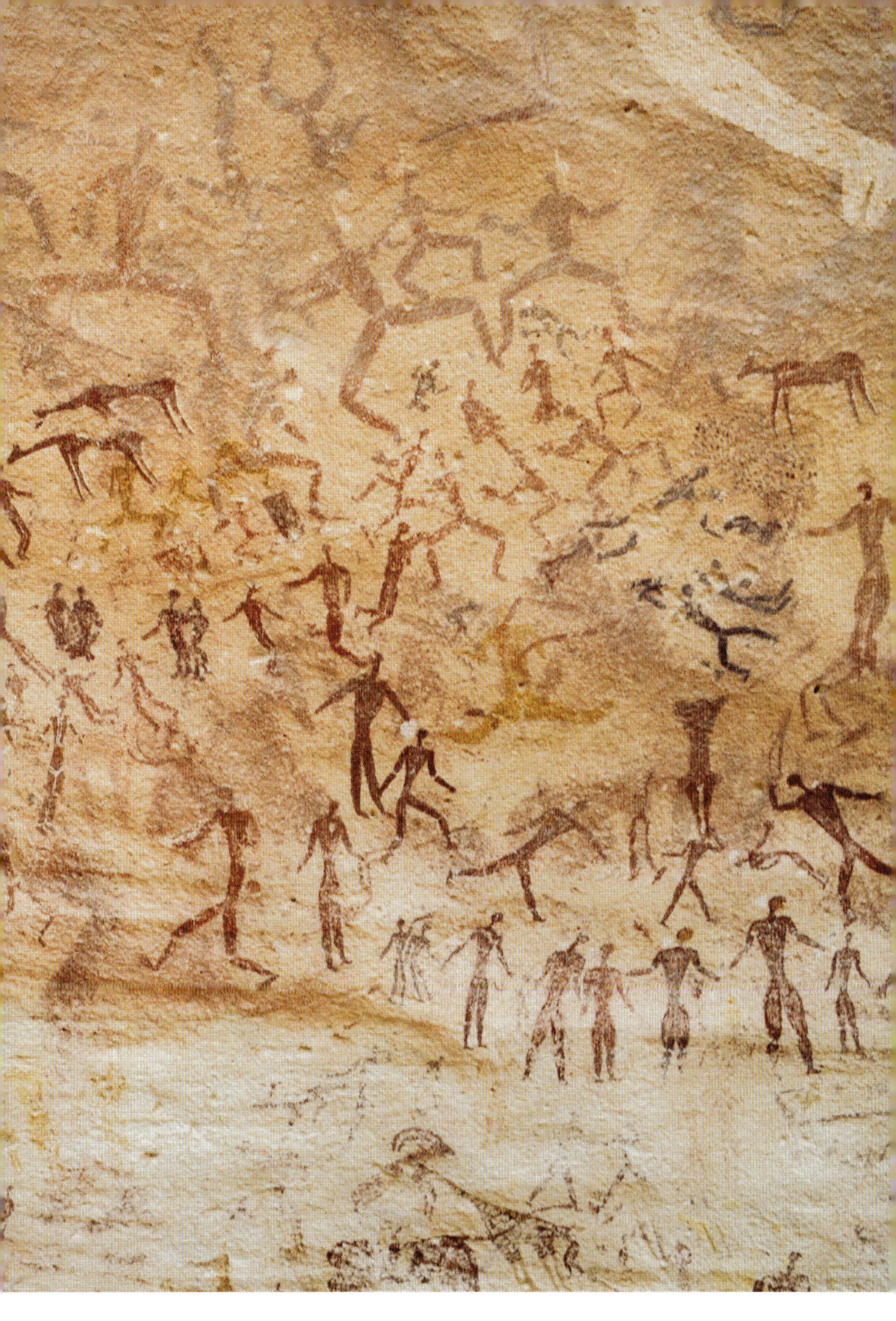

The First Shoes

Big toes provide stability; they help make sustained bipedal motion possible. But our smaller toes also have a tale to tell, indicating that about the same time that people started painting on cave walls, they started wearing shoes. Between 40,000 and 26,000 BCE, the thickness of human toe bones decreased, leading archaeologists to speculate that shorter, thinner toes resulted from foot protection. Although little evidence remains of early footwear, what does endure shows how people adapted to the demands of their climate and topography. While vast swaths of the human population walked shoeless, foot coverings enabled some groups to explore austere terrain ranging from deserts and canyons to mountains and arctic ice packs.

The world's oldest known leather shoe, seen here, is about 5,500 years old. Made from a single piece of cowhide and laced front and back with leather cord, it was found filled with grass, possibly used as insulation, in the Areni-1 cave complex in Armenia. At a US women's size 7, it may have belonged to a woman or a man, given the smaller stature of men in that era. In colder climates, people used bag-like coverings to protect their feet from harsh weather and rocks. The laced leather Jotunheimen shoe, discovered in Norway and dated somewhere between 1800 and 1100 BCE, is the oldest article of clothing found in Scandinavia.

Other early forms of shoe include bison-hide moccasins worn by natives of North America and the thong sandals, predecessors of the flip-flop, of Europe and the Middle East. Made from materials ranging from papyrus in Egypt to rawhide in Africa or rice straw in Japan and China, thongs could be ornamental as well as practical. Most people went barefoot most of the time, but Greeks, Hindus, and Egyptians wore shoes on special occasions. Ancient Greeks did almost everything, from war to worship, barefoot. But it was they who pioneered the platform shoe, the buskin, to give extra height to the most important actors in their plays, thereby introducing the idea that shoe-assisted elevation conferred social status.

Unlike the Greeks, all but the poorest Romans wore shoes, and the society as a whole considered shoes as crucial to physical performance and social standing. Perhaps for this reason they were the first to acknowledge a difference between the left foot and the right. Rather than simply wrapping feet in materials that might gradually conform to the wearer's body, they constructed chiral soles and shoes, that is, pairs adapted to the asymmetry of right and left feet. Then, recognizing the military value of a well-shod army, they issued right- and left-footed shoes to their soldiers.

Although they preferred lightweight sandals for everyday use, Romans frequently donned what can be considered the first modern dress shoes. Called *calcei*, these solid, lace-up shoe-boots were obligatory complements to a toga. They were

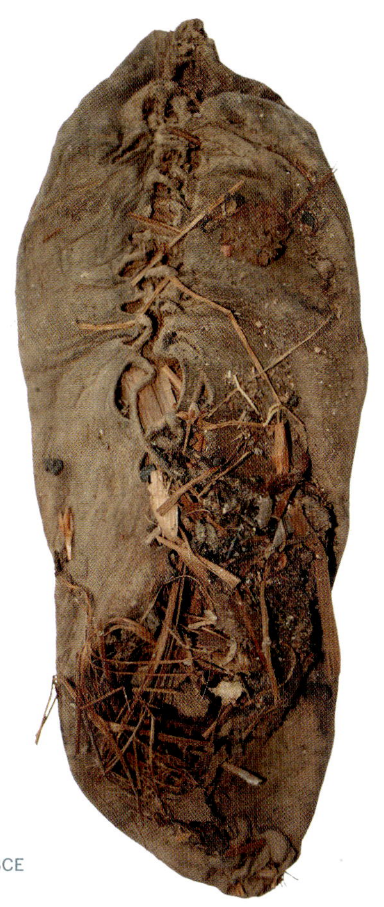

Prehistoric shoe, Areni-1 Cave, Armenia, c. 3500 BCE

worn whenever Romans went out formally for business or entertainment. Different styles accorded with social rank: patricians had crescent-shaped buckles, while senators wore red-dyed *calcei* when they met for affairs of state. Going out to dinner, the upper classes would wear the sturdy *calcei* in the street, then change to lighter slippers once they had greeted their hosts, only to remove their footwear entirely when they reclined on couches to dine. "Time for my slippers" meant that the party was breaking up, as the process was reversed.

Back on the practical front, perhaps the most specialized of all ancient shoes are those worn by a wayfarer nicknamed Otzi the Iceman, whose remains were found in the Tyrolean Alps at an elevation of 11,000 feet. Dating to about 3300 BCE, Otzi's footwear consisted of bearskin and deerskin covers that attached his grass-socked feet to a bark-string net supported by a wooden frame. In short, he was wearing snowshoes. Otzi's presence at such an elevation indicates how specially adapted footwear enabled humans to extend the range of their activities. They are precursors to the high-tech climbing shoes of today and the space boots worn to walk on the moon.

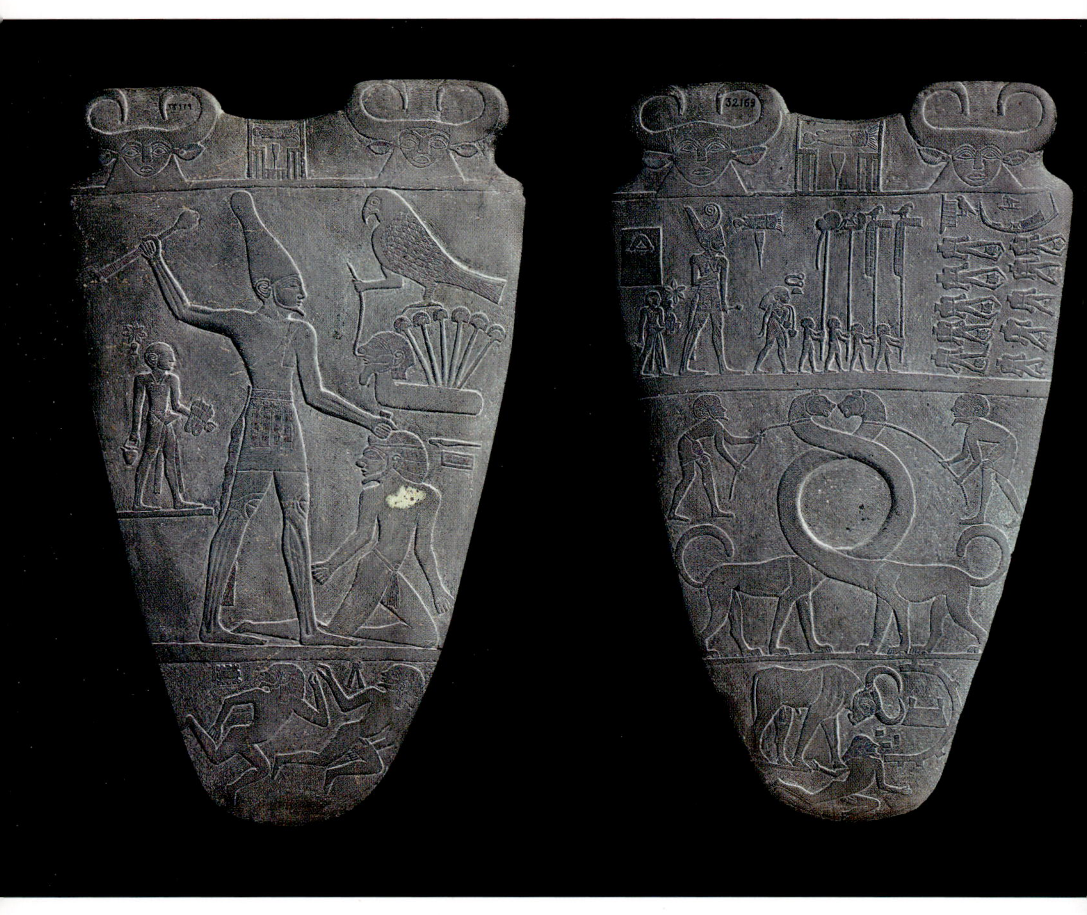

Narmer Palette, c. 3000 BCE

A Royal Procession

Dating from the thirty-first century BCE, the Narmer Palette has been called the "first historical document in the world." With it, walking enters the historical record in the form of a brutal parade of power. Carved on the surface of the two-foot-tall siltstone slab are violent scenes depicting King Narmer's unification of the Upper and Lower Kingdoms of Egypt. They also show that in commemorative propaganda, size matters: the bigger you are pictorially, the more your mighty steps can make your enemies tremble and your subjects cower.

The front of the stone features Narmer in godlike scale, towering over followers and adversaries. Wearing the lotus crown of Upper Egypt, he steps forward to smite a kneeling prisoner. With one fist already planted on the victim's head, he raises his mace to deal a mighty blow. Behind him an attendant bears the king's sandals, which he seems to have removed to do the heroic work of unifying Egypt. On the back of the stone, now wearing the papyrus crown of Lower Egypt, Narmer stands head, shoulders, and torso above his standard bearers. Solemnly they process toward a row of decapitated bodies that testify to Narmer's conquest.

This display of regal bloodlust is even more remarkable given the symbolic function of the flat slab it is carved on. Ceremonial palettes dealt with appearances in more than one sense. As stylized versions of actual palettes where high priests would grind cosmetics in temple rituals, such palettes testify to their own artistry as well as the accomplishments of those they commemorate. The face paint they evoke would adorn statues in the temple, while the palette stone would year after year and century after century exhibit the official story of Narmer's might. Scholars debate whether Narmer actually achieved the full conquest the palette claims. The story told by his stone might be propaganda or just wishful thinking. Either way, the ostentatious stride of the king toward his enemies signals a fearful resolution. For Narmer, to walk is to act without mercy.

The Narmer Palette rounds out its message with pictures of defeated towns and more victims. Meanwhile, its hieroglyphics and animal divinities confer suprahuman authority on Narmer, providing the civic and religious trappings that have embellished victory parades ever since. Taken together, the stone's vignettes constitute a procession of bloody deeds that both commemorate and subjugate; they brag and warn. In compact form, the Narmer Palette anticipates the triumphs of the ancient Romans, those miles-long parades of prisoners and plunder that made victory walks into a form of mass entertainment and turned the heroic general, his face painted Mars red, into a demigod for the day.

Walking and Working with Animals

It's the beginning of something. An ordinary man walks behind a plow pulled by two oxen. The long, semi-companionable working relationship of man and animal plods into artistic life, in the form of a painted wooden sculpture. His feet sunk into the soil he has just plowed, the brown man leans forward to urge the beasts onward with his raised stick. Meanwhile the black-and-white oxen stare stolidly ahead, looking a bit puzzled by the whole arrangement. Someone will follow behind man and beasts, putting seeds in the narrow cut that the rudimentary wooden plow has opened. Civilization, so often defined in conjunction with the rise of agriculture, declares itself.

It's also the end of something. The Paleolithic hunter-gatherers, who painted cave walls and who by many accounts "worked" only twenty hours per week, have turned into the agricultural laborers of the Neolithic period. Nomadic groups moved just a few miles each day (still-extant bands average about six), but covered thousands in the course of a few years. Their farmer descendants, however, found themselves attached to the soil they tilled. By 10,000 BCE the nomadic existence of many social groups had been reshaped into a sedentary form by the farming of cereals and the domestication of cows, sheep, and pigs. Along with the use of pack animals, the invention of animal-drawn plows about 3000 BCE furthered the transition to a trade- and crop-based economy. The increasingly complex social organization of Bronze Age Mesopotamian and Egyptian peoples tied their growing populations to the land through a combination of legal and economic constraints. With their hierarchies, taxes, written records, and settled urban populations that had to be fed, defended, or turned into armies, Egyptian authorities created an intricate feudal system with little room for individual mobility. The human original of this plowman would have walked to work and walked behind the plow as work. But he could not walk away from this work. The oxen would have been leased to him by the state so that he could farm land that he rented from the state.

As an artifact, the painted plowman faced a further form of bondage. Wooden models of daily life were used as what museum curators now call "burial equipment." They stood by in corners of the tombs of high officials, ready to provide whatever goods or services might be required by the dead. This man bent to his furrow in a tomb for about 3,600 years, in case his master needed some plowing done in the afterlife.

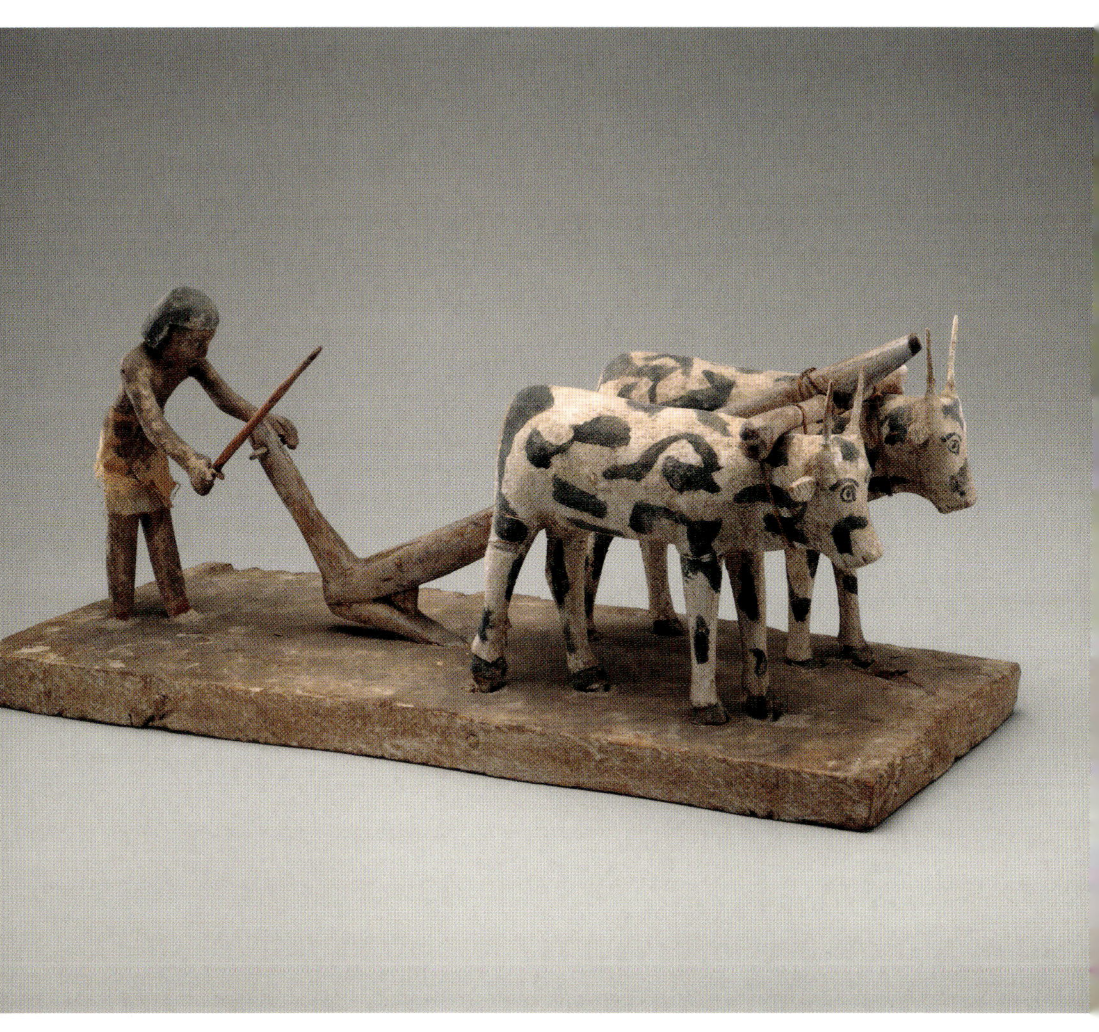

Model of a man plowing, burial equipment, c. 1981–1885 BCE

Marching into Battle

There was a time when barefoot soldiers could conquer the world. In the eighth century BCE, unshod Greek soldiers called hoplites (from *hopla*, "heavy equipment") trained themselves to walk slowly in unison toward the enemy. Their tight formation was called the phalanx. Although the ancient Near Eastern soldiers of Sumer and Egypt were perhaps the first to march into battle in block formation, the concept of the marching phalanx is most strongly associated with the Greeks because of their tremendous success with the technique. In their left hands they held large round shields, overlapped to cover their bodies, while in their right hands they carried long spears to push their adversaries relentlessly backward until their lines broke.

The phalanx was a lethal feature of the interminable city-state conflicts, but the Athenians and their allies the Plataeans also used it to save Greek civilization with the historic victory over the Persians at the Battle of Marathon in 490 BCE. A century later, Philip of Macedon and his son Alexander the Great trained their nearly invincible armies with extra-long fifteen-foot spears called *sarissae* that made their phalanxes especially deadly. Undefeated in battle, Alexander led his troops from Greece to India, constructing one of the largest empires of the ancient world.

The Chigi Vase, made in Corinth about 650 BCE, lays claim to being the first to depict Greek forces marching in formation. The vase is remarkable not only for its subject matter but also for its pioneering use of polychromy. The colors allow the artist to distinguish between the darker, reddish bare skin of the soldiers' arms, legs, and feet, and the lighter-colored metal greaves that they wore to protect their shins. Meanwhile their overlapping shields follow the time-honored device, dating back to prehistoric cave art, of using echoing forms to create an impression of dynamic action. From the Parthenon gift-bearers to Futurist pedestrians, subsequent representations of walkers will use these repeated, superimposed legs, arms, and torsos to evoke a flurry of motion.

In an unusual feature, the vase suggests the sound of battle: a tunic-clad flutist provides music that must have been rousing and strongly cadenced, to keep the men in step and propel them with deliberate strides toward their enemies. If warfare is organized violence, then the tactical, artistic, and musical organization of this scene succinctly communicates how the Greek soldiers did their damage with a highly disciplined walk. As the Roman military historian Vegetius later observed of the marching step: "Nor is anything of more consequence either on the march or in the line than that they should keep their ranks with the greatest exactness. For troops who march in an irregular and disorderly manner are always in great danger of being defeated."

Formidable as the Greeks were, their Roman successors added a component that greatly increased their effectiveness. They standardized the notion of pace, the relationship between steps taken, distance covered, and time required, so that the speed of their armies could be calculated and their capabilities practically applied. A Roman pace, or *passus*, was the length of two steps, covering the distance made by a full stride, from the heel strike of a foot to the spot where that heel next touched down. General Marcus Agrippa used his own foot in 29 BCE to regularize the *passus* as five Roman feet. The marching step of the Roman legions defined not only how far they moved in a thousand full strides—one mile (from *mille*, a thousand)—but also how rapidly. As Vegetius wrote in his training manual, soldiers "should march with the common military step twenty miles in five summer-hours, and with the full step, which is quicker, twenty-four miles in the same number of hours." Mercilessly applying this grueling pace to his own men, Julius Caesar rampaged across Gaul on a schedule whose precision would be the envy of any long-distance hiker today.

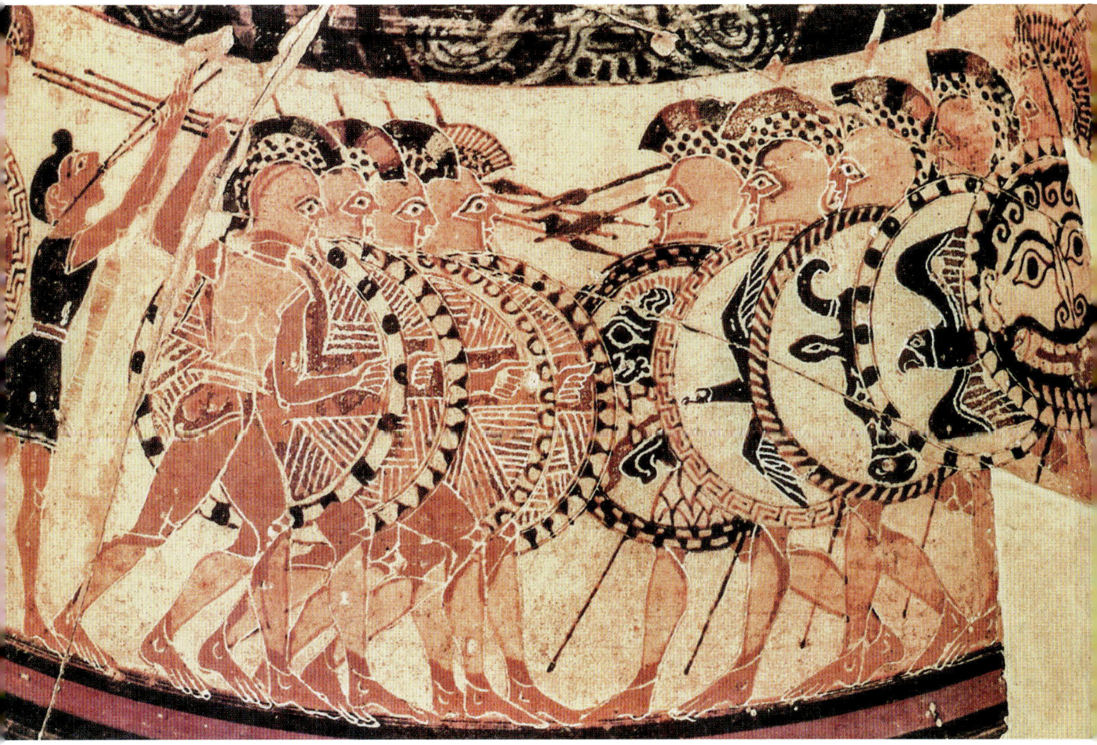

Hoplites marching, Chigi Vase, c. 650 BCE

A Beautiful Step

Put your best foot forward. Egyptian artists had no hesitation about which leg to thrust out when they represented walking. They depicted everyone, from King Narmer down to the lowly plowman, stepping forward with the left foot, likely on the theory that the usually dominant right side of the body anchors the life force of an individual. The resulting statues have a stolid, flat-footed appearance, but the posture introduced a pictorial strategy that would echo through the centuries: a decisive step signifies a person's power to act in the world.

Ancient Greeks followed a similar flat-footed convention for several hundred years. But if Egyptian art portrayed people wielding official power, the Greeks had other ideas about what deserved commemoration. They developed idealized forms of beauty that made the sheer physical presence of a lithe, well-muscled body something to celebrate. Not recognizing any anatomical difference between ordinary men and the gods on Olympus, the Greeks sought to express a combination of divine spirit and corporeal perfection through the flawless proportions of a naked male body.

Around 700 BCE, Greek sculptors began making freestanding life-size figures of young men called kouroi (*kouros* means "youth"). They placed them in cemeteries and shrines to honor the dead or to mark earthly achievements. The stylized torsos are topped with faces that smile in an artificial manner designed to show their remoteness from the trivial concerns of everyday life. The arms of the kouroi hang stiffly at their sides in the Egyptian manner, out of synch with the forcefulness of their stride. The well-rounded Kroisos Kouros, circa 530 BCE, exemplifies the tension between lofty abstraction and determined action found at the end of the Archaic period.

But within a century, at the dawn of the Classical period, something dramatic had happened. Sculptors abandoned the rigid symmetry of their precursors in order to show the grace of the body in motion. With the Kritios Boy (c. 480 BCE), a body both relaxed and vibrant makes its appearance for the first time. It shifts the weight largely onto one leg, adjusting the center of balance, the curve of the spine, and the tilt of the hips and shoulders accordingly, an invention that Renaissance artists would come to call contrapposto ("counterpoise"). These advances culminated in the *Doryphoros* ("Spear Bearer") of Polykleitos (c. 450 BCE), where the weight shift becomes dynamic, and the solid step becomes an active stride. The spear bearer places all his weight on his forward-stepping leg, the right one. The toes of his left foot just touch the ground as he pushes off into his next step. Committed to forward motion, he opens the way for a new concept of physical and emotional

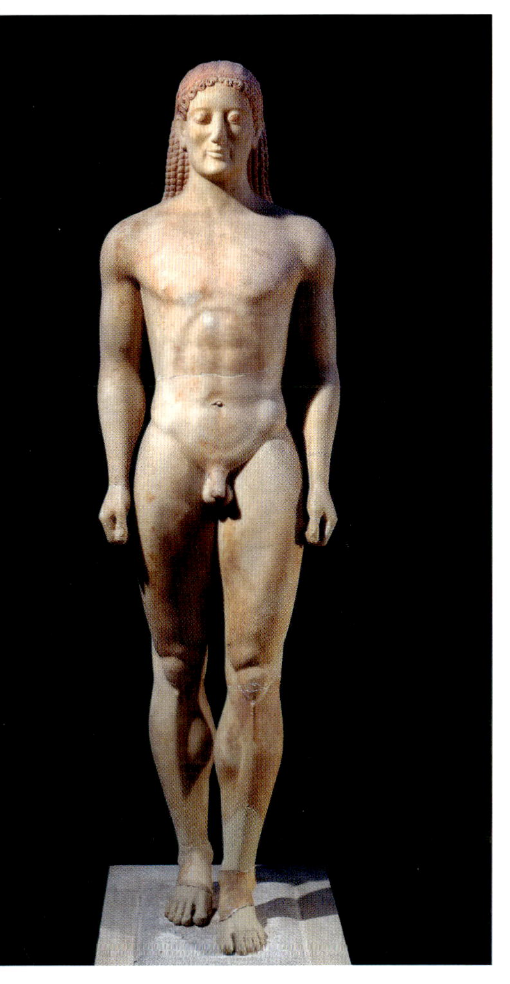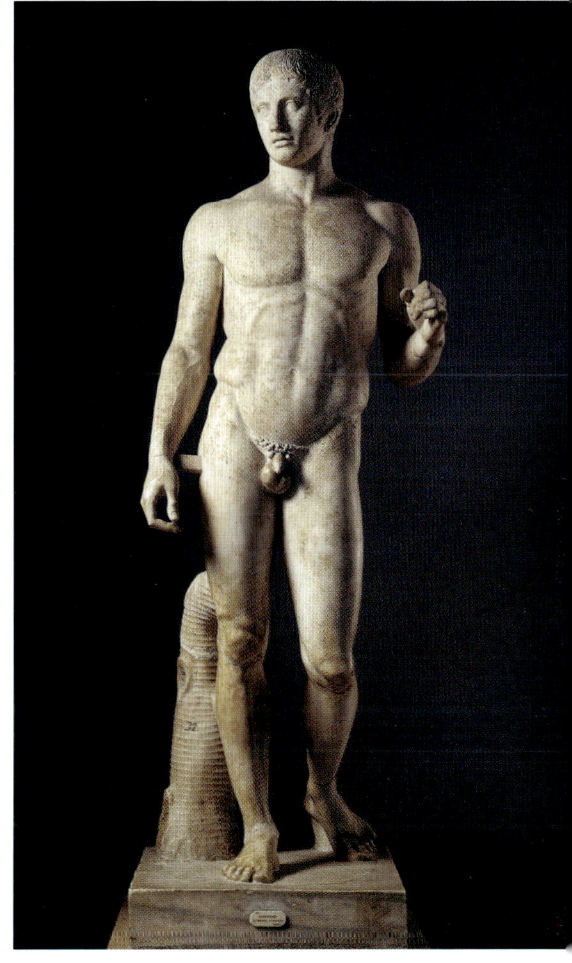

attractiveness, based on the curve of the hips, the slant of the shoulders, the twist of the torso. His casual stride sets the standard for subsequent sculptors, displaying a fully realized action whose natural beauty, whether regarded as human or divine, has never been surpassed.

She Who Steps

She lifts her skirts and trips lightly, briskly, over the smooth marble. Eyes intent on the path before her, she pays no attention to potential spectators peering into her world of stone. All the awkward posing and self-importance that characterize ancient walking sculpture have fallen away. Who is she? Where is she going?

As the male nude kouroi became more relaxed and naturalistic, Greek representations of clothed women, called korai ("maidens"), underwent a similar transition. Like the kouroi, the korai were ideal forms of beauty that could represent humans and deities at shrines or gravesites. In the Classical period after 450 BCE, the dynamic musculature of male statues found its counterpart in the flowing, semi-transparent robes of female statues. Delicately undulating ridges of stone revealed the action of limbs and torsos, as in the monumental caryatids of the Erechtheion. A century later, when this skirt-lifting maiden was sculpted in bas-relief, artists were turning to more intimate scenes to showcase their skill at realistic depictions of everyday activity.

This figure, just over two feet tall, is a fragment of a larger tableau. The context reveals that she is an Agraulid, one of three sister goddesses who spread the nighttime dew. With exceptional dexterity, the sculptor has cut the sweeping folds of her gown and hood to accentuate her forward motion into the night, leading her sisters (surviving in fragments only), who dispense the dew from a dainty pitcher. Perhaps her attentive step is designed to suggest the invisible dew she represents. Or maybe she simply does not want to get her feet wet.

Eighteen hundred years later, in the Vatican Museum, where it still resides, the sculpture caught the eye of a German writer, Wilhelm Jensen. In 1902 he made it the title character of his psychological novella *Gradiva: A Pompeian Fantasy*. *Gradiva* means "she who steps" in Latin, and Jensen imagined his archaeologist protagonist falling in love with the goddess though the beauty of her walk. Smitten, the archaeologist goes to Pompeii so that he can better envision Gradiva's final walk in the moments before the eruption of Vesuvius destroyed the city. Carl Jung mentioned the story to Sigmund Freud, who was so fascinated that he psychoanalyzed the story's characters as if they were real patients. His "Delusion and Dream in Jensen's *Gradiva*" (1906) argues that a single step can trigger deep psychic turmoil—and ultimately save a life. Freud himself visited "Gradiva" in Rome, and had a cast made that he hung on the wall of his study. From there she looked down on his famous couch, the much-fetishized image of obsessive desire. In the *Aeneid*, Virgil had written that "by her gait the true goddess is known." Together, Freud and Jensen insisted that the dew goddess could, by a single step, unlock the Unconscious as well.

     "Gradiva," Roman copy, c. 2nd century CE, of Greek bas-relief, 4th century BCE

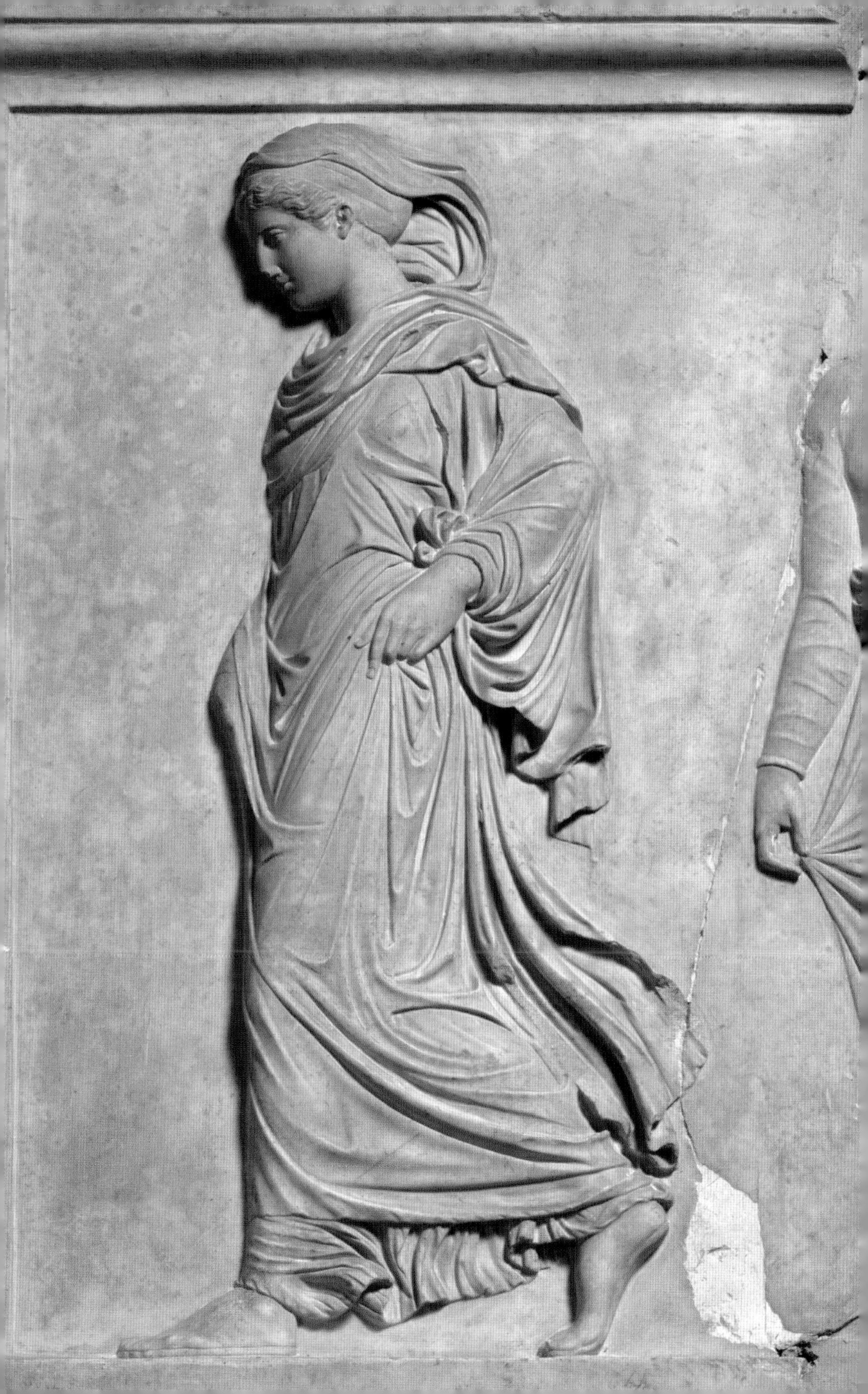

Walking on Stone

With one legendary exception, humans do not walk on water. This puts bridges high on the list of a walker's needs. Their existence reminds us that the story of walking is partly told through its affordances, with durable transportation infrastructure such as bridges, roads, and pathways complementing perishable equipment like shoes and clothing. Among the most practical and long-lived contributions to walking efficiency are Roman bridges, many of which are works of art in themselves. Even after two millennia, they survive by the hundreds, marvels not only of engineering but of beautiful design.

None is more architecturally accomplished than the Alcántara Bridge, which crosses the river Tagus in what is now Extremadura, Spain, near the border with Portugal. Built by order of the emperor Trajan between 104 and 106 CE, the bridge commands its rugged setting through the elegant simplicity of its majestic proportions and dramatic curves. The height of the bridge, 230 airy feet above the water, is balanced by its imposing 590-foot length. A thousand years after its construction, the sight was still so stunning that the medieval Muslim cartographer Muhammad al-Idrisi considered it one of the wonders of the world.

Alcántara means "arch" in Arabic, and the success of the bridge depends both physically and visually on the six symmetrical arches that carry the roadway across the river. The smallest arches at either end are about half the width of the second arches, and the third arches that actually span the river are almost a fifth again as wide. The bridge plays on the emotions of its crossers, gathering in audacity until the human-dwarfing midpoint is reached. There, in the middle of the roadway, at right angles to the supporting arches, stands a seventh, triumphal arch that overshadows walkers coming from either direction. It is as if the designer of the bridge, Caius Julius Lacer, wanted his clients to experience the majesty of the bridge from the river's point of view; they seem to pass beneath the very arches that hold them over the water. The arch itself bears an inscription announcing not only the emperor's patronage but also the fact that twelve local municipalities put up the money to build this bridge. For the Romans, such a bridge did not belong to a single town but was seen as a communal property benefiting the entire region.

Roman bridges would have had far less value if they had not been connected to the extensive network of long, straight Roman roads that dissect the European continent—fifty-three thousand miles of them. And once travelers reached cities, they found well-paved, right-angled city streets, banked by high-curbed sidewalks. Pedestrians could traverse the street on mini-bridges of raised stepping stones, protected from dust, muck, or water below, while cart wheels could roll through the gaps.

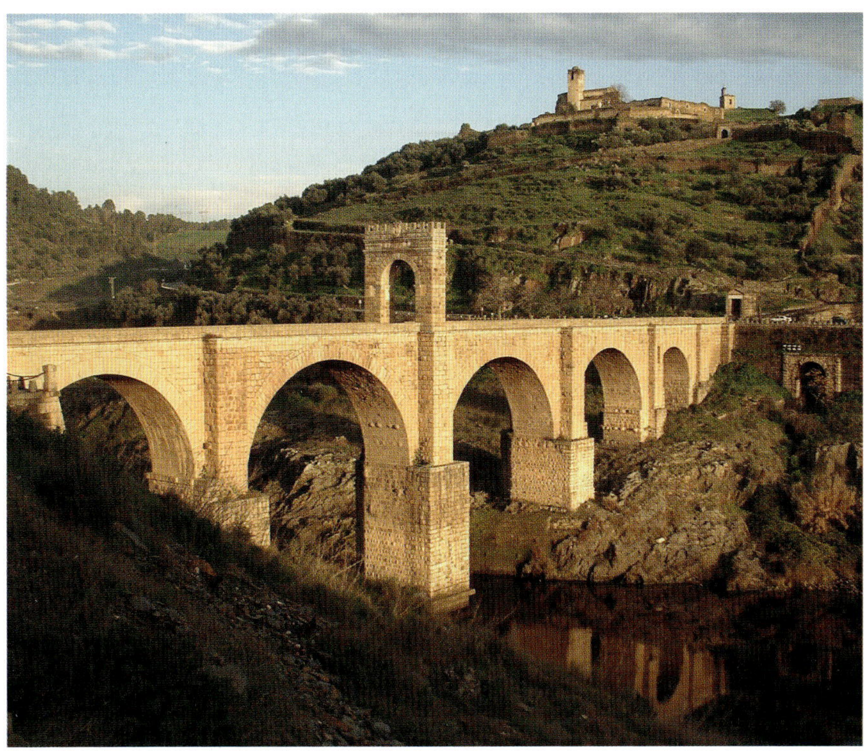

Trajan's Bridge at Alcántara, Spain, 104–6

Bridges and stepping stones make visible at a glance the essential properties of all walking routes: they are connectors that facilitate movement of people and things. Their story continues back past the oldest stone bridges (c. 1300 BCE) and stairs (c. 1500 BCE) to the first paved roads of stone and brick that appeared around 4000 BCE in Mesopotamia and South Asia. At the start of it all lies the humble path, product of the walker's perennial desire to make the way easier. A trail is encoded information, a solution to the problem of getting from A to B with the least expenditure of time and energy. Once in use, every path works toward its own optimization, as corners are cut and surfaces smoothed. If the distance has been cleverly bridged by prior walkers, the mind is freed to travel elsewhere as the body moves surely toward its goal. This enables trails to transport more than bodies and goods; they convey ideas, too.

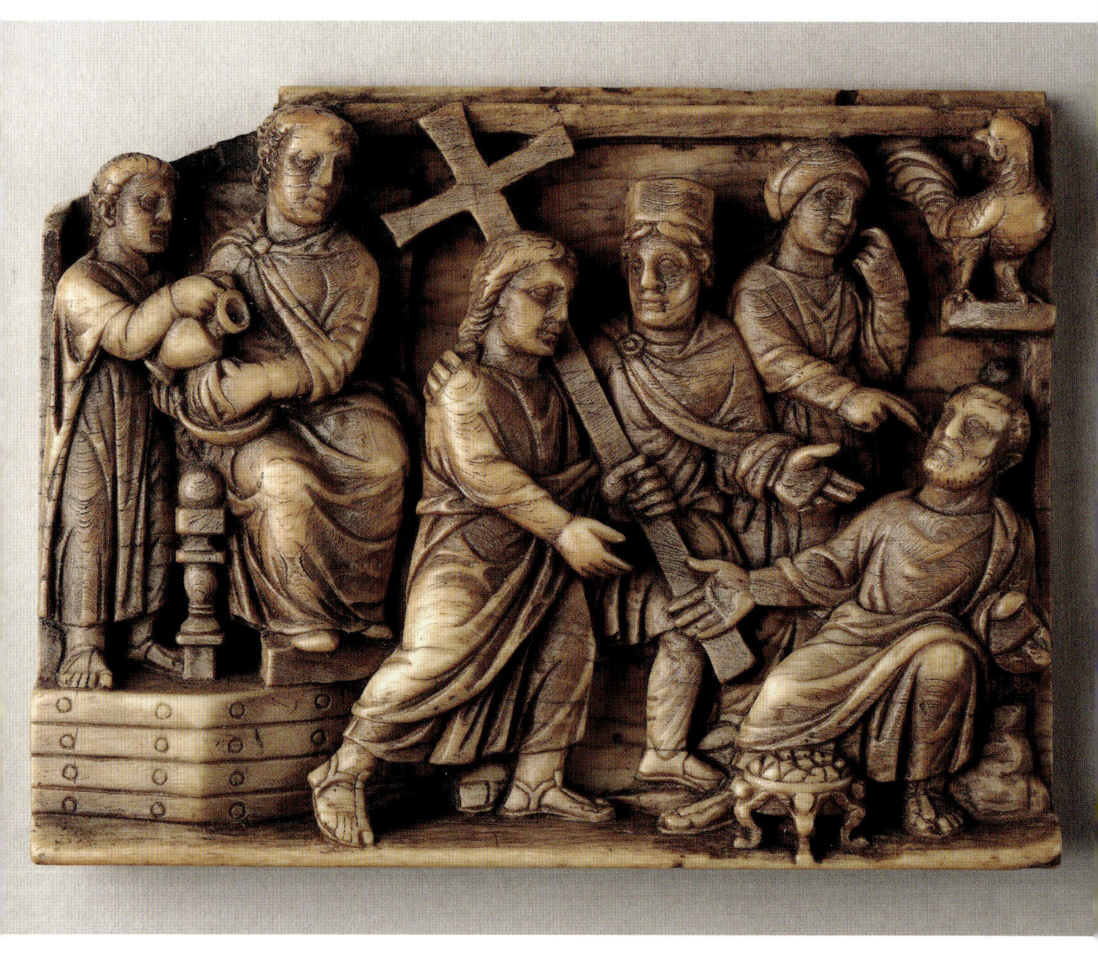

Ivory panel from a casket, Late Roman, 420–30

A Cross to Bear

Jesus was a walker. In the Gospels, he spreads his word on foot, from the crowd-stirring events of his ambulatory preaching to his post-resurrection journey to Emmaus, where he explains the necessity of his death to his disciples. As a Middle Easterner sensitive to rituals of hospitality and humility, he not only allows his hosts to wash his dusty feet after his journeys but takes it upon himself to wash the feet of his apostles at the Last Supper as a sign of his love and submission.

Of all the walks in Western culture, Jesus carrying the cross to Calvary must be the one most often depicted. The oldest known representation is found on a small panel of a carved ivory casket from the late Roman period, about 420–30 CE. Reading from left to right, we see Pilate washing his hands of the decision to execute Jesus; then Jesus striding forward with the cross, guided by a soldier who lays a hand on his shoulder; and finally, Peter denying he knows Jesus as the cock crows. The artist sets the walk at the center of the story, presenting Jesus from the early Christian point of view that stressed his victory over death rather than his agony in facing it. The cross-bearing walk that will turn into a pervasive metaphor for human suffering has yet to take visual shape. Here, Jesus marches in heroic fashion, striding confidently toward the fulfillment of his destiny.

The Stations of the Cross, a series of images and prayers denoting the final steps of Jesus's life, developed in the later Middle Ages from the practice of pilgrims who went to Jerusalem to retrace the exact route Jesus took on the way to Calvary. Gradually establishing a sequence of anguishing events wedded to particular spots on the journey, Franciscan monks created a Via Dolorosa that, with the aid of standardized scenes, could be replicated elsewhere. By the seventeenth century a Catholic Christian could metaphorically follow in Jesus's final footsteps by saying a series of prayers at designated places in a church. Outdoors, pilgrims walked specially designed itineraries marked by pious sculptures, each depicting one of the fourteen stages that had come to define the crucifixion narrative. Over the centuries and all over the world, popes, priests, and private individuals have carried crosses on Good Friday to emulate a fatal journey that paradoxically promises eternal life.

Walking Impaired

Why is an amputee walking with his crutch on top of a decorative capital D? His platform is the first letter of a medieval musical manuscript that begins with the phrase *Diffusa est gratia* ("Grace is poured"). The words from Psalm 45 are often interpreted as a prophecy of the Messiah. What is the link between this vigorous crutch user and Christian salvation?

From ancient times, able-bodied walking has been haunted by the fear of impairment. The answer to the legendary riddle of the Sphinx—"What goes on four feet at dawn, two at midday, and three in the evening?"—recognizes that people only temporarily enjoy the gift of a sound step. Crawling babies and cane-supported elders demonstrate that two-legged walks do not define the human condition. Looking for an allegorical image of Old Age, a medieval illustrator of the *Romance of the Rose* depicted an aged nun bent over her crutches, contemplating the yellow leaves of autumn outside her cloister wall.

As a walking aid, the crutch signals limitation even as it helps overcome it. As early as 1500 BCE, Egyptian wall painters depicted active-looking crutch users, possibly stricken by polio. The Greco-Roman aversion to deformed bodies caused the lame to disappear from both public life and classical art. But Christianity's stress on healing by faith and the forgiveness of sins opened a place for crippled people in the art of medieval Europe. If some Christians thought that sin could cause infirmity, more people seem to have believed that the afflicted approached Jesus through their suffering, and deserved charity accordingly. The earliest surviving image of Jesus, painted on a baptistry wall in Syria about 235, shows him miraculously healing a lame man. It's likely the moment at the Bethesda pool in Jerusalem where Jesus says, "Take up thy bed and walk" (John 5:8). The panoply of Catholic saints includes many who today are described as patron saints of persons with disabilities, including Saint Anthony of Padua, patron of amputees, and Saint Servulus of Rome, who was a full paralytic.

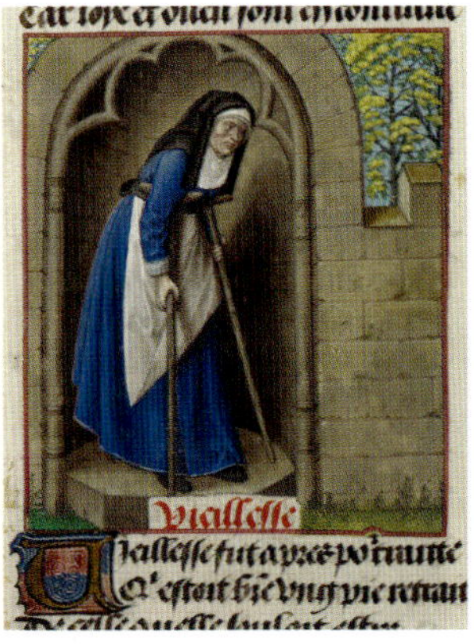

The ravages of leprosy, polio, war, hard labor, and accidents meant that medieval artists had plenty of models for their images of affliction. One of the most popular saints, Saint Martin of Tours, was venerated for cutting his cloak in half on a winter's day to share with a naked beggar, often depicted as an amputee. In secular scenes, artists readily included crutch users as part of everyday life along the road or in town squares. Hand

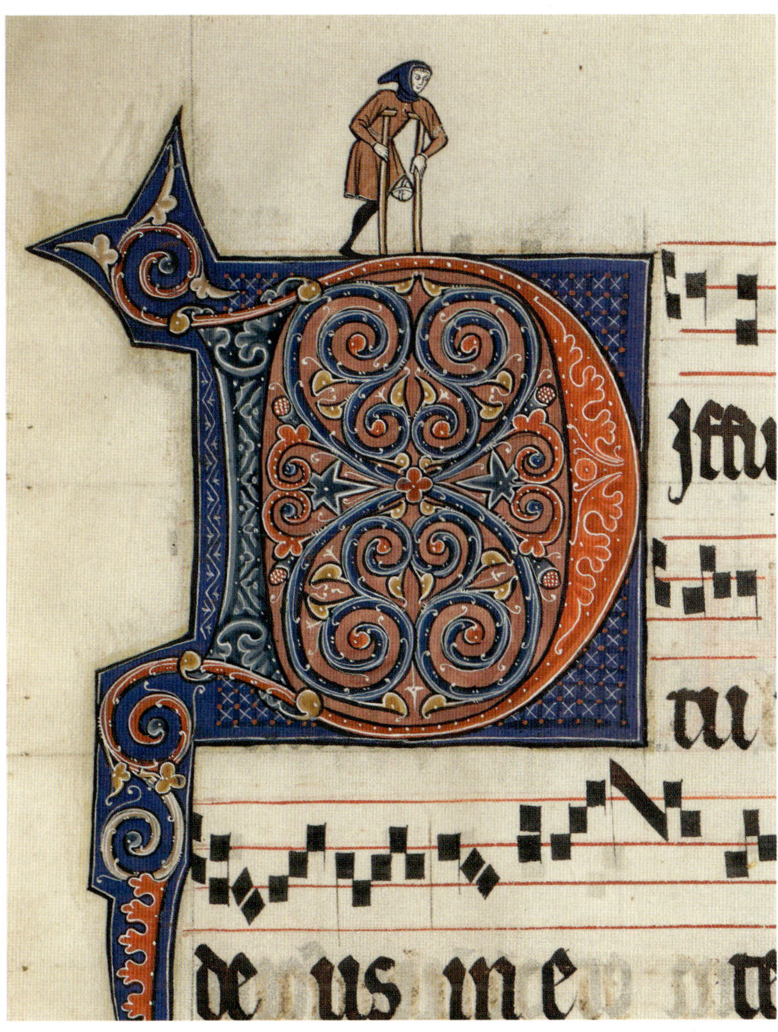

crutches and two-pegged leg supports can be seen in *The Fight between Carnival and Lent* (1559) by Pieter Brueghel the Elder, and most famously in Brueghel's *The Beggars* (1568). To return to the musical illumination: with his above-the-knee amputation, the lithe, determined figure who swings his body forward into the words of a song about the coming of the Messiah shows that all kinds of walkers will receive Christ's blessing: "Grace is poured into thy lips: therefore God hath blessed thee for ever."

Pilgrimage

Amid the many reasons for walking, the pilgrimage to a sacred site has always commanded special respect, combining both physical determination and spiritual motivation. For Christians, pilgrimages belonged to a biblical tradition that was almost inseparable from long journeys on foot: the expulsion of Adam and Eve from the garden, the nomadic travels of Abraham, the wanderings of Moses and his people for forty years in the desert, and the flight of Joseph, Mary, and infant Jesus from Bethlehem into Egypt. During his peripatetic preaching, Jesus proclaimed himself as the Way, so that no matter where they traveled, devout followers could be said to "walk" with him.

Most pilgrimages are inspired by precursors, people who have made the trip earlier and claimed that travel to this place will bring the faithful closer to God. Western Christian pilgrimages to the Holy Land gained popularity due to the efforts of two women. The first was Saint Helena. The mother of Constantine, the first Christian emperor, she went to Palestine in 326 CE, spending several years identifying sites connected with the life of Jesus. She was believed to have located fragments of the True Cross. The second was Egeria, possibly a French nun, who in 380 CE journeyed to the Holy Land. She visited many biblical sites, including Mount Sinai, and wrote the earliest account of a Christian pilgrimage.

Sporadically cut off from the Holy Land by religious wars, European pilgrims frequently turned to more accessible sites associated with apostles, martyrs, and miraculous events. Foremost was the seat of Christianity, Rome. The city was overwhelmed with penitents after 1300, when Pope Boniface VIII granted a plenary indulgence—full remission of sins—to those who made the journey in the right frame of mind. Another destination was the cathedral of Santiago de Compostela in Spain, whose approach roads became the renowned Camino de Santiago, or Way of St. James. Today it still stretches across northern Spain, trod by thousands of people each year.

Of all medieval pilgrims, those on the Camino were the most recognizable. Undertaking a demanding trek that could last several months, they wore the symbol of Saint James, the scallop shell, on their hats, and carried long staffs and leather supply bags called scrips. The scrip might contain a wooden bowl or have a spoon poking out of it, both ready to receive alms. Summing up such a journey in a single scene has always been a challenge for artists, but the limners of this image, the Masters of the Gold Scrolls, had a ready stock of conventions to draw upon. This representation of Saint Jodicius of Brittany, a hermit who lived by a river in the forest, shows him bearing the requisite staff, scrip, and three scallop shells on his hat. The shells are echoed by the three towers of his implied destination in

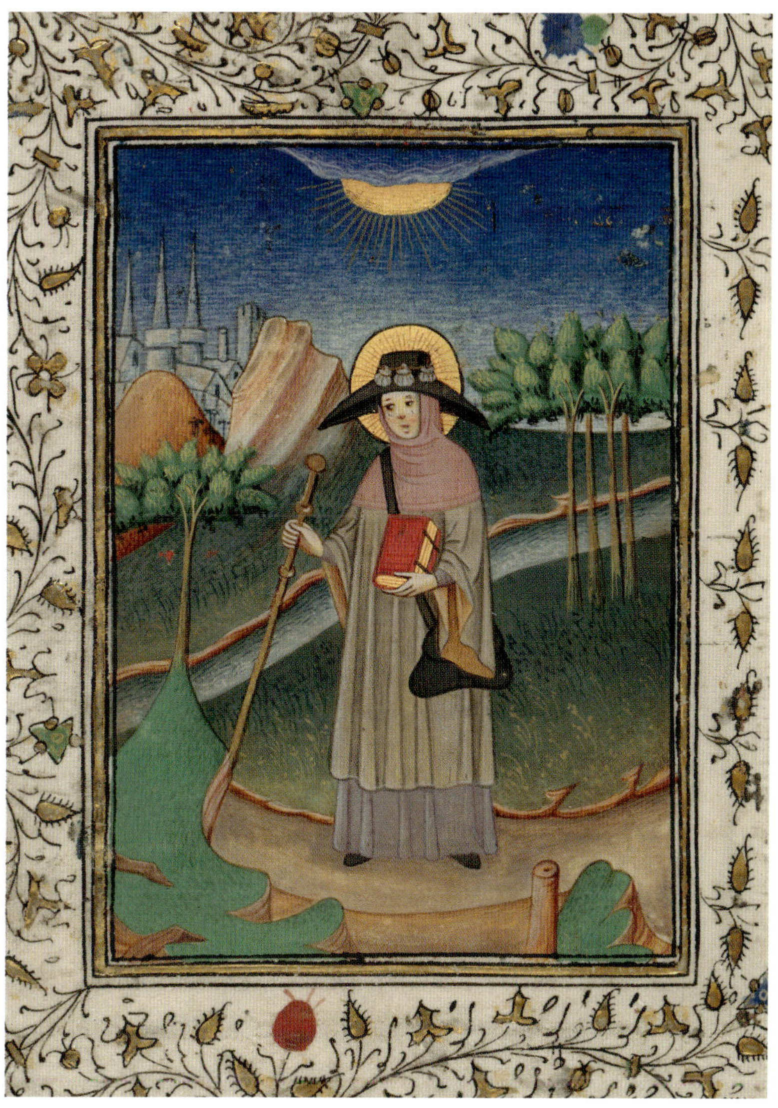

Masters of the Gold Scrolls, *Pilgrim on the Road to the Shrine of Saint James*, Belgium, perhaps Bruges, c. 1440

the background (seen from the front, the cathedral of Santiago has three towers). Often mistaken for a woman because of his delicate features and pious robes, Saint Jodicius looks a bit distressed by the river that blocks his path. But God's approval shines down from a cloud above, and the pilgrim himself radiates spirituality through a resplendent answering halo.

Converging on the Cathedral

Medieval pilgrims took literally the concept of *homo viator* ("man the wayfarer"). They regarded human life as a journey, a physical and spiritual trek through this world to the next. By making their way, they brought themselves closer to a Christ who declared himself "the Way, the Truth, and the Life" (John 14:6). All of their itineraries were in effect part of one long symbolic walk, from the locked gates of Eden to the open doors of the heavenly New Jerusalem. Along their paths they could pray for aid from many saints, including Saint Christopher, patron saint of travelers, who was said to have carried the Christ Child himself across a raging torrent. At the end of a major pilgrimage, a cathedral such as those in Rome, Santiago, or Chartres would welcome the devout. There, they could visit restorative shrines and see relics of venerated saints.

A cathedral represents a microcosm of religious walking and instruction. Perhaps the most complex work of sculpture ever produced in the West, one that needs to be walked around inside and out to be understood, a Gothic cathedral is a pilgrimage in itself. At Chartres, the focal point was the Sancta Camisa, believed to be the covering worn by Mary at the time of Jesus's birth. But first, worshippers would study the detailed and prolific statuary on the doorways: the life of Mary on the north side, apostles and martyrs on the south, and Christ in majesty at the Second Coming over the main entrance. Once inside, they would walk the labyrinth, symbolically retracing their lives and their progress toward salvation, and then make the circuit of the ambulatory chapels and the crypt. All the while they proceeded in the multicolored light of the famous stained-glass windows.

Of the hundreds of stories retold in glass medallions and vignettes, the double narrative of the Good Samaritan window stands out. Pilgrimage is its theme. Paid for, appropriately, by the shoemakers' guild, the window begins its story at the bottom with an advertisement, the signature panels in which the shoemakers work with leather and donate the window. Then several panels show Jesus telling the parable of the Jew who was beaten and robbed on his journey. Ignored by his own priests, he is finally rescued by a good man from Samaria, a place traditionally hostile to Jews. The story takes the viewer only halfway up the window. Seemingly disconnected, the images of the top half depict Adam and Eve, Cain and Abel. But the window makers intentionally used the events from Genesis to present a well-known medieval commentary on the Gospel parable.

While modern audiences might believe they should imitate the Good Samaritan and help others, medieval Christians saw themselves as endangered walkers, dependent on God's grace to see them to safety. The beaten traveler is their forefather Adam, representing humankind. He has lost paradise and must wend

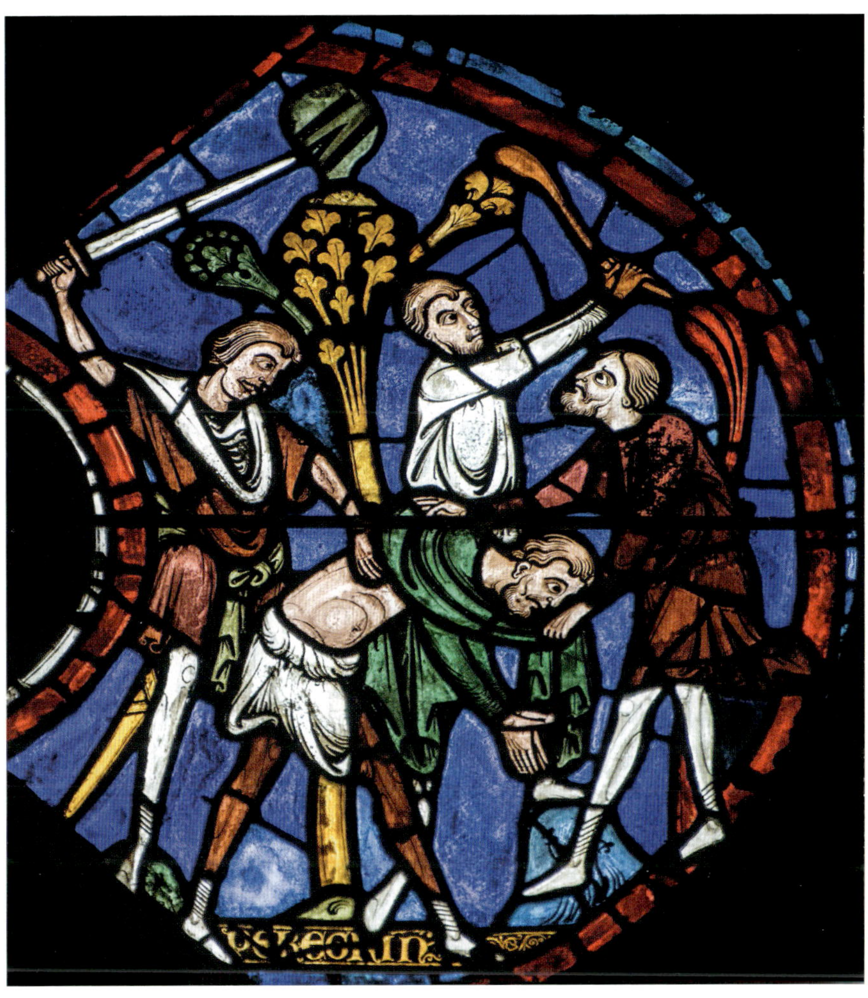

Good Samaritan Window, panel 7, Chartres Cathedral, 13th century

his way through a perilous world. The robbers who thrash him are devils whose evil is repeated in the tale of Cain and Abel. The unhelpful priests are the outmoded Law of the Old Testament. The Good Samaritan is Jesus himself, who by his sacrifice will rescue and heal the poor wanderers of the earth. At the top of the window, Christ in majesty holds the bread of the Eucharist, symbolizing the welcoming meal that can now reward the long-suffering pilgrim, right here at this cathedral.

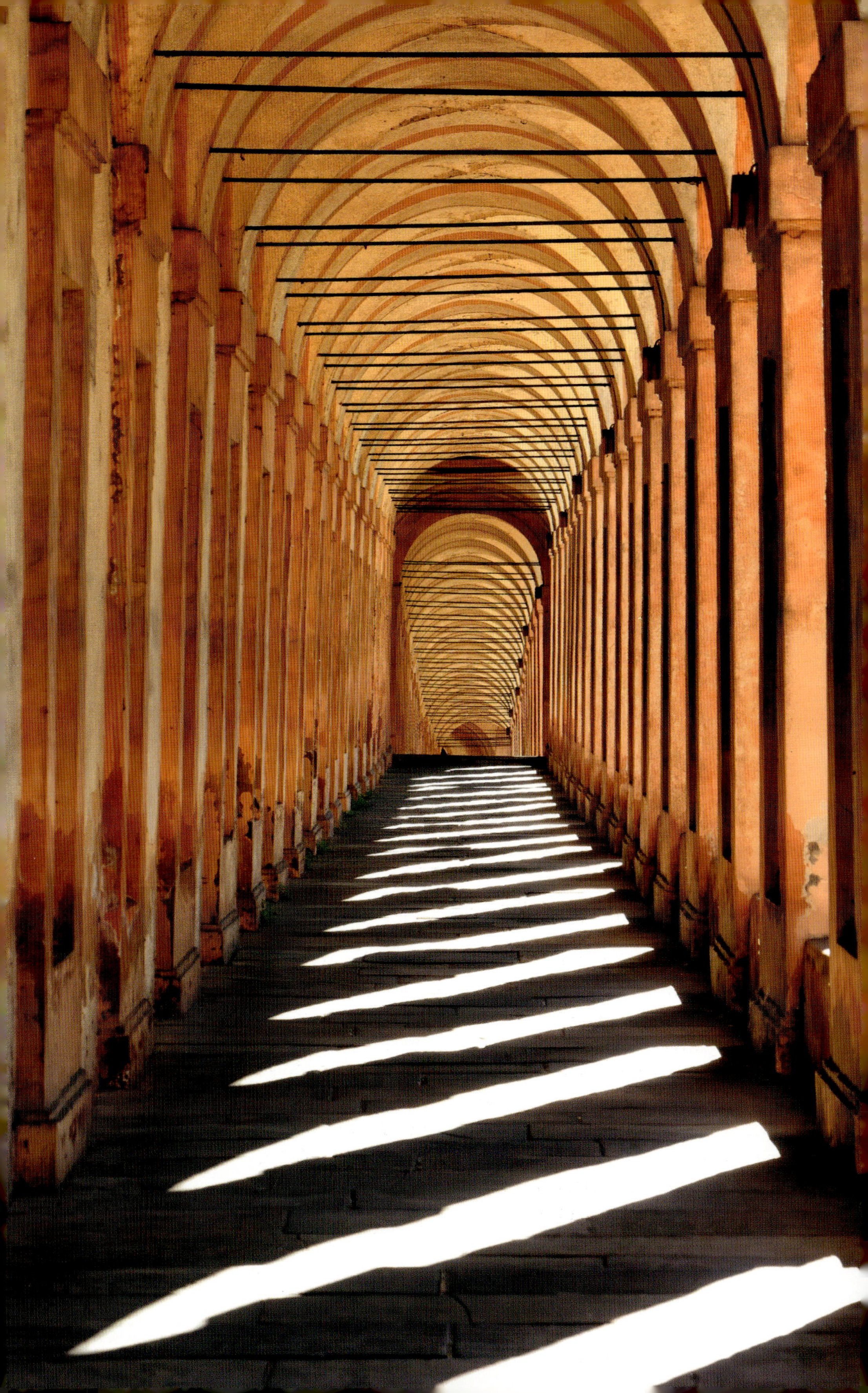

Covered Walking

Stoae, colonnades, porticoes, arcades, cloisters: covered walkways provide pedestrians with a rare amenity, sheltered spaces that are free of traffic and protected from summer heat or cold winter rain. Whereas pilgrims walk exposed to the elements, town dwellers and members of religious orders can stroll comfortably under roofs and arched vaults designed for their convenience.

In ancient Athens teachers and students, merchants and customers, met under roofed colonnades, especially the Stoa Poikile, where the Stoic philosophers gathered. In ancient Rome the porticos of public buildings and temples did similar service. From the Middle Ages on, the recreational and commercial life of European towns was carried on beneath arcades. Technically speaking an arcade, whose name comes from the Latin word for a curved archery bow, is a series of arches supported by columns. Decorative "blind arcades" run along a solid wall and have little depth, but functional urban arcades such as those at the Colosseum in Rome (and at modern sports stadiums) provide a deeper space that can be used as both a walkway and an informal marketplace. Often, as in the famous rue de Rivoli in Paris, permanent shops can be set up not only under the arcade but inside the main street wall of the buildings. In the religious adaptation of arcades, the cloister, nuns and monks meditate while pacing arched passageways built around the four sides of a central garden.

In the later Middle Ages, the people of Bologna built sheltering arches into the very fabric of their city. After the university opened in 1088, enterprising house owners built additional rooms out over the street, supported by columns, to rent to students. By the thirteenth century regulations decreed that the arcades had to be built high enough for a man on horseback to pass beneath. There are over thirty-eight miles of roofed walkways in Bologna, and the ensemble is now a UNESCO World Heritage Site.

Foremost is the world's longest covered walkway, the Portico di San Luca, which stretches over two miles. Climbing to the Sanctuary of the Madonna di San Luca on a hill above the town, the seventeenth-century colonnade features 666 arches and passes fifteen chapels along the way. It enables residents to reach the shrine easily, but its primary purpose is to protect the venerated image of the Madonna, said to have been painted by Saint Luke. Every spring since 1433 it has been carried into the city to ensure that the winter rains will stop. During her sheltered procession the Madonna emulates Bologna's citizens, long accustomed to covered walkways. To this day the sacred image follows in the footsteps of profane pedestrians, touring the city with a roof over her head.

Out of Eden

Driven from paradise, Adam and Eve take what from the Christian perspective is the most significant walk of all time—at least until Jesus carries his cross to Calvary. Their sin of disobedience sets human life in literal motion, and creates the necessity for Jesus to intervene through his sacrifice. In shame and despair, humankind's parents are forced from Eden's gates by a sword-wielding angel who points the way forward. Having failed their future offspring by eating the forbidden fruit, they embark on the painful wandering that henceforth will define the human condition. Anthropologically speaking, this is the mythic moment when the Golden Age idyll yields to the toilsome occupations of farming and herding.

Painted on the wall of the Brancacci Chapel in Florence, Masaccio's *Expulsion from the Garden of Eden* marks a huge advance in the depiction of walking. It is an equally giant step for Renaissance art. No painting to this point had conveyed such physical and emotional drama. Tormented energy ripples through the naked bodies of the wretched sinners, projecting the inner anguish that propels them into exile. The angel drives them, but their guilt drives them harder. Eve howls in woe; Adam covers his face as if to hide from the sight of himself. He steps with the left leg, she with the right. They may be symbolically out of step, but the pair will have to work together.

Masaccio's master, Masolino, had also painted Adam and Eve in the Garden, on the opposite wall of the Brancacci Chapel. But then he went off on another commission. In his absence, the twenty-four-year-old apprentice turned his back on the master's vacant-looking proprietors of Eden, who float idly in space, listening to a snake with a full head of hair. Working for himself, Masaccio thrust real people, stripped naked and exposed to the core, out before the judging eyes of God and Man. Adam and Eve can flee, but they cannot escape the knowledge of what they have done. It seems as if they would gladly depart the painting itself, for their cruelest punishment is sensing that they must endure this agony forever.

Art historians praise Masaccio as the first to construct believable pictorial space in which three-dimensional figures act under the force of gravity. The achievement goes deeper than that, into the actual space in which the fresco was created. Masaccio has designed his work so that the same light that falls through the chapel window seems to cast the light on the limbs of the exiles. The mortal daylight of Florentine reality glares on their painted flesh, as it does on the bodies of those who visit the chapel. Binding spectators to their first parents, it casts their shadows backward toward Eden. Faint but forever following, the unshakeable shadows of their sin dog their footsteps.

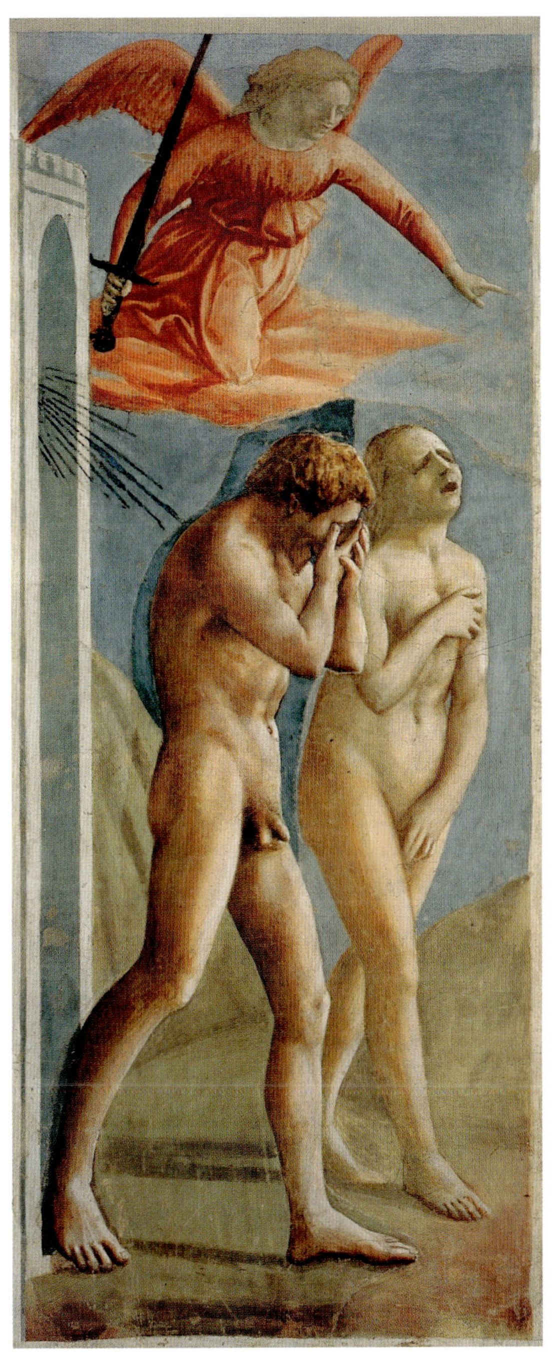

Masaccio, *Expulsion from the Garden of Eden*, 1425

Walking on Water

The Judeo-Christian tradition has no shortage of miraculous walks. Moses parted the Red Sea and strode on through; Saint Peter healed the sick of Jerusalem with his shadow as he passed by; Saint Denis traveled several miles with his head in his hand, preaching repentance, after he was beheaded by Romans at Montmartre.

But from an artistic point of view, the most attention-catching walk belongs to Jesus, as he walks on water. As told in the Gospels, after the miracle of the loaves and fishes, Jesus retires to a mountain to pray while the disciples go on ahead in a boat on the Sea of Galilee. Then, as they battle a windstorm in the night, they suddenly see him walking on the water, and cry out to him. In Matthew's version alone (chapter 14), Peter starts to walk toward Jesus on the water, but sinks when he perceives his danger. Reprimanding him for lack of faith, Jesus takes him by the hand and calms the storm when they get into the boat.

In his stunning painting *The Miraculous Draft of the Fishes*, Konrad Witz creates a technical and theological tour de force that tells this and two other watery stories at once. This is the first European painting of an actual landscape, and by setting biblical events amid the known features of Lake Geneva and the Graian Alps, with Mont Blanc in the background, Witz shows his audience how divine actions can permeate the mundane world of the present. He has painted the reflections and distortions in the water, down to the ripples caused by the oars, with unprecedented accuracy.

The central action of the painting conflates two versions of the miracle wherein Jesus enabled the apostles to catch a mighty haul or "draft" of fish. In the first account (Luke 5), Jesus sits in the boat and bids them put down their nets to make the miraculous catch. In the second version (John 21), Jesus appears on shore after his resurrection and makes the same command, at which Peter plunges into the water in his eagerness to greet his arisen savior. Witz shows both events. First he sets Peter and Jesus in the boat at the left of his painting, and then he portrays them a second time more centrally, with Peter up to his shoulders in deep water and Jesus standing over him near the shore. Jesus casts no reflection, indicating his divinity. His commanding figure floats above the dark, deep water that does not soak his robe. He looks sternly down at the thrashing Peter, whose outstretched hand alludes to a third story, the earlier moment told by Matthew when Peter attempted to walk on water and had to be saved. Like the stained-glass parable of the Good Samaritan, the painting tells viewers that to walk faithfully in the world, on land or water, one must be sustained by divine assistance.

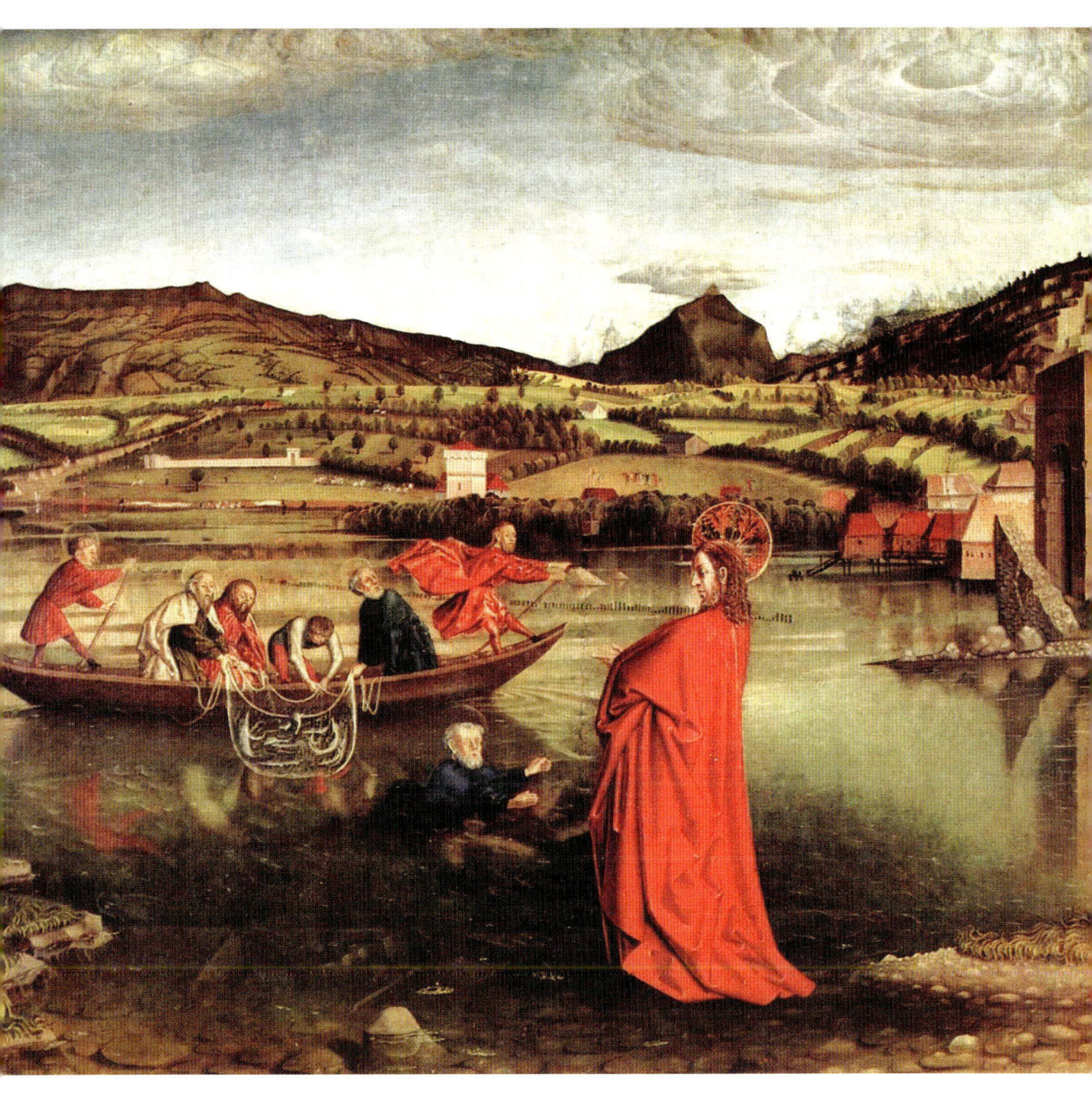

Konrad Witz, *The Miraculous Draft of the Fishes*, 1444

Wandering Jews

For more than three millennia, the holy texts of Judaism have explored what it means to be a wandering people. Among the oldest visual records of Jewish migration are the illustrated Haggadahs from the early Renaissance, ritual guides to the festive seder meal of the Passover. Joel ben Simeon, the illuminator of what is now called the Washington Haggadah, chose a jaunty, well-dressed young man to illustrate the moment in the seder that urges those present to "go forth and learn" about the arduous travels of their people. The text suggests that Judaism is a matter of continued cycles of exile, return, and reward. In the face of that diaspora, the concluding words of the seder, "next year in Jerusalem," convey the determination that Jews will one day return home to find spiritual redemption.

With his shouldered lance and pouch of supplies, ben Simeon's explorer walks briskly toward greater understanding. Representing Jacob and the subsequent migration of the Jews into Egypt, he may also be a portrait of the itinerant artist himself. Ben Simeon circulated between Italy and Germany to ply his trade, crossing the Alps twice. He made no fewer than six versions of this walking figure to illuminate various Haggadahs. Sporting a feathered cap and bright tunic, the walker blithely ignores European regulations prescribing that Jews should dress in a manner that would distinguish them from Christians.

Yet since the thirteenth century, the nomadic history of the Jewish people has been intertwined with another story, the Christian-manufactured legend of the Wandering Jew. The Jew is supposed to have mocked Jesus on the way to the crucifixion, whereupon Jesus replied, "I shall stand and rest, but thou shalt go on till the last day." Condemned to travel the world until the Second Coming, the ragged itinerant is haggard and worn. Sorrowfully, he tells his story to all he meets, seeking to convert both Jews and lukewarm Christians to follow the Way of Jesus.

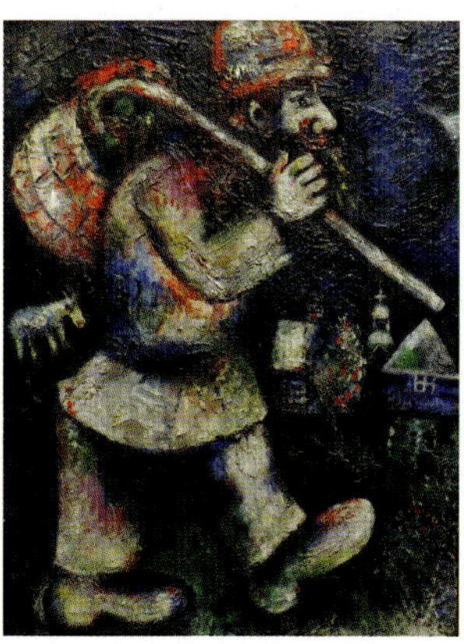

The legend grew at a time when Jews were being expelled from England (1290), from France (1289, 1306, and 1394), from Germany (1348), from Austria (1421), and from Spain (1492). Having banished Jews and confiscated their property, Christians used the story of the Wandering Jew to imply that the forced migrations were the Jews' own fault. Fact imitated fiction, as the legendary Jew's ceaseless steps came to personify the Diaspora of the later Middle Ages.

But gradually the Wandering Jew drew admiration as well as scorn. In the nineteenth century

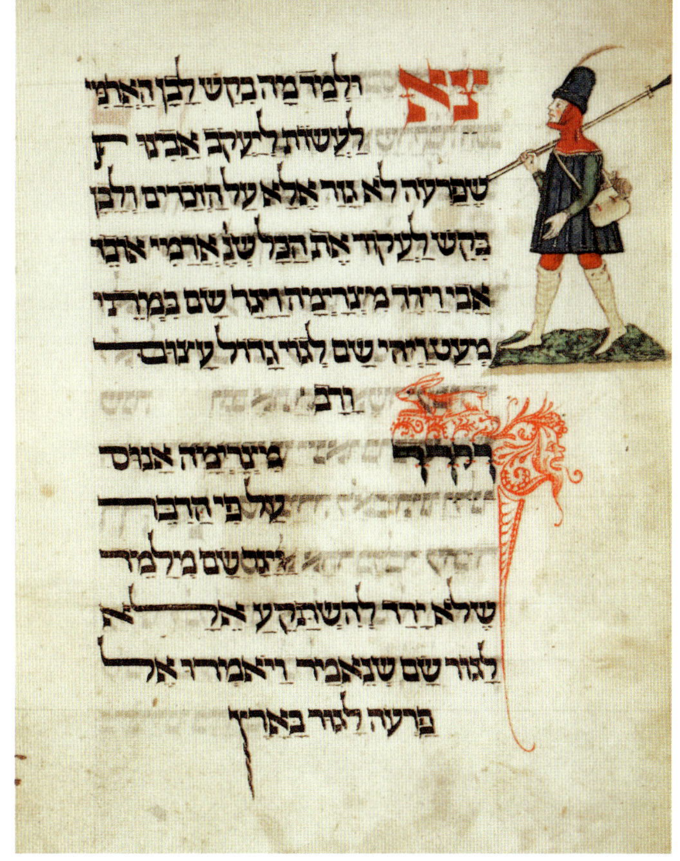

◄ Marc Chagall, *The Wandering Jew*, 1923–25

▸ Joel ben Simeon, traveling figure, Washington Haggadah (detail), 1478

the torment of his endless journeys attracted Romantic writers, who saw him as a Promethean figure whose suffering echoed—and may have inspired—the Flying Dutchman and the Ancient Mariner. Radicals regarded the Jew as representing the endless struggles of the working class. Around 1900, recognizing the heroic power of this haunted figure, Jewish writers, artists, and intellectuals began defiantly adopting the Wandering Jew for their own purposes.

Viewing the Diaspora as a paradoxically unifying condition, Zionists argued that Jews themselves could grant the exile rest by returning to settle in the Promised Land. Reclaimed as an image of resistance to persecution, the weary wanderer has appeared in paintings, fiction, opera, film, graphic novels, and video games. Perhaps his most memorable literary reincarnation is Leopold Bloom, the peripatetic protagonist of James Joyce's *Ulysses* (1922), while the Russian painter Marc Chagall made the wanderer's sturdy form a leitmotif in his scenes of village life. Told and retold, the tale of the Wandering Jew continually confronts Western society with an outcast who refuses to accept that exile will not ultimately bring reward.

A Hell of a Walk

No walking tour has ever taken its participants to such depths or heights. In the *Divine Comedy* (1320) Virgil leads Dante through the darkness of hell and purgatory, then hands him over to Beatrice for a dazzling circuit of heaven. In the first century and a half after the manuscript began to circulate, the poem took its place as one of the monuments of European literature. With the invention of the printing press in the mid-fifteenth century, its fame accelerated and new editions proliferated.

In a bold move for a leading painter, Sandro Botticelli provided some images for the first illustrated edition of the *Inferno* in 1481. But the engraver was not able to emulate the artist's subtle style, and the edition was not a success. Meanwhile

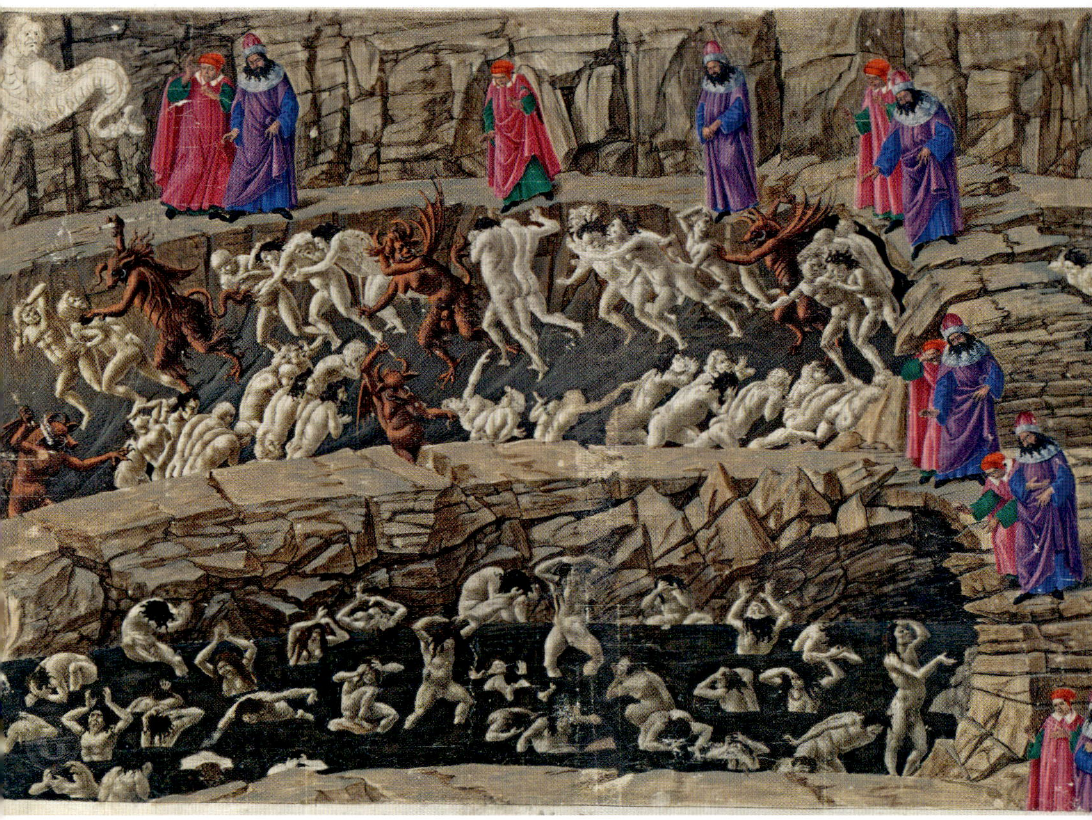

Sandro Botticelli, *Divine Comedy*, canto 18, c. 1490

Botticelli himself could not let go of the project. Possibly on a commission from Lorenzo di Pierfrancesco de' Medici, he began work on a revolutionary book design. His *Inferno* would open vertically, upward, with the illustration on the upper page and the full text of the canto on the sheet below. Overall, the format was about twenty-five inches high by nineteen inches wide. The visual story of each page began in the upper left corner and proceeded across and downward, echoing the way the text, set in four vertical columns, would be read from top to bottom and left to right. Since each picture summarized the action of the whole canto, its entire narrative and thematic sweep could be taken in at a glance, drawing the reader deeper into the Inferno. To turn the page was to move to a new canto and a new part of hell. Thus, as they looked and read, Botticelli's audience would emulate the downward progress of Dante and Virgil.

Choosing not to illustrate one scene per canto but all hundred-plus verses of each one, Botticelli created an intricate and complex work whose achievement rivals that of his *Primavera* and *The Birth of Venus*. Laboring from 1489 to 1505, he produced ninety-two full-page pictures, almost all of them silverpoint drawings. The book was never published, but four fully-colored pages survive to reveal how Botticelli led his viewers deep into his vision of hell.

In canto 18, Virgil and Dante visit the eighth circle. Their path curves steeply downward along the rim of the stone trenches of Malebolge, where those souls who committed fraud are whipped. Prodding them are spiky-winged devils who would become classics of their genre. Botticelli depicts his touristic pair six times, as they stop in different spots to interrogate sinners. Standing out brightly against the pale tormented bodies, the bearded Virgil wears blue and violet robes. Dante sports his characteristic red Florentine cap above magenta robes. Inside the first trench, pimps and seducers make a futile effort to escape their punishment, imitating their own trafficking by scurrying in an endless circle. In the trench of the base flatterers below, the sinners find themselves wallowing in excrement, literally covered in the metaphorical shit they spewed. In the bottom left corner of the image, Botticelli's heroic voyeurs show the audience how lucky they are. They step down out of the repulsive scene, prompting readers to do the same by turning up the page.

A Miraculous Procession

As long as social groups have been proud of their own values and accomplishments, there have been processions to proclaim the fact. Processions display the cohesiveness of parading groups, even if their members fight among themselves for positions of precedence. They walk in orderly fashion, usually bearing proofs of their affiliation, to make public their collective identity. They might be bound together by force, law, faith, or mutual advantage. They might be gown-clad academics or clergy, they might carry in their midst documents, maces, holy objects, or badges of office. Usually they do not walk far, but arrange their route so that public attention and group solidarity coincide. They might be observing a marriage, a death, an anniversary, a triumph, a sacrifice.

And sometimes one procession is cause for another. In 1369 the Scuola Grande di San Giovanni Evangelista in Venice received from the Kingdom of Jerusalem a special gift, reputed to be a piece of the True Cross. The Scuola, a charitable institution run by the leading citizens of Venice, placed the relic, which it still owns to this day, in a reliquary. Soon thereafter they began the practice of taking it out for an annual tour of Venice, the most emphatically pedestrian of the world's great cities. One year the crowd was so dense at the bridge of San Lorenzo that the jostled reliquary fell into the water. Miraculously, it floated, then hovered over the canal. It evaded those who wanted to save it, until the master of the Scuola, who had been the first to accept it as a gift, dove in and reclaimed it for his confraternity.

Further processions produced more miracles. A madman was healed at the Rialto Bridge, while in St. Mark's Square a tradesman who knelt before the relic prayed successfully that his dying son might live. In 1496 the Scuola decided to commission nine paintings of the Miracles of the True Cross. Gentile Bellini, official painter for the Doges of Venice, did three of them.

Painting events that had taken place decades earlier, Bellini decided that the real miracle was the city of Venice itself: its tumbledown, watery beauty, the magnificence of its institutions, the united purpose and beliefs of its citizens. The procession, he saw, does not finally belong to its organizers. Anyone can run ahead or curiously follow, becoming part of its progress, swelling its numbers, increasing its importance. Amid the packed throng at the bridge of San Lorenzo, the white-robed confraternity discover how limited is their control over their own pageant. They can only watch as the miracle of the floating relic unfolds, praying like Caterina Cornaro, queen of Cyprus, on the left, and the reverent gentlemen in the right foreground, the artist among them. A loincloth-wrapped Moor, held by the hand of a woman behind him, hesitates on a boat landing just above them, peering down into the water. Not everyone who witnesses a procession will want to plunge into it.

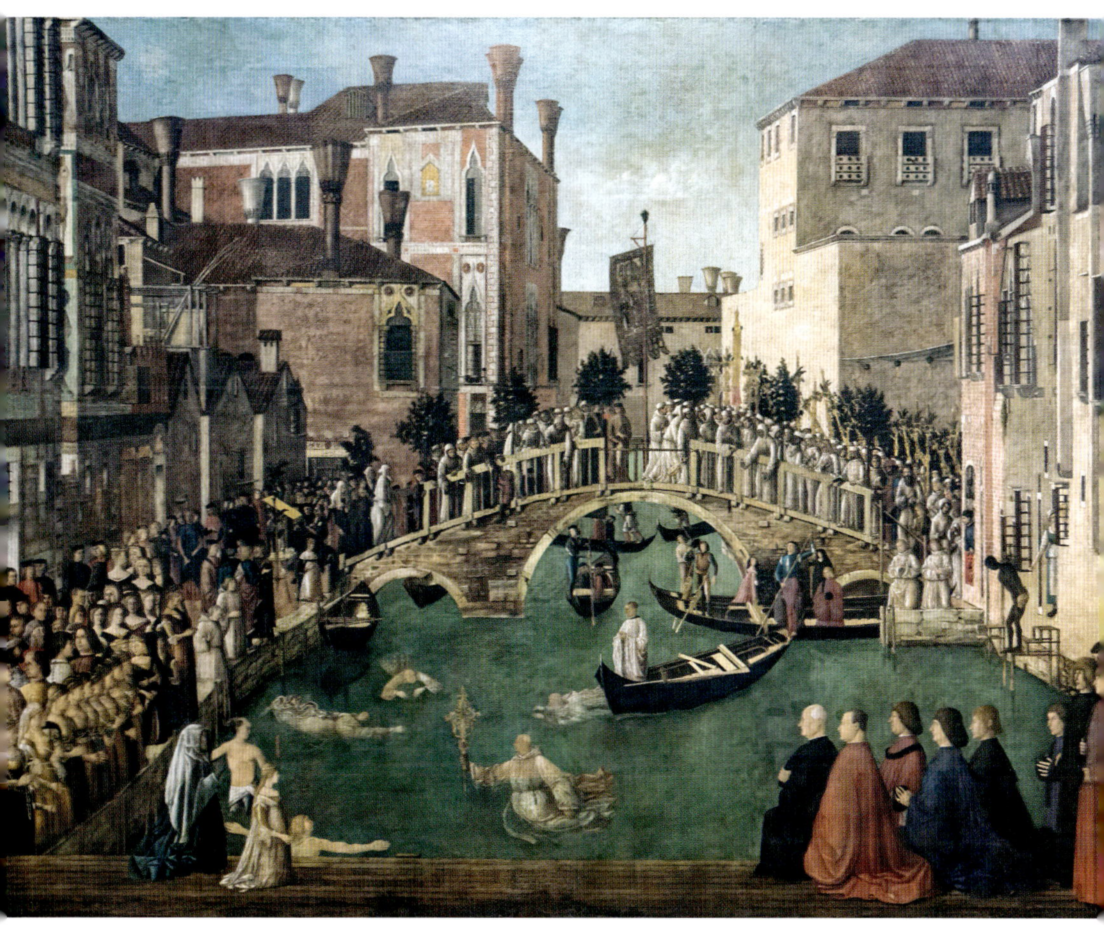

Gentile Bellini, *The Miracle of the Cross at the Bridge of S. Lorenzo*, 1500

Peripatetic Philosophy

Does taking a walk make you a better thinker? Since ancient times, many of the world's most famous philosophers have thought so. The pedestrian routines of Thomas Hobbes, Immanuel Kant, Søren Kierkegaard, Friedrich Nietzsche, and Jean-Jacques Rousseau are often cited as anecdotal evidence, and modern scientific study confirms it: memory, creativity, perception, and problem-solving are all greatly enhanced when the body is in motion. But when people walk, what should they think about? "Higher things," in the realm of abstraction, or down-to-earth observations of what they see in front of them?

In 1509 the painter Raphael posed the question in visual terms, imagining a strolling debate between Plato and Aristotle. Raphael's figures occupy the center of a stunning mural, *The School of Athens*, painted for Pope Julius II in the Vatican. The subject was Aristotle's Academy, a philosophy school that operated in Athens from 335 BCE. It flourished under Aristotle's direction, and continued until the Roman invasion in the first century BCE. Aristotle's followers were called "peripatetic" because of the *peripatoi* or covered walkways that ringed the Lyceum building where they met. The name blended with the later belief that Aristotle walked while he lectured, thereby cementing the relationship between ancient philosophy and ambulatory discourse.

Using the school as a focal point, Raphael took it on himself to portray the most important philosophers of ancient Greece, from the respected Socrates to the much-mocked Diogenes. Giving his philosophers a monumental classical setting, Raphael sought to convey their viewpoints through the disposition of bodies in space. Their thoughts take corporeal form as they spread across marble steps, engaged in animated conversation and physically performing their metaphysical stances. Over twenty figures balance each other on either side of the mural's central axis, indicating the tug-of-war nature of the contest.

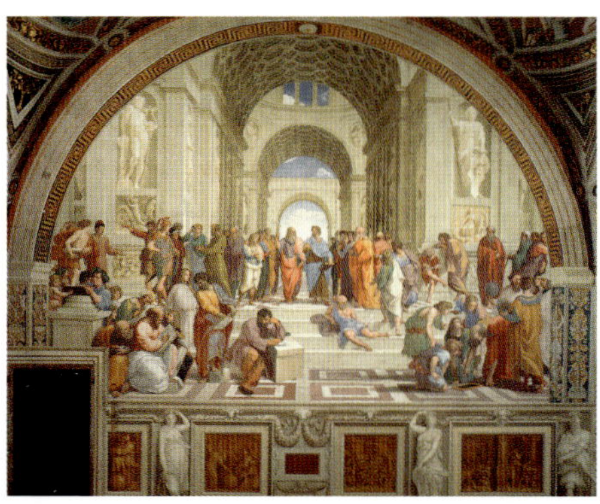

In a virtuoso use of perspective, Raphael located the central debate between Plato and Aristotle at the convergence of the room's architectural lines, connecting the vaulted space of the philosophers with that of their viewers in the Vatican. Plato, given the features of the ultimate Renaissance man, Leonardo da Vinci, points upward toward heaven, alluding to his theory of

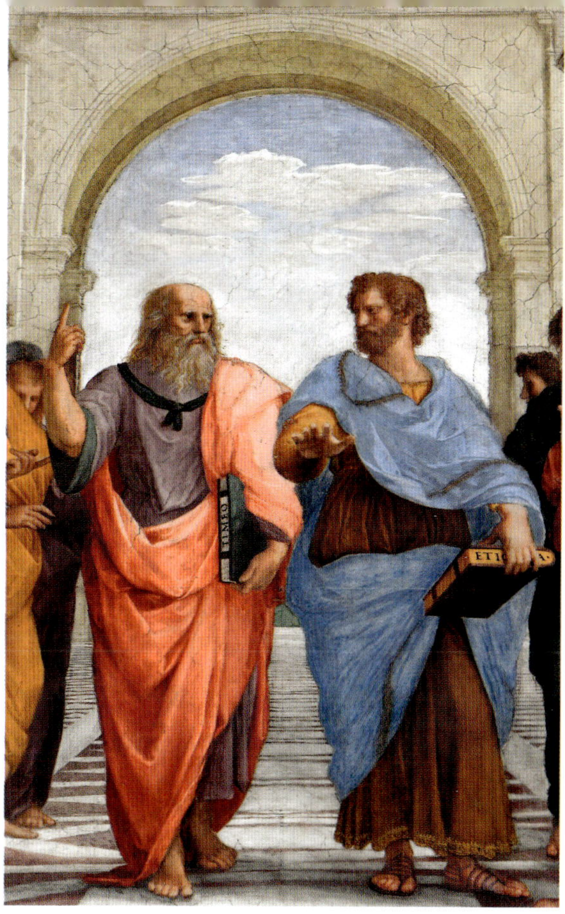

▸ Raphael, Plato and Aristotle walking and disputing, *The School of Athens* (detail), 1509–11

◂ Raphael, *The School of Athens*, 1509–11

abstract, ideal forms. Aristotle, portrayed as a younger man, extends his hand palm downward, as if to push the discussion back toward the material world he treads. Their feet echo their ideas: the barefoot Plato lifts a foot, while the sandal-clad Aristotle has his feet firmly planted.

Although the battle of philosophies appears evenly matched, Raphael gives the last word to art: Aristotle's outstretched hand, located close to the point toward which all the perspective lines converge, thrusts outward at right angles to the picture plane. Dramatic foreshortening makes it look as though the hand extends toward the viewer. The gesture calls attention to the creative hand of the artist, who encompasses a world of thought through the skill of his paintbrush. Raphael silently proposes a theory articulated by the twentieth-century Austrian writer Thomas Bernhard: "If we observe very carefully someone who is walking, we also know how he thinks."

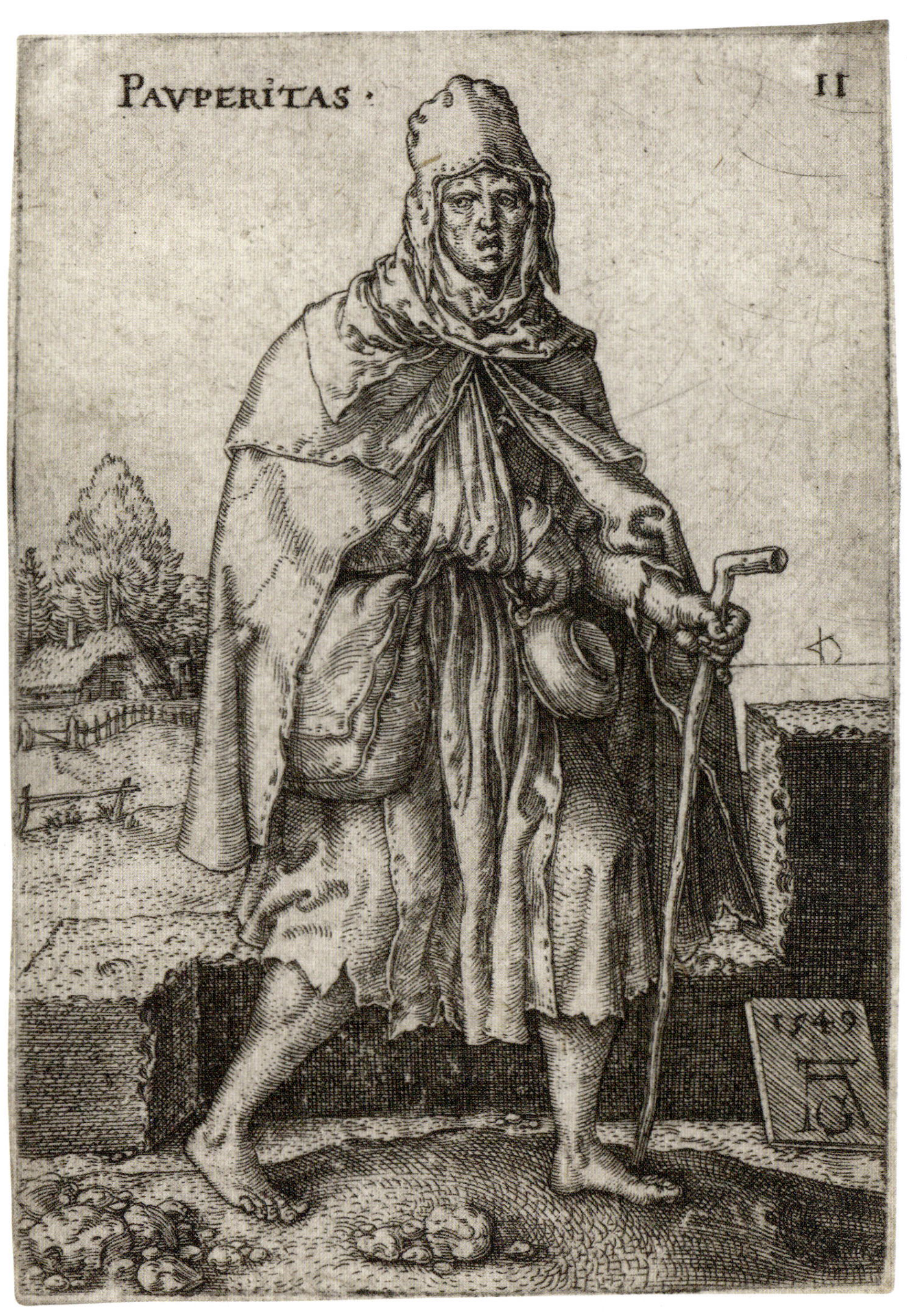

Heinrich Aldegrever, after Cornelis Anthonisz., allegorical figure of Poverty as a wandering vagabond, 1549

Vagrants, Vagabonds, and Beggars

In the Judeo-Christian tradition, the first punishment was walking. Having eaten the forbidden fruit, Adam and Eve were forced from Eden on foot, to wander the world and learn what hard work and mortality meant. The first criminal, Cain, was sentenced by God to be "a fugitive and a vagabond in the earth." To ensure that the punishment endured, "the Lord set a mark upon Cain, lest any finding him should kill him" (Genesis 4:14–15). Western culture has, ever since, regarded vagabondage as both a punishment and a proof of deserving punishment.

For many, mere poverty has been their crime. Medieval and Renaissance authorities presumed vagabonds to be criminals or unlicensed beggars, and acted accordingly. Disease, famine, war, and economic turbulence drove hundreds of thousands onto the road in the Middle Ages. Later, church reforms and the dissolution of monasteries closed many charitable institutions, sending new classes of indigents out on the highways. Unlike pilgrims, who chose to walk in church-sanctioned directions and could ask for food, those who walked from necessity were subject to suspicion, assault, imprisonment, and worse.

In Heinrich Aldegrever's engraving of a work by Cornelis Anthonisz., the allegorical figure of Poverty, "Pauperitas," is presented as a ragged vagabond walking barefoot on a stony road. The farm in the background suggests dispossession, the arm in a sling, that he is unable to work. Leaning on a walking stick and carrying an empty pot to receive food or drink, the haggard figure regards the viewer dolefully, perhaps wondering if alms will be forthcoming.

For all his woes, he was lucky to be Dutch. The cruel insecurities of British householders can be traced in the flurry of laws that targeted the homeless in late medieval and early Renaissance England. In the wake of the labor shortage after the Black Death, the 1379 Ordinance of Labourers sought to keep workers from traveling to seek better pay. It declared that any able-bodied wanderer would be subject to branding and whipping. In the Vagabonds Act of 1530, Henry VIII created the category of "sturdy beggar." Any such would be "whipped until the blood streams from their bodies" for a first offense, have an ear cut off for a second, and executed for a third. (Infirm people, however, might obtain a beggar's license and seek alms as if they were plying a trade.)

Under Edward VI's Vagabonds Act of 1547, "if it happens that a vagabond has been idling about for three days, he is to be taken to his birthplace, branded with a red hot iron with the letter V on his breast, and set to work, in chains." Elizabeth I updated the act in 1572 by defining people without jobs, homes, or land as "rogues" and adding them to the vagabond category. By 1597 unlicensed beggars over eighteen could be executed or transported to Virginia, subject to hanging if they returned. The myth of the jolly vagabond lay almost three centuries in the future.

Walking Blind

And if the blind lead the blind, both shall fall into the ditch.
—*Matthew 15:14*

Pieter Brueghel the Elder's *The Blind Leading the Blind* depicts Jesus's Gospel warning about what happens when the faithful put blind trust in sightless leaders. In classical times, blind individuals were often held in reverence due to the belief that the gods had given them special insight. During the medieval period, as subjects of Jesus's miracles, they merited mercy and alms. But the Protestant Reformation emphasized faith rather than good deeds, and it tended to regard blind people as having been punished by God. They might be real or potential criminals who warranted suspicion, scorn, and mockery. Many of the sightless had little choice but to become wandering beggars.

Brueghel approached this subject with a combination of satire and sympathy. His individualization of his characters, along with a brilliant design, has made this one of the world's most recognizable paintings.

Knowing the parable, Renaissance viewers might have jumped quickly to the conclusion that these men are spiritually blind, deserving to spend time in a ditch. The men's clothing—hats, cloaks, staves, a cross on a chain, and well-padded purses—makes them look more like wealthy pilgrims than starving beggars. They may represent false priests and hypocritical holy men like the Pharisees that Jesus condemns. Yet this interpretation loses punch when one realizes that Brueghel has troubled to give four of the men medical conditions specific enough for doctors to identify, including pemphigoid, phthisis bulbi, corneal leukoma, and enucleation.

The dynamic composition tells a story open to several readings. Arranging his beggars in a left-to-right downward arc, Brueghel gives a pre-cinematic impression of one man caught in six stages of a staggering plunge into a ditch. Yanked forward by their linked staves, the figures spread out as their speed increases. But there is a gap between the two on the right, who have lost control, and the remaining four, heading for the brink. Here Brueghel interposes an actual landscape that includes the Catholic church of Sint-Anna at Dilbeek in Belgium. On his toes, the crucial blind man raises his head to face the steeple. Will the church's presence, sensed if not seen, prevent his fall? Or is the church doctrinally responsible for his plight? Or merely coldly indifferent?

Brueghel leaves open the possibility of salvation, but he does not shy away from considering the opposite fate. Blindness may be less the subject of the picture than the affliction of its audience. The man who has stumbled beyond recovery turns his empty eye sockets toward the painting's viewers. You too? he seems to ask.

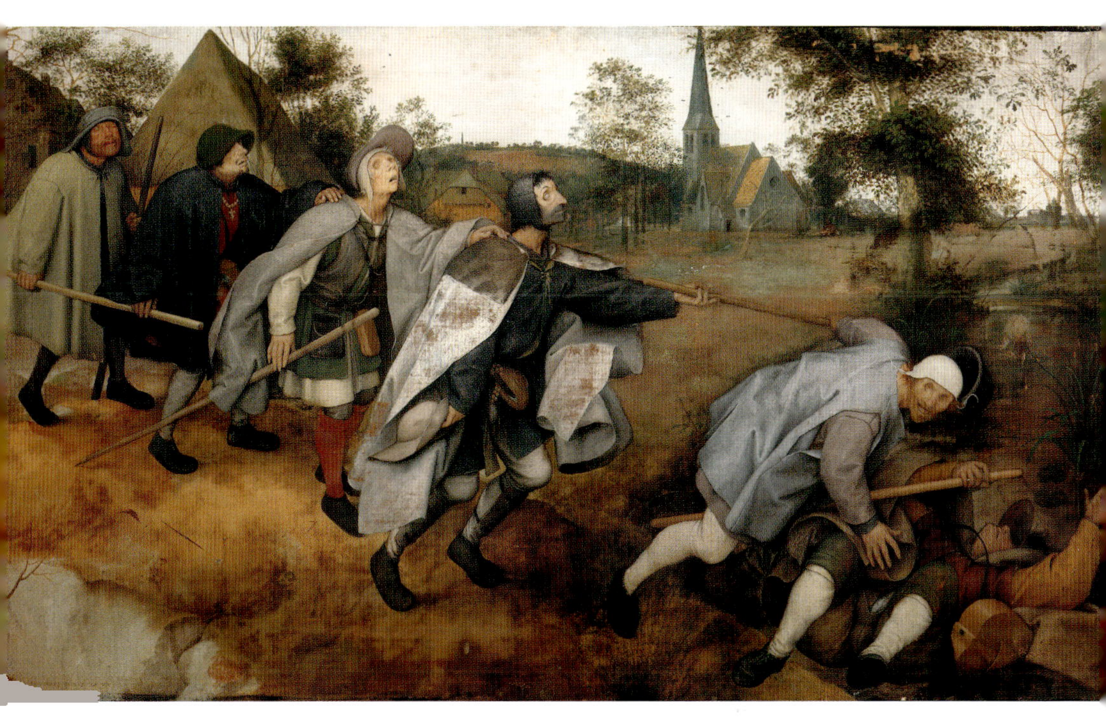

Pieter Brueghel the Elder, *The Blind Leading the Blind*, 1568

High Heels Arrive

In the Middle Ages, harlots were color-coded essential workers. Saints Augustine and Thomas Aquinas, not to mention most civic authorities, agreed that if prostitution were eliminated, lust would destroy the social order. To distinguish "public" women from "honest" women, Pope Clement III ordered that prostitutes dress in a manner that signaled their profession. Yellow was the most common color that sex workers were forced to wear—in Leipzig, Pisa, Venice, and Vienna, for example—while striped hoods were required in London and Bristol, and striped tunics in Marseilles. In Florence a working woman had to don an elaborate outfit that included gloves, bells in the hair, and high-heeled slippers.

But the prescribed heels were a misstep. After 1400, almost all women of social standing apparently wanted to wear them. Originating in the Middle East, the fashion came to Spain in the form of elaborately decorated cork-soled platform shoes called chopines, which women wore ostentatiously visible below the hems of their dresses. In Italy the shoes were made of wood and hidden by the dresses, with tantalizing results. The height of the shoes, up to twenty inches, not only increased women's stature and provoked curiosity about their true height; it also required them to lengthen their skirts to reach the floor. In this way they could show off their wealth in the form of costly textiles. And because they were hidden, the shoes acquired the status of sexy underwear, to be guessed at but rarely seen.

In 1588, however, a pioneer of the interactive book, Pietro Bertelli, took advantage of the licentious reputation of Venetian women to publish a series of fashion plates in which courtesans did yield some of their coquettish secrets. He applied the lift-the-flap format of Renaissance medical books to expose not internal organs but underwear and enticing body parts, soliciting the active engagement of his well-to-do masculine customers. Suggesting that love does not always have to be blind, this engraving depicts a courtesan with a hinged dress that an admirer, if smitten by the cupid flying beside her, could lift to reveal her ten-inch charms.

Laws that forced prostitutes to wear chopines muddied social distinctions. High heels and low-cut dresses could be worn by both common streetwalkers and "honest" courtesans. The latter category included highly educated daughters of respected families, women able to amass considerable wealth and personal influence. Venetian rulers passed sumptuary laws forbidding women to dress above their station—in a literal sense, since in 1430 the height of chopines was limited to three inches. But there seemed to be no way to prevent noble women from imitating prostitutes, and vice versa. The taller the woman, the richer her family, the higher her social status, and the more enticing—if she could manage to walk gracefully—the shoes beneath.

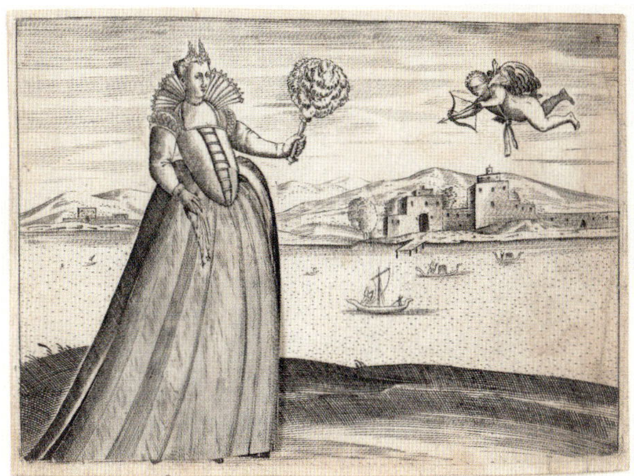

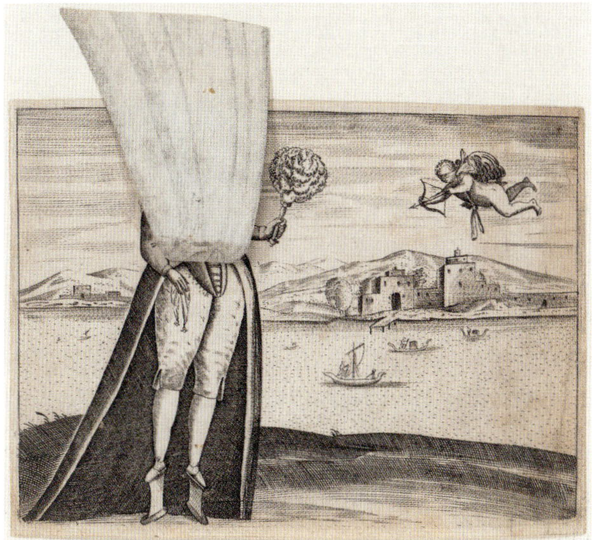

Pietro Bertelli, publisher, *Courtesan and Blind Cupid*, c. 1588

Pietro Bertelli, publisher, *Courtesan and Blind Cupid*, c. 1588, movable skirt lifted

If the shoes were really tall, a woman might need an attendant on either side to help her balance. But the key to social success was a studied way of lifting a foot without bending the knee. A treatise on courtly dance explained that "this extension keeps her body attractive and erect, besides which her chopine will not fall off." If a lady can master the technique, the author concluded, "she will seem to be on chopines only three fingerbreadths high, and will be able to dance flourishes and galliard variations at a ball."

The Pilgrim's Progress

Often regarded as the first novel in English, John Bunyan's *The Pilgrim's Progress from This World to That Which Is to Come* unfolds like a hiker's nightmare. Treacherous bogs, expensive towns, vicious monsters, early nightfall, and poor directions plague Bunyan's hero. Luckily, it's only a book, and a dream in a book at that. Medieval Catholic pilgrims slogged toward shrines, but English Puritans could take the perilous journey allegorically, reading Bunyan's spiritual adventure while staying safe at home. In fact, it's a meta-narrative journey, since Bunyan's protagonist, an everyman named Christian, reads while he walks. Deeply worried about what he finds in the Bible, Christian resolves to travel to the Celestial City. Unable to convince his wife and children about the dangers of their hometown, the City of Destruction, Christian departs alone, staggering under a metaphorical burden that torments him more than a sixty-pound backpack. It represents the weight of his knowledge of sin. He will not find a way to release its straps until he climbs the steep hill of Calvary.

Over twenty places near Bunyan's Bedfordshire home in southeast England have been identified as possible sources for the geographical features of Christian's journey. Bunyan may even have based the itinerary on the route he himself often took from Bedford to London. In contrast to its earlier checkered reputation, the metropolis had acquired, after the Great Fire of 1666, a "Celestial City" aspect, dazzling visitors with the dozens of church spires designed by Sir Christopher Wren.

Unlike the road to London, Christian's way is anything but straight or well marked. In the *Divine Comedy* Dante was shepherded expertly by Virgil and Beatrice. Christian, however, belongs to the self-reliant Puritan tradition, and must fend for himself. Ravines, walls, fences, and wild beasts bar his way. A still greater peril comes from the unreliability of his fellow travelers, whose names—Obstinate, Pliable, Talkative, Ignorance—reveal the poor advice they offer. Along the way, Christian and his readers encounter spiritual snares that take on physical form: the swampy Slough of Despond, the alluring Vanity Fair, and the terrifying Valley of the Shadow of Death.

For centuries the most reprinted book in England, *The Pilgrim's Progress* has been a paradise for artists and illustrators. They have visualized its events in media ranging from engravings, oil paintings, and animated films to graphic novels, manga, and video games. The very first image, seen here, appeared opposite Bunyan's title page in 1679, telling the story in condensed form. In the background, carrying his burden and reading his Bible, Christian heads uphill from the City of Destruction toward the Celestial City. Meanwhile, in the foreground, his author dreams it all, unperturbed by the lion lurking below him. Bunyan's fearless slumbers convey a

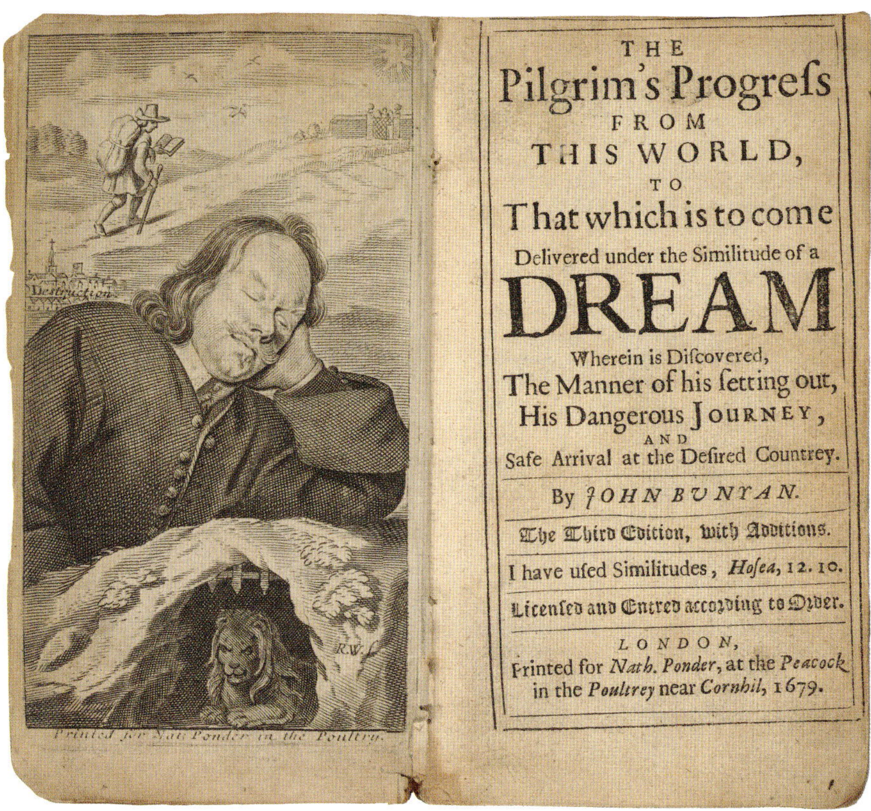

John Bunyan, *The Pilgrim's Progress*, frontispiece and title page, 1679

Daniel-in-the-lion's-den message about the blameless steadfastness of his faith. Like the prophet Daniel, Bunyan was imprisoned for his beliefs, and it was in prison that he began this work. The portcullis gate raised above the lion's head shows that the lion (who also figures in the dream, testing the faith of pilgrims) is free to attack Bunyan but, as in the biblical tale, chooses not to harm a true believer. On the title page, the central word DREAM is capitalized and placed level with Bunyan's eyes and forehead to stress the prophetic, God-sent nature of Bunyan's vision. Like Bunyan's hero Christian, readers will learn to see the world in a new light.

The Pilgrim's Progress remains the most widely read book ever written about a walking journey. Its current rival, *The Lord of the Rings,* reverses the journey but not the moral message. Throwing the corrupting Ring into the fires of Mount Doom at the end of his epic trek, the Hobbit Frodo accomplishes for Middle Earth what Christian does for his own soul, shedding the burden of despair and putting to flight the powers of darkness.

Walking with the Sun King

In the art of the Middle Ages and the Renaissance, most walking has a religious purpose. But while pious people struggled on the straight and narrow path, a far-reaching social transformation was gathering momentum. Parts of the wicked world were turning back into gardens, not through prayer but through the pleasure-minded decrees of royalty.

The nobility took the first step. In the sixteenth century aristocrats were advised to walk for their health, and when the weather did not permit strolling in gardens designed for the purpose, they turned to indoor galleries, such as the famous one spanning the river Cher at Chenonceau. Later they hung paintings on the walls to give them something to look at as they did their laps.

The next step involved a larger group of the wealthy, what might be called "society," who gradually gained access to former royal preserves over the course of the seventeenth century. The Jardin des Tuileries in Paris was opened to the public in 1667, following London's Hyde Park, opened by Charles I of England in 1637. Formerly Henry VIII's hunting ground, Hyde Park became a popular recreation area, especially known for its May Day parades. In Vienna, royal consent allowed nobles and persons of distinction to frequent the Prater Park on the Danube River. As enclosed places whose access could be controlled by royal whim, such parks were often used for elaborate shows, such as fireworks on royal birthdays or celebrations to mark victories and marriages.

Standing at the center of European fashion, Versailles and the court of Louis XIV decisively changed the status of walking. As "the most public palace in Europe," Versailles welcomed visitors of social standing, whom it stunned with its lavish demonstration of power and opulence. Newcomers strained for a glimpse of the king, while habitués made it their business to be seen daily by his majesty, presenting as devoted and charming an appearance as possible. Under the keen eye of the Sun King, how people walked demonstrated who they were. Each step became a performance designed to enhance the status of the walker. With luck and skill, a courtier could use a walk to become Someone on earth rather than a humble soul in heaven.

When the king, seen here in red stockings about 1700, walked at Versailles, he liked to have his entourage properly arrayed. In landscape paintings, the peasants who labor in the background providing scale and minor activity are called staffage. For Louis XIV, even nobles could play that role. Their courtly presence reflected his glory visually as well as politically.

As Étienne Allegrain's painting shows, persons of consequence had to develop a style to move gracefully down a garden path. It was de rigueur to affect a godlike

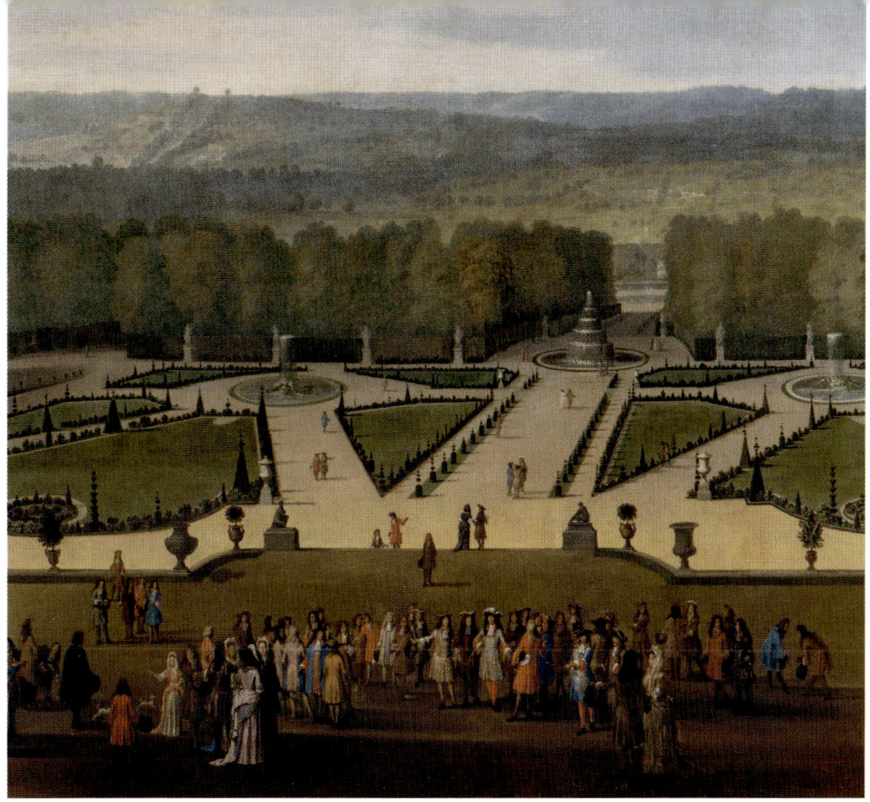

Étienne Allegrain, *Louis XIV Taking a Walk, Seen from the North Parterre of the Gardens of Versailles* (detail), 1688

superiority of motion that nevertheless showed proper respect for social hierarchies, particularly if the monarch was present. The latest in virility was high heels for men, and the newly important schools of ballet, encouraged by the king, taught them how to make polished progress around the grounds. In fact, the toe-turned-out style of walking in ballet derives from the way earlier courtiers finessed their steps in big boots fabricated more for warfare than showing off.

The court rituals that required an elegant company to promenade ostentatiously in an elegant spot grew organically from the magnificent gardens of Versailles. In fact, the gardens were open to courtiers and the public well before the palace itself was finished; manners evolved to suit the setting. Laid out in the 1660s by André Le Nôtre (seen standing proudly to the right of the king in Allegrain's painting), the gardens provided eight hundred hectares of lawns, parterres, canals, and statues. The celebrated Water Walk led strollers past fourteen fountains adorned with sculptures of tritons, satyrs, and cherubs. The king himself enjoyed conducting his most eminent guests around the grounds, pointing out its subtleties and splendors. Louis even wrote out four different itineraries for visitors to follow—becoming in effect a royal tour guide to his own domain.

A Good Walk Spoiled

"A good walk spoiled," runs the famous definition of golf. Perhaps no social activity voluntarily undertaken has engendered as much frustration. Only on a golf course can a pastoral stroll in the company of friends routinely produce misery and despair. Yet for centuries people have been unable to resist golf's demonic attraction. In Scotland, traditional home of the sport, the first document to mention golf is James II's law banning it in 1457, because it took too much time away from learning archery. King James IV, the first monarch known to have had his own set of clubs, reinstated golf in 1502. Development of courses soon followed. The Old Course at St Andrews dates to the later sixteenth century, the Musselburgh Links to 1672, and the standard eighteen-hole course was approved at St Andrews in 1764.

Along with clubs, ball, and terrain came rules. The oldest existing regulations, many of which apply to this day, were set down in Edinburgh and Leith in 1744. Few sports expect better behavior than golf; courtesy to other players matters as much as ability with a club. This is not surprising, given golf's walk-intensive character. In an era when social precedence determined every step that gentlefolk took, from who might stroll at the center of a group to who had to cross a stile or a stream last, rule makers recognized that the game was not an escape from society but an extension of it. Fierce as the competition might be, the sociability of golf requires each player to think first of the respect due to other participants. Concern for athletic performance is not allowed to disrupt the rituals of deference, and while scrupulous honesty is expected, players observe each other's behavior near the ball with hawklike intensity.

Although golf was not introduced into the United States until 1888, three of its four major tournaments now take place there, and it was in the United States that the sport's fundamental nature was legally contested. Is the walk on a golf course, whether wretched or rejuvenating, a necessary component of the game? A good golfer will walk five miles around a standard course, and unpracticed amateurs considerably more. The potential fatigue of golfers, even if they have caddies to carry their clubs, has long been considered part of the physical challenge.

But in 2001 a disabled golfer named Casey Martin successfully sued to compete in professional tournament play. The US Supreme Court ruled that a disabled golfer had a legal right to ride in a golf cart, since an impairment requiring a cart would produce sufficient fatigue getting to and from the ball (about a mile's worth of painful walking). A continuous walk between shots was not deemed essential. In opening up play to the disabled, the decision tacitly implied that the primary rule of golf is not about the body; it lies in consideration for one's opponent. Secure in the knowledge that tribulations await all golfers, no matter how short the trip to

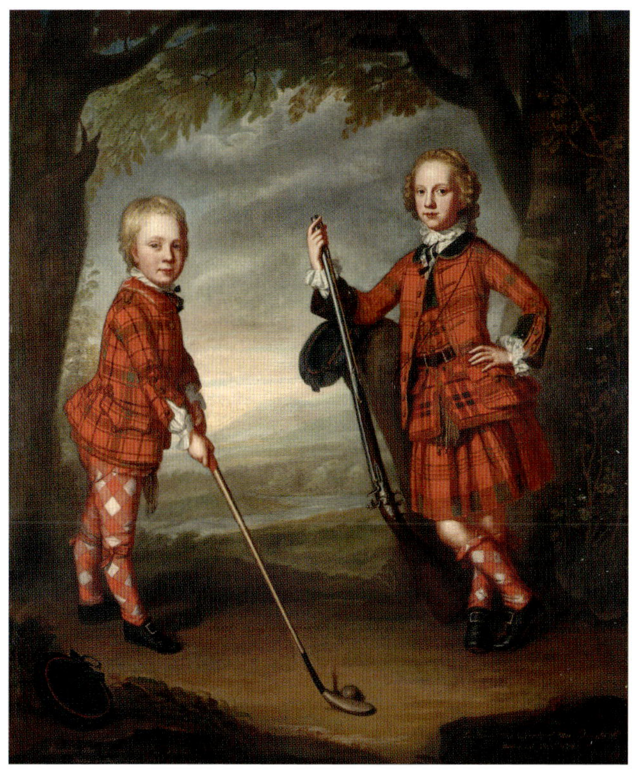

Unknown artist (attributed to William Mosman), *Sir James MacDonald, 1741–1766, and Sir Alexander MacDonald, 1744/45–1795* (*The MacDonald Boys Playing Golf*), c. 1749

the ball, duffers and professionals alike gallantly extend courtesy to fellow victims of their obsession.

Back in the eighteenth century, the tartan-clad MacDonald brothers were doubly ready to make their shots. There's no cart or course visible, but young Alexander has a textbook grip on the ancestor of a fairway wood. Meanwhile, his elder brother James looks supremely confident that he will bag a birdie or two—with his fowling piece. Setting golf on a par with shooting as an aristocratic pursuit, the portrait asserts the socially elevated nature of a game that would later become a favorite of American presidents and those who want to strengthen their position on the social ladder. In its more immediate context, the bloody attempt of Bonnie Prince Charlie to gain the British crown in 1745, William Mosman's painting reassures viewers that the moors in the background will be used for sport, not slaughter. The tartan is no different from a fox-hunting outfit, it seems to say; dressed for a good tramp outdoors, these Scots know how to play by the rules.

Picture Perfect

"Pictures to walk into," the English upper classes called their country parks. While French aristocrats promenaded around symmetrical royal gardens, the very notion of landscape—a concept dating from seventeenth-century Dutch painting—was evolving to meet a growing English demand for more varied scenery. "All gardening is landscape painting," declared the poet Alexander Pope in 1734.

The key figure in the transformation was William Kent, who in the 1730s redesigned the English garden so that it took its inspiration not from architectural motifs but from an idealized conception of nature. Previously the great estates such as Blenheim Palace and Castle Howard featured formal gardens adorned with statuary and floral designs, in the style of Versailles. But Kent drew his ideas from the paintings of Claude Lorrain and Nicholas Poussin, paintings in which Greek divinities wander in pastoral playgrounds of an imagined Golden Age.

Through a skillful deployment of pictorial effects, Kent and his successors, such as Capability Brown and Humphry Repton, pulled observers deep into garden vistas. Great lawns rolled down to an artificial lake or a rerouted river, highlighted by an off-center bridge that created the urge to cross it. Winding paths brought strollers past edifying allegorical statues and philosophy-inducing ruins. Distant classical temples or Gothic ruins functioned as eyecatchers, inviting spectators to mount expeditions toward viewpoints where still more "wild nature" awaited. The very notion of scenery came from theatrical sets, and Kent expertly juggled his artifices to create a three-dimensional work of art whose biggest selling point was how "natural" it looked.

Kent had his greatest success at Stowe House in Buckinghamshire, where he worked from 1731 until he died in 1748. The owners of Stowe, their guests, and respectable-looking tourists, drawn by the property's fame, could wander the extensive grounds in all seasons. Rather than display its charms from a central viewpoint, Stowe evolved into an unfolding panorama that required a sustained walk to sample its ingenious marriage of nature and culture. Freed from a set itinerary, visitors could make their own discoveries of prospects and nooks that Kent had artfully prepared for them, including a Temple of Ancient Virtue and a Temple of British Worthies.

An appreciation of Kent's much-discussed "improvements" could even be acquired without making an expedition to Stowe. Those planning a trip or wanting a souvenir could admire Jean Baptiste Claude Chatelain's painted sample of Stowe's attractions, seen here in George Bickham's engraved version of 1753. Captioned in both English and French to reach the growing market for picturesque prints, Chatelain's scene groups several of the features that captivated strollers.

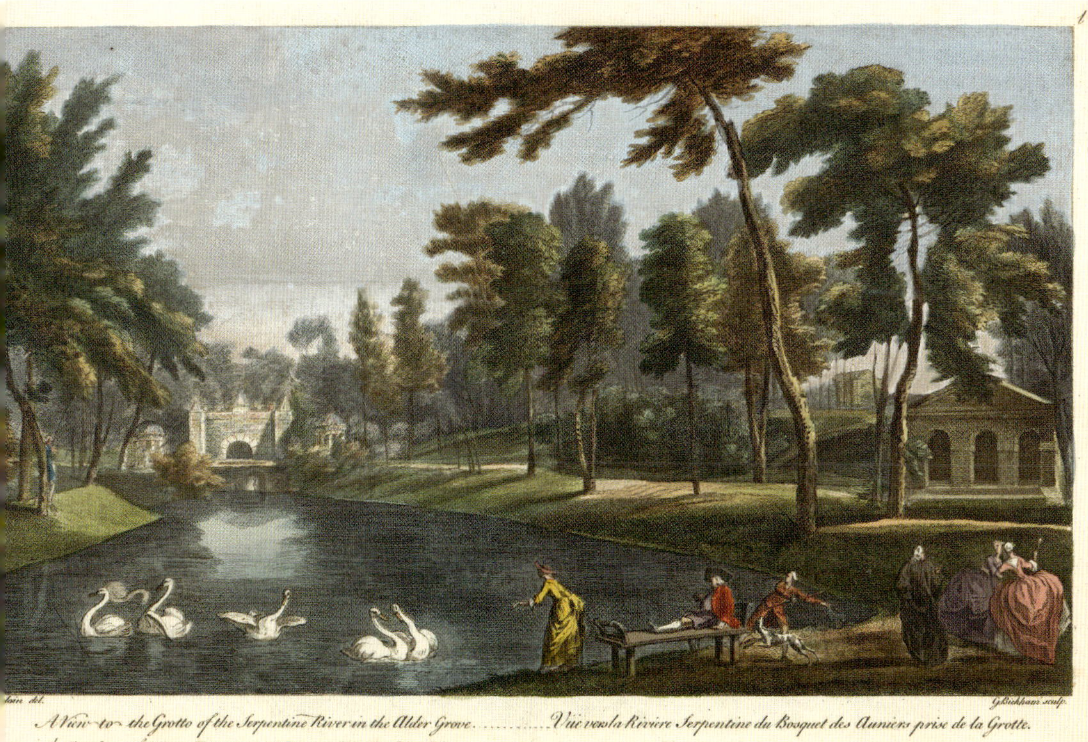

Jean Baptiste Claude Chatelain, artist; George Bickham, engraver, *A View to the Grotto of the Serpentine River in the Alder Grove in the Gardens of Earl Temple at Stow, in Buckinghamshire*, 1753

A sinuous river leads past faux temples to a bridge and a grotto, while shady pathways beckon from both banks. In the foreground, possibly at the start of a morally elevating promenade, a black-robed cleric raises a remonstrative finger toward two frolicking young ladies. Meanwhile a boy tosses a stick for his dog, a rotund gentleman rests a leg on a bench, and another young woman feeds the swans. Leaving a walk past virtue-engendering statues for another day, a gentleman angler leans negligently against a tree to adjust his bait, completing the picture of exquisitely engineered idleness.

Yet for all Stowe's beauty, Kent's most significant innovation was invisible. "Kent leaped the fence, and saw that all nature was a garden," as Horace Walpole famously put it. In fact, Kent removed the fence altogether. He let the garden blur back into woodland and pasture by using a deep ditch and sunken wall to keep animals out.

The device permitted the eye to travel from the great house outward to nature without impediment, as if looking at a painting. The trench was called a ha-ha because people reportedly exclaimed "Aha!" when they came upon it. At Stowe the ha-has extend over four miles, encompassing over four hundred acres. Unseen from vantage points near the house, the ha-ha concealed gardeners, farmworkers, and cattle as they moved about the estate, helping owners and their guests preserve the fantasy of idyllic, labor-free leisure.

Kent's innovations had far-reaching effects on the entire European relationship to nature, overthrowing the French formal style and influencing landscape design in France, Germany, and even Russia. Subversive in more than concept, the apparent "natural liberty" of the English park evolved into a political statement. Not only did it encourage the independent meditations of the walker but it also spoke, through its winding paths and untrimmed horizons, about freedom from the social tyranny of the old order. With help from human artifice, Nature took the upper hand.

Public Parks

For some people, the most important thing about a walk is where it is taken. Gabriel de Saint-Aubin specialized in painting the French aristocracy at leisure as they brought their elaborate courtly rituals out into the open air, to see and be seen against a backdrop of pastoral harmony. Parisian promenades demanded ornate dress, ambulatory know-how, and beautifully made accouterments such as fans, canes, and swords. Ideally, the strollers would look as intricately adorned as the trees that arched over them.

In their quest for visibility, the upper classes were aided by the growing popularity of landscaped gardens, which in urban areas took a new form, the "public" park. Carefully regulated by the monarchs and nobles who owned the land, these urban green spaces were at first hedged round with rules that prevented any casual mixing of social classes. Open to certain groups at certain hours, with plenty of bouncers at the gates, the groves and alleys of well-fenced gardens provided the European elite with an informal arena for self-promotion and gossip. As early as 1616 Queen Marie de Medici of France established the Cours la Reine in Paris, where nobles could walk at fashionable hours, undisturbed by the presence of commoners. Although the gardens of Versailles became more accessible to commoners under Louis XV, men's admission was still dependent on their wearing the requisite silver buckles and sword, even if these could be rented at the gate.

By the 1760s, rigid class segregation was easing. Here Saint-Aubin gives pride of place to a young lady who lifts one of her capacious skirts with delicacy, while her escort points his toe with studied grace. But to the left, an aged beggar has managed to get in. He approaches a seated foursome, his hat outstretched for a coin. The beggar's presence indicates that a transition is underway. For the moment he seems an intruder, an exception proving the rule that parks belong to the decorative classes. But change is coming.

The Revolution might have been avoided, some thought, if only there had been more parks. Benevolent rulers like Charles Theodore, elector of Bavaria, believed that if they could provide enough good walks in agreeable surroundings, they could keep common people happy and ease class tension. Already in *Julius Caesar* (1599), Shakespeare's Mark Antony calms an angry Roman mob by telling them that Caesar had left them in his will "All his walks, / His private arbours, . . . / And to your heirs for ever,—common pleasures, / To walk abroad and recreate yourselves." Even earlier, in 1592, the viceroy of New Spain decreed the first public green space in the New World, the Alameda Central Park in Mexico City, overlaying an Aztec marketplace with Spanish gardens. Just a few years after Saint-Aubin's painting, Emperor Joseph II of Austria opened the former royal park of the Prater in Vienna for public entertainment (1766), and Charles Theodore, his eye on the revolution in France, opened the English Garden in Munich (1789). Built on the model of country parks in Britain, the English Garden is often regarded as the first modern public park because it was expressly designed to encourage the relaxed mingling of citizens from all social strata.

As the perceived value of outdoor walks increased, society's leading lights began to walk farther afield, beyond fenced gardens, and for more than social display. Writers promoted the idea that walking abroad was instructive, like being in a library: "He does not see a book, but everyone he sees serves as a book," wrote François de Grenaille in 1641. Eighteenth-century doctors such as the influential Theodore Tronchin, friend to Denis Diderot, Jean-Jacques Rousseau, and Voltaire encouraged walking for health.

Delicate sensibilities were also protected by a new form of road, the boulevard. The word itself came from the German *bollwerk* ("bulwark"), and was transferred from ramparts to roadways because the first of the *grands boulevards* were built by Louis XIV along the route where the city wall of Louis XIII had stood. All over Europe the defortification of towns produced walks on the razed or elevated ground of former ramparts. Those in Paris went further, combining park, path, and carriageway so that walkers and riders could observe each other and socialize if they chose. A central lane allowed for slow promenading in carriages, while strollers enjoyed the side alleys, shielded by trees from the traffic, a scheme still employed in Paris today. Traffic separation allowed for social separation: because the boulevards circled the city rather than entering it, they were not working streets, full of common people plying common trades. By knowing where to go and when, stylish *promeneurs* could enjoy parks without having to face the public they were ostensibly designed for.

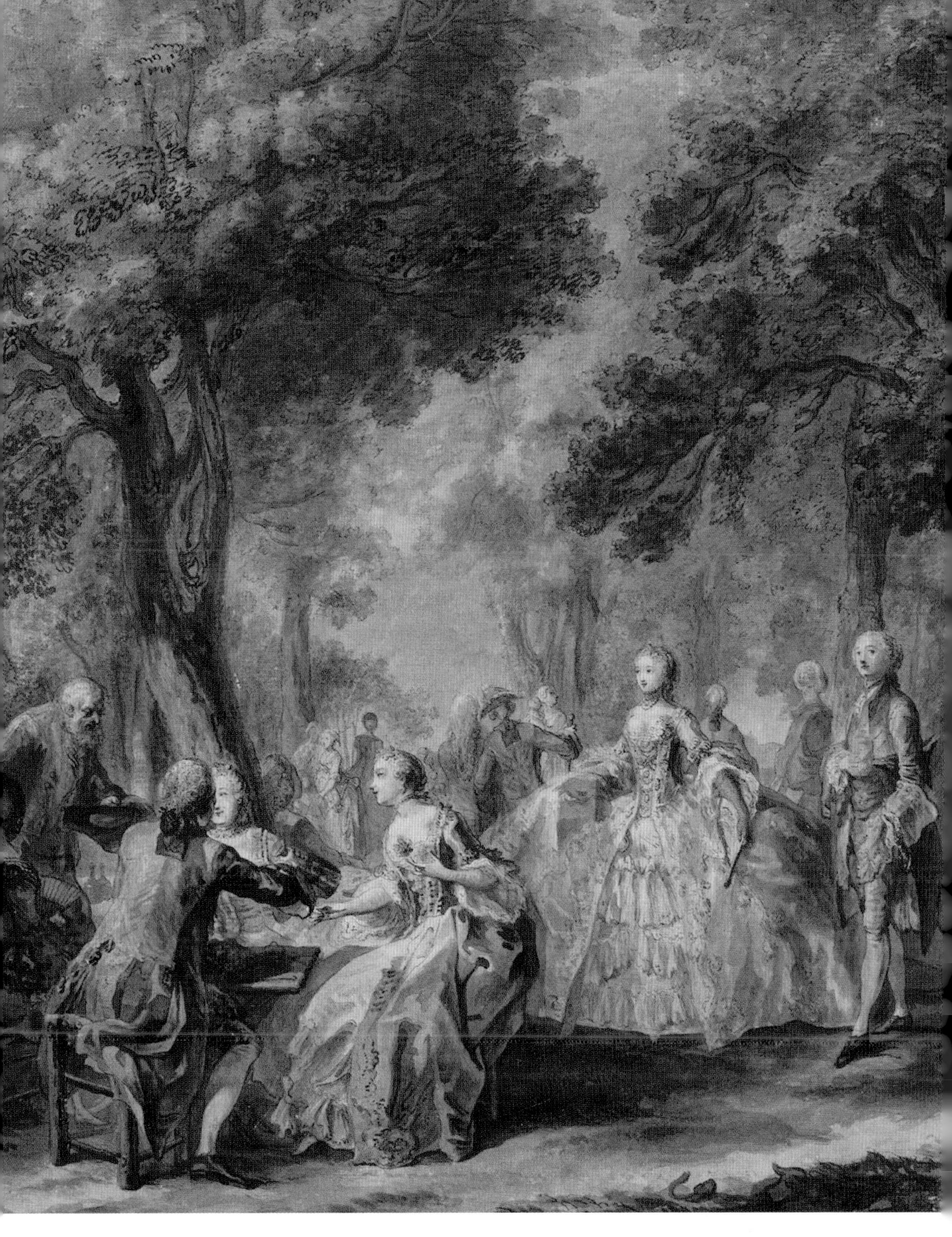

Gabriel de Saint-Aubin, *Society Taking a Promenade*, c. 1761

The Walk of Self-Discovery

No one promoted the idea of walking for its own sake more successfully than Jean-Jacques Rousseau. It was staying out late on a walk at age fifteen that led him to run away from his native Geneva, since he returned after the city gates were closed for the night. For the rest of his life Rousseau wandered the continent, producing innovative works that were as much reviled as praised: works on music, government, botany, love, and education, and the first modern autobiography, the uninhibited *Confessions*. His life, he said, was a surrender to "the pleasures of going one knows not where."

What made Rousseau so influential was not how much he walked but how emotionally he expressed what walking did for him. He put into words what walkers before him must have felt, but never thought (or dared) to say. First and foremost, walking made him feel intellectually alive. "I can only meditate when I am walking," he told the readers of *Confessions*. "When I stop I cease to think; my mind only works with my legs." For Rousseau the thinking walk was only one step toward an elusive goal that few before him had ever considered: how to be oneself. Having made enemies all over Europe by proclaiming the corrupting power of civilization, Rousseau struggled unceasingly to pierce the barriers that, he believed, life in society builds between individuals and their true being. "Never did I think so much, exist so vividly, and experience so much, never have I been so much myself . . . as in the journeys I have taken alone and on foot. There is something about walking which stimulates and enlivens my thoughts. . . . The absence of everything that makes me feel my dependence, of everything that recalls me to my situation—all these serve to free my spirit, to lend a greater boldness to my thinking."

Like most utopias, Rousseau's walks were founded on negatives: nothing that made him feel insecure would be allowed to intrude on the healthy joys of a good hike. Walking his way to mental freedom and self-identity, he taught readers how they could do the same. Instead of regarding walking as a class indicator, Rousseau promoted it as a means to renounce hierarchy altogether. Walking, one could get back to the state of nature, a nature that Rousseau regarded as almost synonymous with one's inmost self.

This portrait hints at how Rousseau's reputation developed. During his lifetime no one had thought to paint Rousseau in the sort of woodland setting he idolized. In 1840 Swiss artist Charles Gleyre used a 1764 pastel bust portrait of Rousseau by Quentin de La Tour to design the full-length out-on-a-botanical-walk image that Jean Charles Thévenin then engraved for a growing audience of admirers. Gleyre made sure to include Rousseau's walking staff and gathered flowers as proof of the writer's oneness with nature. "Brightly colored flowers, the varied flora of the

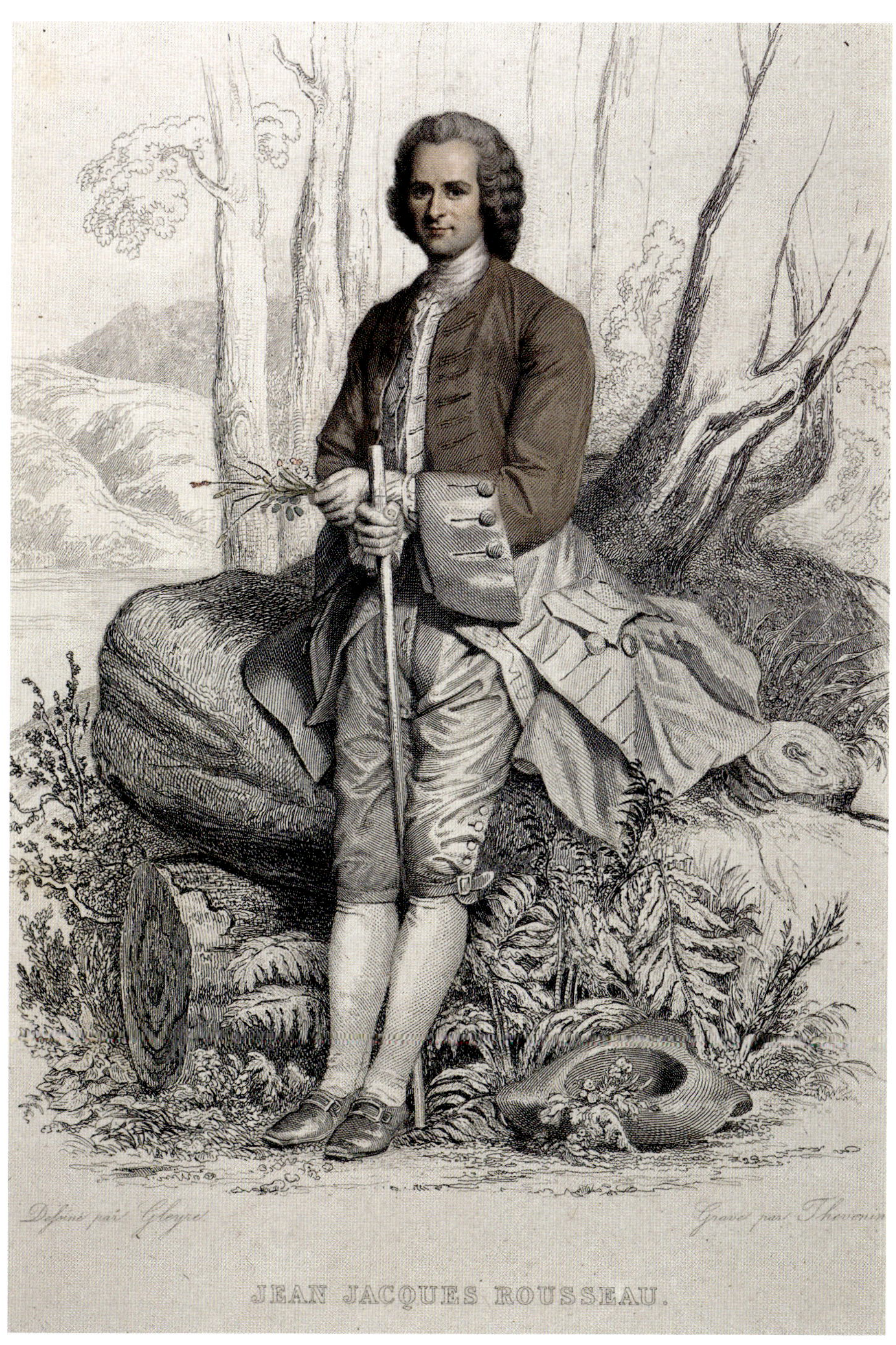

Charles Gleyre, artist; Jean Charles Thévenin, engraver, *Jean Jacques Rousseau*, 1840

meadows, cool shade, streams, woods, and greenery, come and purify my imagination," Rousseau wrote in *Reveries of a Solitary Walker*. But with Rousseau's portrait head grafted on to the body of an imagined forest wayfarer, Gleyre also illustrates Rousseau's contention that the brain and body need not worry about each other once launched on a rustic path. The walking body releases the mind to be at peace with itself.

By the time Rousseau died in 1778, the natural-looking English landscape style had reached France. He was buried near Paris on the Isle of Poplars in an artificial lake on the estate of his friend the Marquis de Girardin, who had designed his grounds according to principles enunciated in Rousseau's own writing. Soon the tomb became a pilgrimage site, where France's greatest apostle of nature was honored by poets and philosophers, monarchs and statesmen, as well as by major players in the Revolution that Rousseau's political theories had helped to set in motion. Marie Antoinette, Georges Danton, Maximilien Robespierre, and Napoleon all paid their respects to a man who was never happier than walking away from everything they represented.

Night Walks

"What things to see when all eyes are closed! Peaceful citizens! I kept awake for you; alone, I explored the night for you. For you, I entered the haunts of Vice and Crime!" With this proclamation Nicolas Edme Restif de La Bretonne, the man who coined the word *pornography*, introduced himself to Parisian readers in 1788, just a year before the French Revolution began. Claiming to have spent a thousand and one nights roaming the city, he promised to reveal its secrets one night and one story at a time. Influenced by Jean-Jacques Rousseau's *Reveries of a Solitary Walker*—and sometimes called "the Rousseau of the gutter" because of his libertine tastes—Restif turned Rousseau's peripatetic format from rural introspection to urban sensationalism. Over the course of ten volumes that spanned the years of the Revolution, the author unflinchingly detailed his encounters with spies, cheats, thieves, abusers, the wicked, the passionate, the wronged, and the unlucky. "I exposed my health, my life, my honor, my virtue," he boasted—all to show his innocent readers the snares that await them in the depth of the night.

Admired by the Surrealists, *The Nights of Paris* belongs to a long tradition of exposés that guide the would-be urban adventurer through an eerie dreamscape where lawless passions rule. Such works have a single modus operandi whether they are poetic, like John Gay's *Trivia, or The Art of Walking the Streets of London* (1716), or muckraking, like George Foster's *New York by Gaslight* (1850), or surrealistic, like Philippe Soupault's *Last Nights of Paris* (1928), or even historical, like Matthew Beaumont's *Nightwalking* (2015). Starting from the premise that each nocturnal step brings the unwary traveler closer to disaster, they suggest that only the book in hand can shepherd the reader safely through the physical and moral dangers they luridly, almost lovingly describe. Sex, murder, and betrayal lurk at every corner, so better to read about the experience than undergo it. "Prepare for Death, if here at Night you roam, / And sign your Will before you sup from Home," warned Samuel Johnson in "London" (1738).

To get the lowdown on nightlife, urban reformers such as Charles Dickens or Jacob Riis often took a police escort. Restif, however, seems to have been a policeman himself, or at least a police spy. The text hints that the Nocturnal Spectator, as he often calls himself, was more on the job than on the prowl. He carries a baton and pistols, wears the police-standard blue coat, and seems able to summon the watch whenever the need arises. He would have been aided in his work by the famous Parisian streetlamps, the *réverbères*, which reflected their oil-fueled light toward the innocent and guilty alike. Invented in 1745, the *réverbères* were by 1766 being strung on ropes along streets and across intersections at regular intervals. Just before the Revolution, some were fixed to lampposts, providing a convenient spot

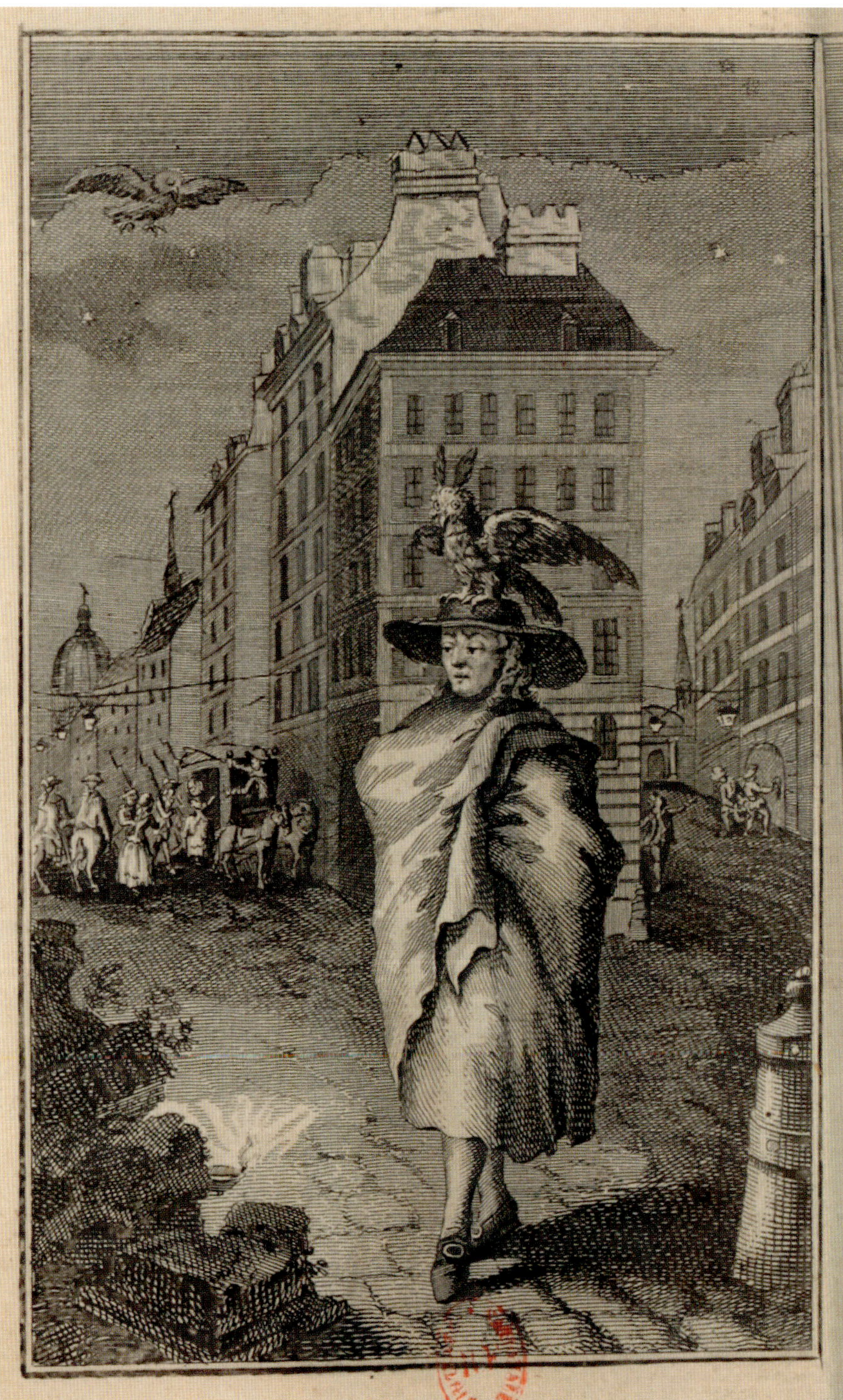

for a mob wanting to *lanterner* or hang a victim. As Lord Byron wrote in *Don Juan,* "on their new-found lantern, / Instead of wicks, they made a wicked man turn."

In Jean-Michel Moreau's frontispiece for *Les nuits de Paris* (*The Nights of Paris*), the artist captures the willful thrill of the nighttime promenade. Rope-strung *réverbères* illuminate two crimes in progress. On the left, an abduction: men force young women into a waiting coach as the mounted watch arrives in the nick of time. On the right, housebreakers attack a door while a watchman on foot runs to the corner to sound the alarm. More striking than the crimes, however, is the depiction of the author. Wrapped in a cloak, he stalks the streets with an owl perched on his hat. Unperturbed by the transgressions in the background, the "Owl-Spectator," as Restif calls himself on the opening page, walks in an aristocratic manner, toes turned out, toward a small oil lamp that represents his midnight toil as a chronicler of crime and vice. Anticipating the desires of his readers, he dares the city to show him something sensational, some dark deed of nocturnal audacity that he has not seen before.

Jean-Michel Moreau, known as Moreau le Jeune, "The Owl-Spectator, Walking at Night in the Streets of the Capital," frontispiece for *Les nuits de Paris*, 1788, by Nicolas Edme Restif de La Bretonne

The Women's March to Versailles

Women were the central figures in one of the most decisive civilian marches of all time. Marches and mobs had challenged power before, on the streets of ancient Rome and near London during the Peasants' Revolt of 1381. But never did they have so direct an effect on the fate of a nation as in the march to the king's palace at Versailles in October 1789.

Captioned with the rallying cry "To Versailles, to Versailles," this engraving was made just two or three years later for an illustrated history of the French Revolution that came out in installments from 1791 to 1796, recording history as it happened. Republished in a complete format in 1798, 1802, 1804, and 1817, the book combined information and propaganda so effectively that it had a large and positive influence on how the Revolution was regarded all over Europe. Here the anonymous artist depicts a cohort of women harnessed to a cannon and surging forward with pikes and spears. A marcher at the forefront turns back to encourage her companions. A less robust middle-class woman to the rear pauses, looking dazed and faint. She wears a tricolor decoration on her hat, but seems to be having doubts about the bloody cries of her working-class sisters-in-arms. A few men fill in the background, but the image glorifies the determination of the women, whose bold action inspired countless others throughout the Revolution.

The vigor of the crowd's forward motion, tempered by the visual brake of the doubtful individual, sums up in a glance the stirring yet disturbing events that began to unfold on the morning of October 5, 1789. A crowd of angry women gathered at a market in the working-class district of the Faubourg Saint-Antoine in Paris. Most were fishmongers who, by tradition, expected protection from the king in exchange for their fervent support. But near-famine conditions had tested their loyalty to "Papa," as they called Louis XVI. Suddenly a woman on the edge of the crowd began beating a drum. Enraged at the high prices of bread, the women stormed off toward the city hall. Surging through streets and marketplaces, they gathered weapons and allies as they went. At the city hall, now numbering ten thousand, they ransacked municipal stores of arms and food.

Then they turned their attention to a new goal, the palace of the king at Versailles. There the royalists and reformers of the National Assembly were engaged in urgent negotiations about citizens' rights. Fearing that their own needs would be ignored, the Parisian crowd decided to bring the king back to Paris, to conduct discussions in public view. Pulling cannons they had seized at the city hall, the crowd marched through the rain for six hours, waving pikes and swords, some calling for Marie Antoinette's head.

At Versailles a delegation of women placed their demands before the king. After

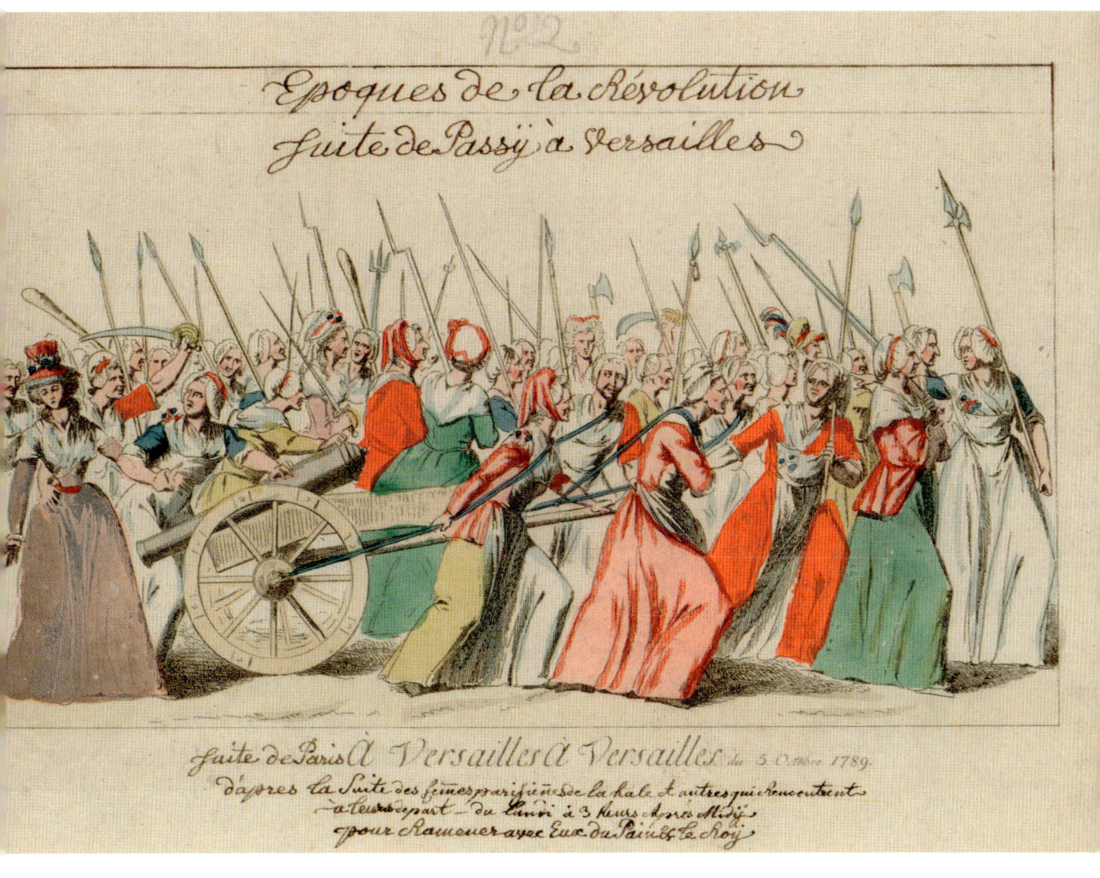

Unknown artist, "To Versailles, to Versailles," c. 1792, in *Tableaux historiques de la Révolution française*, 1791–96

an uneasy night in which the crowd swelled to about sixty thousand, a militant group broke into the palace, killed many of the guards, and nearly captured the queen. Army officers, reluctant to attack the crowd, brokered a deal for the king and his family to return peaceably to Paris. The journey took about nine hours. The triumphant procession waved both loaves of bread and the heads of the slaughtered guards on the tips of their pikes, brandishing them in sight of the royal family as they made their way into the city. Along the way the marchers shouted, "Here is the baker, the baker's wife, and the baker's little boy." About thirty-six hours after the first drumbeat, the women's march concluded. It had broken the power of the monarchy, made the king a virtual prisoner, and, through the invasion of the palace and the assembly, presented so clear a forecast of mob rule that both royalists and moderates alike pulled back from the political process. Many fled the country. Revolution was now inevitable.

Walking Tours

Suddenly tourists were everywhere, many of them traveling on foot. The vogue for "picturesque" landscapes brought English sightseers, cooped up on their island during the French Revolution and its aftermath, out into the countryside in droves. They roamed over Scotland, Wales, and the Lake District, looking for views they could capture with Claude glasses and watercolors. The trend was set in 1782 with the publication of William Gilpin's *Observations on the River Wye, and Several Parts of South Wales, etc. Relative Chiefly to Picturesque Beauty.* Gilpin not only introduced the concept of the picturesque to a wide audience, he explained to his readers how to locate naturally occurring picturesque landscapes as they traveled. His book helped make the Wye Valley one of the most visited places in Britain.

For many, the majestic ruins of Tintern Abbey were the highlight of a such a tour. With this view of the chancel and crossing, the nineteen-year-old J. M. W. Turner joined the growing number of watercolor artists who took advantage of the medium's portability to produce fresh-looking, apparently on-location portraits of newly fashionable ruins and scenery. Here, Turner contrasts the elegant tracery around the windows and arches with shrubs and vines that pull the finely carved stones back to nature. Responding to Gilpin's criticism that the tidied-up site would be more picturesque if strewn with "rough fragments of ruin," Turner obligingly adds large chunks of fallen masonry to his foreground. He places two gentlemanly figures, with their frock coats and knee breeches, in the left foreground to stand in for his viewers, as they muse on the lessons of the scene. They presumably belong to the new religion of nature worship, cast into relief by the crumbling remains of the monastery that once flourished here. The men's discreet presence allows the tree-sprouting arches to dominate, even as their small stature serves to remind viewers that all human efforts will eventually be dwarfed by natural forces.

Turner's work opens up a further dimension in the exploration of the Romantic landscape, the fruitful gap between first encounter and later impression. How much of what a walker experiences and records is influenced by memory? Turner's carefully composed watercolor was actually painted two years after he had originally sketched the site when he was only seventeen, during his own tour of picturesque places in 1792. A few years later, in 1798, a young William Wordsworth and his sister Dorothy walked up the Wye Valley to Tintern Abbey with their own past experience very much in mind. Wordsworth had first visited the locale in 1793 at the age of twenty-three, and now, on the verge of publishing *Lyrical Ballads*, the book that would make his name, he made the five-year distance between encounters the subject of one of his greatest poems, "Lines Written a Few Miles above Tintern Abbey, on Revisiting the Banks of the Wye during a Tour, July 13, 1798."

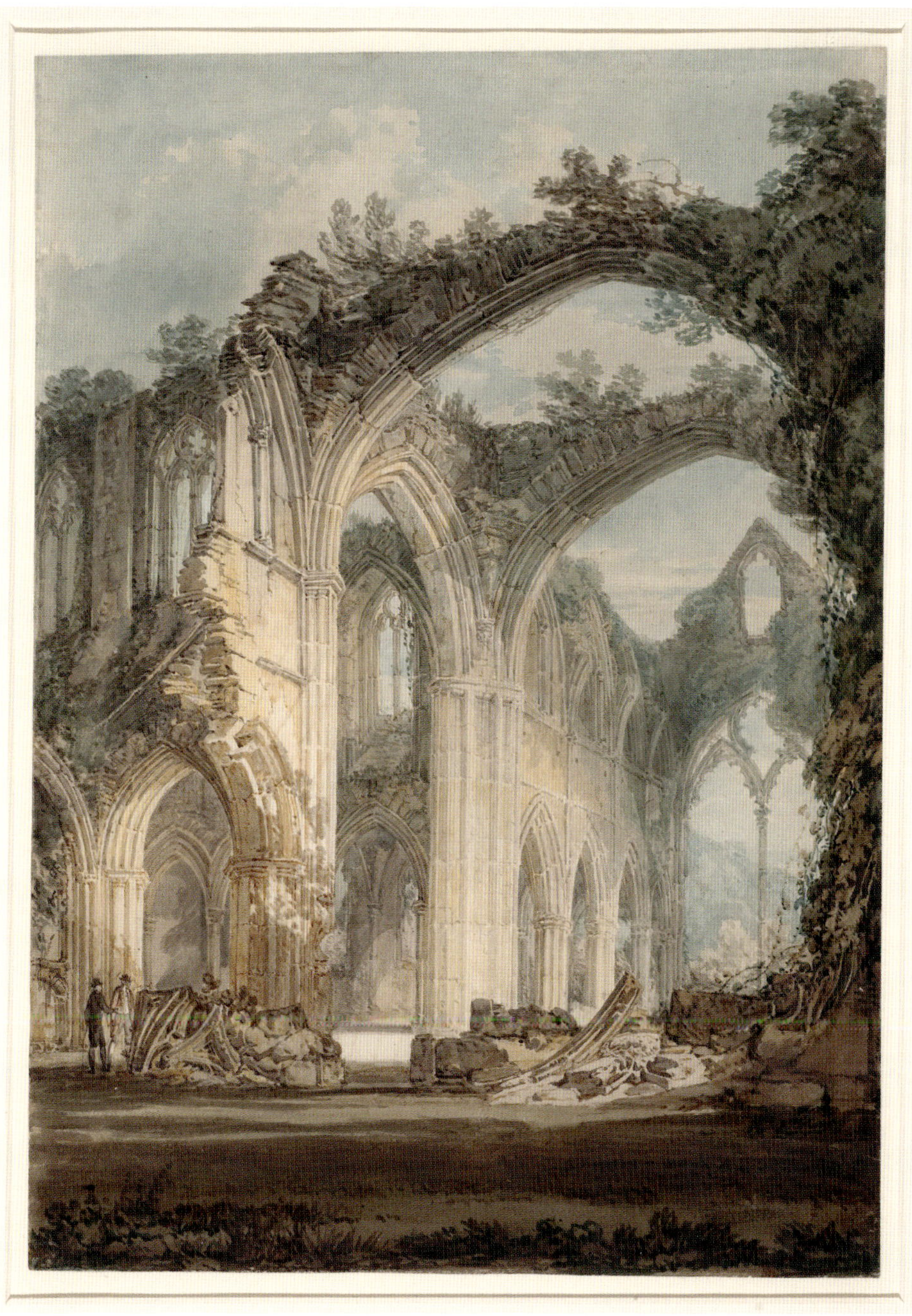

J. M. W. Turner, *Tintern Abbey: The Crossing and Chancel, Looking towards the East Window*, 1794

Pioneering though their poetry and painting might be, Wordsworth and Turner were following fashion in their choice of itineraries, caught up in the same cultural shift that left landowners reeling. Since antiquity, aristocrats had used walls, hedges, and fences to separate themselves from an implicitly hostile world, full of common people and untamed natural forces. Their protected gardens provided them safety, comfort, and an opportunity to show that they were as cultivated as the land they owned. But when the English fashion in landscaping demanded that their own domains look as "natural" as the world outside their walls, they found themselves defenseless before a troubling question: What was wrong with walking in nature itself?

Nothing at all, according to a growing number of enthusiastic walkers who seized trend-setting power from the upper classes. They began in the late eighteenth century to take multiday journeys on foot in the name of personal freedom and self-discovery. Embracing Adam and Eve's punishment, they left the garden willingly for the enticing wilds outside the gate. Against prevailing norms that associated foot travel with poverty and criminal behavior, they walked to improve their health, their knowledge of nature and society, and above all their spiritual well-being. Rebellious and middle class, they walked because they wanted to, not because they had to. Taking advantage of safer and better roads, they left highways, coaches, postillions, and overcrowded inns behind to travel at their own rate, through whatever landscape stirred their souls.

As the meditative walks of Wordsworth and others became widely known, they inspired legions of admirers to follow in their footsteps. "There is a joy in every spot made known by times of old / New to the feet, although each tale a hundred times be told," the poet John Keats wrote during his 1818 journey in northern Britain. Just as Wordsworth had visited places described by Jean-Jacques Rousseau, Keats shouldered his knapsack like Wordsworth, writing that "to make a sort of Prologue to the Life I intend to pursue, . . . I will clamber through the Clouds and exist." But weakened by his strenuous program, Keats contracted the tuberculosis that ended his life three years later. He ought to have said of Wordsworth's walking what he had already remarked of Milton's poetry: "Life to him would be death to me."

The Romantic Walker

Whether out for a day's excursion or an extended tour, sensitive wanderers of the Romantic era transformed walking from a practical necessity into a form of revelation. They gloried in nature, but the inward spiritual journey was as important as the physical one. No one pictured the encounter of walker and wonder better than Caspar David Friedrich. Regarded as more eccentric than prophetic during his lifetime, Friedrich has emerged as the central figure in German Romantic art. "The artist should paint not only what he sees before him," Friedrich said, "but also what he sees within him." In his paintings Friedrich repeatedly shows that the point of a walk is to stop and look—not at conventionally pleasing scenes, but at awe-inspiring depths, distances, and heights.

Every landscape painting takes its audience on a walk, but Friedrich repeatedly puts walkers, back to the viewer, in his pictures as active elements. They intensify the experience of being drawn in to the sublimity of the scene. It is as if we onlookers have taken the same walk as these *Rückenfiguren* ("figures seen from behind"), and caught up to them just as they are arrested by a sight that then holds us too. In *Chalk Cliffs on Rügen*, Friedrich depicts a moment, imagined or remembered, from his honeymoon on the Baltic island. His wife Caroline points down toward the vertiginous spot where the sea approaches the cliff; the painter, on his hands and knees, peers into the gulf before them; and their companion, heedless, stares out at the distant horizon.

As usual with Friedrich, these completely absorbed strollers seem to urge the painting's viewers to join in their intense acts of looking. Here Friedrich offers a choice: to peer into the frightening abyss below, or outward toward the unreachable, invisible juncture of sea and sky. Either way, the curve of the cliffs and the overhanging branches focus the sight like the pupil of an eye. What's unusual is that the painter exhibits a sense of humor about the incident. No lady of Caroline's standing would walk abroad without covering her head. Her hat must have blown off; obeying her gesture, the artist awkwardly inches forward to see if he dares recuperate it. The painting follows the same perilous path: Friedrich risks undercutting the reverent atmosphere that he habitually portrays, but grounds himself in the belief that the spiritual power of these depths and distances cannot be shaken.

Friedrich is exceptional too in allowing women to share in such sublime moments, as he does here and in *Man and Woman Contemplating the Moon* (1824). The Romantic walker—generally white, male, and middle class, free of childcare and fearing neither rape nor starvation—has been criticized for pretending to have a universal message that in reality only a few could heed. Yet even at the turn of the nineteenth century, certain creative women found ways of making the landscape

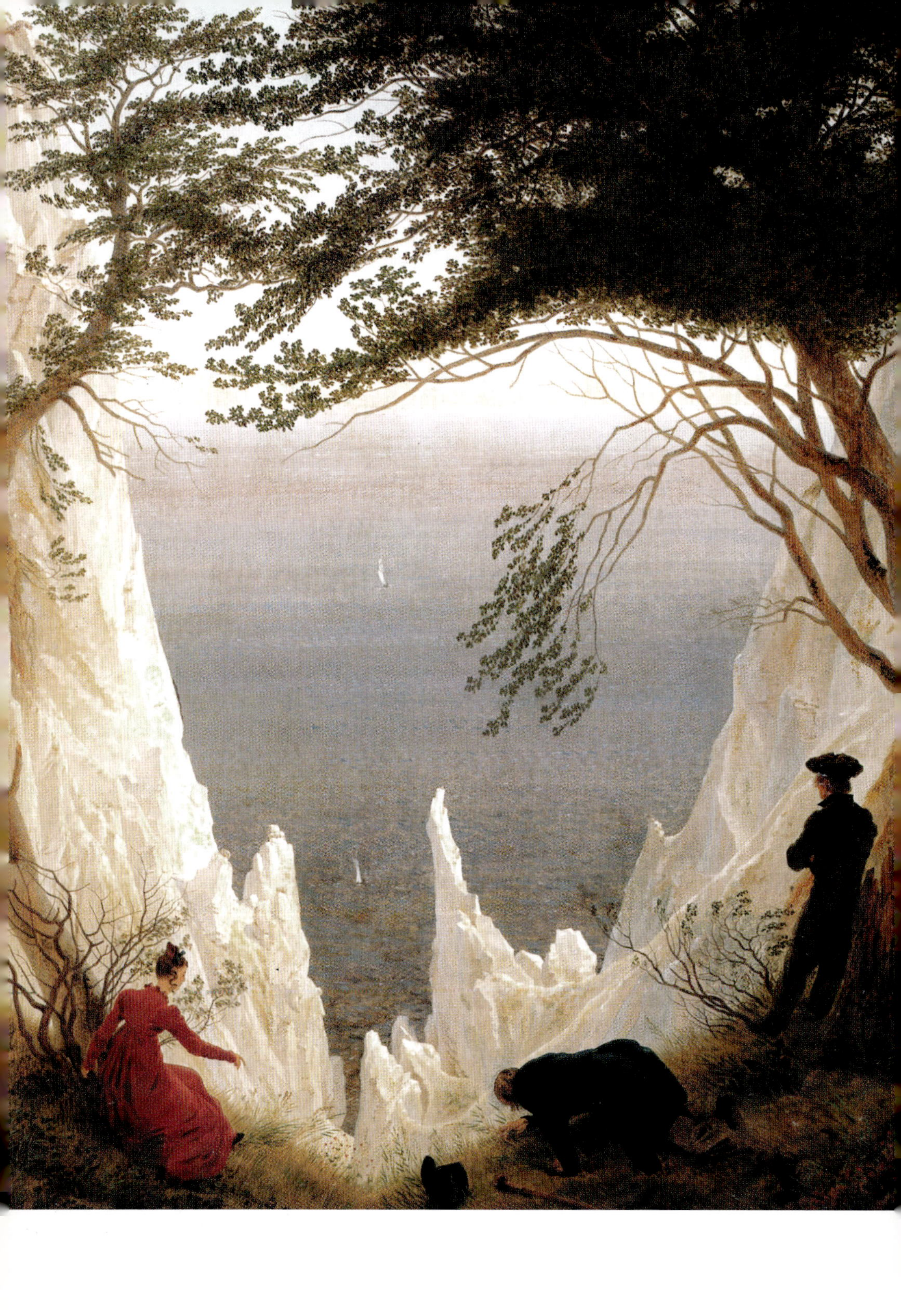

work for them, using its representation as a form of cultural capital. Of all English authors, Jane Austen best captured what a walk can deliver in the way of emotional uplift, romantic opportunity, and plot development, whether it be Elizabeth Bennet's daringly vigorous tramp across muddy fields to nurse her sick sister or the Dashwood sisters' excursion into the ecstasy of the picturesque: "They gaily ascended the downs, rejoicing in their own penetration at every glimpse of blue sky; and when they caught in their faces the animating gales of a high south-westerly wind, they pitied the fears which had prevented their mother and Elinor from sharing such delightful sensations. 'Is there a felicity in the world,' said Marianne, 'superior to this?'"

One of the great walkers of the era was Dorothy Wordsworth. Her journals, pillaged by her brother William for his poems and travel books, record dozens of twenty- to thirty-mile days, mixed with vivid descriptions of the Lake District and beyond. One day Dorothy was so transported by the experience that she simply noted, "Walked I know not where." The spirit of Friedrich and the Wordsworths, and even of Austen's characters (though they might not have admitted it), can be summed up in a sentence from one of their successors, the Scots American naturalist John Muir: "I only went out for a walk and finally concluded to stay out till sundown, for going out, I found, was really going in."

Caspar David Friedrich, *Chalk Cliffs on Rügen*, 1818

Crossing the Street

Where is the profit in walking? Dr. Theodore Tronchin and Jean-Jacques Rousseau argued convincingly for its physical and psychological benefits. Designers of gardens placed allegorical statues of virtues in strategic spots to ensure a moral payback for strollers. The fashion for edifying sculpture and inscriptions went so far that in 1831 German poet Ludwig Tieck wrote satirically, "One need only push some criminal or godless debtor gently through the garden gate and then, after two hours, let him out at the other side as a convinced believer and a man of virtue."

For simple monetary reward, those who tended street crossings knew that a few feet of mud were a sure source of income. They could exact a penny toll for sweeping a path or providing a board over which the "better" classes could walk. Ancient Roman cities had functional sidewalks and raised crossings, but circa 1800 most Parisian streets still followed the narrow, multipurpose medieval model: the upper classes kept close to the walls, forcing the lower orders into the central gutter. Although protected pedestrian paths were legislated in England by the seventeenth and eighteenth centuries, and sidewalks ordered in Paris in 1790, the reality did not keep pace with the law. A wet crossing generated economic opportunity even as it created a social free-for-all.

The painter Louis-Léopold Boilly specialized in mildly humorous genre scenes that sympathetically depicted incidents in the life of the rising middle class. Here a finely dressed bourgeois family—father, mother (carrying a lapdog), a boy, a girl, and a baby held by a nursemaid—hesitates to pay its toll to an old soldier in a patched coat whose outstretched right hand indicates that he is the one maintaining this plank crossing. A working woman with a basket uncomplainingly puts money into his other hand, but the top-hatted paterfamilias makes a dismissive gesture. The delicate footwear and stockings of the family stand out on their plank pedestal, contrasting with the more sturdy and somber dress of the other pedestrians. The population density of Paris meant that rich, poor, and in-between circulated in close quarters, jostling each other in the packed streets. Unlike nobles who could promenade through private gardens and spacious boulevards, separated from common people (as well as their own children), Boilly's awkward family must self-consciously make its conspicuous way through a heterogeneous crowd. Showing an alternative to the plank, a man in the background carries a woman over a puddle, while colored umbrellas frame the action across the picture plane.

As usual, the social walk has a symbolic edge. The well-to-do family shuns the crowd around them as much as they do the mud below their feet. The plank itself may represent the precariousness of bourgeois life, while a pointy Phrygian cap

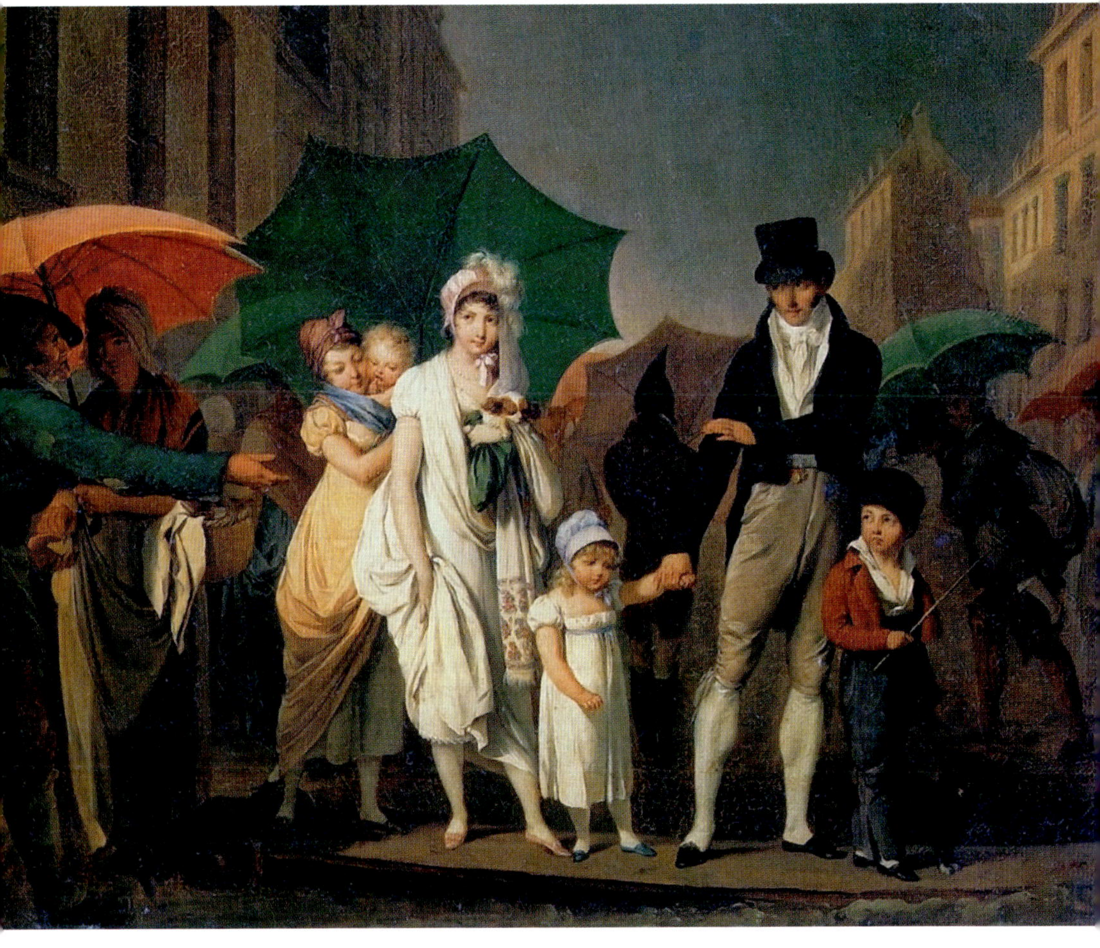

Louis-Léopold Boilly, *Pay to Pass*, c. 1803

that looms in the background between the two halves of the family group recalls the violence of the Revolution. Boilly himself had had a run-in with the Committee of Public Safety during the Reign of Terror. He may have been thinking of the Enlightenment philosopher the Marquis de Condorcet's ironic words, written before he fell victim to the Revolution he supported: "The human species . . . walks with a firm and sure step on the path of the truth."

Arcades

At the turn of the nineteenth century, the newest thing in walking was the covered arcade, ancestor of the modern shopping mall. Like Louis-Léopold Boilly, the German artist Georg Emanuel Opiz delighted in capturing moments when peripatetic social transactions came out in the open. But for Opiz the transactions could be sexual as well as commercial. In Paris, a city where window shoppers and streetwalkers shared the same turf, Opiz found a ready audience for images that stressed the liveliness of the pleasure market at the original shopping center, the Palais Royal. Here Opiz records the preliminary dalliance between elegantly uniformed soldiers and equally elegant but scantily gowned prostitutes.

The Palais Royal was already a gathering place for Parisian aristocracy, thanks to its spacious garden, art gallery, and proximity to the palaces of the Louvre and Tuileries, when it was converted to commercial use in 1784. Deeply in debt, the owner, the duc de Chartres, decided to surround his garden on three sides with ornate commercial arcades over which were built stylish lodgings. The complex eventually featured two theaters, a circus, forty underground shops, and, on the garden level, over one hundred boutiques, cafés, bookstalls, hair salons, tea rooms, jewelers, furriers, and other upscale retailers. In 1786 the wood-covered Galerie de Bois opened on the fourth side of the garden, providing an Arabian-style bazaar to complement the fastidiously maintained shops lining the palace walls.

The well-to-do had congregated before, but the commercial context was a game changer. For the first time, people shopped as a leisure activity, coming together to bask in the glow of commodities that many could not afford. While the makeshift stalls located in the colonnades of Italy and the market archways of England were open to everyone, the permanent boutiques of the arcades aimed at a high-end clientele. Protected from the elements and the sight of the poor, the social elite could relax, promenade, and shop, while the rising middle class could aspire to imitate them.

The Palais Royal and its successors not only pioneered the use of large windows to attract customers to their goods but also were the first to use gaslighting and display fixed prices. Spared the trouble of bargaining, spared concerns that they were paying more than other customers, the clientele of the arcade could size up where they stood on the economic ladder. If the newly social nature of shopping might reveal their (lack of) affluence, it also provided the double-edged compensation of window shopping. Whether seeking goods or pleasures, strollers could at least covet what they could not acquire. By the time of the Revolution the Palais Royal was the most famous, and infamous, commercial site in Europe.

The idea that everything had its price encompassed the best-known nocturnal

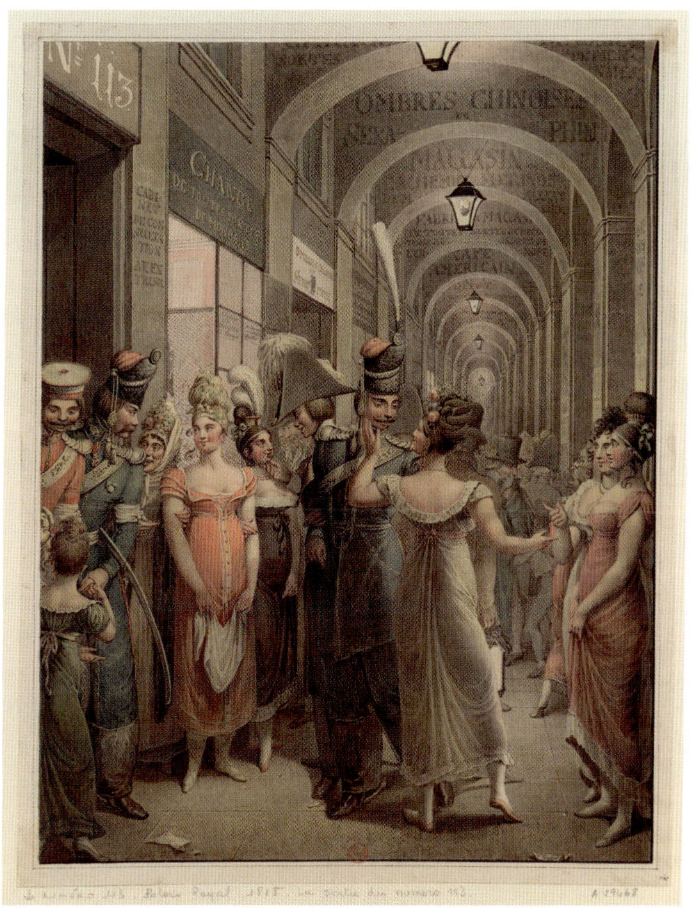

Georg Emanuel Opiz, *Palais Royal*, 1815

activity at the Palais Royal, prostitution. Under the novel flare of gaslights, the promenading pleasure seeker could find plenty of human merchandise available for temporary hire. Over six hundred women and men were said to lodge in and near the arcades, serving the soldiers, libertines, carousers, and steady streams of bourgeois clients. Next door to the notorious gambling den at No. 113, and in front of a shop advertising "all sorts of monetary exchange," Opiz sets up a visual equation between two professions, soldiering and prostitution, that prize flamboyant head dressing and a robust physique. Some of the French bourgeoisie may be seen in the background, but in the wake of the Battle of Paris in 1814, Opiz has chosen invading Russian Cossacks as his chief shoppers. If their presence alludes to Napoleon's defeat, Opiz makes it clear that French women hold no grudge toward the tourists. Commerce conquers all at the Palais Royal.

London Flamboyance

From 1816 to 1828 the British illustrator George Cruikshank published an annual drawing satirizing the latest fashions. *Monstrosities of 1822* captures the moment when tight pantaloons, shoulder padding, high collars, and pinched waists made the flower of British manhood look particularly ridiculous. Cruikshank chose Hyde Park Corner in London as the location for his see-and-be-seen parade of upper-crust fashion plates. In the eighteenth and nineteenth centuries, Hyde Park and its tony thoroughfare, Rotten Row, were *the* places to ride one's horse, parade in one's carriage, or stroll with studied nonchalance. Timing was crucial: just before midday during the week and a bit later on weekends, the richest equestrians and pedestrians of London would enter the park from their houses on the western edge of town. An average of more than a duel a year had been fought in the park in the preceding century, but by 1822 rivalries were contested with the cut of a coat, the tilt of a cane, or the twirl of a parasol.

The Georgian stroller was not an ordinary walker. Outfitted for a proper promenade, dandies and coquettes used posture, gesture, and dress to participate in a

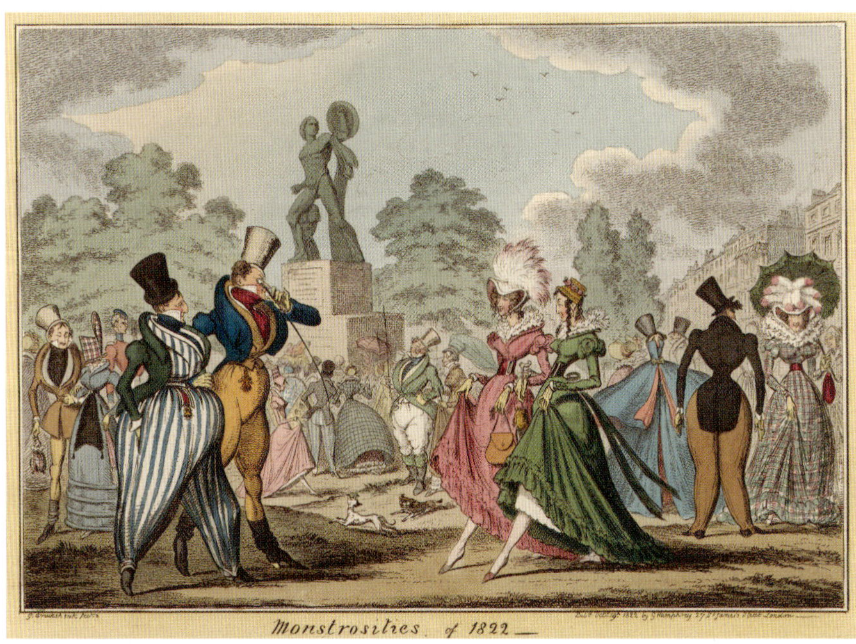

George Cruikshank, *Monstrosities of 1822*, 1822

ritual whose every nuance would be noticed by others of their set. The social and sexual dynamics of the era demanded that society's leading lights put their wealth and grace on show whenever they stepped into this erotically charged arena. At the center of the skirmish shown here, two puffed-up gallants, stuffed into form-fitting cutaway coats and matching waistcoat-and-trouser pairs, pause to ogle two slim-profiled women who advance toward them, skirts seductively raised. At a transition point between the light, clinging fabrics of the Regency and Victorian hooped skirts, the women in Cruikshank's scene wear wide-ruffed collars and a variety of bonnets, from attention-grabbing feathers to simple affairs adorned with flowers or sun-shielding visors. For both sexes, the ballet-inspired pointed-toe style of French court walking was still very much in vogue. In an ironic twist on Caspar David Friedrich's landscapes, Cruikshank uses an eye shape in the clouds to remind his viewers that Someone is always watching. Here the rich must endure the ever-critical stare of Society itself, in the form of Cruikshank's caricature.

The pretense-mocking nude statue that gathers a crowd in the background is not an innocent bystander. Unveiled only a few weeks earlier, it was widely mocked for its own pretense in depicting the Duke of Wellington, victor at Waterloo, in the guise of a naked Achilles. As the first unclothed statue to be publicly installed in London since the time of the Romans—and embarrassingly paid for by the contributions of British women—the heroic figure had to contend with pointed comments on the size of its fig leaf. Cruikshank mercilessly satirized the statue in another drawing, where he lent Achilles just one practical article of clothing: Wellington boots. Here he has deliberately omitted the hero's sword, as if to say that he must make his way in the public eye in a vulnerable, all-natural manner, in contrast to the frippery on display beneath his pedestal.

The Underground Railroad

When her master saw her, he said, "Well, Bell, so you've run away from me."
"No, I did not *run away*; I walked away by day-light."
—*Sojourner Truth,* The Narrative of Sojourner Truth

While the leisured classes of Europe were worrying about the kind of figure they cut on a stroll, a less fortunate American population could only imagine what it would be like to walk unnoticed into freedom. Courageous or not, most enslaved people were unable to follow Sojourner Truth's defiant path away from bondage. Knowing the punishments that awaited them, they ran till they could run no longer. If they were lucky, they might pick up a ride on the Underground Railroad—a curious railroad, since the customers generally transported themselves. They might be ferried across a river or a lake, they might catch a wagon or a boat sailing north, but mostly they walked—up to twenty miles at a stretch, usually in the dark.

For it was not really a railroad, and it was not underground. It was a covert network of guides and safe houses that operated by night, helping enslaved people escape northward out of the slaveholding states of the American South. Its first "lines" were laid by Quakers in the 1790s, before railroads were even invented, in the wake of the Fugitive Slave Act of 1793. The operators of the escape routes grew to include abolitionists, clergy, Native Americans, and freeborn or escaped African Americans, without whom the network could not have functioned. When actual railways spread in the 1830s, abolitionists borrowed the terminology to code their messages: "conductors" guided "passengers" to "stations" or "depots" where they could hide and rest until a "stationmaster" made arrangements to move them onward. According to John Rankin of Ohio, one of the Railroad's most active conductors, "they who took passage on it disappeared from public view as really as if they had gone into the ground. After the fugitive slaves entered a depot on that road no trace of them could be found."

When the harsh Fugitive Slave Act of 1850 required all US citizens to assist in the recapture of escapees, it gave the Railroad a full head of steam, making its operation as urgent in the North as in the South. The Railroad's densest branch lines stretched on both sides of the fortieth parallel and the Mason-Dixon Line, across Iowa, Illinois, Indiana, Ohio, Pennsylvania, and Maryland, also reaching down into Virginia, up through New York and New England, and across the Great Lakes to Canada. Only in Canada were escapees finally and legally free. Difficult as the journey was, the Railroad provided an invisible pathway to freedom for an estimated hundred thousand people before 1850, and then perhaps five thousand per year until the Civil War broke out in 1861. If discovered, stationmasters and conductors

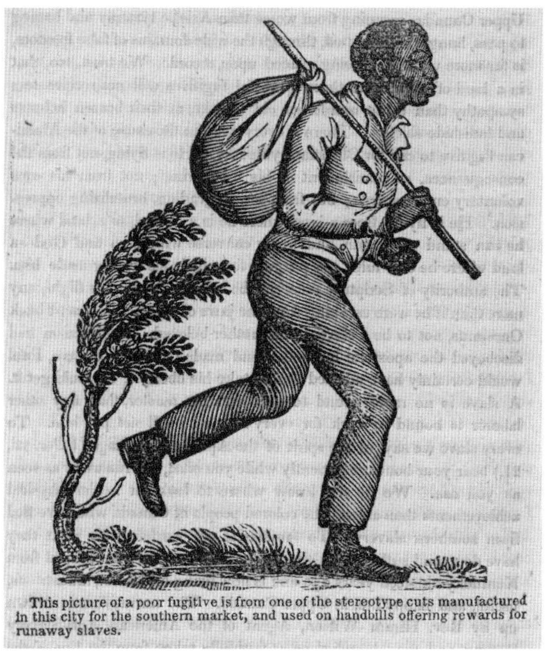

This picture of a poor fugitive is from one of the stereotype cuts manufactured in this city for the southern market, and used on handbills offering rewards for runaway slaves.

Unknown artist, "The Runaway," in *The Anti-Slavery Record*, 1837

could not be forced to betray others, since they worked independently on their own sections of the escape route.

This woodcut of a stereotypical "runaway" was widely reprinted to accompany notices offering rewards for the return of "lost property." An abolitionist newspaper in New York reproduced it to inform its readers that it was made locally, exposing how Northern business was tangled in the web of slavery. Like many of its genre, the image depicts a fugitive with stick and bundle, a tree in the background. It acted more as a headline than a picture of any actual fugitive, who would be verbally described in a paragraph beneath.

Generic as it was, the image did strive to paint a flattering portrait—of the slave owner. The apparently excellent state of the runaway's health and clothing (solid shoes, smart waistcoat, long trousers) indicates that he has been well treated. His ample bundle may conceal a generously provided wardrobe, or goods to which he had access. The windblown tree may suggest that he is stealing away under cover of a storm. But it also shows that the wind is at his back as he dashes toward freedom. If the fugitive had the good fortune to connect with the Railroad in Maryland, the conductor might have been the indomitable Harriet Tubman, who in thirteen raids brought seventy people to safety. As she later said of her eight years on the line, "I never ran my train off the track and I never lost a passenger."

The Self-Guided Walk

If your idea of a good walk is ambling along a well-maintained forest path, guided by colorful marks on trees and stones, then the person you have to thank is Claude-François Denecourt. More than anyone else, Denecourt shaped the way most people hike in nature today. A former sergeant in Napoleon's army, Denecourt became in the 1830s the self-appointed curator of the natural beauties of the forest of Fontainebleau, a hundred-square-mile nature reserve about forty miles from Paris, where French kings used to hunt. In an era when any kind of tourism required taking a local guide, Denecourt presciently believed that people would enjoy nature all the more if they could find their own way to the most interesting sites. In 1839 he published his first guidebook, accompanied by a map that could be bought separately.

In the history of walking, maps hold a special place. With simple lines they visually link distant places that walkers will have to bridge with their own steps. Promising a continuity of travel that reality constantly imperils, the map becomes a precious object, to be carefully protected, anxiously consulted, and occasionally reviled. Endeavoring to spare his readers unnecessary turmoil on the trail, Denecourt innovatively used different colors to trace out five distinct itineraries, all of which aimed to delight the visitor. Promenade 1, for example, outlined in green on the map, took walkers on a counterclockwise loop from the former royal chateau past spots whose Denecourt-given names sought to stimulate the public's curiosity: the Eagle's Nest, the Cliff of the Fat Beech, the Rock of the Two Sisters, and the Lair of the Druids.

What made Denecourt's guides so successful was their practical approach. He took care to explain how long his routes would take, and how they were interconnected. Reminding readers that "the tableau of nature's grandeur should be the work of painters and poets," he declared that his humble mission was to point out places where they could admire such beauty as if they were artists themselves.

Popular as Denecourt's walks were, people kept getting lost in the maze of forest paths on their way to the wonders he described. So in 1842 Denecourt blazed his first trail, leading to the scenic overlook of Mont Chauvet. In 1847 he brought out the first guidebook dedicated to exploring the forest solely on foot, by means of following the blue paint marks that he himself dabbed on trees at judicious intervals. Denecourt chose the color blue not for visibility but for its associations: a still-loyal ex-soldier, he evoked the shade of his uniform and the republican values it represented. By the time of his death in 1875, he had created over ninety miles of blue-blazed trails, described in seventeen editions of his guidebook.

Still used today, the trails reveal that Denecourt had an artistic sense of his own. Intrigued by the way that weather had shaped the components of the landscape, he singled out over a thousand natural features (coded in blue capital letters). Some seventy of them appeared already on the 1839 map. Often Denecourt made up stories about faces in the rocks, bodies in the trees, or fantastic creatures eroded into being by wind and water: "The seven- or eight-hundred-year-old oaks," he said, "which had braved a thousand storms, seemed to bend and beg me to wind my meandering path under their shade."

For all this, Denecourt had a ready audience. The Barbizon school of painting, so-called after a village in the forest where artists such as Jean-Baptiste-Camille Corot, Charles-François Daubigny, and Théodore Rousseau congregated, was well established in the 1830s. The artists who lugged their easels into the woods and up boulders or hills in search of a good viewpoint mark a decisive shift in the history of landscape painting. They turned away from idealized "historical" canvases populated by gods and kings, and toward the direct representation of actual places that could be studied on location under a variety of lighting conditions. The Barbizon artists focused on visually unpretentious scenes of accessible locations, "pictures to walk into."

The area became so recognized for its contribution to French art that in 1853 the government declared fifteen hundred acres in certain scenic zones to be off limits for logging. Declared an artistic reserve, this designated nature sanctuary was gradually enlarged, becoming in 1861 the world's first national park, eleven years before Yellowstone National Park in the United States. Picturesque art rather than enlightened ecology was the driving force, as Denecourt's marked trails showed thousands how easy it was to walk into a masterpiece.

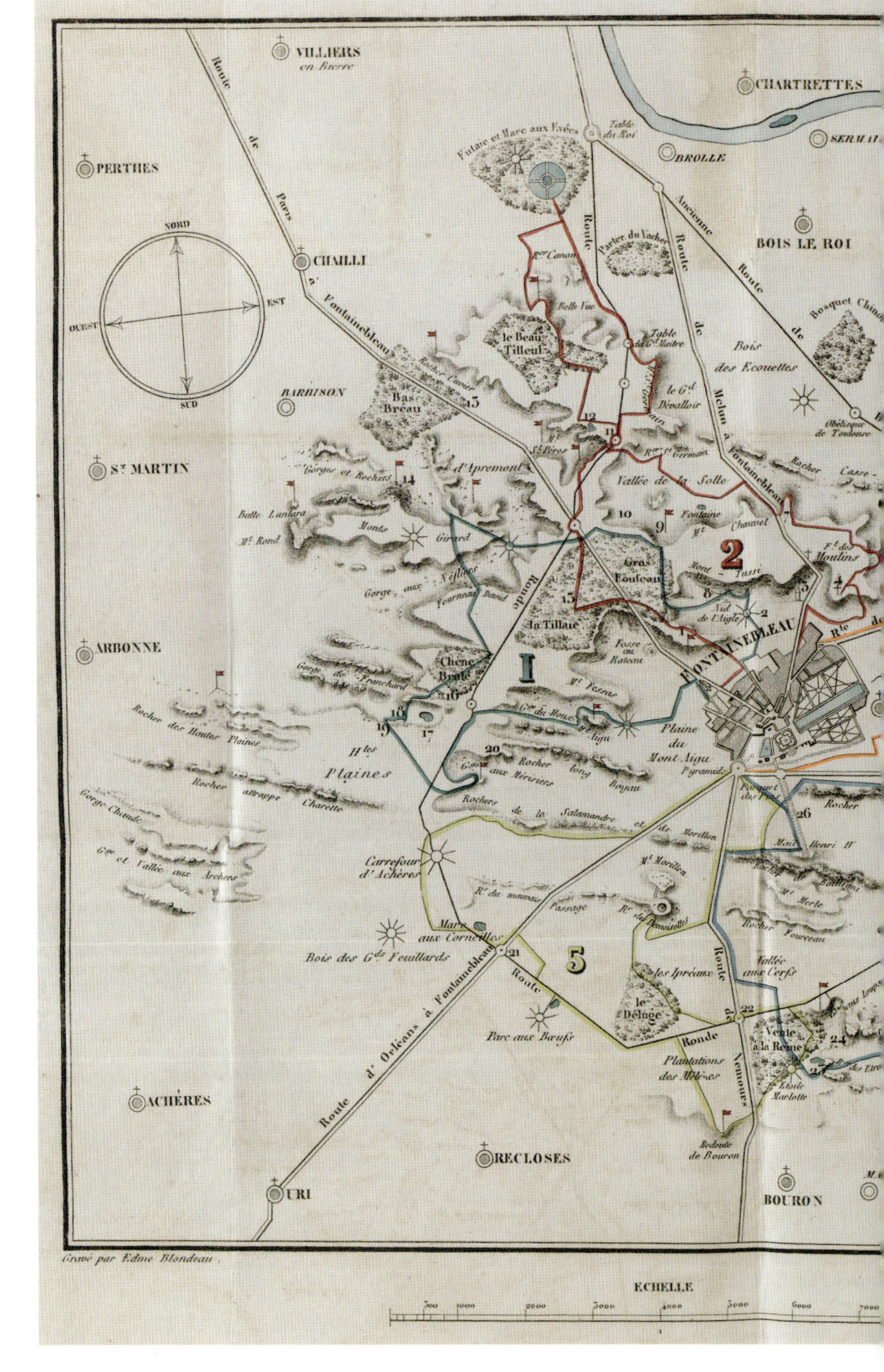

Gravé par Edme Blondeau.

ECHELLE

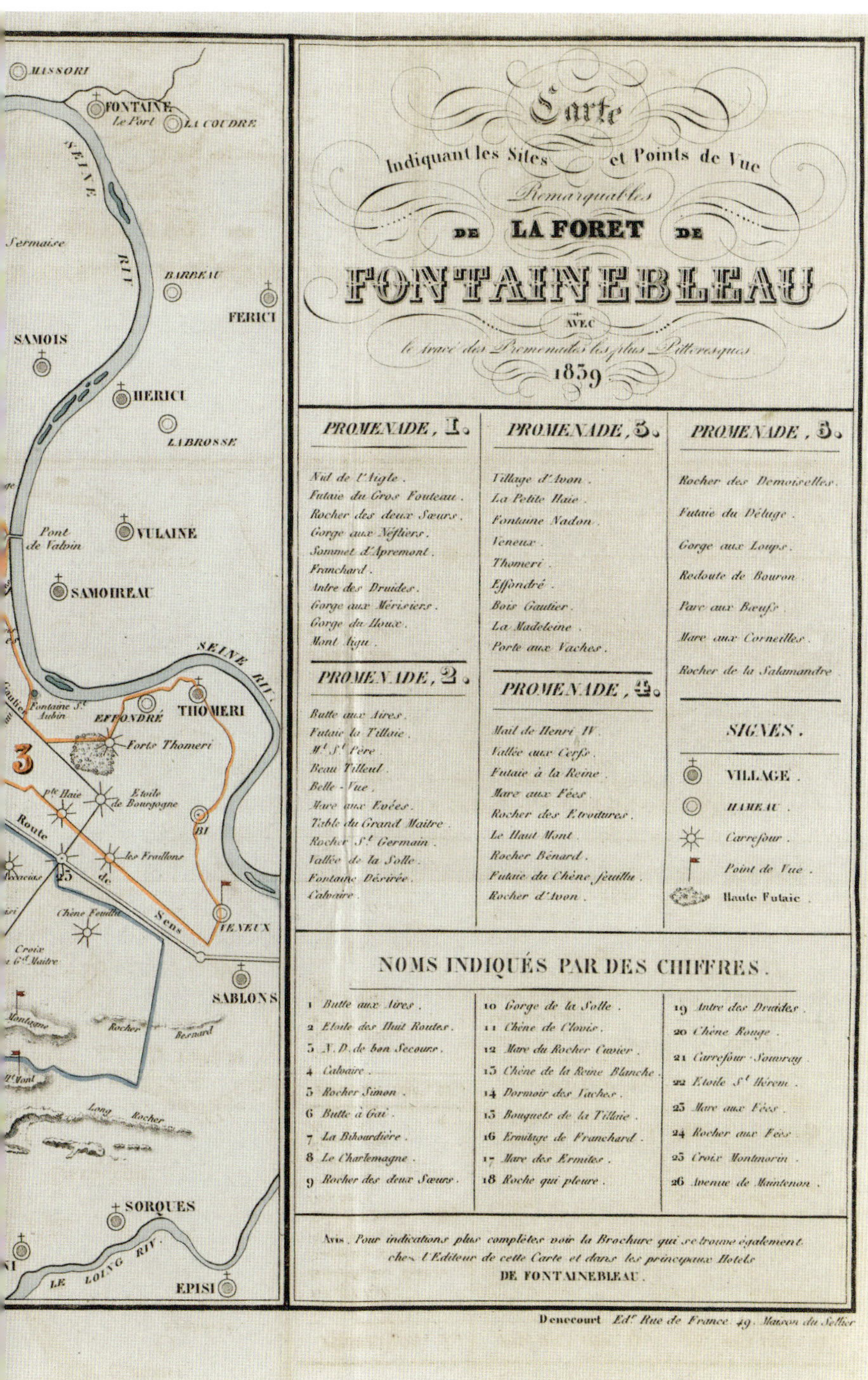

Edme Blondeau, engraver, *Map Indicating the Notable Sites and Viewpoints in the Forest of Fontainebleau, 1839*

The Flâneur

Few cities entice walkers as Paris does. Only Paris can lay claim to having created a distinctive type of walker, the flâneur, a person emblematic of modernity and yet profoundly resistant to it. While the roots of the noun *flâneur,* the verb *flâner,* and the overall concept of *flânerie* go back to an Old Norse word for wandering without a fixed goal, it was in the mid-nineteenth century that the flâneur took literary and visual shape. As much a creation of journalists as an actual category of pedestrian, a flâneur is an intelligent man of leisure out on a stroll. He is open to new impressions and fascinated by anything he has not seen before, from a new shopping arcade to an enterprising beggar. An omnivorous consumer of the urban spectacle, he holds himself aloof from the social mechanisms he analyzes. While he may have aristocratic pretensions, he may equally be a struggling writer or artist looking for material.

Paul Gavarni, a popular illustrator and flâneur himself, drew this generic portrait for a book on Parisian characters. With his top hat, cane, and long-tailed overcoat, Gavarni's figure gazes up at some novel sight the viewer is left to imagine. The accompanying article by Auguste de Lacroix defines the flâneur as someone who can walk, look, and think at the same time: "The observer at rest is only half an observer; the true observer is the flâneur . . . a man of subtle intelligence who ceaselessly explores everything, the human species above all." Crucially, he is a Parisian: "We do not admit even the existence of a flâneur anywhere but Paris."

The most sustained effort to show the world what a flâneur looks like came in the same year as Gavarni's image, from Louis Huart's collection of essays *Physiologie du flâneur* (1841). Humorous vignettes by various artists depict the flâneur admiring everything from dogfights to graffiti, even as he trips over a beggar's crutch or gets splattered with mud by a passing coach. Huart describes the flâneur as subject to pickpockets; he wanders erratically not due to genius but because he is avoiding his creditors. Still, says Huart, "What separates the Man from the brute is that the Man knows how to waste his time." To be truly human is to be a flâneur.

By the 1860s, however, the flâneur had come to seem emblematic as well as amusing. Baron Haussmann's transformation of central Paris gave the flâneur, with his critical skepticism, an enlarged arena of analysis, the *grands boulevards*. For the poet Charles Baudelaire, the flâneur was the one person qualified to become "the painter of modern life" because of his insatiable desire to understand the crowds in which he felt himself a perpetual outsider: "For the perfect *flâneur,* for the passionate spectator, it is an immense joy to set up house in the heart of the multitude, amid the ebb and flow of movement, in the midst of the fugitive and the infinite."

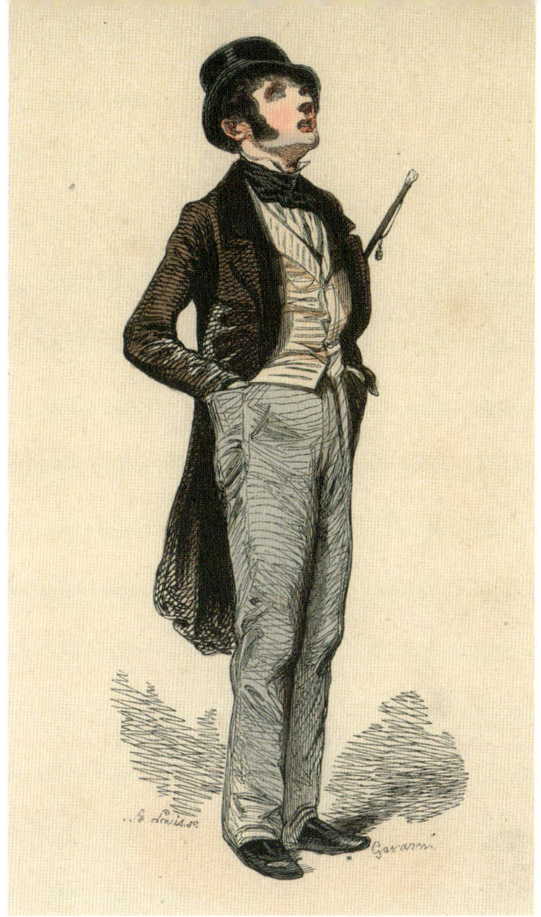

Paul Gavarni, "The Flâneur," in *Les français peints par eux-memes*, 1841

Today, thanks especially to the Marxist critic Walter Benjamin, the flâneur has become the quintessential figure of modern urban life.

Was there a female counterpart, she who has been called the "invisible flâneuse"? Most women would have had trouble fulfilling Baudelaire's famous description of the flâneur's aim: "to see the world, to be at the centre of the world, and yet to remain hidden from the world." A Parisian woman who dawdled on a street corner would not "remain hidden from the world" for long. And yet determined women have often managed to circumvent the society that constrained them. For female flâneurship, all paths lead back, by way of Virginia Woolf, to the novelist George Sand (Aurore Dupin), who braved public outrage to don men's clothing. Decades before Baudelaire, Sand discovered the pleasure of mingling multitude and solitude. Going out for a walk in Paris in the 1830s, she wrote, "No one paid any attention to me, and no one guessed at my disguise. . . . No one knew me, no one looked at me, no one found fault with me; I was an atom lost in that immense crowd."

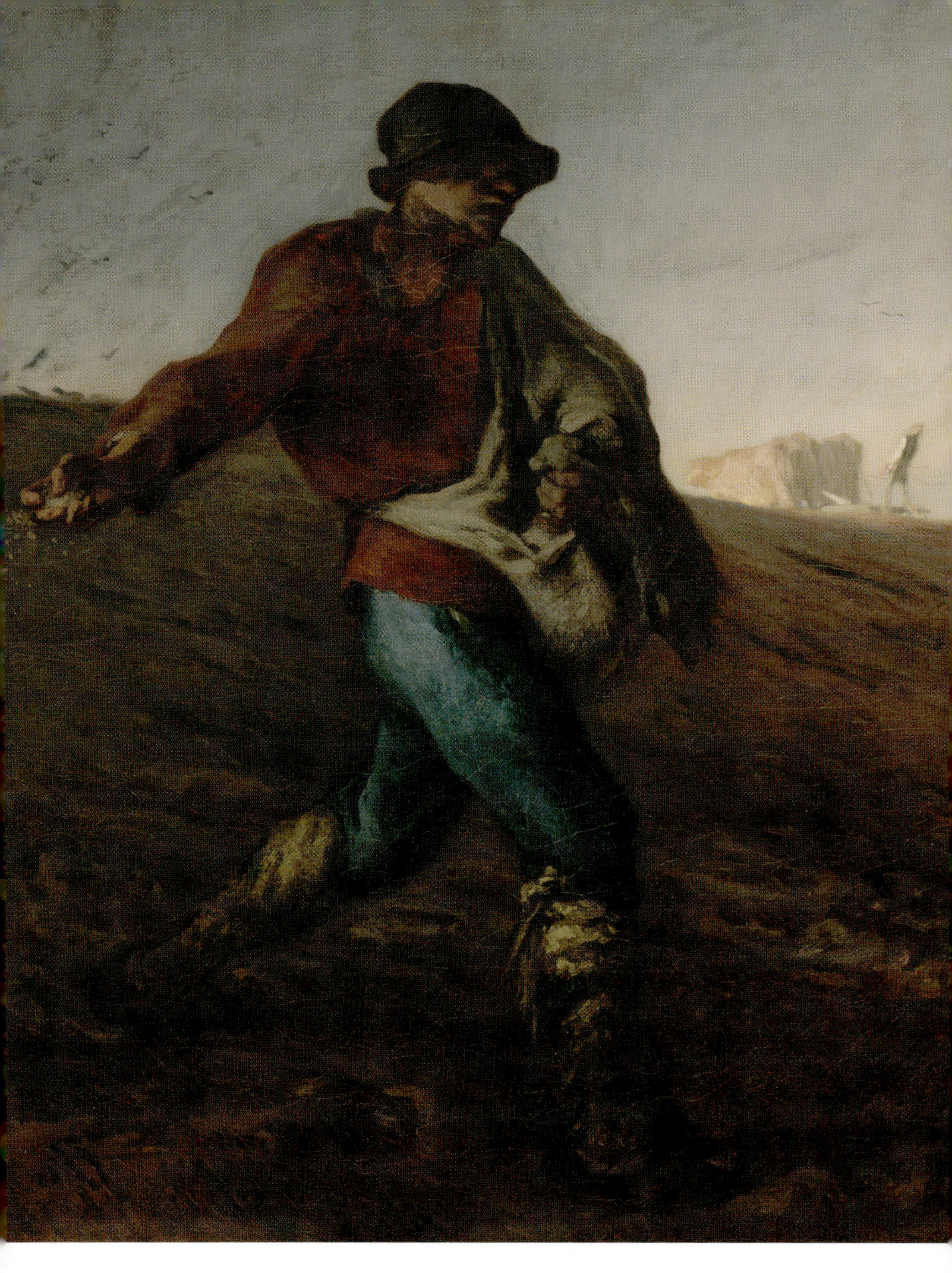

Jean-François Millet, *The Sower*, 1850

Walking Work

When landscape painting emerged in the fifteenth century, many of the people who worked the land were still legally tied to it. In illuminated manuscripts such as the *Très riches heures* of the duc de Berry, or later in the works of Pieter Brueghel the Elder or Jacob van Ruisdael, peasants bend to their tasks, as much a part of the countryside as the leaves on the trees. Eighteenth-century landowners kept farmhands out of their idyllic vistas by relegating them to the ditch of their ha-has. But by the mid-nineteenth century certain painters had decided to bring peasants and workers out of the background. In *The Sower* and *The Laundress*, Jean-François Millet and Honoré Daumier celebrated the heroic stature of the laboring poor.

To the dismay of art critics and the anxious bourgeoisie, who preferred to see workers engaged in quaint rituals or humorous genre scenes, Millet's sower and Daumier's laundress fill the foregrounds of their painted worlds. The strength of their bodies is unmistakable. While the sower works with the earth and the laundress with water, the sympathy of the artists unites them. "My dream is to characterize the type," Millet wrote of his subjects. His peasants and Daumier's townsfolk are imposingly allegorical in their simplicity and stature. Unashamedly they declare the muddy nobility of agriculture, the tender power of the working mother.

In the 1840s Millet learned from Daumier, who was passionate about sculpture, how to give his figures solidity and presence. He makes his sower nine heads tall, instead of the usual seven, and by assigning the viewer a low vantage point, he makes the figure loom even larger. The broad sweeping motion of the sower's right hand activates a complex system of diagonals that thrust into the air with the scattered seeds and plunge into the earth with his muscular stride. In the background a man plows with a pair of oxen, opening the earth to receive the seed that a flight of crows, circling on the left, waits to attack. In this battle to survive, Millet has used grimy shades of primary colors—red coat, yellow boots, blue britches—to carve his laborer out of the gathering darkness. Radical as Millet seemed, within a few decades his motif, modified into a female Ceres representing the Republic, would take on the force of a cultural icon, represented on French coins and explored over thirty times in works by Vincent van Gogh.

In contrast to the open stride of Millet's sower, Daumier's laundress and child laboriously climb stairs to reach the level of the viewer. They trudge up from the open-air laundry barges anchored on the Seine, as if wrenching themselves out of the underworld. Grasping her mother's hand, the child places a foot firmly on the top step. Her other hand clutches a clothes paddle, as if beating the laundry is the only game she can play, until it becomes the only job she can have. Like Millet,

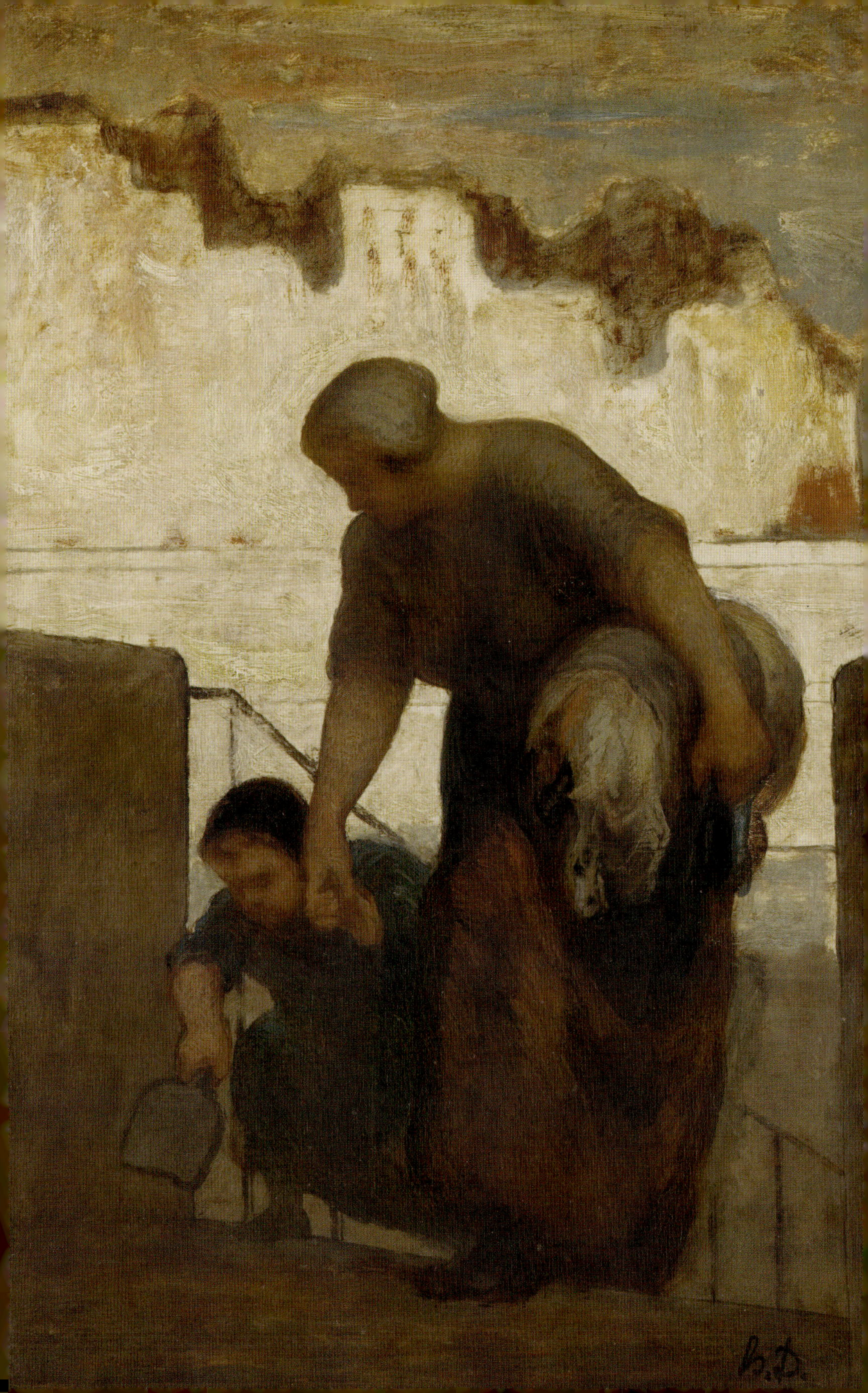

Daumier has given his figures primary colors—the blue of their dresses, the yellow-tinged laundry, the raw red of the washerwoman's hand—to stand out against the paler background of houses across the river, rumpled as a dirty sheet.

The glowing evening light behind the sower and the laundress suggests that they do not share in the prosperity of the society they labor for. But they both nurture hope, in the form of seeds and progeny. Millet's crows may eat the seed; bundles of laundry may soon bend the back of Daumier's child. But for now the figures move inexorably forward, monumental as Michelangelo's biblical characters. Feeling the determination of their step, it is up to the viewer to take notice and get out of the way.

Honoré Daumier, *The Laundress*, c. 1863

A Walk Captured

Three young chimney sweeps trudge along a wall of the Quai Bourbon in the glare of the morning sun, with the houses of Right Bank Paris forming a background across the river Seine. Arranged in ascending order of size, their faces mere profiles, they walk into photographic history: this is one of the earliest depictions of people in motion, frozen forever in the warming light. In 1838 Louis Daguerre had been the first to photograph human life, a distant man having his shoes shined during a seven-minute exposure of a Parisian street. Now in 1851 Charles Nègre decided to put the faster, more flexible calotype process to the test. Nègre knew that his paper negative, unlike the single-image daguerreotype, could produce an unlimited number of prints, should his picture come out well. He might not get Daguerre's crystal-clear detail, but he would be able to take a picture in less than a minute. It would have to be staged, deliberately held motion, given the exposure time, but the *impression* of movement could be conveyed.

Nègre situated his chimney sweeps in the forefront of his scene in bright sunlight to decrease the exposure time. The left-to-right walking stance, enhanced by the out-of-focus blur of the background, enabled Nègre's viewers to read a photograph for the first time as a stop-action document. Until then, most photographs shared with paintings a static, composed, studio-style construction. But Nègre was in the process of inventing the snapshot, giving the novel impression that the scene had been caught and *extracted* from the ongoing rush of events.

Even so, the sweeps may have been posed as a study for a painting, since Nègre himself was an accomplished artist. The "painters of modern life," as Baudelaire styled them—illustrators, caricaturists, portraitists, and more—were rapidly learning to exploit photographic technology for their own needs. Even as photography undermined the market for portraits, it opened the public's eyes to new ways of seeing, constructing a compelling model of visual reality that painters could imitate or reject at their peril. The chimney sweeps form a dynamic group, even if the hats, soot, and harsh light render them nearly faceless. Their personalities emerge instead from their postures and clothing. Looking a bit weary, the taller lad on the left leans forward, his weight on both feet, his sack weighing him down. The middle sweep, hands in pockets, shuffles forward in a relaxed, casual way, clearly in no hurry. But the third, a mere child, looks lively and energetic. Having surged ahead of the others, he vigorously pushes off with his left foot as his right leg awkwardly crosses over it, knee bent.

The sweeps have a robust quality despite the soot that clings to them. The way they move their softer, rounded forms against the sharply etched stone wall of the quay suggests how they will scrape their bodies through unyielding fireplaces and

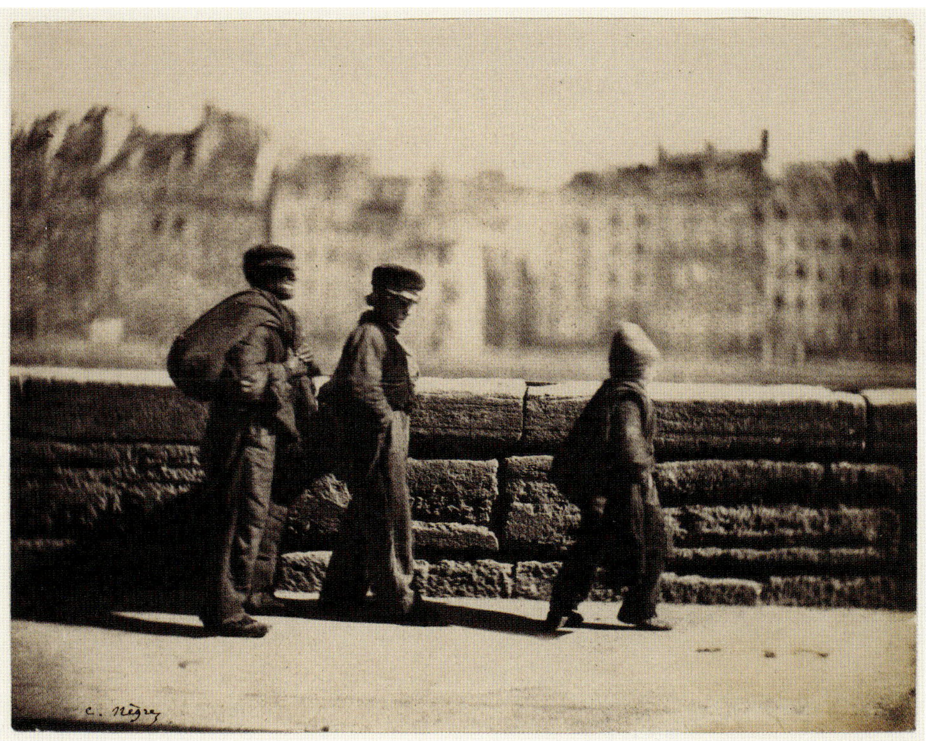

Charles Nègre, *Chimney Sweeps Walking*, 1851

chimneys. Seen in the longer term, the contrast between flesh and stone brings into crisp focus the way in which the people documented in photographs live forever in a medium that highlights the ephemerality of human life. Collectively, the chimney sweeps take a giant step for photography, a decisive stride into the as-yet-unphotographed future.

Freedom Dress

When in the 1830s George Sand slipped into men's clothing to enjoy anonymity as she stalked the streets, she noticed how much easier it was to move around in trousers and boots than in flimsy feminine footwear: "I can't express the pleasure my boots gave me. . . . With those little iron-shod heels, I was solid on the pavement. I flew from one end of Paris to the other. It seemed to me that I could go round the world." Sand walked incognito, but within two decades feminist leaders in the United States launched an overt attack on the constrictions of women's clothing. Engaging the support of women in Britain and the Continent, they started a sustained movement for "Freedom" or "Reform" dress that lasted until the 1920s, when shorter skirts and the right to vote coincided with the death of the corset.

Amelia Bloomer was not the first to wear the garb that has come to bear her name, but her prominent defense of billowing Turkish trousers or "bloomers" empowered women and outraged men in equal measure. Bloomers got their start in 1849 when a health magazine asked its readers to find a less harmful alternative to the tight corsets and heavy skirts then in fashion. Collectively they came up with variations on a short-skirt-and-trousers theme that echoed Turkish dress. Over the next two years ordinary women, as well as famous activists such as Elizabeth Smith Miller and Elizabeth Cady Stanton, adopted a pantaloon style. Then in March 1851 Bloomer announced to readers of her temperance journal the *Lily* that she too wore the baggy trousers, providing instructions on how to make them at home.

By the summer of 1851 bloomers were all the rage. There were songs ("I Want to Be a Bloomer"), dances ("The Bloomer Polka"), and satirical comments aplenty. More stereotyped than accurate, pictures proliferated of Amelia Bloomer wearing a full but short skirt over pantaloons pulled tight at the ankle. Armed with a parasol, she was invariably depicted as being out for a genteel nature walk in dainty slippers that would have made George Sand wince and Elizabeth Bennet despair. As the fashion swept America, some adventurous travelers dared to pack their bloomers for a trip abroad. Under the headline "Bloomerism in Edinburgh," the *Times* of London reported that "comments, characterized by freedom more than politeness . . . followed the unblushing Bloomers. . . . we learn that the ladies are Americans." The mocking that dress reformers had to endure is summed up by the *Punch* cartoon that followed: amid the jeers of street urchins and the stares of ladies in full skirts, two American women stride obliviously down a British street, further savaging gender norms by puffing cigars as they go.

Within a few years bloomers had gone out of style. Amelia Bloomer herself stopped wearing them in 1857 when she judged that the new hoop skirts and crinolines allowed sufficient freedom of motion. But if the fashion faded, the idea

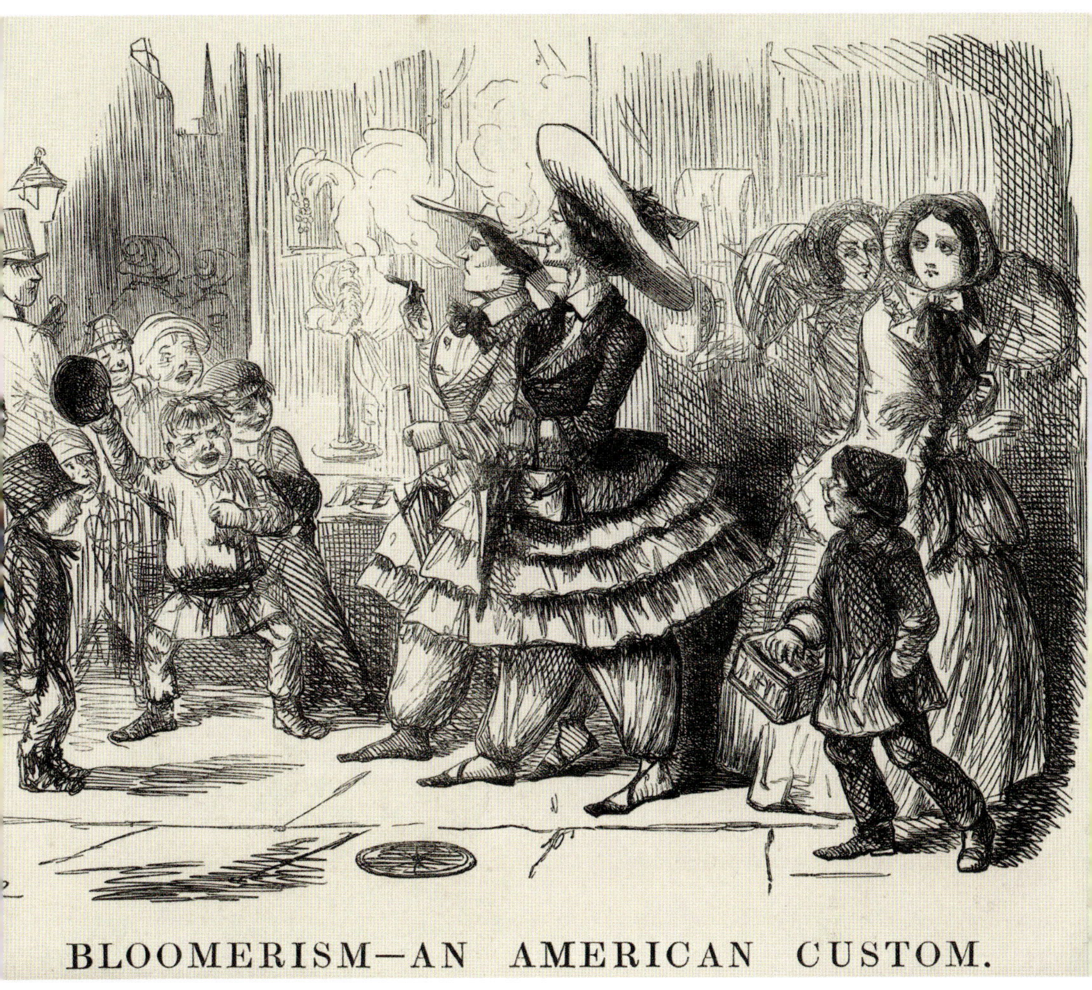

Unknown artist, "Bloomerism—An American Custom," *Punch*, 1851

behind it refused to die. In 1881 Lady Florence Harberton founded the Rational Dress Society in London, which soon had sister organizations all over Europe. Lady Harberton actively modeled practical clothing, bringing new life to the trouser-skirt outfit that emerged as a popular cycling costume in the 1890s. Since then, women's trousers have never left the fashion scene, backed by Bloomer's timeless logic: "Let men be compelled to wear our dress for a while, and we should soon hear them advocating a change, as loudly as they now condemn it."

Caught in the Act

> We never understood it thoroughly until the time of the instantaneous photograph.
>
> *—Oliver Wendell Holmes, "The Physiology of Walking"*

In 1859 the American poet, physician, essayist, and inventor Oliver Wendell Holmes produced the first illustrated essay on the mechanics of walking, a process he jokingly called "balanced vertical projection." What most struck Holmes was how precarious the whole affair was. "Walking . . . is a perpetual falling with a perpetual self-recovery," he said. "It is a most complex, violent, and perilous operation, which we divest of its extreme danger only by continual practice from a very early period in life." Employing the book illustrator F. O. C. Darley to delineate the unexpected positions he discovered in photographs, Holmes pointed out that "no artist would have dared to draw a walking figure in attitudes like some of these."

To study walking, Holmes took advantage of two recent advances in photographic technology. The first was shorter exposure times that enabled photographers to capture people in mid-step on a city street. "Instantaneous" snapshots of big cities like New York and Paris then proliferated because of a second innovation, the stereoscope. This handheld device enjoyed a runaway popularity in the 1850s because it added to photographs a hugely attractive feature: depth. Two photographs of the same subject, taken a short distance apart (often with a double-lensed camera) and viewed side by side through the stereoscope, caused the brain of a viewer to believe it was seeing in three dimensions. The device enjoyed a revival in the mid-twentieth century as a children's toy, the View-Master color slide viewer that, like its ancestor, initially showed landscapes and tourist sites.

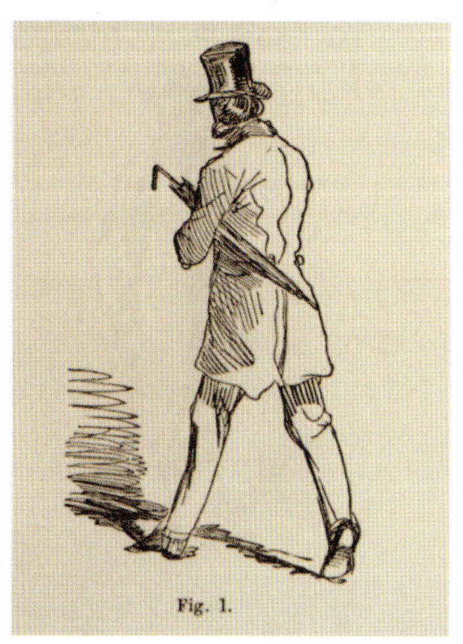

The overall effect gave people an incentive to linger over the abundant details of something they had never been able to see before, one frozen second in the life of an apparently solid world. The swing of a leg that would have blurred into nothingness in the 1840s was held fast in the vise of chemistry only a decade later. Fascinated by photography, Holmes himself invented a version of the stereoscope in 1861, which he deliberately did not patent, so that its wonders could reach as many people as possible.

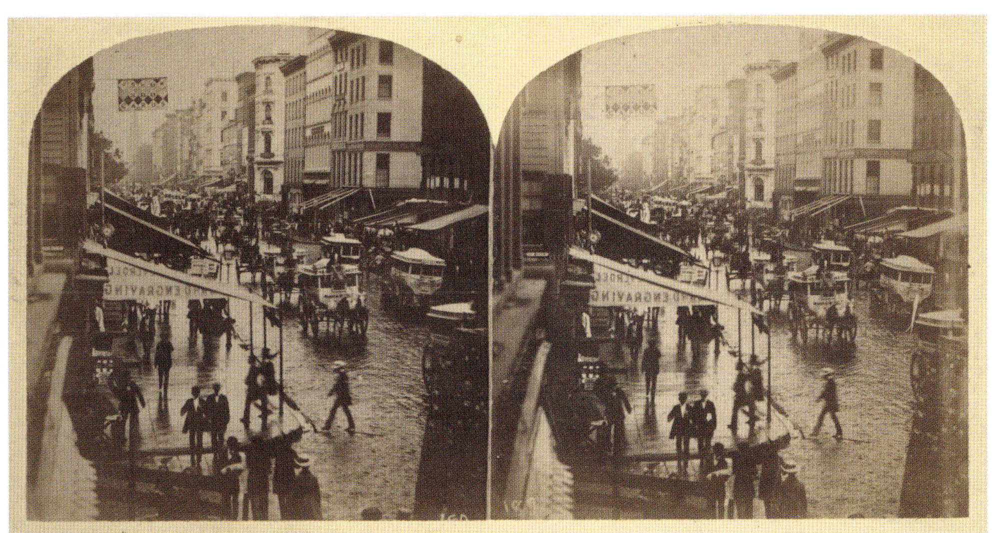

▶ Edward Anthony, *Broadway on a Rainy Day*, stereoscopic view, 1859

◀ F. O. C. Darley, "Walker Drawn from Stereoscopic View," in Oliver Wendell Holmes, "The Physiology of Walking," 1859

Of the hundred thousand stereo views that Holmes claimed to have studied, many were the work of the enterprising Edward Anthony, who with his brother Henry ran the largest photo supply store in the United States. His stereoscopic scene of a rainy day on Broadway catches some of the positions noted in Holmes's essay: the almost vertically raised heel of the trailing leg, the bent knee of the unweighted leg as it pendulums forward, the heel strike of the firmly descending front foot. "Every foot is caught in its movement with such suddenness that it shows as clearly as if quite still," Holmes wrote of Anthony's images in 1861, connecting modern American photography to ancient Greek statuary; "Motion is as rigid as marble if you only take a wink's worth of it at a time."

The Long Walk

In 1946 George Orwell wrote that "in our time, political speech and writing are largely the defense of the indefensible. . . . Millions of peasants are robbed of their farms and sent trudging along the roads with no more than they can carry: this is called *transfer of population* or *rectification of frontiers*." From ancient Assyria to modern Kosovo, temporarily powerful groups have forced weaker parties to depart from their homelands, little caring how many died on the way. All continents and almost every country have tales to tell about forced relocation, about death marches that scarred the survivors and their descendants forever. In the United States, the Orwellian euphemism of the "Indian Removal Act" (1830) only poorly concealed the federal government's armed displacement of sixty thousand Native Americans during the 1830s, a series of events now better known as the Trail of Tears. Members of the Cherokee, Chickasaw, Choctaw, Seminole, Creek, and other nations were driven from ancestral lands in the southeastern United States and forced to march over a thousand miles to reservations west of the Mississippi, largely in the area that is now Oklahoma. The sufferings of the Cherokee in 1838 were especially severe. Almost half of the sixteen thousand starting the journey perished along the way.

Few contemporary visual records remain of the Trail of Tears. But something had changed by 1864 when the US Army pushed the Navajo, or Diné, people from their territories, in the name of protecting them from settlers and enemy tribes. Those who survived what the Navajo came to call "the long walk" were met by a new form of exacting record-keeper, the army camera.

From 1864 to 1866, in over fifty different forced marches, about nine thousand Navajo walked eastward more than three hundred barren miles from what is now Arizona to Fort Sumner and the Bosque Redondo Reservation in the present state of New Mexico. Along the way many were treated cruelly and left to die by their army escort, or harassed, raided, and killed by traditional enemies. Once they arrived at the poorly chosen site, which lacked food, clean water, firewood, and shelter, they were photographed. In many ways photography is the imperialist tool par excellence, with its rhetoric of taking, shooting, capturing, and documenting—all rights reserved—what must yield to the superior force behind the lens.

In this arrival photograph, the huddled subjects keep a literally guarded distance from the observing lens. The earthworks in the foreground separate the watching soldier, bayonet fixed, from his blanket-wrapped prisoners. The shallow rampart evokes the military history of westward expansion, with soldiers gathered in forts pitted against larger populations—not only warriors but women, children, the elderly—spread across a rugged yet domestic space. Tellingly, the camera surveys

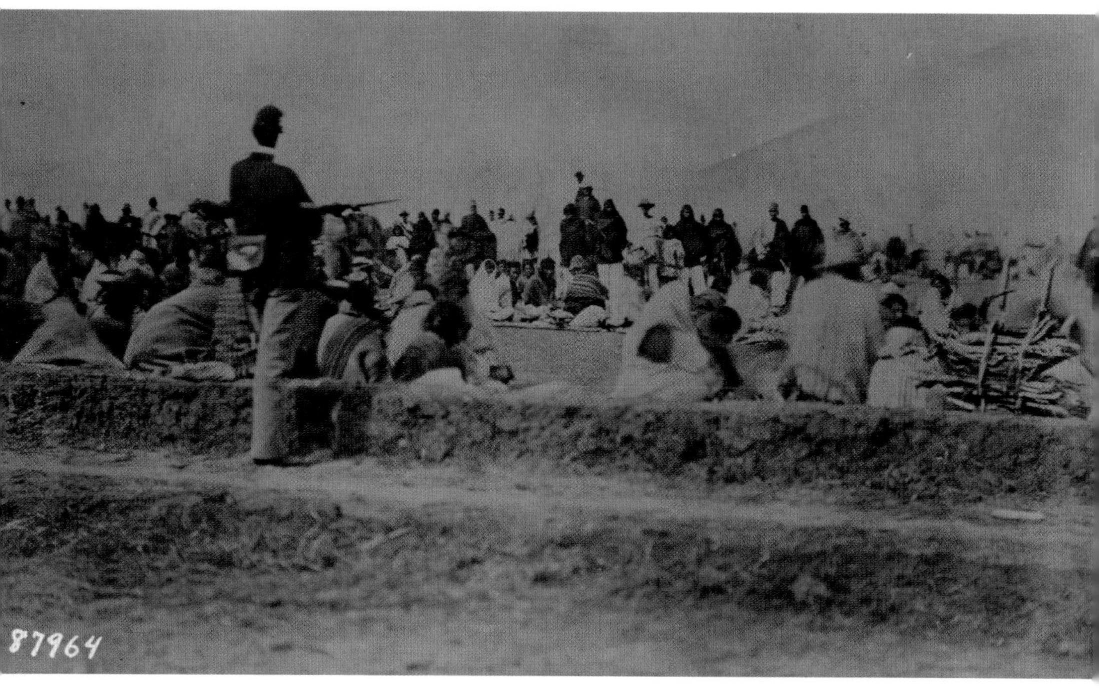

Unknown photographer, Navajos under guard after a forced march to Fort Sumner, New Mexico, c. 1864

the out-of-focus mass of indigenous people from inside the makeshift bulwark, reinforcing a message as old as colonization: it's a few of us against all of them. Subsequently filed away in a government office, the photo replicates its content. It stands watch over this moment, testifying that might made right, and the removal took place in an orderly fashion.

Some two thousand Navajo died while interned at Bosque Redondo. The administration of the reservation was so evidently a disaster that the Navajo were able to negotiate a new treaty. Native American trails had laid the foundation for future American transit and transport; Native American guides had helped colonists find paths that enabled them to spread across the country they would seize. Now, in 1868, the Navajo survivors refused to be "guided" in return. They departed together in a unified trek, "the long walk home." Laboriously they retraced their steps to regain portions of their former lands. They arrived home bonded more strongly than ever by the needless ordeal that has since helped define them as a people.

Terrific Apparition

Do traffic lights serve the interests of vehicles or pedestrians? The first effort in that direction was intended to save the lives of walkers. In the 1860s London was the world's largest city, with a population approaching four million. Some of its bridges were crossed by over a hundred thousand people a day, and several died each week in accidents involving vehicles, horses, and pedestrians. In front of the Houses of Parliament, the intersection of three streets, fed by heavy traffic coming off Westminster Bridge, was particularly dangerous. London policemen had directed traffic for over a century at this spot, but they could hardly be seen in the tangle of tall coaches and heavy wagons that carried passengers and advertising signs on their roofs. So in December 1868 the Metropolitan Police installed a twenty-foot-high semaphore tower there. Red arms extended horizontally to signal "Stop!" The arms relaxed by forty-five degrees to indicate "Caution."

Designed by railway signal engineer John Peake Knight, the apparatus was topped with gaslights for night use, shining red for "Stop" and green for "Caution," as was the custom on train lines. The semaphore was manually operated by a policeman because no one believed that traffic would stop for the signal alone. Ten thousand leaflets, addressed to riders and drivers, were printed by the police department to explain the operation to Londoners. "Caution" meant proceed "with due regard to the safety of Foot Passengers," while "Stop" meant halt clear of the intersection "to allow the passage of Persons on Foot."

An illustration entitled "The New Street Semaphore at Westminster" shows a typical nineteenth-century every-which-way mix of traffic. A stagecoach, its horses briskly trotting, enters from the left; a boy crossing-sweeper makes a path for a man with a bundle under his arm; a working man accosts a gentleman and lady as they approach the signal pole. A policeman stands with his back to the column, looking in the direction of two women whose full skirts crease as they turn to face something outside the frame. And a sandwich-board man partially hidden behind the signal pole advertises the *Illustrated Times*, the weekly newspaper in which this picture was printed. No one is paying the slightest attention to the signal.

According to the humor magazine *Punch*, however, they did notice the twenty-foot-tall figure at night. It loomed out of the winter fog, waving its arms and frightening the populace with the red or green glow of its cyclopean eye. Despite the concerns of *Punch*, the public responded unexpectedly well to the giant's directions, leading a newspaper to predict that "similar structures will no doubt be speedily erected in many other parts of the metropolis."

But a gas leak under the pavement caused an explosion in January 1869, seriously injuring the policeman on duty. The stoplight experiment was ended, and

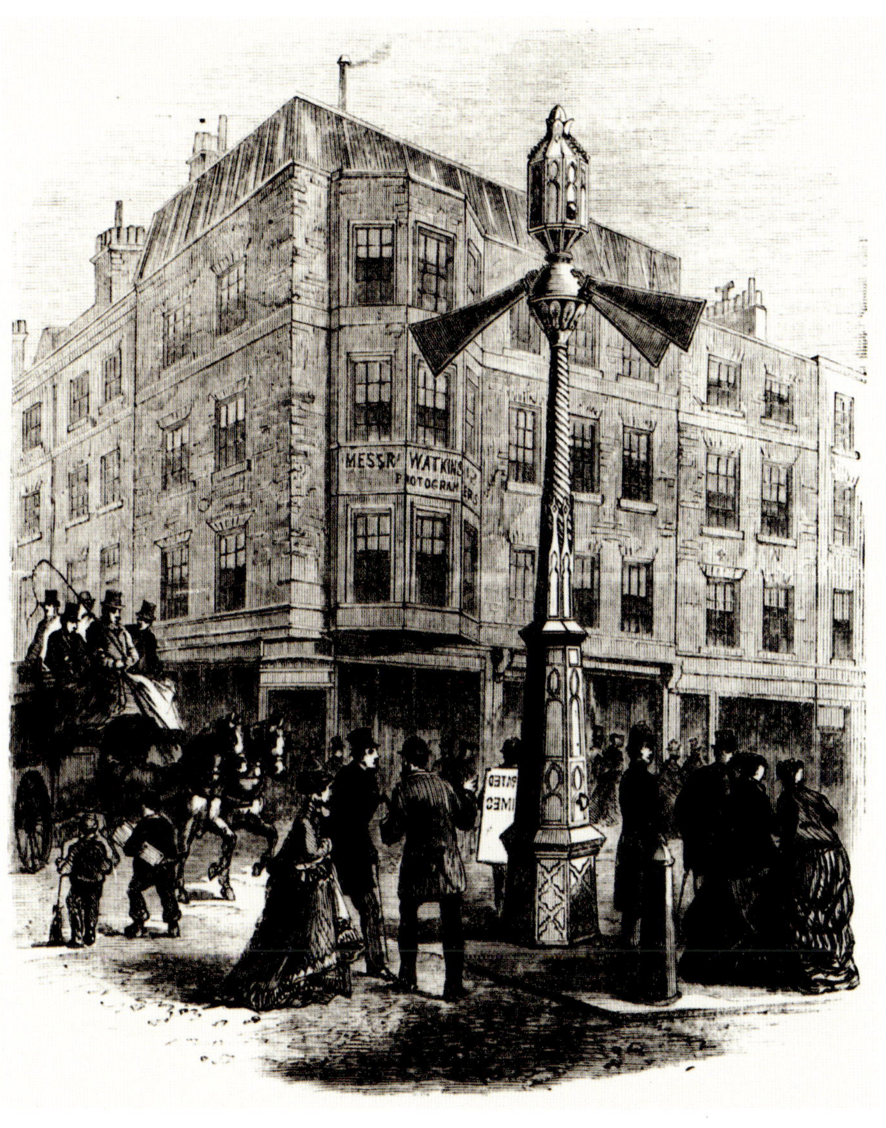

Unknown artist, "The New Street Semaphore at Westminster," *Illustrated Times*, January 16, 1869

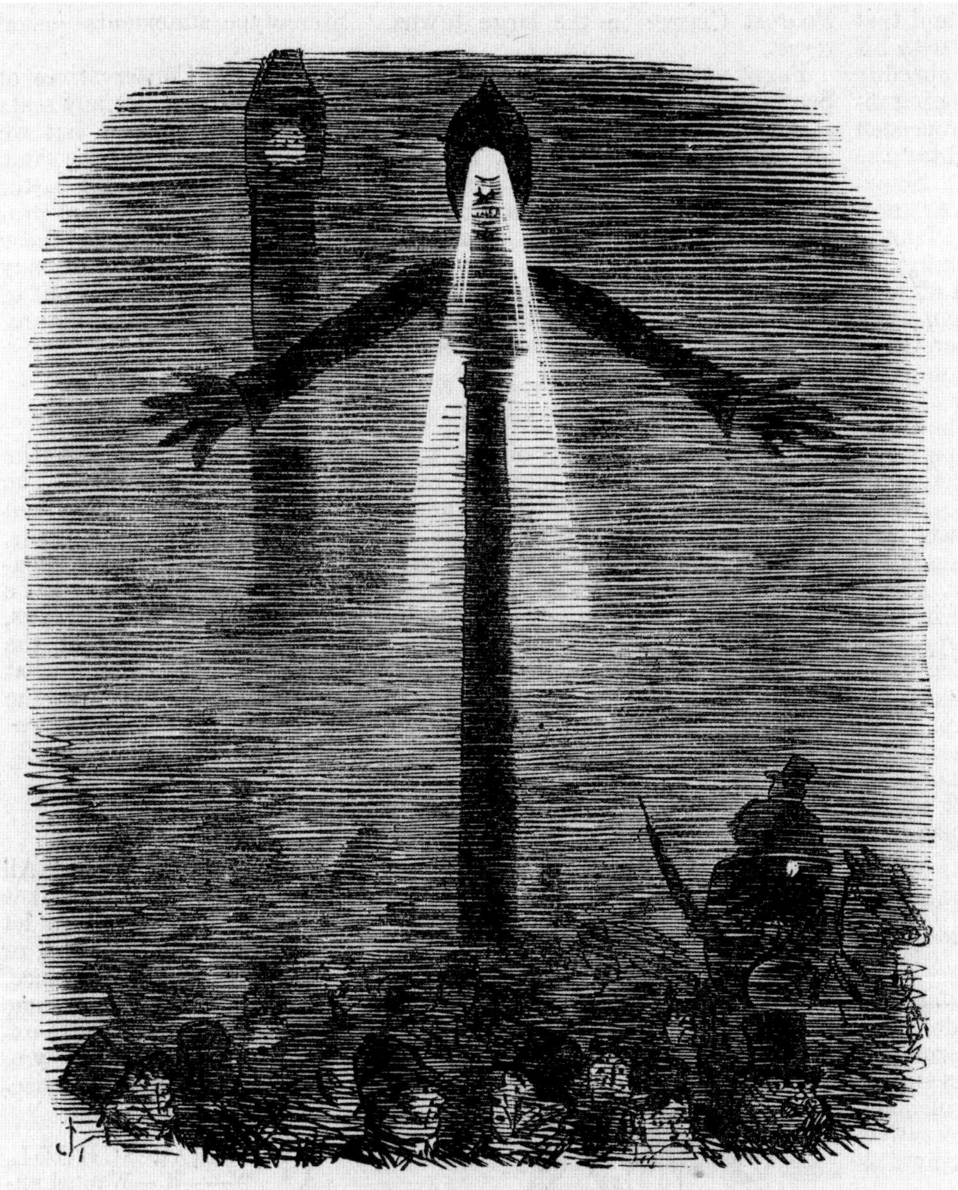

TERRIFIC APPARITION

Seen during the Recent Fog at Westminster.

the semaphore arms remained in the "Caution" position until the end of 1872, when the structure was removed because the city would not pay for its repair. Eventually J. P. Knight, the inventor, was called upon to pay over three hundred pounds for the expense of running it, plus its gas bill. While various forms of traffic light appeared elsewhere in the next half-century—there was one in Toledo, Ohio, by 1908 and another in Paris by 1912—the next signal was not installed in London until 1926, in Piccadilly Circus. By then automobiles had provided an even more lethal reason to control traffic, and walkers had lost the right to use streets as they chose.

Unknown artist ("L. T."), "Terrific Apparition—Seen during the Recent Fog at Westminster," *Punch*, 1869

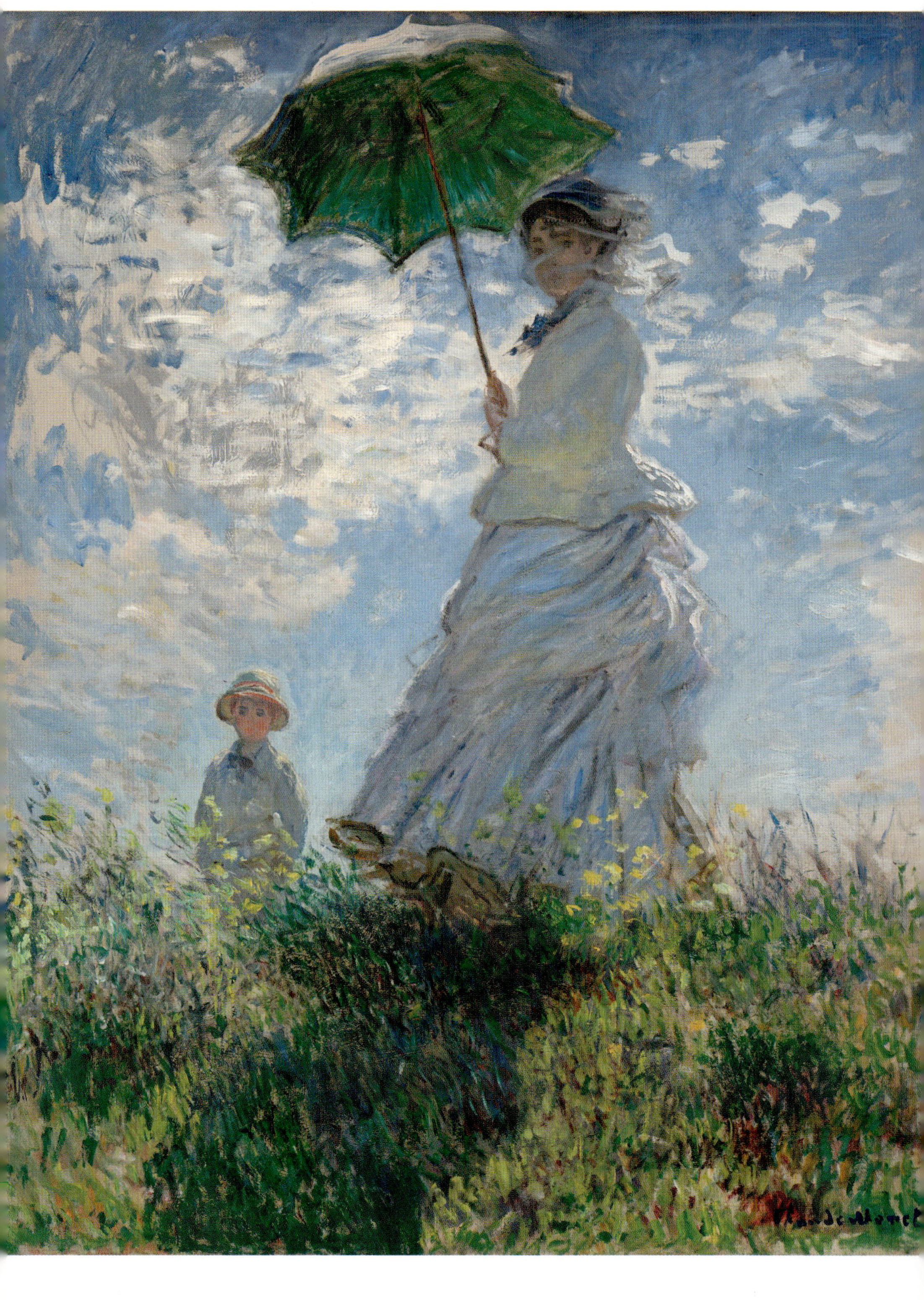

A Sunday Walk with Madame Monet

No picture better sums up the ethos of Impressionism than *Woman with a Parasol*, apparently painted outdoors in a single session. Madame Monet and her son pause during a country walk to look down at the artist, who has strayed from the path. The low viewpoint sets Camille Monet on a pedestal, lending her an appearance every bit as monumental as Jean-François Millet's *Sower*. It's Monet's largest canvas of the decade, turning his wife into a casual, triumphantly impermanent statue that incarnates the breezy radiance of the day. Her pose seems ready to change with the next flutter of her veil. What made Impressionism seem so "outdoorsy" was not so much that painters worked en plein air as that the subjects themselves were depicted in action: bathing, boating, picnicking, and above all, walking.

Here the story of the walk is told in the interaction between people and accessories. A parasol and a shadow, echoing each other in grass-green color, link the woman's figure to earth and sky, filling the frame from top to bottom. The figures and landscape interpenetrate each other. Sky-blue paint in Camille's dress flashes above and below the glowing reflection of the yellow flowers on her dress beneath her elbow, while her white veil ribbons match the paint strokes of the clouds to either side of her head. Monet's flurried brushwork lays down a thick blanket of vegetation at her feet that becomes incorporated in the hem of her dress. Meanwhile, seven-year-old Jean Monet waits patiently in the background, half hidden below the ridge, watching. He could just as easily be the young Marcel Proust, who took such walks with his family during these same years, walks that structure the first volumes of *In Search of Lost Time*.

Emblem of the democratizing tide of the nineteenth century, *Woman with a Parasol* announces that middle-class leisure, in the form of a well-dressed woman taking a walk, has become a subject important enough for a major painting. No anecdote is told, no great event is shown, and yet a crucial historical process unfolds. Like Monet's *Poppy Field, Argenteuil* (1873), which represents his wife and son on another outing, this painting celebrates what the poet Charles Baudelaire only half ironically called "the heroism of modern life." Instead of anonymous peasants working the land, or noted aristocracy surveying their dominions, here bourgeois strollers traverse at their ease the countryside they neither till nor own. Like other holiday walkers, Monet's family become a fleeting possession of the landscape that hosts them. They belong only to the sight, and will as soon be gone as the shadow at Madame Monet's feet.

Claude Monet, *Woman with a Parasol: Madame Monet and Her Son*, 1875

A Walk in the Rain

When it comes to walking the city streets, Gustave Caillebotte's *Paris Street; Rainy Day* makes perhaps the most compelling statement of nineteenth-century modernity. Big as a shop window, the canvas invites quizzical awe at the drizzly expanse of the new metropolis that the artist puts on clinical display. During the 1850s and 1860s Baron Georges-Eugène Haussmann had transformed Paris, demolishing hundreds of buildings, displacing three hundred thousand people, and creating new squares, boulevards, train stations, and parks. In addition to the homeless, Haussmann left in his wake hundreds of disgruntled artists and writers yearning for the past. The poet Charles Baudelaire famously lamented "Old Paris is no longer. The shape of a city / Changes faster, alas! than the human heart." But many residents, not to mention subsequent generations, celebrated the result. For them, Haussmann's effort to bring light, sanitation, and aesthetic harmony into a still-medieval labyrinth succeeded in producing the world's most walkable city.

Among the fifty miles of roadway that Haussmann cut through the old quarters were the streets around the place de Dublin, close to where Caillebotte grew up. In his life-size painting of strollers moving south along the rue de Turin, with the rue de Moscou and the rue Clapeyron diverging from the square behind, Caillebotte took stock of what had happened to his once-intimate neighborhood. He drew in an original manner on two of Impressionism's vital resources, the compositional daring of Japanese woodcuts and the varied ways of seeing that photography was now imprinting on visual consciousness. Umbrellas cut off a head or a taxicab, while the frame slices off half of the man in the right foreground. The middle ground zooms into sharp focus between the misty, slightly fuzzy softness of fore- and background. The crispness of the lamppost and the shoes of the man crossing behind it, along with the toe push and the heel strike of the other street-crossers, could have come from Edward Anthony's stereoscopic shots of Broadway.

One has only to recall other paintings from the era to see how different Caillebotte's vision is. Pierre-Auguste Renoir's *Pont Neuf* (1872) brims with vibrant color, but the awkward poses of his walking figures fit with the story that, struggling, he sent his brother Edmond out to pace up and down as a model (twice). Meanwhile Monet's *Boulevard des Capucines* (1873) tips up its picture plane so much in the Japanese style that the dashed-in pedestrians bristle like pushpins rather than Parisians.

Despite its snapshot casualness, *Paris Street; Rainy Day* reveals that Caillebotte constructed his space every bit as artfully as Haussmann did his avenues. The horizon line and the carefully centered lamppost (a holdover from the 1830s) cut the picture plane into quarters. The post dissects the right-hand vanishing point of

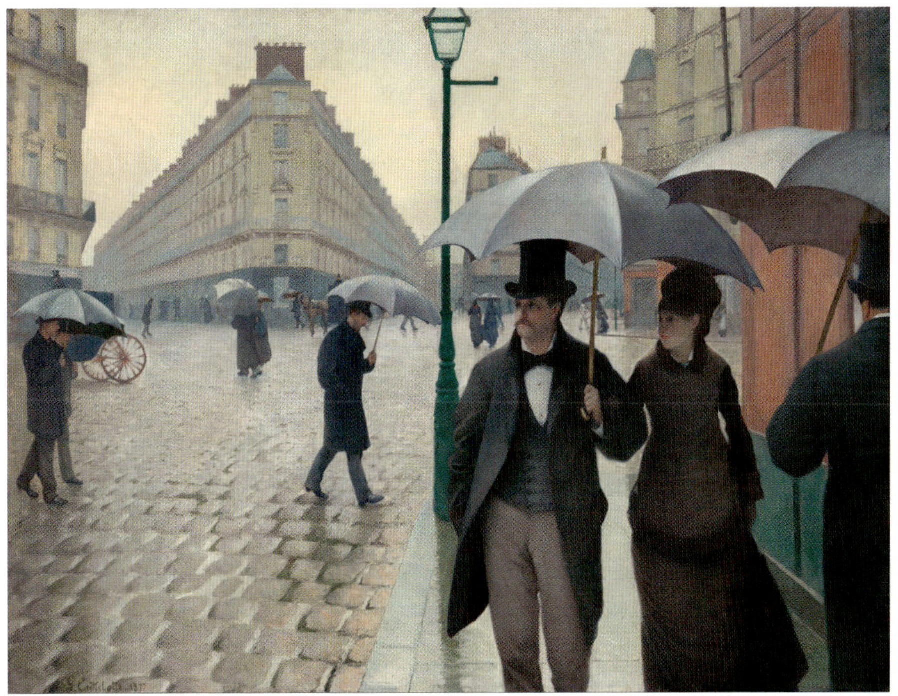

Gustave Caillebotte, *Paris Street; Rainy Day*, 1877

the unusual two-point perspective, exactly on the level of the male protagonist's eyes, separating the close-up sidewalk space from the receding street area. Almost any cityscape offers a path into the scene, but here the half-figure in the right foreground who could stand in for the viewer is instead blocked by the approaching couple. This town looks empty and feels cramped; he would have to step into the street to get past.

Relegated to the background, the workers that once crowded the narrow streets have been reduced to a maid in a doorway, a headless workman carrying a ladder, and the top halves of two cab drivers. But the reigning middle-class do not look any more at ease in the city they now dominate. Nobody looks at anybody; they use their umbrellas as isolation chambers. With gazes as serenely vacant as the bare cobblestones that take up a full quarter of the canvas, Caillebotte's monumentally mundane couple stare off into the empty distance, disengaged from the broad, stony streets where they have yet to learn how to feel at home.

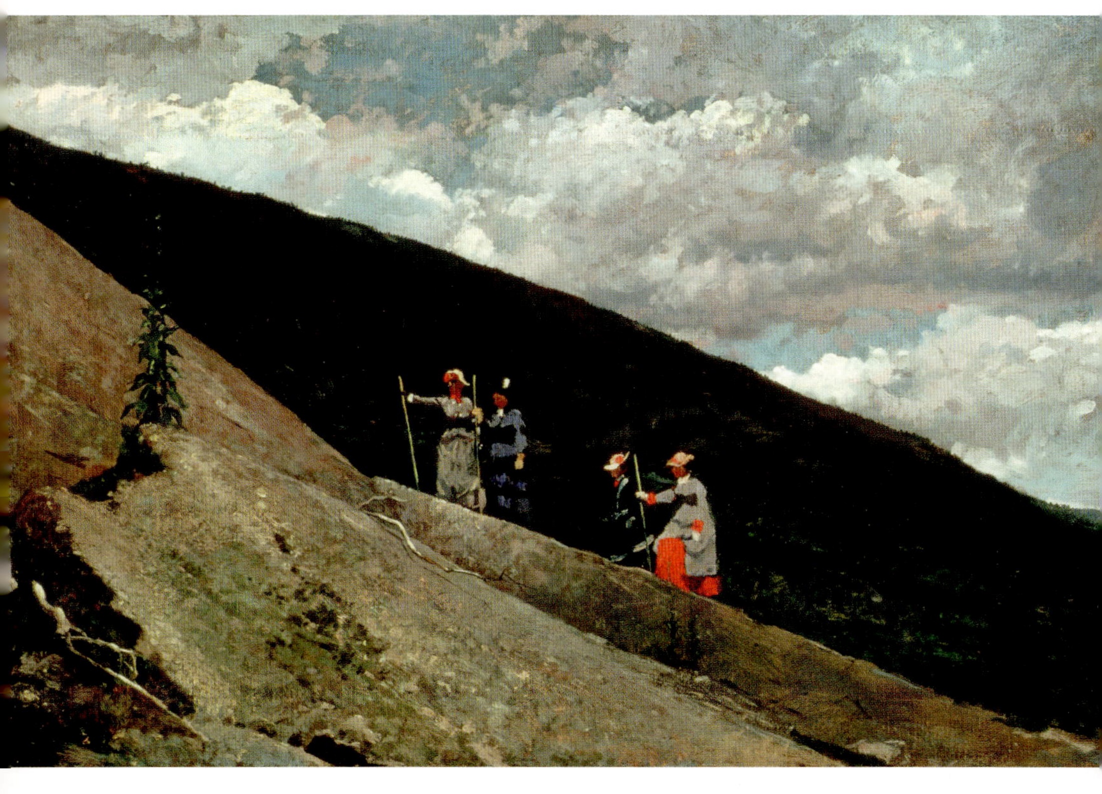

Winslow Homer, *In the Mountains*, 1877

crowd but also a cultural advantage: pedestrianism was "their" sport. It had evolved from wagers placed by eighteenth-century noblemen on whose footman could cover a distance faster. The betting spread to the general public, as competitors from all classes battled over who could walk the farthest in a given time. In 1788 a lawyer's clerk, Foster Powell, walked a hundred miles in 21 hours 35 minutes. Soon more complex challenges arose. Captain Robert Barclay Allardice, "the Celebrated Pedestrian," walked one mile in each of one thousand consecutive hours in 1809. Women had their own stars and records. In 1864 Emma Sharpe duplicated Allardice's thousand-hour challenge, and in 1877 Ada Anderson walked a thousand half-miles in a thousand half-hours. In 1878 she walked fifteen hundred miles in a thousand hours, earning the title of "Champion Lady Walker of the World."

At the Agricultural Hall in London, the aging Weston defied British dominance. He launched into his characteristic shambling gait with grim resolve, walking and jogging a world-record-breaking 550 miles in 142 hours. Ever the showman, he waved British and American flags on a final victory lap. Seventy thousand people witnessed his triumph, and even more turned out to give him a hero's welcome in New York on his return. His record lasted only a year, shattered by Haitian-born Frank Hart, "the Negro Wonder," who covered an astonishing 565 miles in a six-day run-walk at Madison Square Garden in 1880.

Undaunted, Weston rediscovered long-distance walking in the real world. At the age of seventy he rambled from New York to San Francisco in 105 days and then, unsatisfied, walked back in 87 days at the age of seventy-one. A crowd of five hundred thousand people cheered his final miles. Weston spent his later years promoting walking for the sake of health, having lived long enough to see what automobiles were doing to the national physique. His warnings about the dangers of cars came true in 1927, when he was hit by a New York City taxicab. He was eighty-eight. He died two years later, never having walked again.

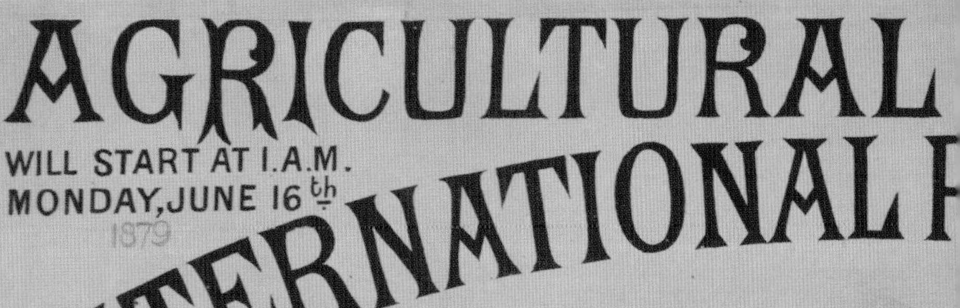

AGRICULTURAL

WILL START AT I.A.M.
MONDAY, JUNE 16th
1879

INTERNATIONAL

COMPETITORS

CHARLES ROWELL
(HOLDER OF THE BELT,)
(CHAMPION of the WORLD)

JOHN ENNIS.
(CHALLENGER)
CHAMPION of AMERICA.

BLOWER BROWN.
(CHAMPION of ENGLAND)

DICK HARDING.
("THE JOLLY YOUNG WATERMAN"
&
E.P. WESTON.
THE EDITOR
OF THE
SPORTING LIFE
HOLDS THE STAKES & WILL
OFFICIATE AS REFEREE.

WESTON   HARDING   BLOWER

CHAMPIONSHI

ADMISSION 1/-   A FAIR FIELD AND NO

Montague Chatterton & Co Lit

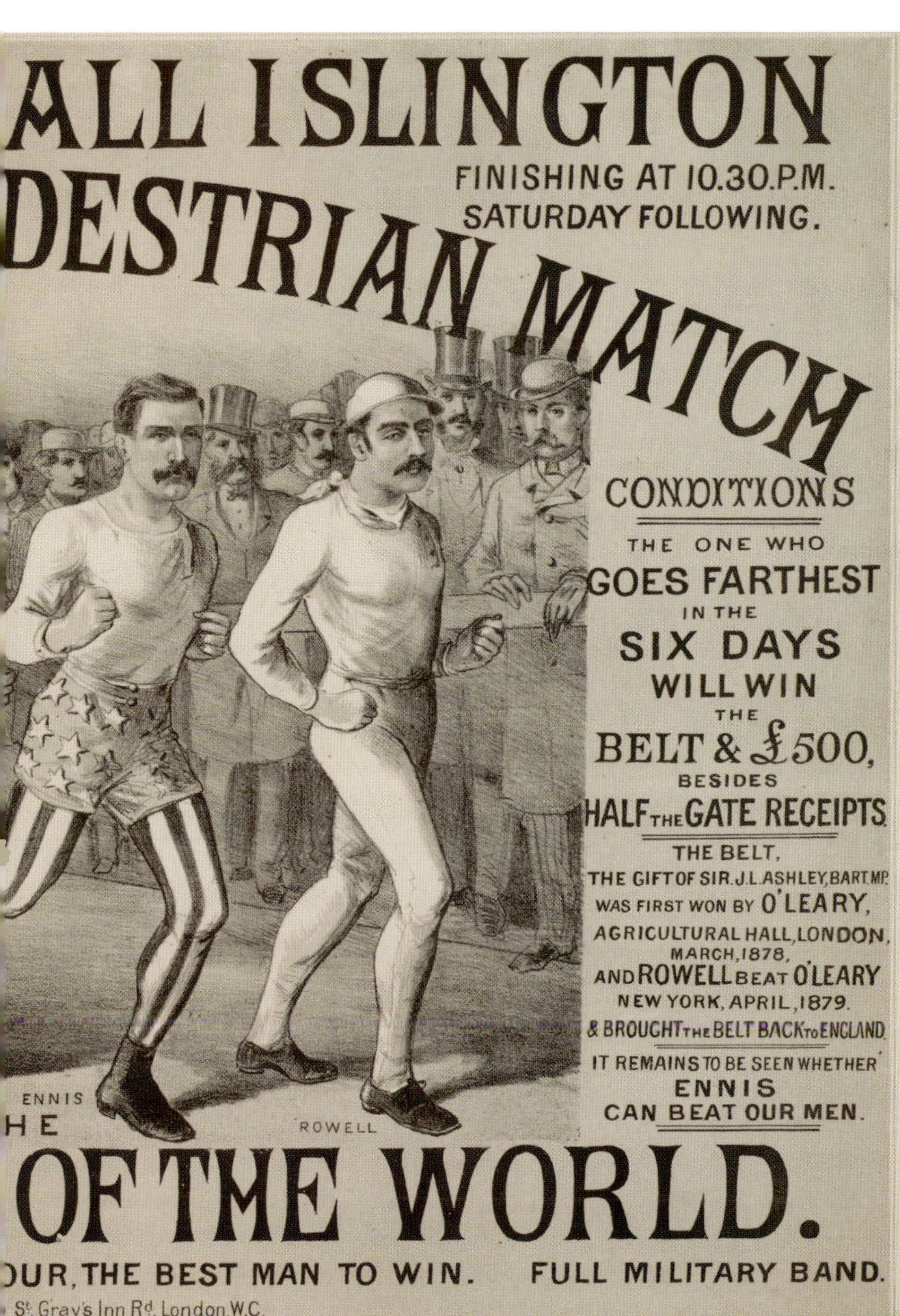

Montague Chatterton and Co., advertisement for Astley Belt Competition, 1879

The Shrouded Stride of Liberty

A vigorous step unites two world-famous incarnations of Liberty, yet most people don't notice the connection. Because they are accustomed to seeing a head-on image of the Statue of Liberty, a gift from France to the people of the United States, even visitors to New York Harbor miss the energy and symbolism of Liberty's dynamic pose. But replace Liberty's torch with a tricolor flag, imagine a barricade, and the American icon becomes recognizable as a toned-down version of Eugène Delacroix's militant painting *Liberty Leading the People*. Controversial with monarchists in France, Delacroix's artistic call to arms supported the French Revolution of 1830, which overthrew the last of the Bourbon kings. His incarnation of Liberty, a bare-breasted, flag-waving freedom fighter with roots in Roman slave rebellions, would have been too radical for the American public. So when the French sculptor Frédéric Auguste Bartholdi designed his colossal statue *Liberty Enlightening the World*, he gave Liberty decorous classical robes and replaced her rifle and bayonet with a book whose open page shows the date of the Declaration of Independence. Charging into battle, Delacroix's Liberty gains visual momentum from the horizontal base of dead bodies that she surges over to make her attack. In place of the French corpses whose inert, upended legs counterpoint the assault of living revolutionaries, Bartholdi slipped a broken shackle and chain under the American Liberty's feet.

And this is where the Statue of Liberty's message became muffled. Bartholdi's aim was to signify the emancipation of African Americans, and in fact the original idea for the statue came from his friend Édouard René de Laboulaye, president of the French Anti-Slavery Society. As a lesson for his own countrymen, Laboulaye wanted to commemorate the vital step toward freedom taken by the US government in winning the American Civil War. But thanks to the height of the pedestal, the shackle and chain are nearly invisible from below. They are further obscured by the drapery that covers Liberty's advancing left leg. Only by viewing the statue from its right side can one see the lifted heel and the strong diagonal of the right leg. Echoing the torchbearing arm, the step is meant to communicate Liberty's bold advance toward universal freedom.

Finally, the meaning of the enlightening torch and the energy of the stride were cloaked in a maternal embrace by the famous words gracing the statue's pedestal. Emma Lazarus's sonnet "To the New Colossus"—written in 1883 to raise funds to build the statue's base—called Liberty the "Mother of Exiles." Lazarus imagined the

Frédéric Auguste Bartholdi, *Liberty Enlightening the World*, 1886

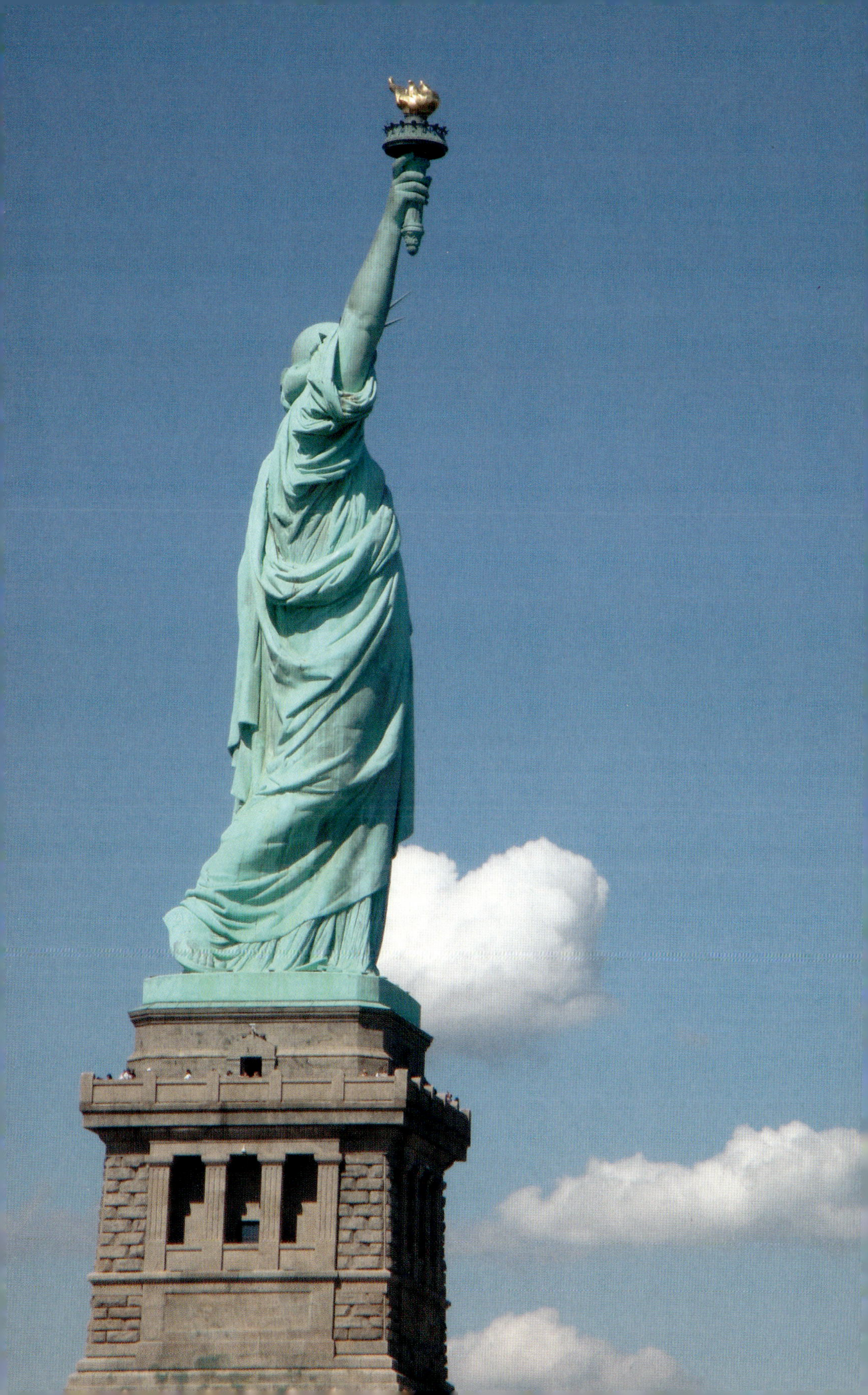

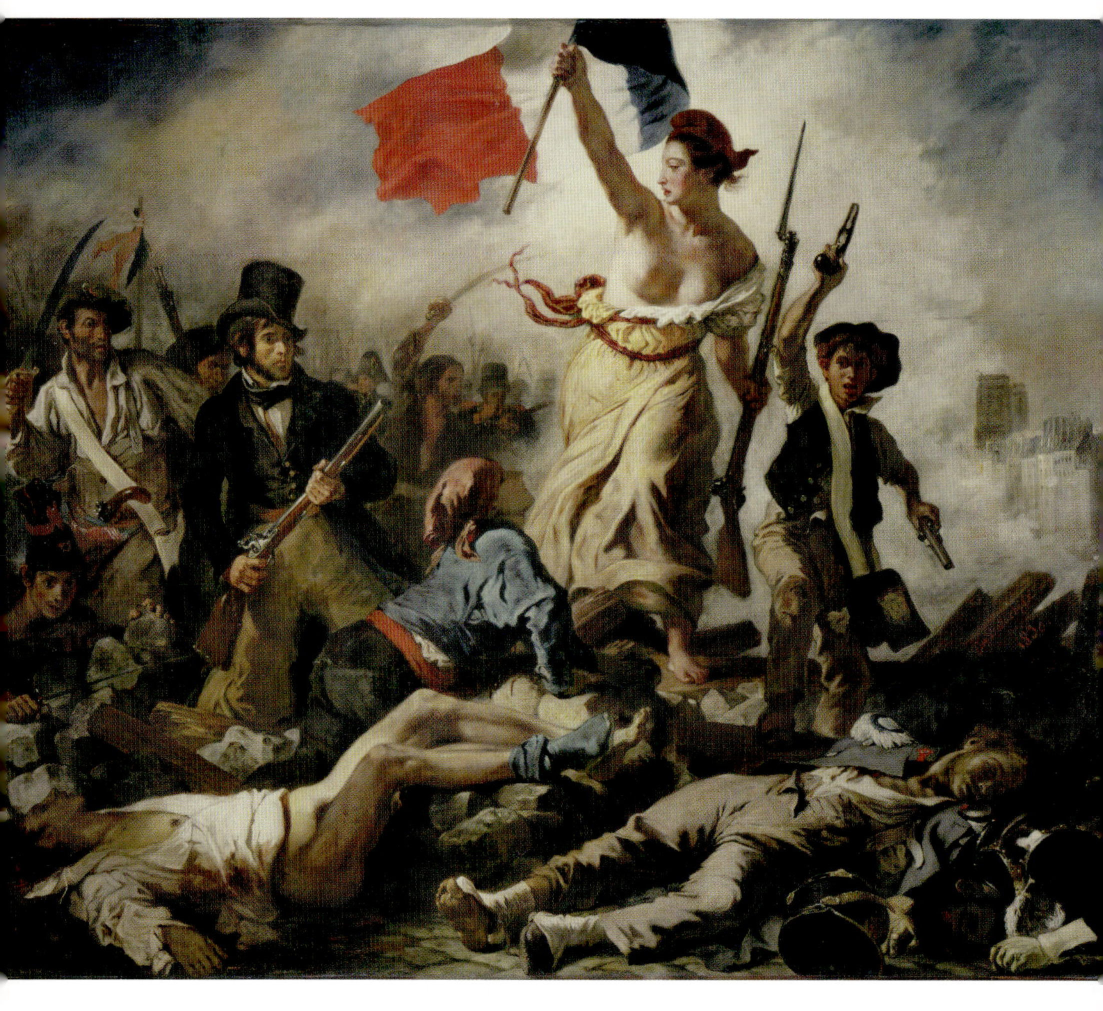

Eugène Delacroix, *Liberty Leading the People*, 1830

statue declaring compassionately: "Give me your tired, your poor, / Your huddled masses yearning to breathe free." After the poem was joined to the pedestal in 1903, immigration overshadowed emancipation in the statue's interpretation.

More comfortable with the idea of religious freedom than racial equality, the American public aligned the statue with the prevailing mythology that saw Americans as weary pilgrims arriving in a promised land. Unlike Delacroix and Bartholdi, who envisioned Liberty aggressively leading the way into a more egalitarian world, Lazarus thought that those who glimpsed Liberty in the harbor would be exhausted from having had to struggle out of Europe. Domestic rather than dynamic, the rewritten colossus waits patiently for the immigrants she will nurture. Slavery forgotten, Mother Liberty offers a warm welcome and a place to rest: "I lift my lamp beside the golden door!"

Portrait in Shoe Leather

What may be the most famous shoes in all of art history are the heavy, high-topped black clodhoppers that Van Gogh painted in 1886. Their laces askew, their uppers scuffed and deformed, Van Gogh's work shoes nonetheless appear proud of their appearance, thanks to the dramatic spotlight the artist sets them in. He was not the first to give special notice to a pair of shoes—the wooden clogs in Jan van Eyck's *Arnolfini Portrait* (1434) have drawn attention for centuries. But the intensity of Van Gogh's depiction has convinced generations of admirers that his well-traveled shoes have a story to tell.

And indeed few things matter more to the walking body than the shoes it wears. Shoes can provide comfort, a sense of style or power, a strong athletic performance, or an agonizing path of pain. Shoes are personal; with luck and time, they adapt to the body so well they seem an extension of it. They may telegraph not only the general social status of the wearer but also elements of a more intimate biography.

It was this line of thought that created a controversy. Van Gogh's shoes gained notoriety in 1935 due to an essay by the philosopher Martin Heidegger, who read in them the life story of a peasant woman:

> In the stiffly rugged heaviness of the shoes there is the accumulated tenac-
> ity of her slow trudge through the far-spreading and ever-uniform furrows
> of the field swept by a raw wind. On the leather lie the dampness and rich-
> ness of the soil. Under the soles slides the loneliness of the field-path as
> evening falls. In the shoes vibrates the silent call of the earth . . .

In 1968 the art historian Meyer Schapiro proved to the satisfaction of many that philosophers should not interpret paintings. He scolded Heidegger for wrongly presuming that these were women's shoes, and not noticing that Van Gogh gave a more perfunctory treatment to peasant shoes on the documentable occasions when he drew them in a real-life context. Moreover, the artist painted battered work shoes many times during the 1880s. Portraying them from the front, the back, the side, or flipped over to reveal a worn or hobnailed sole, he was clearly investigating their formal properties. Finally, Schapiro revealed that in fact Van Gogh had bought the shoes himself in a Paris flea market in 1886. They did not fit, but the artist wore them around long enough for them to acquire a character worthy of being painted. It was clear to Schapiro that Van Gogh treated his *own* shoes as if they were individual sitters, calling the result "veridical portraits of aging shoes."

It's a subtle point, but a compelling one: the shoe portrait may reflect the shoe's life, not the wearer's. Finding that the shoes have further tales to tell, subsequent critics have granted them plenty of narrative power: they may bespeak a

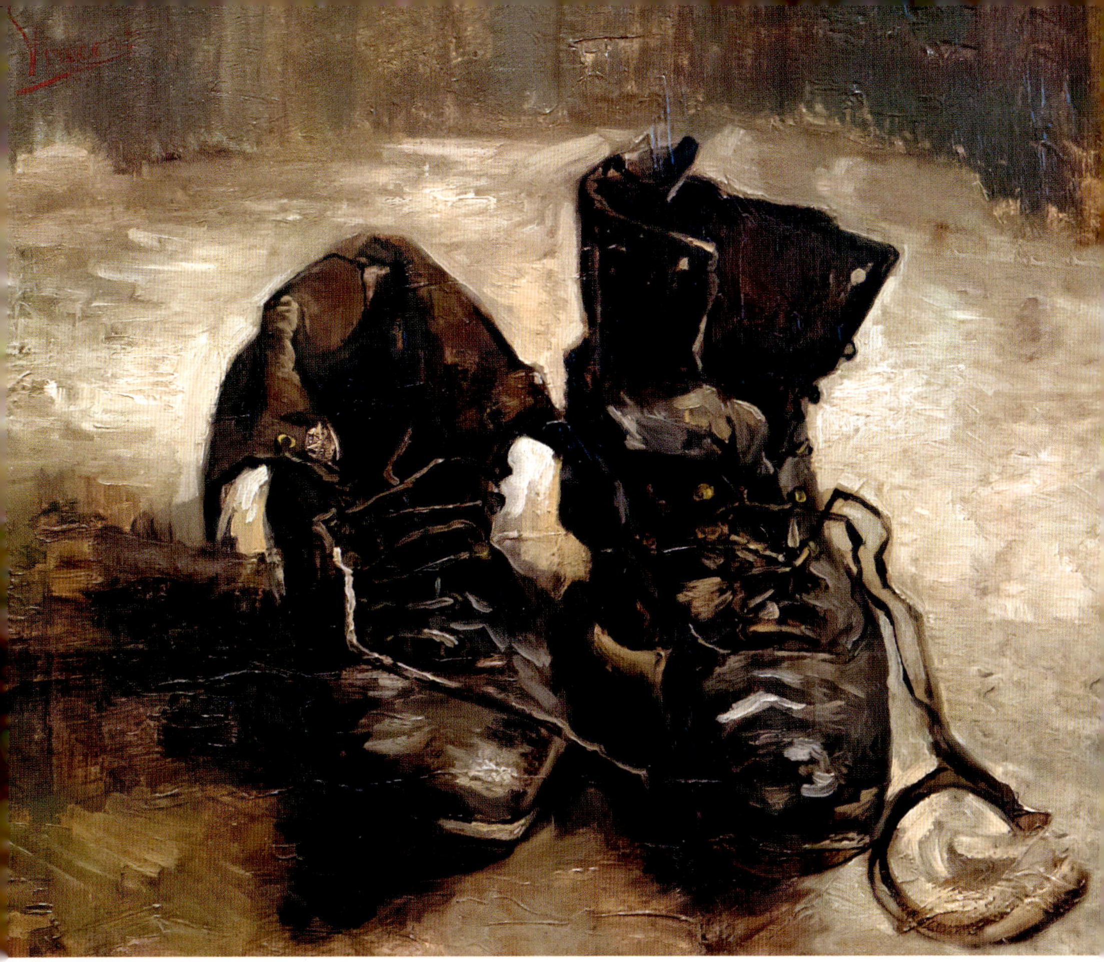

Vincent van Gogh, *Shoes*, 1886

Milletesque glorification of agricultural labor or criticize its unrelenting toil. (Van Gogh would later copy Jean-François Millet's drawing of a peasant child taking her first steps across a vegetable patch in wooden clogs.) They might offer a leathery record of the owner's passage through life. More narrowly, they might refer to Van Gogh's abortive career as an itinerant preacher, or be a prediction of his future travels in Provence, where he roamed the countryside looking for subject matter, as in *The Artist on the Road to Tarascon* (1888). Van Gogh seems to have deliberately provoked the viewer to think of the shoes as open to interpretation: unlaced, their interiors yawning receptively, they invite all comers to try them on for size.

Disembodied Motion

Étienne-Jules Marey dedicated his life to studying motion. He made important contributions in the fields of medicine, physiology, aviation, and biomechanics, inventing devices to measure heartbeats, blood flow, and muscular movement. In the process he pioneered photographic methods that had a direct impact on the birth of cinema and a lasting effect on modern art.

In 1882, aware of Eadweard Muybridge's efforts to capture the motion of a horse on film, Marey developed his own photographic techniques at his "Physiological Station" research center near Paris. His "photographic gun" could take twelve pictures in a second, at a shutter speed of 1/700th of a second, thanks to a rotating cylinder that moved light-sensitive plates before a shutter whose tubular lens mount made it resemble a rifle. Unlike Muybridge, who took a series of photos using different cameras, Marey preferred to capture all stages of a movement on a single photographic plate. The photographic gun could not keep a fixed viewpoint with a sideways-moving object, so Marey invented "chronophotography." In its perfected form, a single high-speed camera with a rotating shutter moved along a rail, keeping up with its subject and recording its motion in tiny increments, as filmmakers would later do in tracking shots. In 1888 Marey used the first moving paper film, at twenty exposures per second.

When it came to the challenge of documenting the human walk, Marey did not so much want to see a man walking as to see the motion of walking itself. For maximum contrast, he positioned his subject outdoors in bright light, in front of a black background. Then, clothing the walker in black from head to toe, he added reflective tape on feet, legs, arms, shoulders, and head. The highlighting of certain body parts resulted in an unprecedented visual effect. Not only could one graph the trajectory of each arm and leg, or how the head rises and falls, but one could see the whole motion flowing with an unmistakable rhythm, a pattern without a figure to make it. Until that moment, photography had shown the world bodies without motion; now Marey had pictured motion without a body. Part dancing skeleton, part abstract painting, the rippling lines of moving limbs shimmer across his photos like wind ruffling water. The Futurists and other artists took note, lending Marey's scientific images a lasting aesthetic power.

Marey, who would later advise the French army on how to erase personal gaits in order to produce efficient marchers, had found a way to extract the individual walker from his portrait of the walk. In quest of the universal, he suppressed what many people believed was the essence of the walk: its uniqueness to each person. If Romantic walkers implicitly contrasted their enlightening walks to those of the

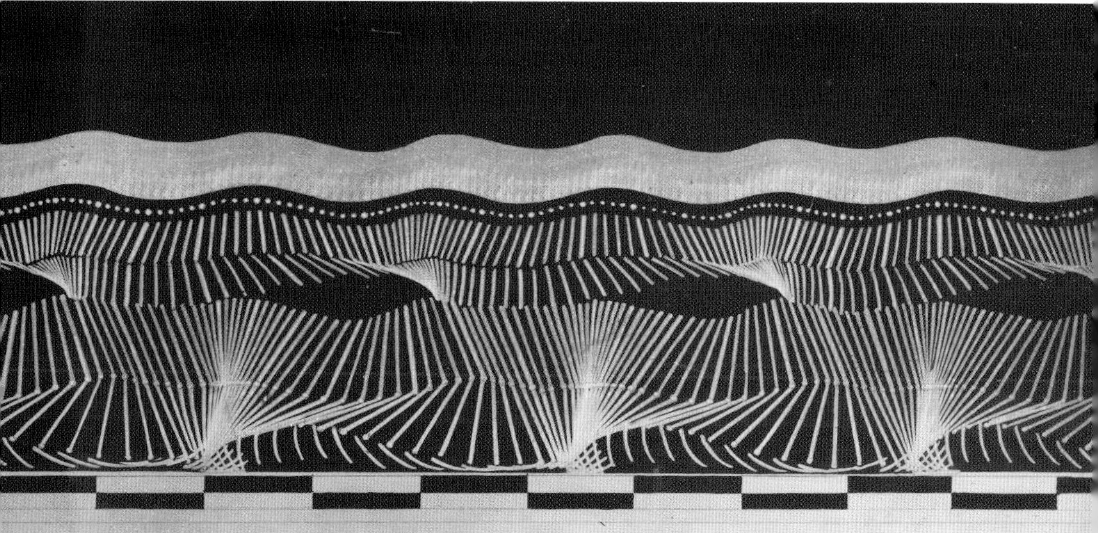

plodding everyman, Marey had created a third kind of walker—generic, decontextualized, stripped of all religious and social significance.

And yet . . . Marey's isolation of key joints and movements via points of light laid the groundwork for motion capture systems that today enable surveillance cameras to identify individuals through gait analysis. There is a short line to be drawn between Marey's nearly invisible walker, marked with points of light yet black-hooded like a political prisoner, and the security apparatus that can identify a masked bank robber or a potential threat to a totalitarian regime. Marey himself sensed the paradox that he had created a legible abstraction. Chronophotography produced, he said, "a luminous trace . . . at once multiple and unique."

The Walk Stripped Bare

English-born Eadweard Muybridge was a respected nature photographer, known for his scenes of Yosemite Valley, when the ex-governor of California contacted him. For years Leland Stanford, a prominent horse breeder, had been convinced that artists were wrong in their depictions of galloping horses. He believed that there was a moment—and not the splay-legged one favored by artists—when a horse had all its legs off the ground, and he thought that an instantaneous photograph could prove it. Taking up the challenge, Muybridge began a new career as a photographer of animal locomotion. His work over the next three decades would have far-reaching consequences for the evolution of motion pictures, animation, biomechanics, and high-speed stop-motion photography. With their subtle increments of action, his sequences would inspire painters, writers, composers, and choreographers.

Muybridge's eureka moment came when he realized that he needed not just faster film and shutter speeds, but more than one camera. By 1878 he had hit on a solution: a bank of twenty-four cameras, spaced evenly at twenty-seven-inch intervals, would fire in succession every twenty-fifth of a second as the horse galloped past, hitting the shutter trip-wires as it went. With a shutter speed of 1/1200th of a second, Muybridge produced a series of crisp shots that proved what a gallop really involved. All four hooves came off the ground, curved under the horse, in mid-stride. Setting painted silhouettes of the photos on a spinning disk and projecting them through what he called a "zoopraxiscope," Muybridge presented his sequences to a California audience in 1880, the first-ever movie show.

In 1881 Muybridge met Étienne-Jules Marey in Paris and observed his stop-motion approach that captured successive movements on a single photographic plate. Each man felt that the other's approach left something to be desired. Marey was a scientist seeking universal principles; Muybridge was an artist not averse to slipping out-of-sequence shots into his galleries. Sponsored in the 1880s by the University of Pennsylvania, where he worked for a while with the realist painter Thomas Eakins, Muybridge used his multiple-camera technique to document a wide variety of everyday motions. He took over a hundred thousand photographs of models, often nude and seen against a gridded background, doing everything from sweeping with a broom and carrying water to playing leapfrog and baseball. The result was a mammoth portfolio of twenty thousand individual images, *Animal Locomotion: An Electro-Photographic Investigation of Connective Phases of Animal Movements* (1887), a work still studied today. The famous opening sequence simply shows a naked man, a walking Adam, moving toward, away from, and sideways to the viewer.

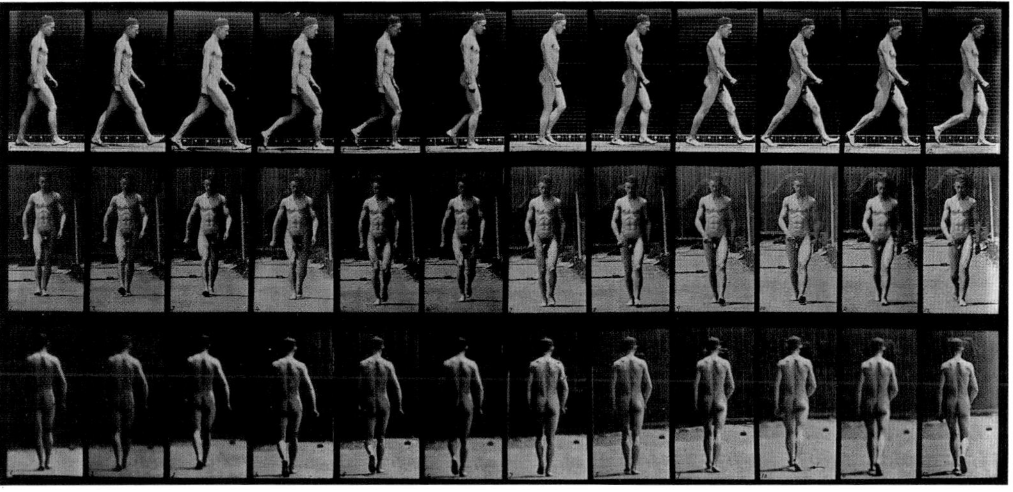

Eadweard Muybridge, nude man walking, *Animal Locomotion*, 1887

On the page, this thirty-six-shot group of photos is only implicitly lively. What is dynamic about Muybridge's work is how the mind and eye, through projection or rapid scanning, can release its potential. If Marey abstracted motion from a body, Muybridge celebrated the body by showing the motion implicit in each frame. He created movie stills before there were movies, truncated stories of actions that are beautiful in their own right.

Pioneering though they were, Muybridge's photos look intently toward a mythic past. Taken outdoors in bright sunlight, they exude a sort of Edenic innocence. His nudes cavort with a bucket or ball as if there were no cares in the world, no sins to force them into clothing or exile them from this stage-set paradise. Exposure after exposure, his relaxed Adams and Eves have nothing to hide from the godlike inquisition of the camera eye.

The Gates Open

For sheer symbolism, it would be hard to conceive a better beginning. Massive doors open and dozens of people flood outward, walking briskly, released from their working day and ready for entertainment. This is the non-plot of the first full-fledged motion picture, *Workers Leaving the Lumière Factory* (1895), a forty-six-second sequence in which the audience can see itself. A mass of individuals is transformed into fascinating flickers of light and shadow on a screen, vibrantly present, tantalizingly remote. The surge of energy at the factory gate embodies the excitement that will soon energize workers everywhere at day's end. As they stream

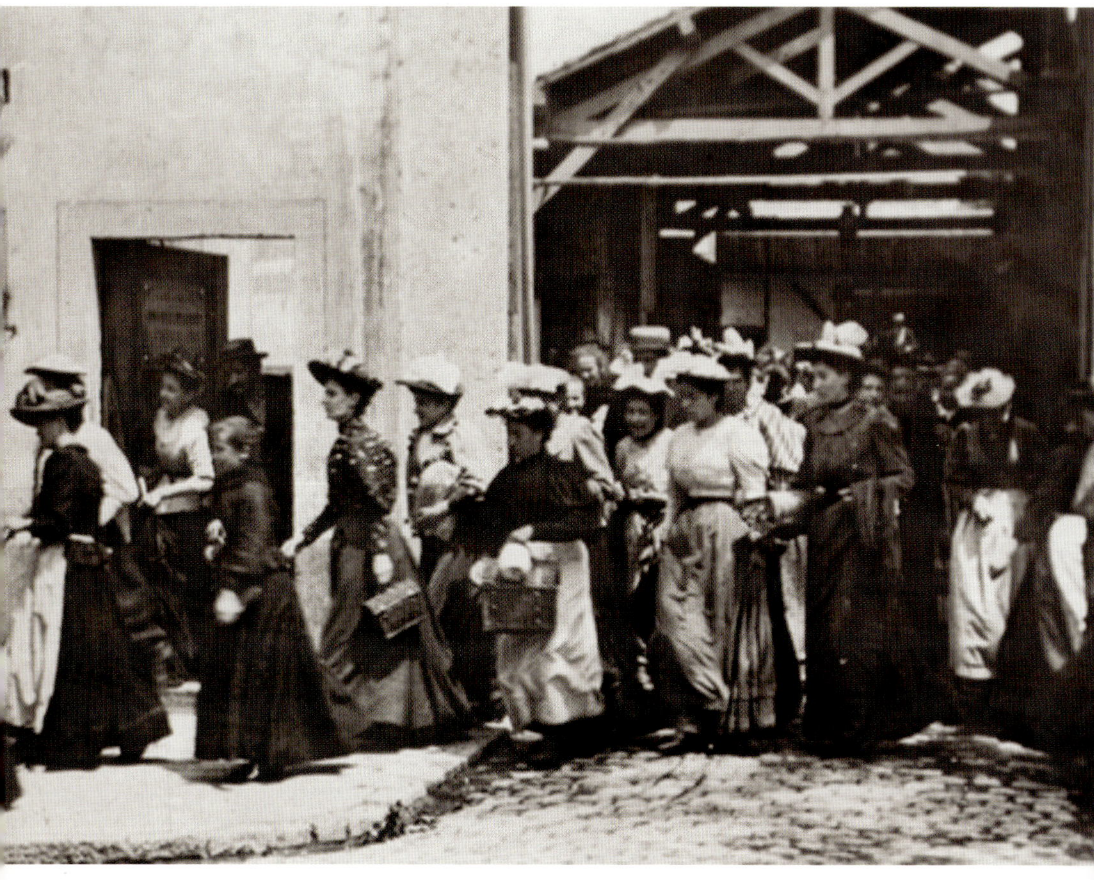

Lumière brothers, *Workers Leaving the Lumière Factory*, 1895

past the camera, Lumière's employees forecast a world in which filmed motion, real or scripted, will outdo every after-work diversion ever created. The mesmerizing shadows of Plato's cave materialize in modernity, promising intangible rewards that will make the chains of life weigh less heavily for an hour or two.

The Lumière brothers, Auguste and Louis, were Lyon-based manufacturers of photographic equipment. They experimented with movies for little more than a decade, from 1895 to 1905. But during that time they produced films all over the world, generating a demand that has never ceased. They began by improving the Cinématographe camera invented by Léon Bouly, adding perforations to the film to advance it in a reliable way. In December 1895 they showed the factory-exiting movie in Paris, on a bill with nine other Lumière films, an event now considered the first commercial motion-picture show. Each filmstrip was fifty-five feet long, about forty-five hand-cranked seconds of playing time. The second film on the bill, *The Sprinkler Sprinkled*, was the first ever comedy film (a gardener gets drenched by his own hose), and the first to feature a fictional plot. Two other films made in central Lyon captured people walking, the first cinematic street scenes.

What the Lumière brothers showed the world, at sixteen frames per second, was a realistic representation of moving people that required no ocular gymnastics. Their film offered *sustained* motion, not limited to a three-second burst as in a flip book (first available in the 1860s) or a spinning mechanism (dating to the 1830s). In long shots, viewers of the Lumière films could follow individual walkers along a street, watch them cross it, and then shift their attention to a trolley as it approached the camera, discharged passengers, and moved off screen.

Much has been made of the (apparently apocryphal) panic of the first audience for *The Arrival of a Train at La Ciotat* (1896). But the coming-at-you effect of *Workers Leaving the Lumière Factory* is in a way even more magical. The tide of workers surging forward is powerful enough to rejoice a socialist, or cause a *bon bourgeois* to shudder. Most of the workers are women, full skirted and sporting flowered hats. A large dog gets in the way. Male and female alike give their friends playful shoves as they part ways for the evening. Many walk out arm in arm, while a few guide bicycles that they pedal away in a rush. Off they go in different directions, right, left, and straight past the camera, changed from "the masses" into humans in the course of only a few liberated steps. Hitherto, artists had sought the essence of a personality in a static pose. Henceforth, the fluid subtleties of style and sway would define the walk and the person, each one unique. From Charlie Chaplin to Mae West, from John Wayne to Greta Garbo, a compelling walk would be a path to stardom, to be endlessly admired and imitated.

What the Walker Heard

A skull-faced, androgynous figure—wide-eyed, open-mouthed, hands raised in horror to cover its ears—recoils from a sight, a sound, or a thought. It's one of the world's most iconic images, but what Edvard Munch is actually saying in *The Scream* may be lost in the volume of its primal cry. What is clear is that it started with a walk.

In his diary in early 1892, Munch noted: "One evening I was walking along a path, the city was on one side and the fjord below. I felt tired and ill. I stopped and looked out over the fjord—the sun was setting, and the clouds turning blood red. I sensed a scream passing through nature; it seemed to me that I heard the scream. I painted this picture, painted the clouds as actual blood. The color shrieked." Contrary to what many believe, Munch imagined his appalled figure not screaming at all, but *registering* a scream, recoiling from the sound of nature's agony. And indeed, the original German title of the painting for its first exhibit in Berlin was *Der Schrei der Natur* (*The Scream of Nature*).

Because the image is so compelling, endless efforts have been made to track down a real-world stimulus. It's possible that the bloodred sky originated in the eruption of the Indonesian volcano Krakatoa, whose ash caused lurid sunsets in Europe. Yet Munch would have had to remember that sky from 1884, eight years earlier. Alternatively, scientists propose that Munch had in fact seen a red sky very recently, in the form of nacreous clouds, a high-latitude phenomenon that produces iridescent colors very like those in the picture.

But did the scream emanate from nature or from within the artist? A fundamental question the painting poses is whether a walk—and its representation—is about the world encountered, or the interior life of the person walking. The setting of the painting, a street in Ekeberg, outside Oslo, has been identified. Munch used it and the same diagonal composition in other paintings, such as *Despair* (1892) and *Anxiety* (1894). In the neighborhood were a slaughterhouse and an asylum, from which screams might have emanated. Munch was likely in Ekeberg to visit his sister, a manic-depressive patient at the asylum.

Perhaps nature's scream is being channeled through the artist. Munch wrote later to a friend, "You know my picture, 'The Scream?' I was stretched to the limit—nature was screaming in my blood." Reinforcing this interpenetration, the androgynous figure's body curves like the lines of the land and sky. Half the canvas is given over to the straight, human-made lines of the walkway and fence, but the wavy lines of the foreground figure show that it has become part of nature, distorted by the sound waves of the scream. If Jean-Jacques Rousseau discovered that walking in the country could put him in joyful touch with his inner self, Munch's traumatized individual argues that a terrifying outcome was possible too.

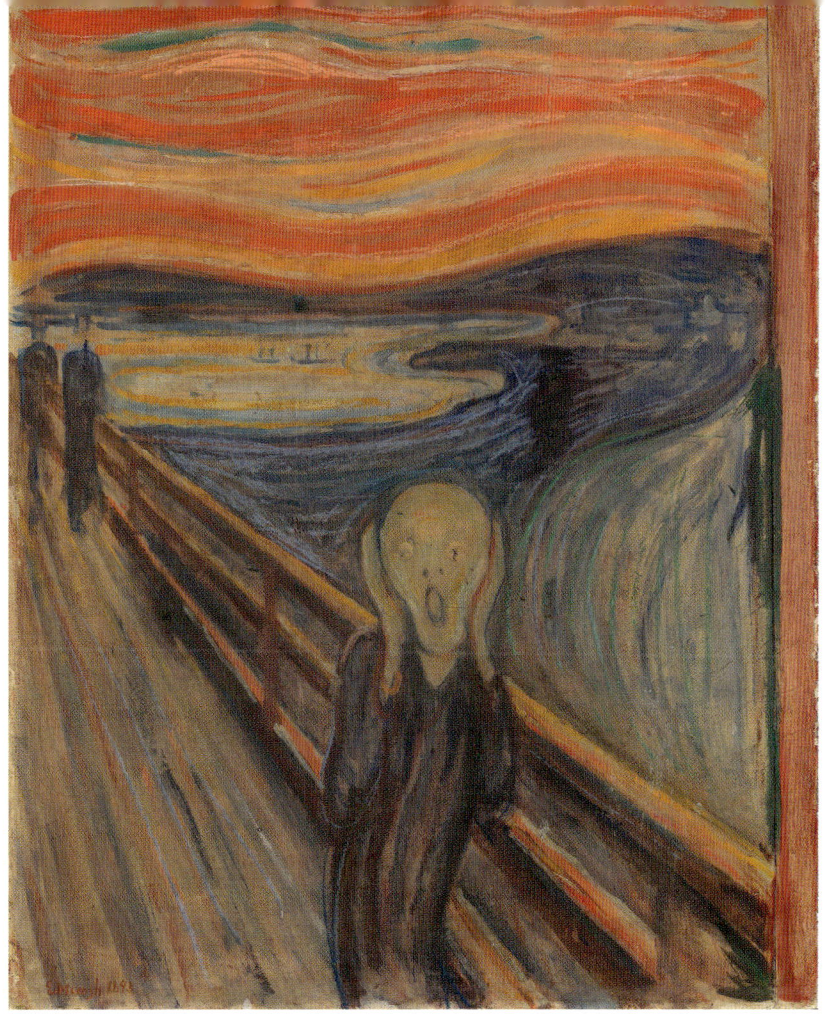

Edvard Munch, *The Scream*, 1893

Munch provided more detail about the walk itself in the bloodred letters he painted onto the frame of the 1895 pastel version of *The Scream*. "I was walking along the road with two friends—the sun was setting—suddenly the sky turned blood red . . . my friends walked on, and I stood there trembling with anxiety—and I sensed an infinite scream passing through nature." The shock that warps the walker's body leaves his companions untouched, like the ships in the distance, with their masts upright on a swirling sea. The walker is part of the scream; they are not. Untouched by the crisis engulfing their friend, they wend their way along the designated path, leaving him behind to deal with his demons alone. Even as it unforgettably amplifies the scream, the painting articulates a corollary truth: the ultimate solitude of the walker, the ultimate inability of any language, spoken or artistic, to say what the walker has experienced.

Walking in Love

Before the internet, before television and film and photography began to drown the world in images, readers lingered over book illustrations, searching them for clues about characters who might become role models or the material of daydreams. And few characters have attracted more attention than those of Jane Austen, whose heroines are always ready to walk themselves into romance or away from ill-mannered suitors. The genteel woman walker—fit, feminine, and self-possessed, agile in word and deed—bursts from the pages of Austen's novels as a disruptive new force in British matchmaking. Surprisingly, for the first eighty years after Austen's death in 1817 her unsurpassed melding of love, looks, and landscape could only be imagined, not seen. An irony of copyright shoehorned Austen's vigorous heroines into stiff Victorian gowns and waistcoats from which they were released only in the 1890s.

What happened was that in 1832, the publisher Richard Bentley obtained the copyright for all the novels. He brought out standard editions until 1886, editions that were the making of Austen's reputation. But the illustrations by Ferdinand Pickering depicted sensitive-looking, wasp-waisted heroines wasting away indoors, wearing billowing skirts and ballroom slippers that would not have lasted five minutes in a muddy English pasture. The reading public did not see Lizzy Bennett or Emma Woodhouse in full stride in their Regency outfits until Hugh Thomson's witty drawings for *Pride and Prejudice* came out in 1894, followed in 1898 by the first color illustrations, made by Charles and Matthew Brock.

The Brocks' lively illustrations of outings and promenades decisively altered the visual perception of Austen. They made clear a central theme of the novels: nothing reveals character like a walk in the open air. For centuries, couples have courted by "walking out together," and Austen exploits the ups and downs of the process by zeroing in on the misunderstandings that can emerge along the way. Recognizing how even a short walk can propel a plot and test a relationship, Austen gives her young ladies and gentlemen a perilous freedom of movement and speech, sending them out into gardens, groves, and country parks a few paces ahead of the larger social group. Out of earshot of chaperones, couples discover that opportunities for revelation, romance, and moral mishap abound. Will he tell her how badly she has behaved? Will she confess her true feelings? Will they enter the wood without waiting for the elder members of their party?

Here Charles Brock captures the moment when the sensible Mr. Knightley proposes to the impetuous heroine of *Emma*. Chastened by her misadventures in matchmaking, Emma listens intently to the earnest words of a man who looks ten years younger than Austen describes him. The characters have fled outdoors to clear their minds and settle their emotions when the walk turns into a

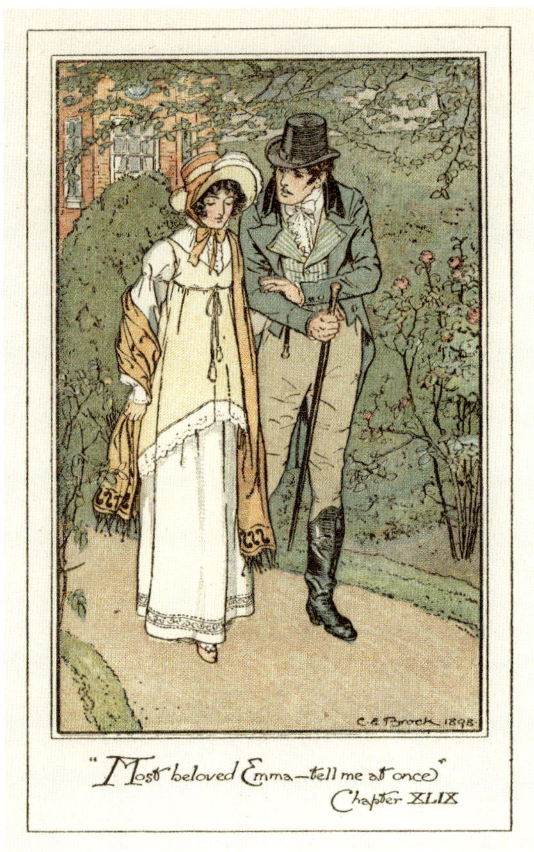

Charles Edmund Brock, "Most Beloved Emma—tell me at once!," 1898

spontaneous proposal that sweeps away all their misconceptions about each other. Mr. Knightley bends urgently toward Emma, his clutched cane signaling his virile desire, while Emma, eyes cast down, symbolically lets her wrap fall from her shoulder, understanding what his offer means.

Working in a clear, linear style, Brock exchanges the monochrome fussiness of Pickering for a simple, gender-and-color-coded treatment of the story. The red ribbons on Emma's hat link her to the romantic roses in the background, as well as the red brick of her father's house, where she will soon live as a married woman. Meanwhile the gray-green of Mr. Knightley's coat enables him to relate comfortably to the flourishing garden and grounds that he will manage along with his own estate. His black riding boot and her pink shoe (matching the blush on her cheek) dominate the foreground. Together they make a pair of feet that will carry the couple—cooperatively, at last—down this garden path to the altar.

The March of History

"The march of modern history," Karl Marx called it in 1848. As depicted in Giuseppe Pellizza's monumental painting, eighteen feet wide and ten feet tall, proletarian workers awaken to their own power. Striding forward to remake the world, Pellizza's resolute laborers so frightened conservatives that the canvas spent most of its first century hidden away in storage. Now regarded as one of the masterpieces of modern Italian art, *The Fourth Estate* turns its drably clad figures into heroic activists whose determined tread literalizes Marx's metaphor. The painting crystallizes the democratizing trend of the nineteenth century, building on the work of Honoré Daumier, Jean-François Millet, Vincent van Gogh, and others to deliver an epic of the people, a collectivity that has discovered a new way to walk: together. These men and women do not demonstrate for a particular cause; they march to show that their unstoppable progress is underway.

The workers pass under an arch that suggests their imminent triumph. Coming from the natural world glimpsed in the background, they cross a dusty factory courtyard, fight-to-the-death gladiators entering the modern industrial arena. With their spokespersons in front, they are mobilized but not a mob. The man on the left sticks his hand, Napoleon-style, in his shirt, a convention in portraiture that indicates calm, decisive leadership. Karl Marx was photographed in the same pose. The indomitable central figure, jacket slung over his shoulder, thumb hooked in his belt, wears his own Arch of Triumph, a distinct curve of sunlight between his shaded upper face and his dark beard. Beside him a barefoot woman, one of only four in the picture, carries a naked baby. The folds of her long dress give her an allegorical look, as she gestures on behalf of Family and Generations to come. Just behind her, two men deep in discussion echo the poses of Plato and Aristotle in Raphael's *The School of Athens*. Aristotle puts his hand out, palm downward, as if to calm his companion. But Plato holds his palms upward, as if to say, "What else can we do?"

At first glance, it's ironic that the technique Pellizza chose to convey the unbreakable solidarity of his workers should be called Divisionism. Successors to Neo-Impressionist painters such as Georges Seurat and Paul Signac, the Divisionists sought greater luminosity by applying small dabs of pure color to the canvas to achieve an intense, almost shimmering effect. But the deeper idea is that the disparate dots of contrasting colors work together in eye and mind, mixing optically, to create solid-looking, unified images. The optical synthesis of many into one—*e pluribus unum*—aims at a transformative vision of the world. As the latest form of pictorial expression, based on scientific color theory, Divisionism attracted

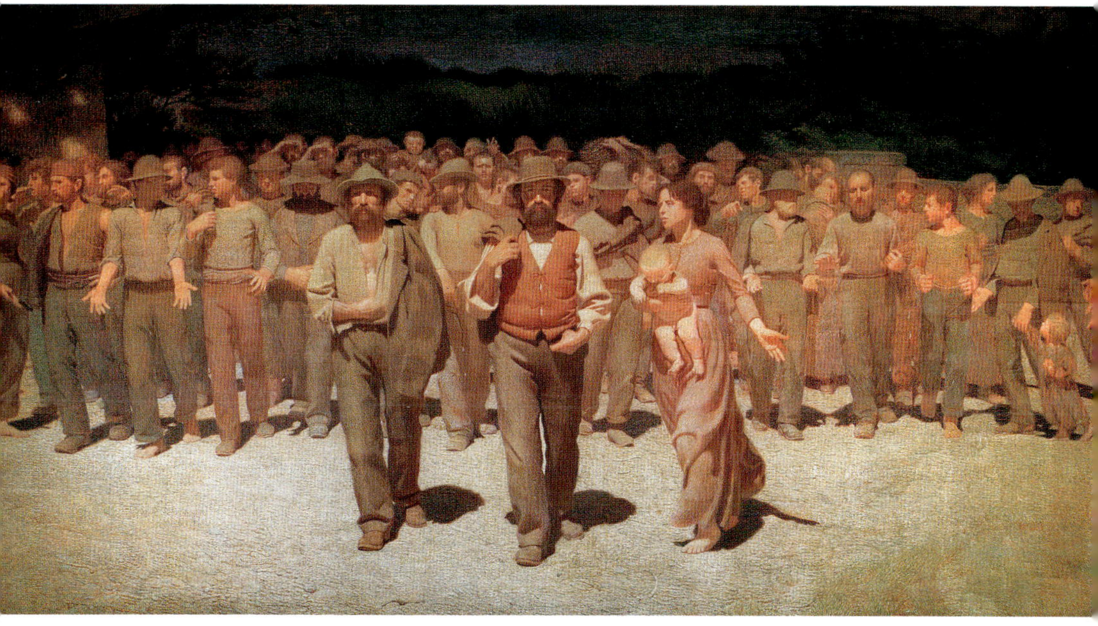

members of the Italian avant-garde in a political as well as aesthetic sense. Anarchists, Communists, socialists, and eventually Futurists would be drawn to the technique.

Pellizza worked on his composition for ten years, erasing strike banners and making his group more symbolic of their class as a whole. The artist's carefully orchestrated point is that this is not a strike over one issue. Rather, it's a picture of the powerful forces that make strikes and battles for a fairer world not only unavoidable but bound to succeed. The title alludes to the major players in the French Revolution: the first estate is the clergy; the second, the aristocracy; the third, the bourgeoisie and common people combined. Following Marx, Pellizza recognizes that an inevitable class struggle separates his laborers from the middle class, requiring them to realize a destiny of their own. As the artist wrote in 1898, "true strength is found in good, intelligent workers who, holding onto their ideals, force other men to follow them or clear the path, because there is no retrograde power that can stop them."

Women Walk for Themselves

Women's suffrage marches began in Britain with a four-hundred-woman parade in 1906, after which its organizer Emmeline Pankhurst declared that women were "awake at last." Finally, she said, "they were prepared to do something that women had never done before—fight for themselves." The term *suffragette,* mockingly bestowed by newspapers, was soon adopted proudly by the militants. On March 20, 1907, a determined group of women tried to force its way into the House of Commons to condemn the failure of the King and Parliament to address their cause.

Dora Thewlis, a sixteen-year-old mill worker from Yorkshire, was the youngest of the seventy-five women arrested that day. She was also the one most prominently condemned by the media, thanks to this front-page photo in the next morning's *Daily Mirror.* Journalists identified her as "one of the attacking party struggling in the grasp of two burly constables." Once her age and background became known, criticism poured in. The press called her "the baby suffragette." The public accused the suffrage movement of exploiting her youth and innocence. The arraigning magistrate told her, "You are only a child. You ought to be in school. Will you go home again?"

Unabashed, Thewlis replied, "I don't wish to go back, sir. . . . It will be an honour to go to prison." Having raised Dora to engage in political debate from an early age, her parents wrote to the court, "We find ourselves in agreement with his Honour when he says that girls of sixteen ought to be at school. But we respectfully remind his Honour that girls of Dora's age in her station of life are . . . compelled in their thousands to spend ten hours per day in health-destroying factories . . . sanctioned by law, in the making of which women have no voice. What wonder is it if Dora should have turned a rebel?" Thewlis was released after a week in prison. She emigrated to Australia a few years later, where women already had the right to vote. Had she stayed in Britain, she would have had to wait until 1928, when she would have been twenty-seven, to cast her ballot.

Equally determined, American women turned the protest march into a long-distance hike. In 1912 a core group of five women walked 170 miles in twelve days, from New York City to the state capital in Albany. They braved winter weather to present to the new governor a document asking that he support a woman's right to vote. Extensive newspaper attention along the way, as the women paused in every town to recruit allies, gave their cause more coverage than they had ever dreamed of. As the *Woman's Journal* commented, "Now the hike along the Hudson seemed a foolish trip and vain / But it gave them advertising from Los Angeles to Maine." The next year thirteen suffragists strode 250 miles in sixteen days to Washington, DC, again in winter, to join five thousand other women in a parade that sought to win over newly inaugurated President Woodrow Wilson. They succeeded, eventually acquiring the right to vote in 1920. The women gained national attention not for their own physical accomplishment but for the fitness of women everywhere—to vote.

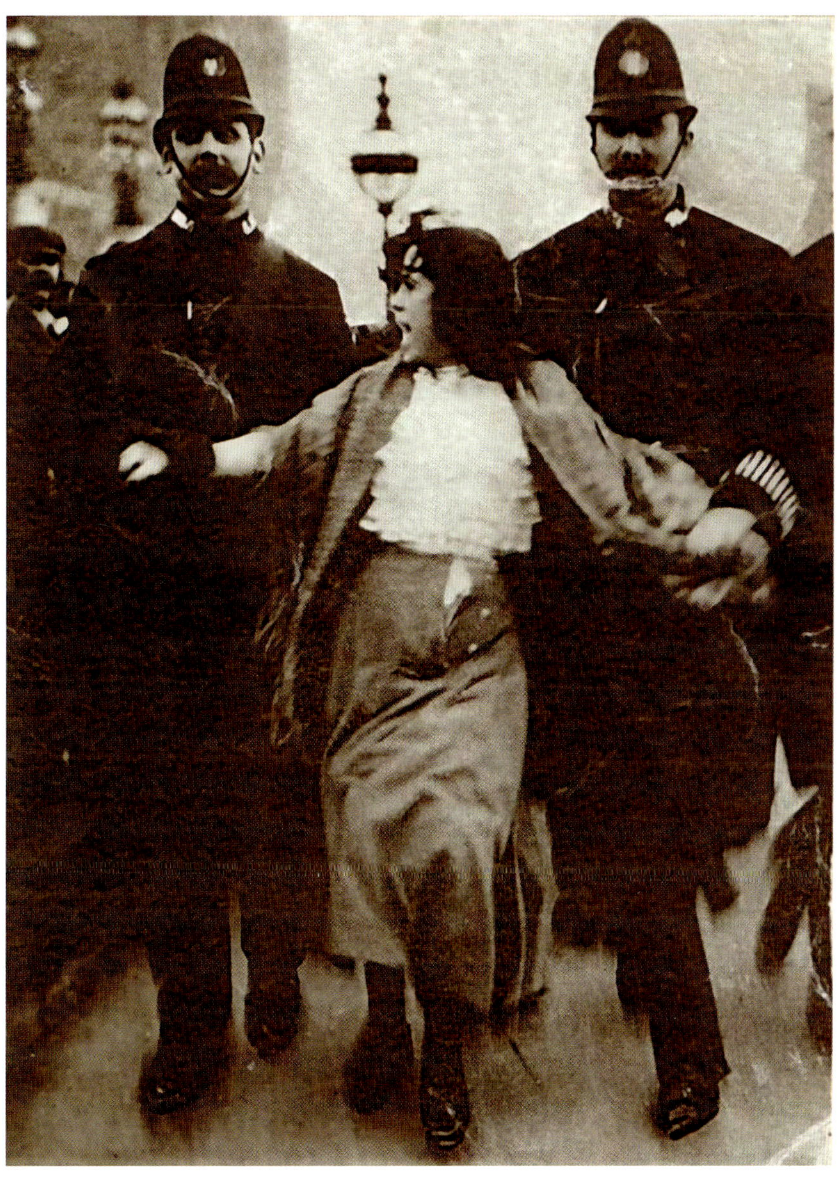

Dora Thewlis being taken into custody, *Daily Mirror*, March 21, 1907

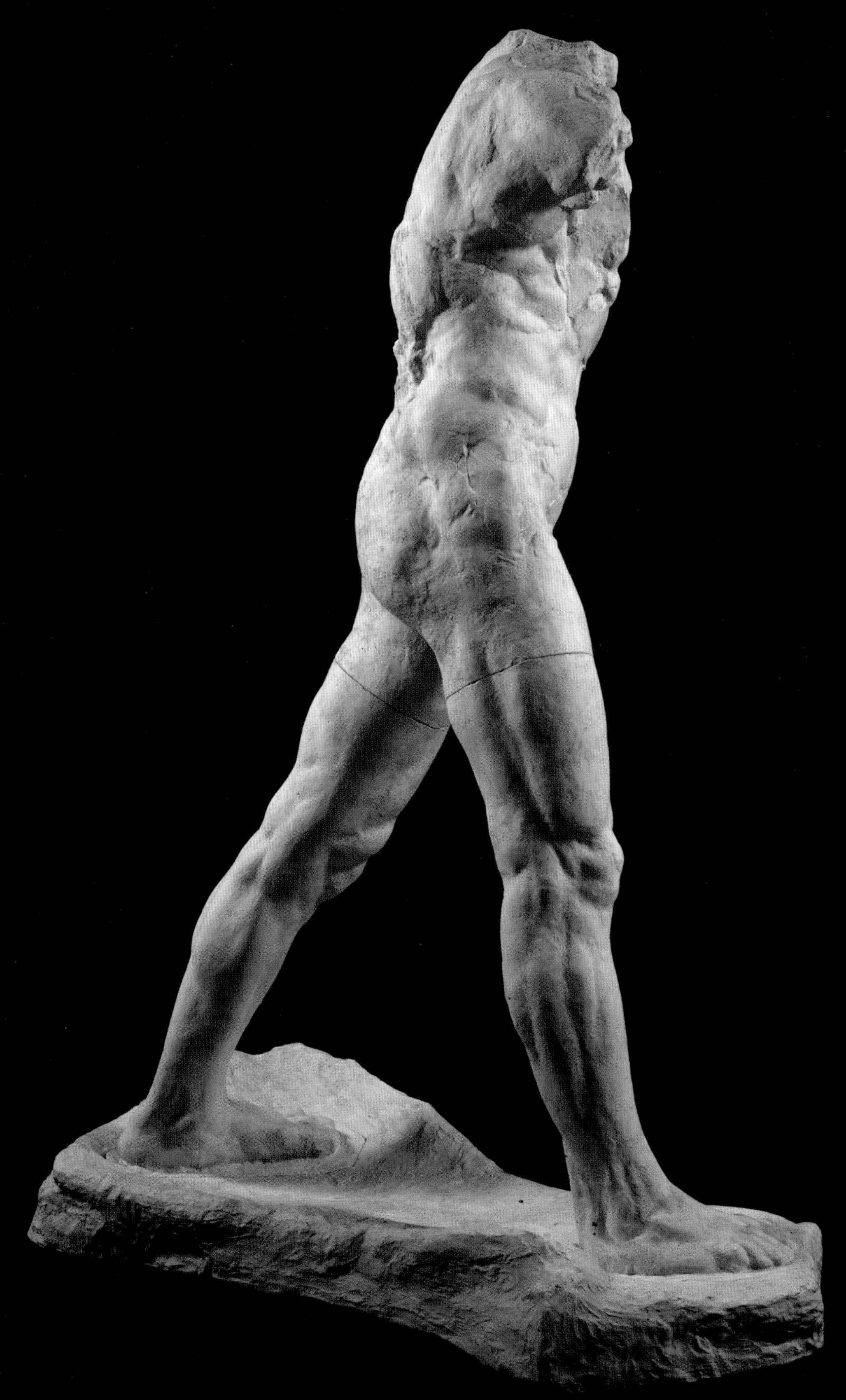

Sculpted Motion

At the turn of the twentieth century, Auguste Rodin transformed sculpture from a classical into a modern art. His greatest works not only represented walking but demanded that viewers walk too, refusing to yield their meaning from a single point of view. *The Walking Man* revitalizes Western sculpture's relation to its classical roots, working with fragmentary and "unfinished" shapes that disdain storytelling. About 1900, Rodin joined the legs and torso of two earlier statues to form a headless, armless, forward-striding composite figure whose mismatched parts, imperfectly merged, lent it a tense dynamic energy. Building on the robust legs and powerful stance of his itinerant *John the Baptist* (first exhibited 1880), Rodin added a roughly modeled torso, begun in the 1880s from classical sources. Before having the assembled figure cast in bronze, Rodin made a larger plaster version, seen here. Its distressed, pockmarked surface made it appear as if it had been recovered from an excavation in Athens or Pompeii.

The absence of head and limbs created a less-is-more archaeological authenticity and amplified another theme in Rodin's work, the value of the fragment. For Rodin, an exquisite broken piece of an antique statue, even nothing but the palm of a hand, could be a complete work in itself: "to contemplate it, to see it live, I don't need the fingers . . . it suffices all by itself because it is true." Rodin presents the walking man to the viewer like a damaged god dug from the earth, no less beautiful or forceful for the limbs he lacks. His absent arms allow viewers to witness both the twist of the torso and the play of light and shadow across its gouged surface.

Changing the title of his work from *A Study for Saint John the Baptist* to *The Walking Man*, Rodin opened his figure to further symbolic resonance. If John the Baptist was a voice crying in the wilderness, the messenger of a new religion who was ultimately beheaded for his faith, then this prophetically headless trunk would become the herald of a revolutionary sculpture, moving away from mythic subjects and polished forms. Stripped of all anecdote, the statue speaks directly of walking humanity itself. Addressing the paradox of a static art that depicts walking, Rodin creates a moving figure with both feet planted firmly on the ground, representing both the start and the end of a stride. It provides not a snapshot but a series of moments and actions. As Saint John becomes an everyman, his holy walk in the wilderness becomes a secular pilgrimage to the very idea of motion. Like the French martyr Saint Denis, who miraculously walked across Paris carrying his severed head, Rodin's figure seems guided by a higher power.

Auguste Rodin, *Walking Man*, plaster model, 1907

A Walk Goes to Pieces

After three million years of human evolution and some forty or fifty centuries of recorded history, one might expect that by the year 1900 there would be few additional ways to depict the walker. Yet the twentieth century would prove exceptionally innovative. The mobilization of the masses—for war, production, consumption, and entertainment—heralded a new era in the representation of walking. Two of the central pictorial developments, the arrival of the motion picture and the creative fracturing of the human body, had particular impact.

No work made the statement more strongly than Marcel Duchamp's *Nude Descending a Staircase (No. 2)*. Reviled when it was first shown in the United States as "an explosion in a shingle factory," the painting caused a ruckus because it sought an abstract image of motion rather than the portrayal of a particular moving body. Never having seen modern art before—Fauvism, Cubism, Post-Impressionism—let alone a semiabstraction derived from Cubist and Futurist principles, the crowds at the landmark 1913 Armory Show in New York were at a loss in front of Duchamp's cascade of clashing monochrome planes.

In the wake of photographic experiments by Étienne-Jules Marey and Eadweard Muybridge, Duchamp wanted to explore how motion could be conveyed in a painted image. "The fact that I had seen chronophotographs of fencers in action and horses galloping . . . gave me the idea for the *Nude*. . . . And of course the motion picture with its cinematic techniques was developing then too. The whole idea of movement, of speed, was in the air." Echoing a twelve-frame sequence from Muybridge's *Animal Locomotion* (1887), a nude woman "Descending stairs and turning around," Duchamp sends his twisting, overlapping concatenation of limbs and torsos down a stairway that starts at the upper right of the canvas. The stairs curve around the rippling body parts to finish beneath the figure's foremost limb at the lower right. It's a past-to-present trajectory, yet Duchamp rejected a strict relation between his picture and an actual descent. "Movement is an abstraction," he said. Therefore one cannot know "if a real person is or isn't descending an equally real staircase."

The title that Duchamp stenciled at the bottom left of the picture was as provocative as the image itself. Over the course of two thousand years, the dynamic male nude of classical Greek statuary had been largely replaced by the languid female nude of Titian, Francisco Goya, Édouard Manet, and Henri Matisse. Such was the weight of this tradition that the Parisian Cubists rejected Duchamp's painting on the grounds, he recalled, that "one just doesn't do a nude woman coming down the stairs, that's ridiculous. . . . A nude should be respected." Viewers felt an erotic frustration over the unbecoming activity of this unsexy bundle of pelvic plates and fanlike limbs. Newspapers mocked both the title and the technique mercilessly:

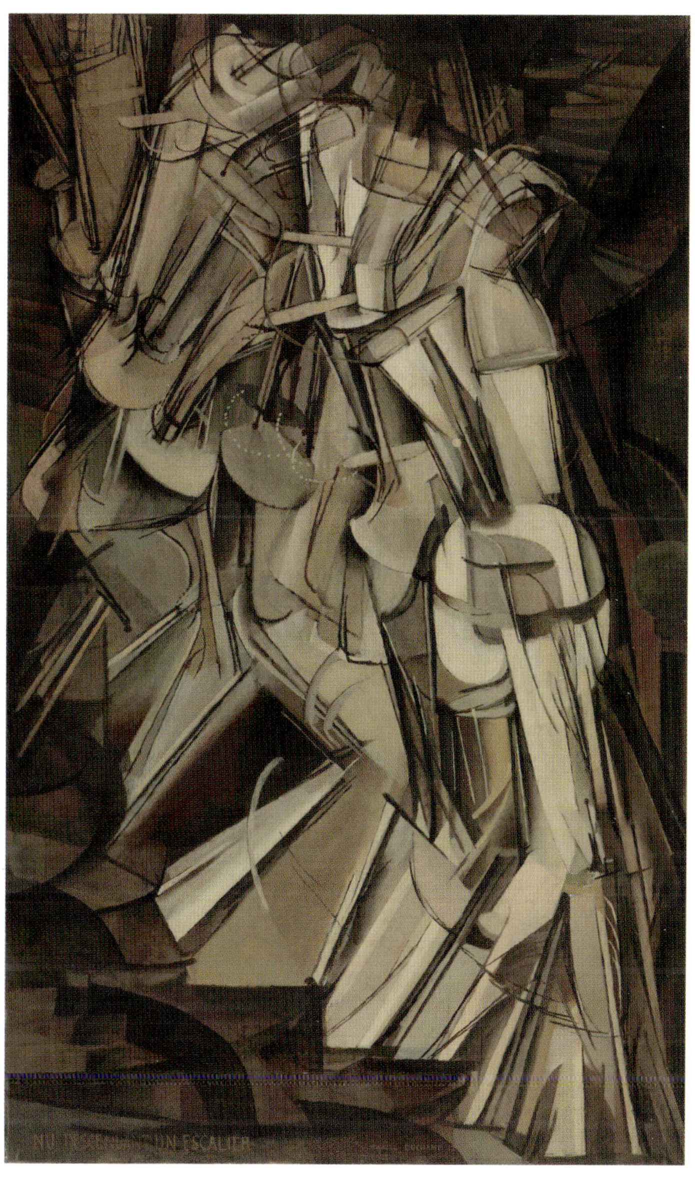

Marcel Duchamp, *Nude Descending a Staircase (No. 2)*, 1912

"The Rude Descending a Staircase (Rush-Hour at the Subway)," ran the caption of one satirical sketch, an angular, angry jumble of pedestrians fighting their way down the picture plane. It was typical of Duchamp that he left any sense of fulfillment up to his audience. "Fundamentally, movement is in the eye of the spectator."

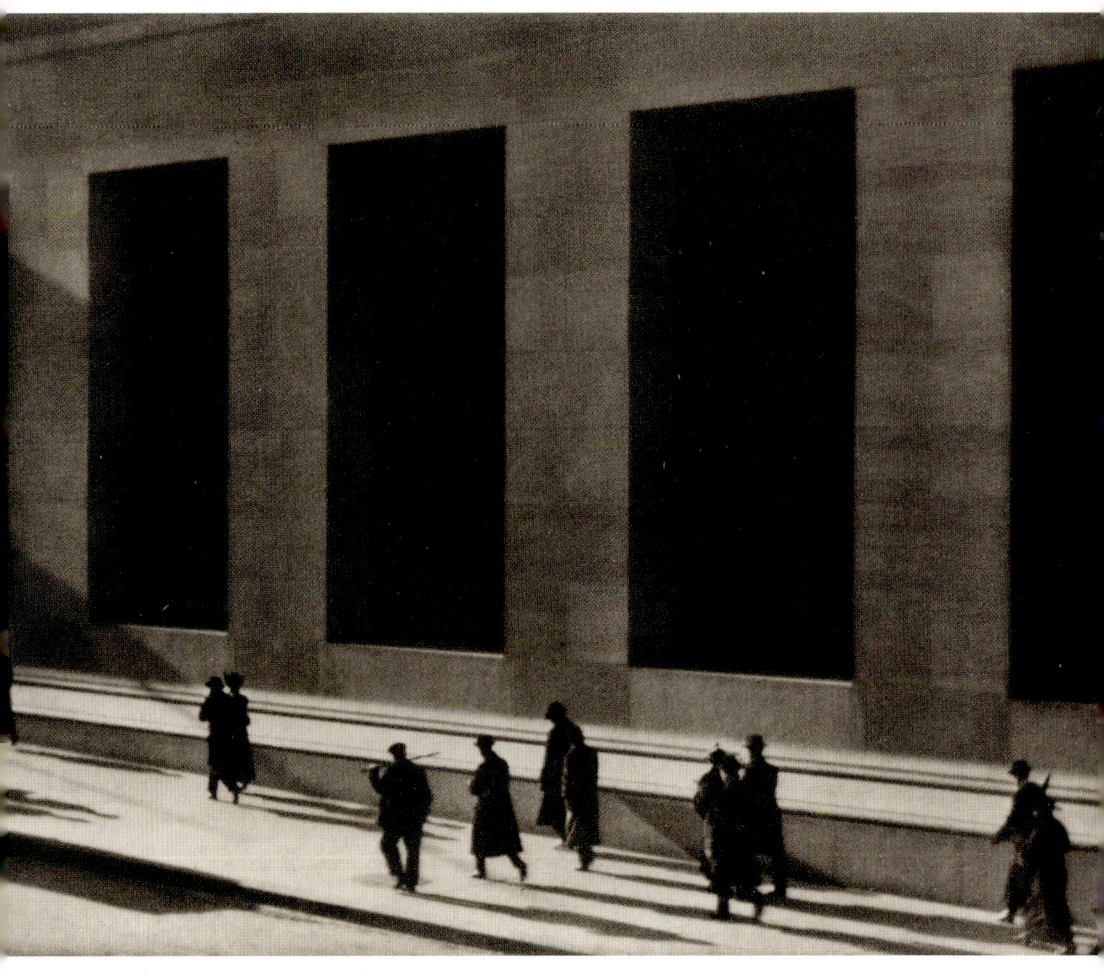

Paul Strand, *Wall Street*, 1915

In the Canyon

Dwarfed by the massive stone facade of 23 Wall Street, a dozen or so individuals make their way through the skyscraper-walled canyon of capitalism. They're heading to work in the early-morning light, long shadows dragging behind them. Having spent the last century acquiring heroic attributes—ranging from the Romantic to the revolutionary—ordinary walkers now confront the implacable forces of free enterprise. Paul Strand's *Wall Street* introduces the grimly resigned, physically diminished walker, the cog-in-the-machine pedestrian, who trudges uphill past the blank, black windows of "the House of Morgan." The plodding people are anonymous, but the fortresslike headquarters of J. P. Morgan and Co., built in 1913, were so distinctive that the bank did not even bother to put out a sign. Associated with Wall Street's power over American life, the building itself seems to have been the primary target of anarchists who exploded a wagon full of dynamite in front of it on September 16, 1920. Collateral damage: thirty-eight passersby dead, several hundred injured.

The cool abstract forms of Strand's *Wall Street* contain but don't defuse that charged social content. The photo has become an icon of American modernity because it marks the moment when art photography decisively turned from the soft-focus Pictorialist mode toward the clean lines of "straight" photography. Having studied with Lewis Hine, known for documenting immigrants at Ellis Island, Paul Strand had a strong social conscience. He expressed it through his own restrained and distinctive style, a meticulous balance of light and dark elements built from simple shapes. In this picture he opposes the human and the inanimate. Three-quarters of the picture is taken up by the dark recessed windows and limestone walls of the bank, whose verticals press down heavily on the narrow band of sunlit street. But in contrast to the ponderous rectangles of stone and shade, the slender uprights of the workers, like the tendril shadows they trail behind them, project an organic life that, although menaced, is not fully subdued.

Visually oppressed by the bank's bulk, Strand's featureless personnel herald the exhausted machine workers of Fritz Lang's 1927 film *Metropolis*, who are pushed literally underground to support the skyscraper dwellers of a dystopian city based on Manhattan. Strand uses the brooding architectural shapes to evoke the intangible forces driving capital markets. The formal values, wherein dark dominates light, imply the monetary values that these stark walls and blind cavernous windows represent. Defenseless, the walkers skirt the edge of an immense cliff that looms dangerously over them. It looks solid enough for the moment, but later viewers of this photograph know that a crash is coming.

The Tramp

It's the most famous comic walk of all time: over the course of two decades, Charlie Chaplin's feisty Tramp waddled his eye-catching way into film history. Duck-footed, lifting his knees too high, he twirls his slender cane and wobbles forward, rocking from side to side, awkwardly acrobatic in his baggy trousers and too-large shoes. "The little fellow," as Chaplin called him, emerged as a fully developed character in *The Tramp* (1915), combining pathos and slapstick in a formula new to Hollywood. Through bravery and cunning he saves a young woman whose heart he is sadly unable to win. From then on, the Tramp penguin-shuffled with comic mayhem through many romantic misadventures, eventually playing the central role in three of the greatest films ever made: *The Gold Rush* (1925), *City Lights* (1931), and *Modern Times* (1936). In the silent era when no language barriers could impede his worldwide renown, the Tramp became the best-known character on the planet: noble in nature, unlucky in love, dignified beyond his circumstances, and physically funny beyond compare.

Hobos and tramps dotted the American landscape in the 1870s, in the wake of the Civil War, a housing shortage, and economic hard times. By the turn of the century there were half a million "knights of the open road" moving from town to town, riding the rails or walking in search of short-term work. When *The Tramp* debuted in 1915, comic actors such as Lew Bloom and Nat Wills had long since made tramp caricatures a staple of vaudeville. So when Chaplin was ordered on short notice to look funny for a Keystone comedy, *Mabel's Strange Predicament* (1914), he decided to assemble a tramp outfit. He recalled, "I wanted everything a contradiction: the pants baggy, the coat tight, the hat small and the shoes large." The mismatch made the man: "I had no idea of the character. But the moment I was dressed, the clothes and the makeup made me feel the person he was." In the absence of dialogue, the Tramp used his walk, shaped by the constraints of his cast-off clothing, to convey his past and his outlook on life. "He actually became a man with a soul—a point of view," Chaplin said. "He wears an air of romantic hunger, forever seeking romance, but his feet won't let him." What the feet did for him, however, was harness the hitherto untapped power of moving pictures to express a unique inner spirit through the medium of the walk.

The Tramp opens with "the little fellow" trudging along a dusty road where he is bowled over twice by speeding cars. In 1915 there were already over two million cars on the road in the United States, and tramps had lost their claim to the highway where once they had been kings. A walker in a mechanized world, homeless and jobless, Chaplin's Tramp has the leisure to save a damsel in distress, using all his cleverness to defend her. But when she makes it clear that she loves a convention-

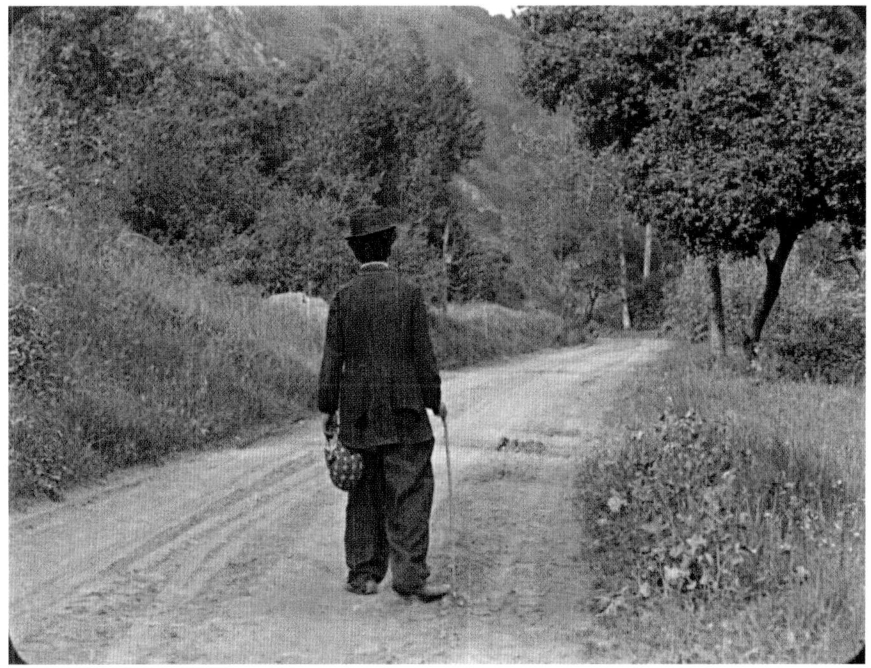

Charles Chaplin in *The Tramp*, 1915

ally handsome and prosperous man, he shoulders his bundle and gallantly returns to the open road, alone. *The Tramp* closes with this classic shot of the disappointed vagabond plodding away. Yet a moment before the film ends, he does a bit of a skip to shake himself up, and then waddles resolutely into the distance. Comically yet nobly, he incarnates Thoreau's ideal: "The Chivalric and heroic spirit which once belonged to the Rider seems now to reside in . . . the Walker—not the Knight, but Walker, Errant."

From Walk of Life to March of Death

Visually, conceptually, it's a brilliant poster campaign. Men from all walks of life "step into their place" in the British army, surrendering their social distinctions to fight their common enemy as a cohesive military force. For the first two years of World War I, until conscription was introduced in March 1916, the British army relied entirely on volunteers. Over two hundred posters like this one were issued through the parliamentary committee that recruited men in their home districts. Literalizing the "walk of life" metaphor and turning the conventional, class-bound idea of "knowing one's place" on its head, the poster asks men to march out of their varied civilian roles and into a self-sacrificing conformity that will save Britain. In so doing, the design provides a graphic translation of Étienne-Jules Marey's motion-study analysis for the French army (also picked up by the enemy Prussians) that transformed individual gaits into synchronized marching steps.

In the poster scene, the occupational class structure of Britain displays itself through headgear. Lower-middle-class bowlers, workingmen's cloth caps, a lawyer's wig, a capitalist's top hat—all describe a social station. Yet soon all will be transformed into the khaki "gor blimey" peaked caps that were worn by both officers and enlisted men during the Great War. Some of the men carry badges of their occupations that gradually become shouldered weapons. Whether you are a farmer with a pitchfork, a tradesman with his tools, a navvy with a pickax, or a horseman with his riding crop, you will end up like everyone else, the poster claims, carrying a rifle with a fixed bayonet.

Of course it was not true. The supposed class-leveling mechanism was controlled by politicians and career soldiers who believed that good officers could only come from the upper orders, and that social rank and army rank should be synonymous. The structures of command remained traditional in the face of a global conflict that utterly changed how wars are fought. With cruel irony, it was the muddy, bloody mess of the war itself, which killed over forty million, that produced in its desolate aftermath the democratizing effect that the poster promised. The "War to End All Wars" was the last in which vast armies actually marched into battle—marching toward the dissolution of the empires they defended. Perhaps the anonymous artist who designed the poster suspected as much: the soon-to-be soldiers tramp off into the distance as a unified force, but they also diminish in size and individuality. They lose even their military identity as they troop like an ever-tinier column of ants toward a final thin, flat line of annihilation.

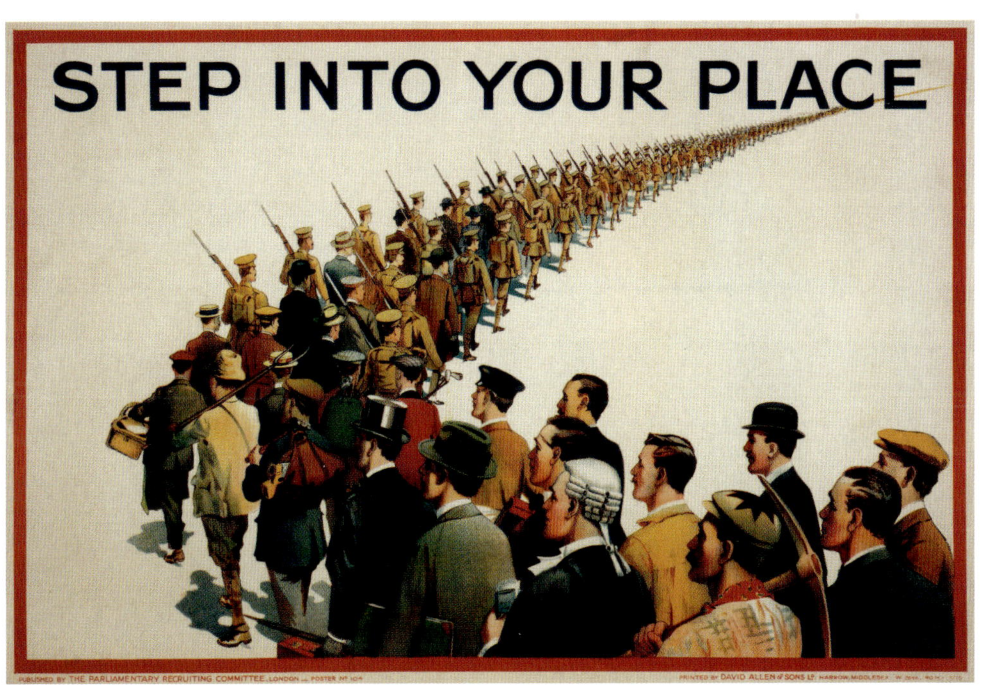

Unknown artist, Parliamentary Recruiting Committee poster, 1915

Into the Sunset

What happens when you send high society's most renowned portrait painter to the front lines? In the summer of 1918, sixty-two-year-old John Singer Sargent visited British and American forces fighting in France, on a commission from the British War Memorials Committee. One day, he reported, he saw "a harrowing sight, a field full of gassed and blindfolded men." They were British soldiers who had been gassed as they went into battle on August 21, 1918, near Arras at the Second Battle of the Somme. Their eyes were wrapped in bandages. Stumbling forward, shepherded by medics, they arrived in small groups at the field dressing station of Le Bac-du-Sud. Sargent made sketches on the spot, but it took several weeks for the haunting scene to push more conventional subjects out of his mind. Abandoning the idea of depicting masses of men and machinery charging into an epic battle, Sargent decided that a true memorial would replace the thrill of attack with its somber aftermath. A general wanted him to focus on tanks as the key modern element of the war, but Sargent intuitively understood that the invisible perils of the war, from mustard gas to shell shock, were even more distinctive.

The result was *Gassed*, a monumental masterpiece twenty feet wide and over seven feet tall. In the place of a triumphal march, Sargent depicts the newly blinded men, each guided by an arm on the shoulder of the man in front, stepping tentatively forward. He breaks his central group of nine casualties into two parts, linked by the outstretched arm of a disoriented soldier. Another group of blinded soldiers and escorts approaches from the right. The three groupings make a triptych of suffering, an altarpiece for the casualties of war.

Sargent revisits Brueghel's *The Blind Leading the Blind* to use the loss of sight as a metaphor for the conflict. But the context offers no biblical lesson, no church in the background to lend a redemptive reading. Instead, we can glimpse between the unsteady legs of the gassed men that still-healthy soldiers are playing a soccer match in the background. War is a game in which some men survive intact to play again the next day, and some don't. The tiny flying ball, near the butt of the rifle left of center, counterpoints the aerial dogfight of biplanes in the far distance on the upper right.

In an ironic reference to the lines of motion and force in Futurist painting, Sargent draws guy lines of medical tents at the right to accentuate the direction in which the procession slowly feels its way. The Futurists glorified speed and war, but here the most dynamic action is one blind soldier awkwardly raising his leg to navigate a step he cannot see.

As the only vertical forms, the new arrivals loom mock-heroically above the invalids who have preceded them. Sprawled in sleep or exhaustion, the bandage-

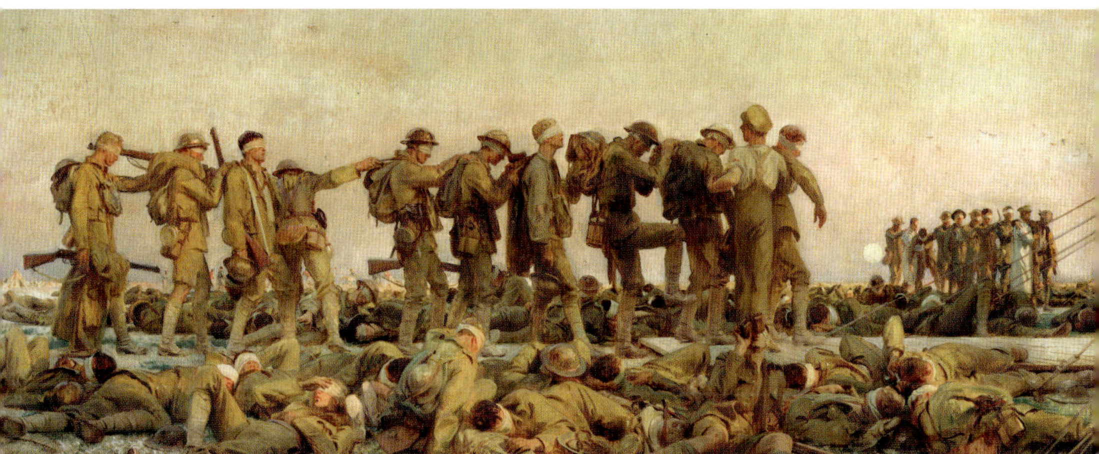

John Singer Sargent, *Gassed*, 1919

wrapped bodies resemble the foreshortened, dozing Roman soldiers who lie at the feet of the risen Christ in depictions of the Resurrection. But the Gospel will not unseal these eyes. All that redeems these figures, spread out across the canvas as if in an allegorical frieze, is the golden light that enfolds them. Henry Tonks, a British artist and surgeon who accompanied Sargent on the trip, wrote: "Gassed cases kept coming in, led along in parties of about six just as Sargent has depicted them. . . . It was a very fine evening and the sun toward setting." As the sun sets on the British Empire, Sargent records what it was like to grope forward in its waning glow.

The Birth of the Long-Distance Trail

If you build it, blaze it, and name it, they will come. Attracted by the challenge, seeking revelation or validation, hordes of secular pilgrim-hikers now swarm the world's long-distance trails. From the Snowman Trek in Bhutan to the Greater Patagonian Trail in Chile, they aim to boldly go where many have gone before. The long-distance phenomenon began with Vermont's 270-mile Long Trail, initiated in 1910 when *hiker* was a new word used in quotation marks, and *hiking* had barely been accepted as a noun. The concept of a dauntingly long footpath took off with the creation of the Appalachian Trail, envisioned in 1921 by American conservationist Benton MacKaye. The first section was opened in 1923 and the overall trail completed in 1937. Stretching 2,200 miles from Georgia to Maine, the white-blazed route crosses fourteen states and takes an average of five to seven months to complete, though fewer than a third of those who start out arrive at the finish.

MacKaye, however, never imagined anyone walking from end to end. Shunning the urban rat race that he believed had led to the suicide of his wife, he charted a path through nature that was equally a psychological route inward. He wanted people to walk toward the purported salvation that nature can provide, "a sanctuary and a refuge from the scramble of every-day worldly commercial life." His plan linked existing paths to improve access to farms and wilderness for city dwellers living along the route. In the 1960s thru-hiking started to become part of the trail's reputation, but more than two million people travel some part of it every year for the original purpose, taking short, restorative wilderness excursions.

As this promotional photo of two hikers scaling skyline boulders shows, at the core of the AT is the geological reality of a mountain chain—and the daunting quest to meet its challenge. Climbing toward adventure and apparently marveling at the magnificent views, these fit-looking but heavily laden young men suggest both the trials and rewards of the rugged trail. The exhilarating allure of these heights is expertly captured by the Forest Service photographer E. S. Shipp's upward camera angle, which gives the textured rocks their skin-scraping due. But a detail suggests that mere agility or dogged determination may not be enough to tame the AT: both hikers wear sidearms. Whether the danger comes from wild beasts (bear, boar, snakes) or fellow humans (there have been thirteen murders on the AT since 1974), the decision to carry a weapon remains a controversial part of hike planning.

MacKaye's original ridgeline path has been extended at both ends. Now starting at Springer Mountain in Georgia, the AT was first planned to connect the highest point in the south (Mount Mitchell in North Carolina) to the highest in the north (Mount Washington). But the Appalachian Mountains do not stop even at the trail's current northern terminus atop Mount Katahdin in Maine. In 1994 Richard Ander-

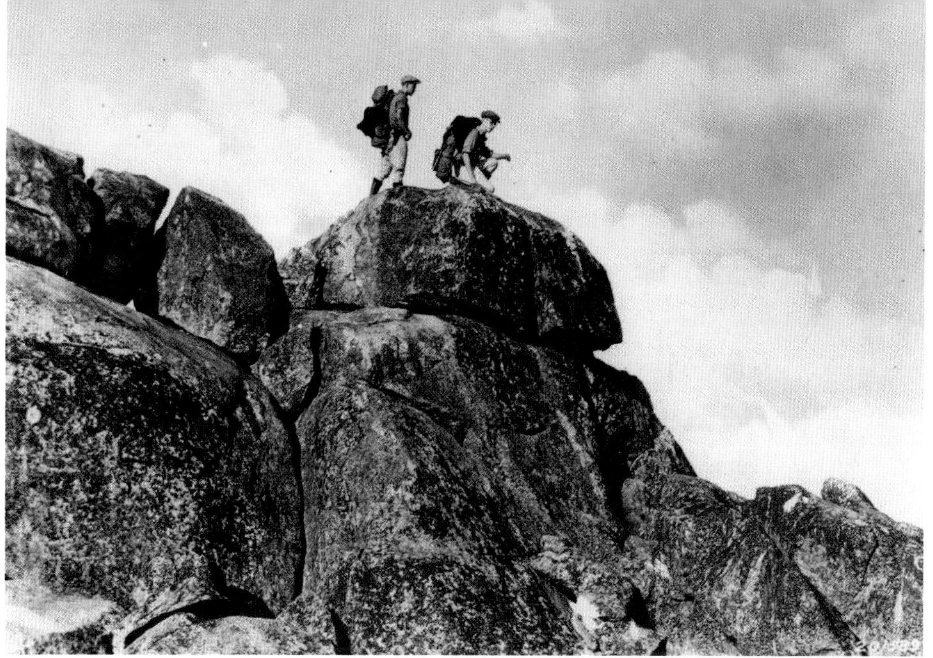

E. S. Shipp, "Above the clouds on sharp top mountain peaks of Otter Country on the Appalachian Trail, Jefferson National Forest, Virginia," 1925

sen proposed the International Appalachian Trail, a 1,900-mile extension through New Brunswick, the Gaspé Peninsula, and then, with the aid of ferries, to Nova Scotia and Newfoundland. Even then, the "trail" continues, since the rock formations it traces belonged 250 million years ago to the supercontinent of Pangaea. Eventually the International Alpine Trail will pass through Greenland, Iceland, Norway, Sweden, Denmark, the British Isles, Spain, Portugal, and Morocco.

With the trail has grown the hunger of walkers worldwide to face not only this challenge but others like it. Well over a hundred long-distance trails cover the planet, on every continent except Antarctica. The compulsion to test oneself against a trajectory and a terrain selected by others is one of the most salient features of contemporary walking. It may seem ironic that the determined, self-reliant people who set out on these paths are, in effect, followers rather than leaders. They have released themselves for days, weeks, months, or even years from the task of charting their way through life. Yet by committing their bodies to a predetermined destination, they have freed their minds to pursue other goals. In 1971, fifty years after he first imagined the AT, MacKaye claimed that the trail's ultimate purpose is "1. to walk; 2. to see; and 3. to *see* what you see!" For the long-distance walker, the ready-blazed trail promises a vision that no other experience can deliver. "The AT as originally conceived," MacKaye said, "is not merely a footpath *through* the wilderness but a footpath *of* the wilderness." Ideally, people do not walk such trails; the trails walk them.

Mass Trespass

It has been called the most successful act of civil resistance in English history. On Sunday, April 24, 1932, members of the British Workers' Sports Federation and the Young Communist League staged a mass trespass at Kinder Scout, a high moorland plateau in the Peak District of Derbyshire. This news photograph captures the exuberant moment when the crowd of ramblers ("hikers" was regarded as a terrible Americanism) streamed toward moorland that the Duke of Devonshire's gamekeepers had permanently cordoned off. Managed for private grouse shooting a few days per year, the open terrain formed a significant part of the 99 percent of land in the Peak District excluded from public use. Determined not to be turned away, the marchers were ragtag in appearance but unified in spirit. Benny Rothman, the twenty-one-year-old organizer of the action, recalled "hundreds of young men and women, lads and girls, in their picturesque rambling gear: shorts of every length and colour, flannels and breeches, even overalls, vivid colours and drab khaki … multicoloured sweaters and pullovers, army packs and rucksacks of every size and shape."

All told, some four hundred walkers from the nearby industrial cities of Manchester and Sheffield joined in the surge that overran the few gamekeepers sent

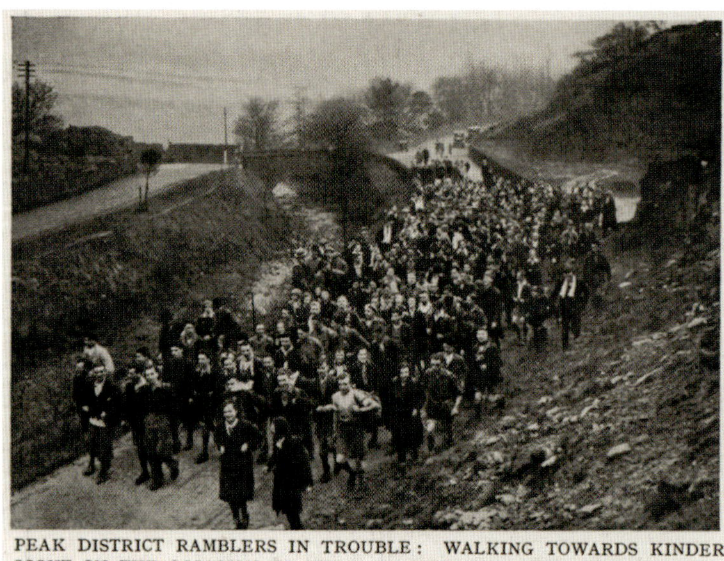

"Peak District Ramblers in Trouble," *Illustrated London News*, April 25, 1932

out to meet them. The ramblers successfully gained the highest point on the plateau, where they held a rally. Five of the leaders were later arrested and jailed. The severe sentences, up to six months' imprisonment at a time when trespass was not a crime, galvanized walkers across Britain. The actions they took—both follow-up trespasses and sustained political action—led directly to the 1949 National Parks and Access to the Countryside Act, and then to the creation of the Peak District National Park a few years later. These in turn helped in the creation of the 268-mile Pennine Way (inspired by the Appalachian Trail), the first of Britain's long National Trails. Collectively, these efforts engendered the Countryside and Rights of Way Act 2000, which guarantees a "right to roam" on areas of "mountain, moor, heath and down" as well as on registered common land.

The ongoing movement toward open access to uncultivated land has been sponsored in many countries by walkers' organizations, working together to protect the environment while encouraging responsible public use. As early as 1866, the Commons Preservation Society used the cover of darkness to remove two miles of railings surrounding Berkhamsted Common, and the same group was active in the creation of the National Trust in 1895. The success of the trespass at Kinder Scout revitalized the Ramblers Association, now the largest hiking group in the United Kingdom. In the United States and on the European continent, walking became a political and environmental force reaching into mainstream culture through organizations such as the Sierra Club, founded in 1892, the French Club Vosgien (1872), the Austrian Naturfreunde (1895), the German Wandervogel (1896), and the International Youth Hostel Association (1932).

Not entirely ironically, the eighteenth-century aristocrat's desire to experience picturesque natural landscapes became in the twentieth century a right demanded by ordinary workers on their day off. Today "freedom to roam" traditions and legislation exist in almost all northern European countries and in Scotland. Both public and private lands are available for low-impact recreation such as walking and camping. About 8 percent of England and Wales is now open access land, with organizations such as the Ramblers advocating further reforms to increase that percentage. Activists point out that the public still has no right of access to 92 percent of England, half of which is owned by less than 1 percent of the population. Still smarting over the seizure of common lands that started in the seventeenth century, many Britons see the trespass as entirely on the part of the ruling class. Three hundred years ago, oral culture produced this classic analysis:

> *The law locks up the man or woman*
> *Who steals the goose from off the common*
> *But leaves the greater villain loose*
> *Who steals the common from off the goose.*

Goose-Stepping

The line between comedy and terror has rarely been so finely drawn. With literal and metaphoric precision, goose-stepping Nazi troops walked all over Europe in the decade after this photo was taken. As George Orwell commented in 1941, such a ridiculous-looking form of military display "is only possible in countries where the common people dare not laugh at the army." Certainly none of the millions of supporters who in the 1930s attended the Nazi Party rallies in Nuremberg, where this photo was snapped, would have dared to laugh. Nor did many nonparty Germans, as Hitler's rise to power led to murder, war, and subjugation. "The goose-step," Orwell claimed, is "far more terrifying than a dive-bomber. It is simply an affirmation of naked power; contained in it, quite consciously and intentionally, is the vision of a boot crashing down on a face."

The step itself began in eighteenth-century Prussia. Called the "piercing step," or *Stechschritt*, the exaggeratedly stiff-legged stride was adopted by Russia in the nineteenth century and spread around the world in the twentieth. Because the step requires balance, unity, timing, and strength to make its striking visual effect, its drillmaster inventor, Prince Leopold I, judged it ideal for turning individuals into a cohesive fighting force. Dozens of nations still use the step today, in armies as varied as those of Chile, Rwanda, Poland, and China. In English-speaking countries, however, its strong association with Nazi Germany decisively ended the goose step's appeal.

That connection was memorably forged by Leni Riefenstahl's *Triumph of the Will* (1935), one of the most influential propaganda films ever made. Documenting the 1934 Nazi rally in Nuremberg, Riefenstahl aimed to convince viewers that Hitler's Germany possessed an unstoppable power. Orchestrated by Hitler's master architect Albert Speer, the congress took place on gargantuan stage sets. In a massive display of disciplined organization, hundreds of thousands cheered and saluted the Nazi flag in unison. The waves of troops that Riefenstahl showed marching in the culminating parade belonged not to the German army but to Hitler's personal forces, raising the glorification of the führer to fever pitch. Riefenstahl overwhelmed spectators with dramatically lit scenes of flags, crowds, and swastikas. No less than the goose step itself, her aerial shots and sweeping, starkly angled perspectives commanded attention across the globe. Hollywood director Frank Capra, charged by General George Marshall to respond, was initially paralyzed by the task, confessing that "Satan couldn't have devised a more blood-chilling super-spectacle."

Yet its blind devotion to fatherland and führer meant that there was plenty to parody in the Nazi self-presentation. Unintentionally, Riefenstahl inspired two

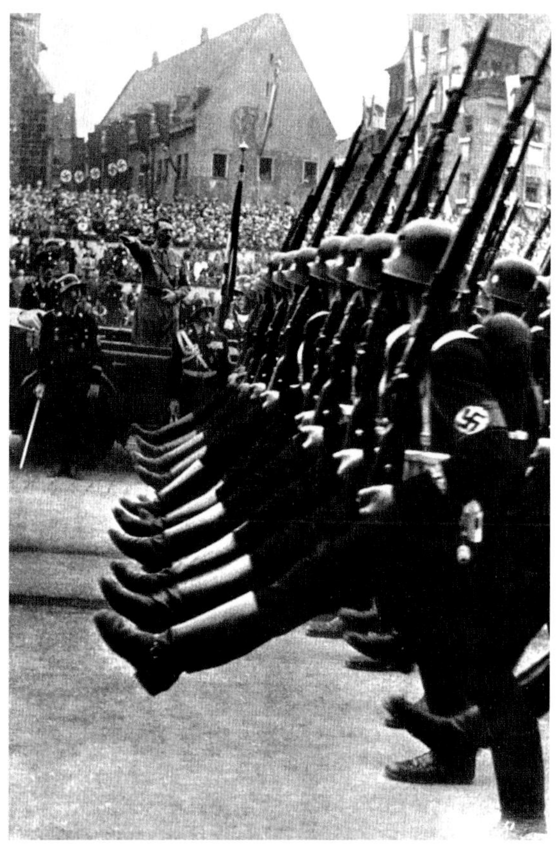

Unknown photographer, Hitler reviews goose-stepping SS troops, Nuremberg, c. 1935–38

comic masterpieces. The first, Charlie Chaplin's *The Great Dictator* (1940), is famous for its savagely funny impersonation of a deranged Hitler. Less remembered is the 1942 short film *Schichlegruber—Doing the Lambeth Walk,* in which Charles Ridley of the British Ministry of Information turned goose-stepping against itself. Reversing and looping the film at key moments, Ridley edited Riefenstahl's marching sequences so that Hitler's troops do silly backsteps, skips, and salutes in time to a popular dance tune, "The Lambeth Walk" (1937). The mockery was heightened by the fact that the Nazis had denounced the song and accompanying dance—popular in Germany as well as Britain—as "Jewish mischief and animalistic hopping." Hitler's minister of propaganda was reportedly so enraged that he placed Ridley on the Gestapo's hit list. As Orwell had predicted, once the Nazi march was seen for itself, it would walk into history—the history of comedy.

Criminalizing the Walker

Pedestrians must be educated to know that automobiles have rights.
—*George M. Graham of the National Automobile Chamber of Commerce, 1924*

By the 1930s the battle was over. The newspapers, the police, the drivers, the dictionaries, and even the so-called criminals themselves agreed: a jaywalker was "one who crosses a street without observing the traffic regulations for pedestrians." It had not always been thus. In early twentieth-century Chicago, for example, the rule was that "all persons have an equal right in the highway, and . . . each shall take due care not to injure other users of the way." Men, women, and children on foot—shopping, walking to work, out for air, or playing in the street—were assumed to have a rightful share of public space. But as motorcars and accidents increased after 1900, the term *jay driver* was coined. It stemmed from the word *jay*, which connoted a rube from the country who did not know how to behave in the city. Jay drivers, joyriders, and speed maniacs were all reprimanded in the press for irresponsibly disregarding life and limb. Electric traffic lights soon spread across the country, starting in Salt Lake City (1912), Cleveland (1914), and Detroit (1920), but they did little to arrest what the *New York Times* called "the slaughter of pedestrians."

Facing stricter regulation, drivers, automobile associations, and the motor industry responded with a single loaded word: *jaywalker*. First used around 1910, the epithet sought to convince urbanites that they were acting like bumpkins if they did not know how to behave in the modern world by yielding to cars. The main strategies of this psychological warfare emerged in 1913 when an Oregon newspaper announced, with some literal truth: "A campaign of ridicule directed toward the extermination of the 'Jay Walker Family' was inaugurated today by the local automobile club. . . . Automobile clubs all over the country . . . will be asked to aid in exterminating 'Mr. and Mrs. Jay Walker and all the little Walkers.'"

Through a concerted campaign of mockery in newspapers, schools, courts, and on the streets, car lobbies sought to convince walkers that they had no rights on the road. Police and newspapers carried the pro-driver bias into their accident reports. Ninety percent of fatalities, the National Automobile Chamber of Commerce falsely claimed, were the walker's fault. Boy Scouts were enlisted nationwide to denounce jaywalking. In 1923 they handed out over six hundred thousand circulars in New York City alone, warning: "DO YOU KNOW YOU ARE GUILTY OF JAYWALKING—WHEN YOU CROSS STREETS CARELESSLY!"

The turning point in the battle came in the 1920s, a decade when a record two hundred thousand Americans were killed on the roads, most of them pedestrians.

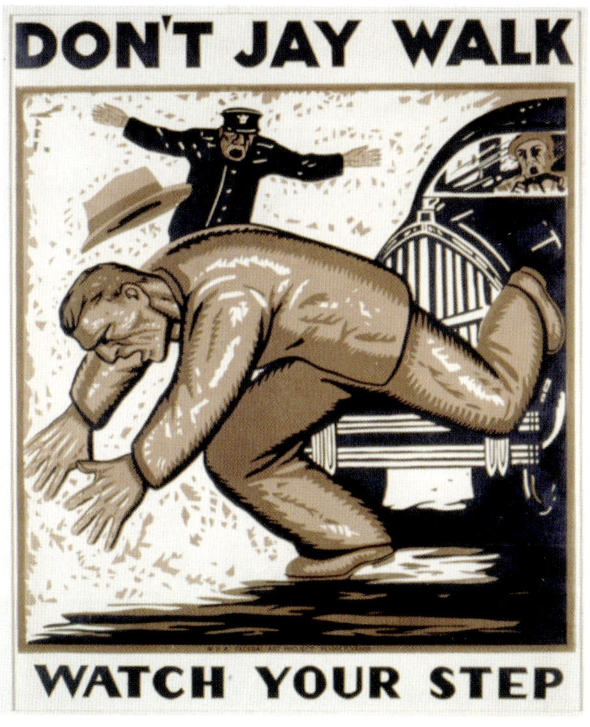

Isadore Posoff, "Don't Jay Walk / Watch Your Step," 1937

Many people favored requiring cars to have governors installed that would limit their speed to twenty-five miles per hour. A looming referendum on the issue in Cincinnati in 1923 shocked the auto industry into a massive "safety" program of car propaganda. It not only defeated the referendum but went on to have jaywalking declared illegal in Los Angeles, whose 1925 traffic code then became the national norm. With lethal power, drivers forced people off the streets. The desire to stay alive caused a de facto pedestrian surrender, regardless of laws that granted them priority in many situations.

As this public service poster from 1937 shows, the US government had by that time accepted that road safety depended on pedestrians steering clear of cars, and not the other way around. "Don't Jay Walk" won out over other possible messages such as "Don't Speed" or "Pedestrians Have the Right of Way." In Isadore Posoff's powerfully schematic rendering, car, driver, and policeman are helpless in the face of the clueless jaywalker, whose falling body fills the frame. It's not clear whether the man has foolishly tripped in front of the car barreling toward him, or whether it's the impact that has sent him flying. The policeman and driver exclaim in shock and frustration, but what can they do? The walker deserves to be hit.

Follow the Yellow Brick Road

"Follow the Yellow Brick Road." When Hollywood mixes messages from *The Pilgrim's Progress* and Homer's *Odyssey* with an American fairy tale, the result is the world's most famous musical journey. The path stands out clearly, in a golden color that took the art directors at MGM a week to settle on. It unfolds alongside a metaphoric trip into the heart of camaraderie. Acquiring and discarding partners along the way, John Bunyan's Pilgrim walked toward the Celestial City to have his soul saved. Dorothy, however, makes faithful friends as she travels to the Emerald City, in search of a way to return to her earthly home. On her odyssey she encounters a Cowardly Lion, a Tin Woodman, and a Scarecrow, all of whom find the qualities they think they lack—courage, heart, brains—by sharing her quest. She assembles an ahead-of-its-time, over-the-rainbow coalition of animal, android, and human members. The true progress of the four pilgrims is less toward spiritual fulfillment (since the Wizard turns out to be a fraud, anyway) than toward the character-building values of love, loyalty, and kindness.

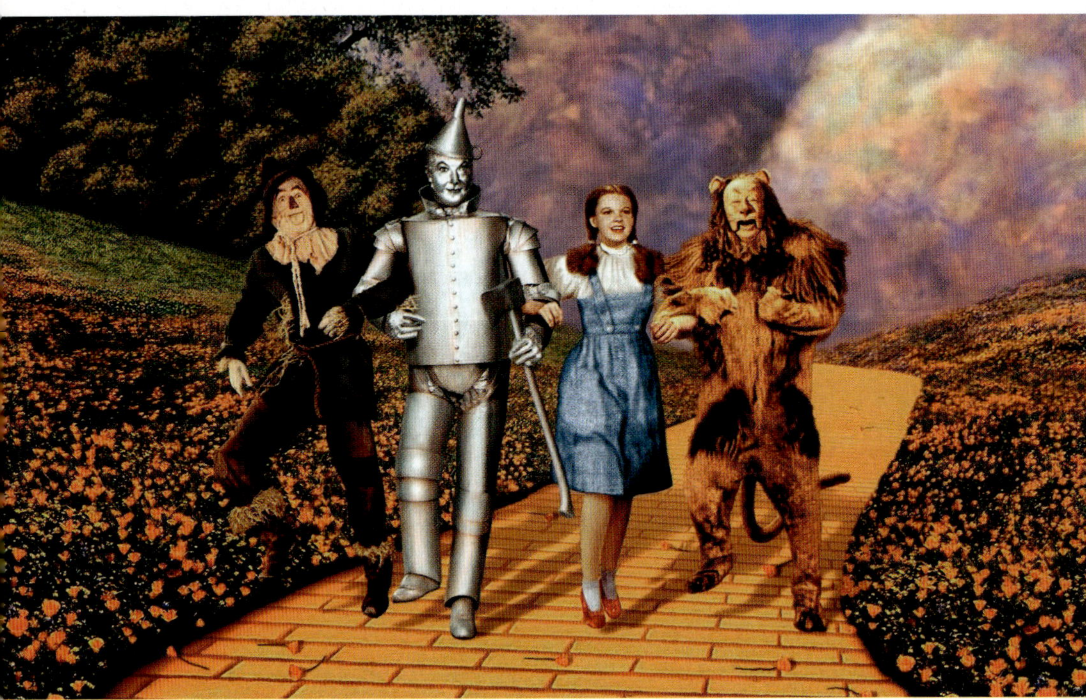

The Wizard of Oz, MGM publicity still, 1939

What does all this say about walking? While the music captures the joy and uncertainty of hitting the road ("We're off to see the Wizard," "Lion and tigers and bears, oh my!"), the plot is goal-oriented. The very qualities for which walking is most prized—new sights, self-discovery, the solidarity of the trail, a deeper understanding of the world and one's place in it—are all only steps toward realizing that "there's no place like home." Having learned their self-worth, the Scarecrow, the Lion, and the Tin Woodman remain in Oz to govern the Emerald City, but for Dorothy the yellow brick road ultimately leads back to monochrome Kansas.

In many ways, this is a cautionary tale. Not only does the Wizard disappoint, and home look dull after the adventure, but Dorothy and her companions march into modernity as watched walkers. Fearing political upheaval (symbolized at the film's start by the tornado), the Wicked Witch of the West responds like any dictator: she monitors their progress through the best available surveillance technology. She tracks them remotely in her crystal ball, while also using the aerial observation of her flying monkeys. As they follow the Yellow Brick Road, the four companions embody the vulnerability of walkers channeled onto an assigned path.

And yet, for all this, could *The Wizard of Oz*, seen by more people than any other film in history, be the most instructive walking story ever? For over two millennia Western culture would probably have nominated Adam and Eve's Expulsion from the Garden for that role. When humanity's anguished parents take their first steps out of Eden, they initiate a Bible-long journey of trial and travail that ends only with a cataclysmic Judgment Day. But instead of a wailing, guilt-ridden couple, fans of Dorothy and her pals can ponder an earth-oriented fable with a rewarding ending. Eluding surveillance, a decidedly mixed foursome goes forth arm in arm to discover its inner strength, amid the wonders of a Technicolor world.

Holocaust Death March

No one will tell them, but they know where they are going: to die. The word, apparently invented in the camps, was passed before they left: this will be a *Todesmärsche*, a "death march." If they don't drop dead from exhaustion, they will be shot if they drag behind, shot if they try to escape, shot if the guards don't know what else to do when they get to the destination. For now, they walk with a brisk step, looking at the camera with cold disdain. Photography's ability to turn people into objects is nowhere more evident than in documentation of Nazi "solutions" to the "problem" of racial purity. These individuals do not play along. With their eyes they speak to us as fellow humans, pushed at gunpoint into the paradox of photography. Like people in any photograph of a certain age, they have already died, but what moves us here is how soon that death is coming.

Between the autumn of 1944 and spring of 1945, as the Allies closed in, Nazi forces moved hundreds of thousands of prisoners out of concentration camps near the eastern front. The prisoners themselves might be Jewish, Romani, homosexuals, mentally ill, or political resisters of various sorts: Communists, socialists, democrats. They trudged with minimal food, water, and protection from the cold. If they were not shot, they still died by the thousands, starving or freezing to death while traveling to, from, or in the boxcars that awaited them at transfer points. Even as photographers methodically documented the marches, the aim was to erase evidence of Nazi atrocities, to employ the survivors as slave labor deeper inside Germany, and even to use them as bargaining chips when negotiating surrender. Earlier in the war, thousands of Jewish prisoners had already been killed on death marches in Poland and Ukraine. Now desperate captors killed thousands even before the marches started.

On the largest single march, fifteen thousand died in the evacuation of Auschwitz in January 1945. Buchenwald prisoners suffered a similar fate in April. In marches from the Stutthof camps between January and May, twenty-five thousand prisoners are estimated to have been shot and drowned. The prisoners pictured here were among the ten thousand forced from the Dachau camp in late April, just ahead of advancing American troops. During a six-day march thousands died, including 1,071 later found in a mass grave on the way. In an irony of the war, hundreds who had been left for dead, covered with snow, were saved by Japanese American soldiers whose own families were at that moment incarcerated in the United States.

Victims of the Holocaust have since been commemorated in many ways, including the step-by-step retracing of itineraries that the prisoners followed to their deaths. One striking—and controversial—reconsideration of the walking memorial was created in 1992 by German artist Guenther Demnig. He placed "stumbling

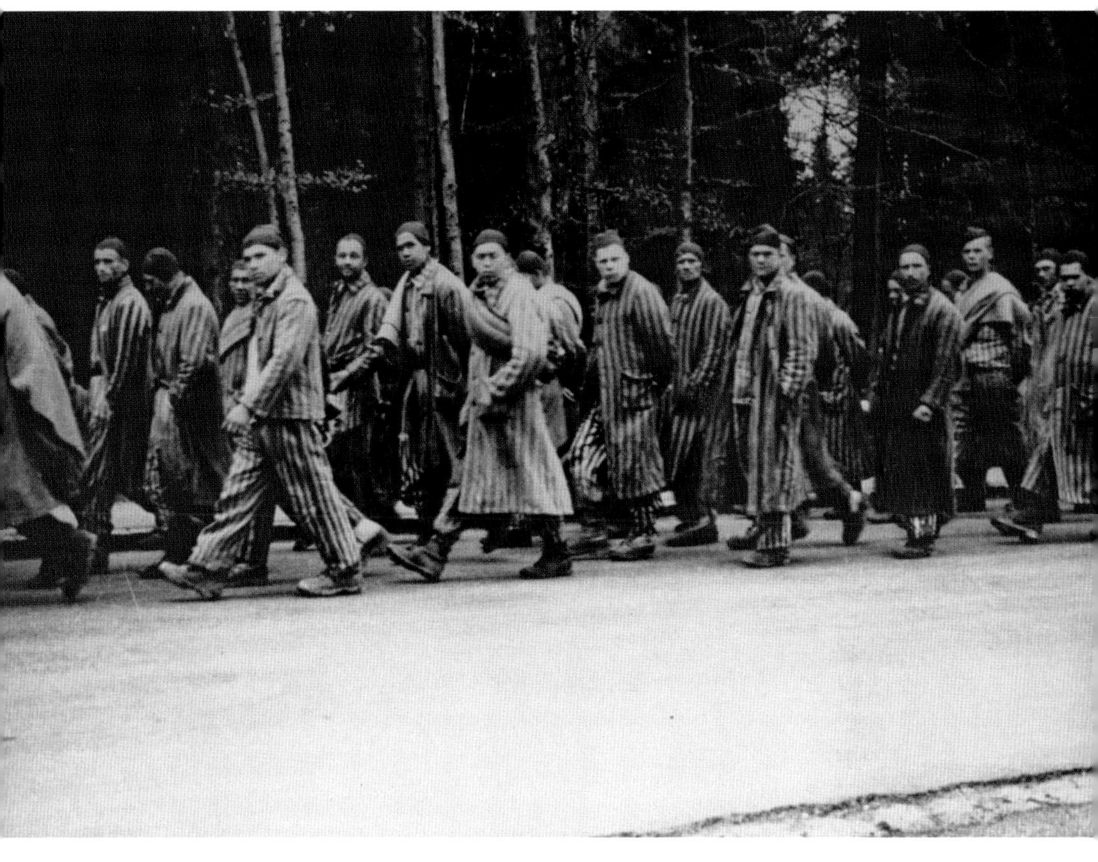

Fritz Melbach, prisoners marching from Dachau, April 1945

stones"—in German, *Stolpersteine*—on streets and sidewalks at the last point where individuals lived or worked before being deported. Each *Stolperstein* is a four-inch concrete cube covered by a brass plaque that states the name and date of birth and, if known, death of the person the Nazis seized. The concept of stumbling stones plays on three meanings: In the German past, someone who tripped over a cobblestone might say, "A Jew was buried here." In German as well as English, a stumbling stone is a problem, an obstacle that needs addressing. And finally, in both languages one can stumble, literally or figuratively, upon something unexpected, including the question of whether a memorial should be walked over. Over seventy-five thousand *Stolpersteine* have been placed by Demnig and his assistants, in twenty countries, making them the world's largest memorial.

The March of Dimes

It started with a clever turn of phrase. In 1938 comedian Eddie Cantor used one of the most durable walking metaphors, "the march of time," to create another kind of metaphoric footstep. Playing on *The March of Time* newsreels, he suggested that President Franklin Delano Roosevelt's new fundraising program to fight polio could become "a march of dimes" across America. It was a twofold stroke of genius. First, it emphasized that small donations could have a major impact. Second, it transformed Roosevelt's ponderously titled charity (the National Foundation for Infantile Paralysis) into a dynamic organization whose ultimate goal—helping polio-stricken children to walk—was signaled in the very first word of its annual campaign, "March." Ten cents was not a negligible amount in the immediate postwar era. It would buy a cup of coffee, a subway token, a magazine, or a bag of popcorn at the movies. But giving a dime to help another child walk was a gesture within the reach of most American children and their parents. In the first months of 1938, letters containing $85,000 in dimes swamped the White House mail room.

Each year from 1946 onward, the March of Dimes poster child played a key role in making the public aware of the crippling effects of the disease, which would reach a peak of twenty-one thousand paralytic cases in 1952. The poster children made visible a condition that the American press had played down in the case of Roosevelt himself, who was not able to walk unaided after an illness, diagnosed as polio, struck him in 1921. But the story told by the posters was resolutely upbeat, emphasizing the progress being made by research funded by the March of Dimes. In a before-and-after scenario, the first poster child, Donald Anderson, who contracted polio at the age of three, was shown twice. In a background scene, he wore a neck brace and arm splint as he mournfully steadied himself in a hospital crib. Then, with a few drawn-in footprints to indicate his progress, a now-robust five-year-old strode into the foreground, where a heading proclaimed, "Your dimes did this for me!" A few years later in 1949, four-year-old Linda Brown was selected for one of the first color posters, pictured here. In the photograph she pushes herself up out of her wheelchair with brave determination, while a caption announces, "Look! I can walk again."

The optimism was not unfounded. In 1955, with significant funding from the March of Dimes, which by then had spent $233 million on patient care, the Salk vaccine was licensed. In the wake of a mass immunization campaign, by 1961 only 161 polio cases were recorded in the United States. Later, with the aid of the Sabin oral vaccine, the disease would be nearly eradicated. The concerted response to polio epidemics had far-reaching results. Rehabilitation therapy developed as a medical field; millions of survivors worldwide contributed greatly to disability

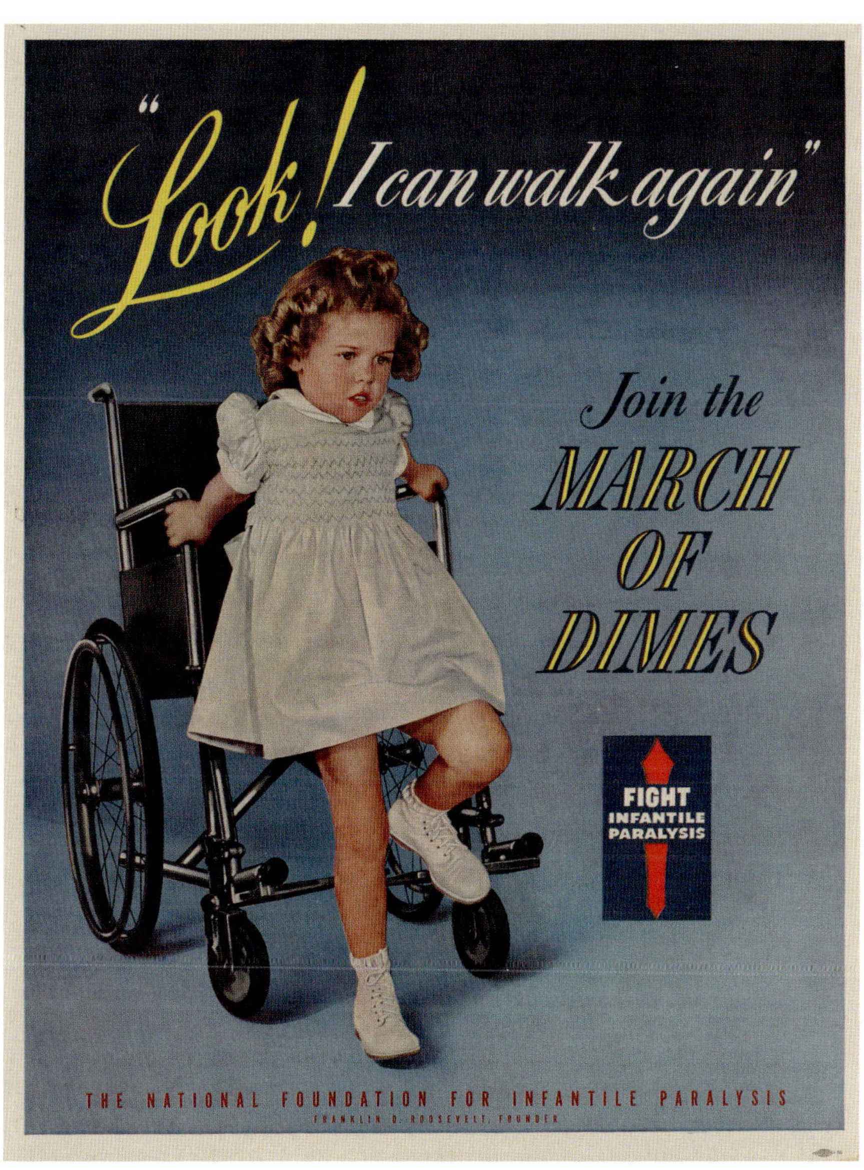

"Look! I Can Walk Again," March of Dimes poster depicting Linda Brown, 1949

rights movements; and the success of the March of Dimes created new models of medical funding, especially at the grassroots level.

Fundraisers rapidly literalized the walking metaphor that the March of Dimes so successfully exploited, creating the modern walkathon. People had raised money before as they walked: the pedestrian athlete Edward Payson Weston solicited funds for his own expenses, while the suffragettes accepted donations to help their crusade for the vote. But in the 1940s and 1950s people began walking to raise money for social benefit, particularly in the area of public health. Taking individual action, in 1948 John Harrison Finger walked thirty-two miles, collecting $1,700 for the March of Dimes, after his daughter came home from school with the request for a donation. Collective fundraising marches began in 1953 in Puerto Rico, when beloved comedian Ramón Rivero crossed the island on a four-day trek of eighty mountainous miles, camping along the way with a few dozen committed supporters, to raise money for cancer research. Rivero encouraged others to share not only in the physical effort but also in the moral satisfaction of having struggled for a worthy cause. In 1970 the March of Dimes launched a spinoff campaign, WalkAmerica (now called March for Babies), that organized the first nationwide walkathons. Since then, the yearly events have raised over $2 billion, as the footsteps of millions of walkers have raised money to fight birth defects, infant mortality, and premature birth.

As time marches on, the March of Dimes model has enabled many to step along with it. Walkathons draw on the classic attractions of walking as a healthy activity that builds community and camaraderie. At the same time they offer special rewards to those who walk on behalf of a friend or relative affected by a particular medical condition. In this regard, charitable walkathons are polar opposites of the original walkathons of the Depression era. In those spectacles of suffering, destitute couples, desperate for prize money, competed against each other in walk-till-you-drop events that could last two or three months.

Walkathons are capitalism's answer to the protest march. Those who walk to aid victims of disease, poverty, or disaster not only demonstrate a pressing need; they also accept that governments are not able or willing to solve the problem. While protest marchers demand social change, nonthreatening walkathoners ask only for the coin of the realm. In 2020, amid the global pandemic, one-hundred-year-old "Captain Tom" Moore raised over thirty million pounds for Great Britain's beleaguered National Health Service by walking one hundred laps of his eighty-foot garden path, aided by a metal-frame walker. Like so many before him, he tacitly recognized a status quo in which public welfare depends on private funding, particularly if it is tied to an ostentatious show of physical effort.

Reading the Walker

It's Italy, 1951. Fifteen men give their full attention to a young woman walking past on a Florentine sidewalk. On her right, the man closest to her, in jacket and tie, bends forward and whistles. Next to him a man, jacket under his arm, hands in his pockets, plants himself in her path. She half closes her eyes and looks straight ahead, clutching her shawl tightly in one hand, her purse in the other, as she takes a brisk step that sways the skirt of her dress backward and leaves her rear foot practically vertical. To her right a man leans forward from his café table, while on her left two men sitting on a motorbike, feet propped on the curb, grin toward her exposed calves.

To some, it is a classic—perhaps *the* classic—photo of a woman receiving unwanted male attention on a city street. The title, *An American Girl in Italy*, draws on stereotypes of sexist, ogling Latin men and innocent, vulnerable American women whose own society, it is implied, protects them from this sort of scrutiny.

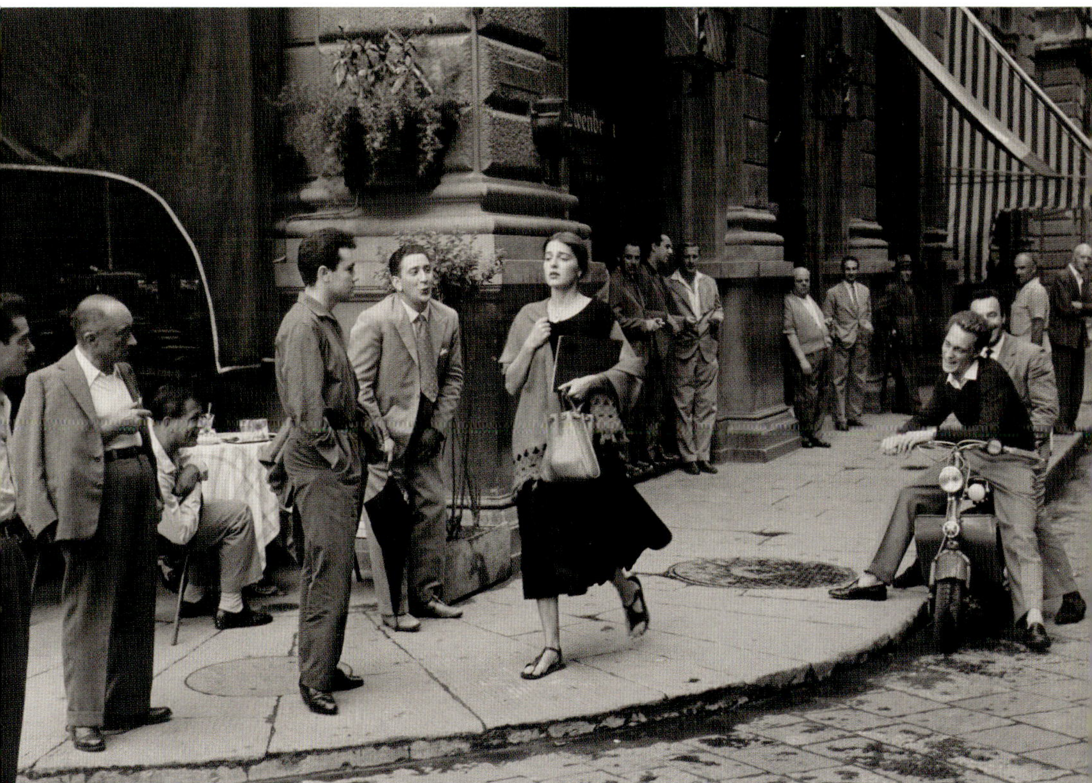

Stay-at-home American women know differently, of course. They have a substantial share in the roughly 80 percent of women worldwide who report having suffered some form of sexual harassment in public spaces.

But the fantasy that the title promotes is further intertwined with the idea of postwar Europe as a sexual playground for Americans with money and time to spare. The photo was published in *Cosmopolitan* magazine in a 1952 story called "When You Travel Alone." Readers were told, "Public admiration…shouldn't fluster you. Ogling the ladies is a popular, harmless and flattering pastime you'll run into in many foreign countries." And in fact the model, Ninalee Craig, twenty-three at the time, recalled in 2017 that she felt far from threatened. "I was thrilled. I was having the time of my life," Craig said. "I was Beatrice walking through the streets of Florence. I felt that at any moment I might be discovered by Dante himself."

How can we know the walker from the walk? Whether this particular image shows Craig suffering the prosaic Inferno of catcalls or enjoying a poetic Paradiso of adoration will depend on how one interprets Craig's facial expression and body language. It may also depend on the words of the American photographer, Ruth Orkin. Apparently the photo was shot on a second pass through the crowd of men, after the two young women realized what they had stumbled onto: "Here was the perfect setting I had been waiting for all these years," said Orkin. "And here I was, camera in hand, with the ideal model! All those fellows were positioned perfectly." In her diary, Orkin noted later that day: "Got idea for pic story. Satire on Am. girl alone in Europe."

Satire, over-the-top cliché, or honest documentary, the picture's power stems from an unavoidable visual point: this is a woman in a man's space. Given how at home they appear, it's easy to credit Craig's claim that "the men were not arranged or told how to look. That is how they were in August 1951." Perhaps Craig, Orkin, and the men all enjoyed each other's fleeting company, for their own sexual and economic reasons. Yet if the photograph shrewdly exploits the cultural assumptions contained in its title, it also transcends the private thoughts of the people involved. *An American Girl in Italy* offers itself as a time-bound symbol of a timeless situation, one in which the walker's body is read like a fantasy novel.

The Catwalk

It's a special way of walking, for a special setting. Fashion models, mostly female, sashay down narrow pathways in front of customers, industry professionals, and the press, showing off the latest in designer clothing. They parade the garments on "catwalks" and "runways," as if they were felines crossing narrow bridges or airplanes accelerating for takeoff. Alert to the metaphors of their location and attire, they perform a ritualized, commercialized walk that takes years to perfect yet must seem natural to its audience. While advice on how to walk has formed part of a gentleman's or lady's education for centuries, in recent times much of walking education has been narrowly directed toward learning how to move in this instantly recognizable, financially profitable way.

Theoretically interchangeable with the clothing's ultimate purchaser, the persons who confidently strut down the runway have practiced this routine to perfection. Advisers to prospective models agree: they should stand tall and straight with shoulders back, leading with the hips and legs, arms and hands relaxed but restrained. The feet are placed one in front of the other, at a pace neither slow nor

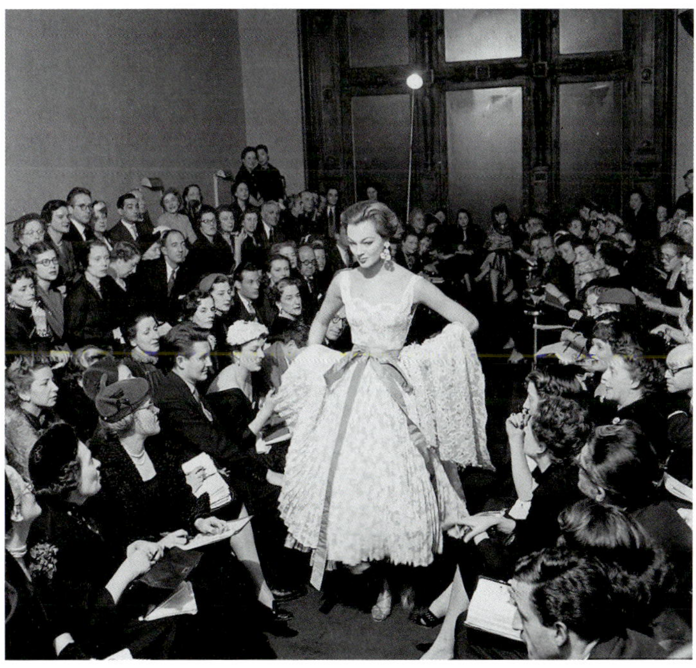

Unknown photographer, Maison de Givenchy, Paris, 1952

fast, to create a natural-looking rhythm to the step, a step that should be subservient to the display of the clothing worn. Eventually models may develop a characteristic style, a stomp, a march, a sway, an attitude, but first the basics must be in place.

Fashion shows using live models date to the 1850s, in Paris at the House of Worth, when Charles Frederick Worth's wife, Marie Vernet Worth, presented his creations on her own becoming figure. Together the Worths changed how dresses were made and sold by requiring their clients to come to them. Worth gowns, selected from the designs that Madame Worth and her fellow models wore, were made in-house. The showroom itself became a high-society gathering place, and Worth was the first to put labels in garments, announcing their provenance. In the early twentieth century, New York department stores ran their own versions of Worth's show, presenting haute couture from Paris as well as locally made versions.

The displays evolved into formal presentations of spring and fall collections. This photo of Givenchy's debut show in Paris in 1952 catches a moment when limited room still required models to navigate a tight catwalk surrounded by journalists and clients. Notebooks were more prevalent than cameras, and the models were not expected to outshine the clothes they wore. In the next few decades, however, the simple parade of dresses would become stylized performances in which the models, gaining as much name recognition as the designers, moved through a carefully engineered space whose lighting, music, and overall theme were as orchestrated as the walk itself. Today, as the model struts by or pauses at the end of the catwalk to strike a pose, dozens of cameras click, whir, and flash, highlighting the perennial paradox of the static walking image. A fluid, integrated motion is cut up and preserved in a potentially infinite number of stills. The walk, like the beauty of the model or the dress, must reside in the eye of the beholder.

Drifting

The sudden change of ambiance in a street within the space of a few meters; the evident division of a city into zones of distinct psychic atmospheres; the path of least resistance that is automatically followed in aimless strolls . . .

—Guy Debord, "Introduction to a Critique of Urban Geography"

There's a word for it: *psychogeography*. In 1950s Paris, Guy Debord and the Situationists came up with a plan to pull the plug on consumer capitalism and its colonization of public space. Rather than go where "the society of the spectacle" wanted them to go—to work, to consume, to surrender authentic feelings to mediatic chimeras based on commodities—Debord and his semi-Marxist collective wandered the streets aimlessly, attuned to the psychic push and pull of microenvironments. They let the city itself guide them, mostly on a subliminal level. *"Psychogeography,"* Debord wrote, "could set for itself the study of the precise laws and specific effects of the geographical environment, consciously organized or not, on the emotions and behavior of individuals."

While Debord's investigations sounded scientific, they were not organized strolls by self-conscious flâneurs armed with clipboards and recording devices. Instead, Debord favored drunken rambles that could last an hour, a day, or a week, depending on the endurance of the participants. Rejecting the complacent walking of their predecessors (flâneurs were too bourgeois, Surrealists too interested in art), the Situationists sauntered toward revolution by resisting capitalist coercion of any sort. "Never work" was Debord's most famous slogan. Their proclaimed method was to construct "situations" in which the true relations between people and social structures could be revealed, and the genuine desires of humans be fulfilled.

The key tool for creating such situations, and acquiring psychogeographic knowledge in the process, is *le dérive*, "the drift." Designed to fight the monotony of the postwar city, the drift is, according to Debord, "a technique of rapid passage through varied ambiances." It's an unplanned, open-ended wander in which small groups of participants forget their social roles, and "let themselves be drawn by the attractions of the terrain and the encounters they find there." Whereas the Surrealists focused on the unconscious forces that drove people from within, Debord and the Situationists sought to locate liberating impulses in the vibrations exuded by certain neighborhoods.

The Naked City, perhaps the best-known visual artifact of the movement, shows a walking figure collaged together from directional arrows and nineteen cut-up pieces of a Paris map. Assembled by Debord and Danish artist Asger Jorn, it strides

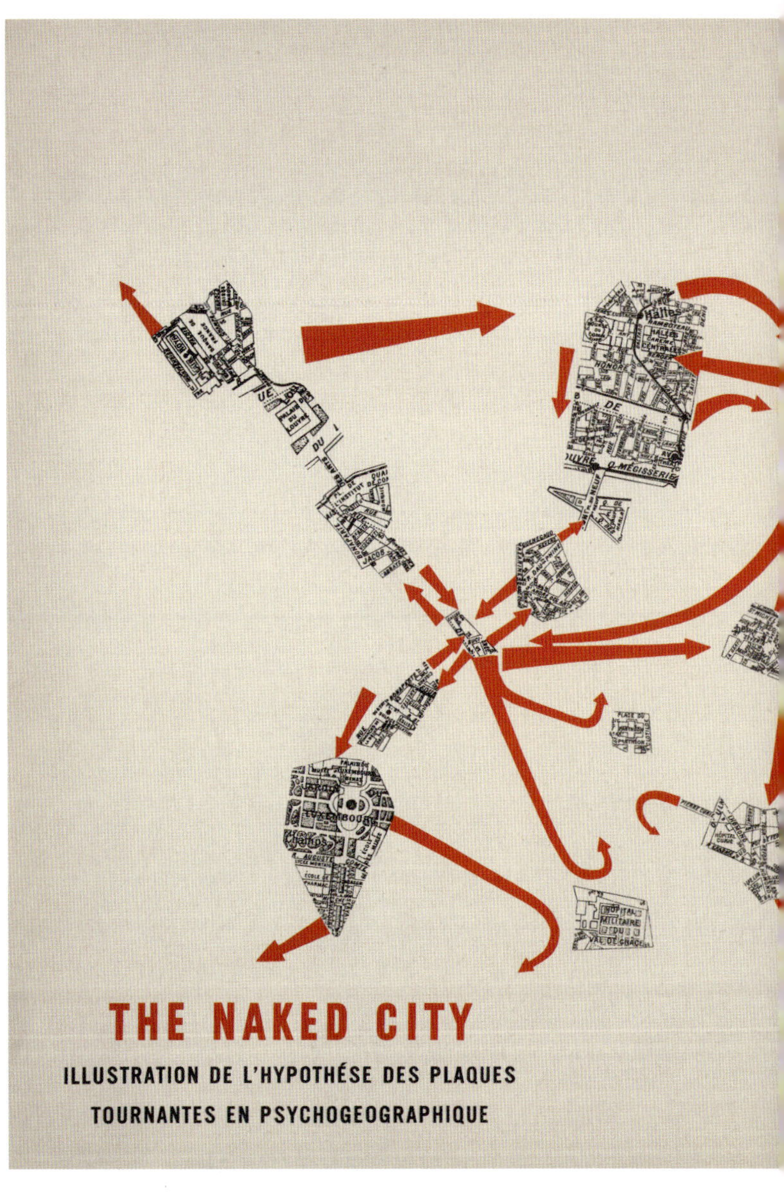

like a Duchampian nude, a leglike vector extended to the left, another straight down, and a flutter of garments streaming off behind, to the right. The collage embodies both vibrant psychogeographical nodes (the mapped areas) and energy transfers (the red arrows) that can propel drifters into other luminous zones—perhaps by taxi, to save time. With a title taken from the film by Jules Dassin (1948), itself borrowed from Weegee's book of photographs of New York (1945), the collage proposes itself as a transmedia drift, stripping the city bare of its socioeconomic

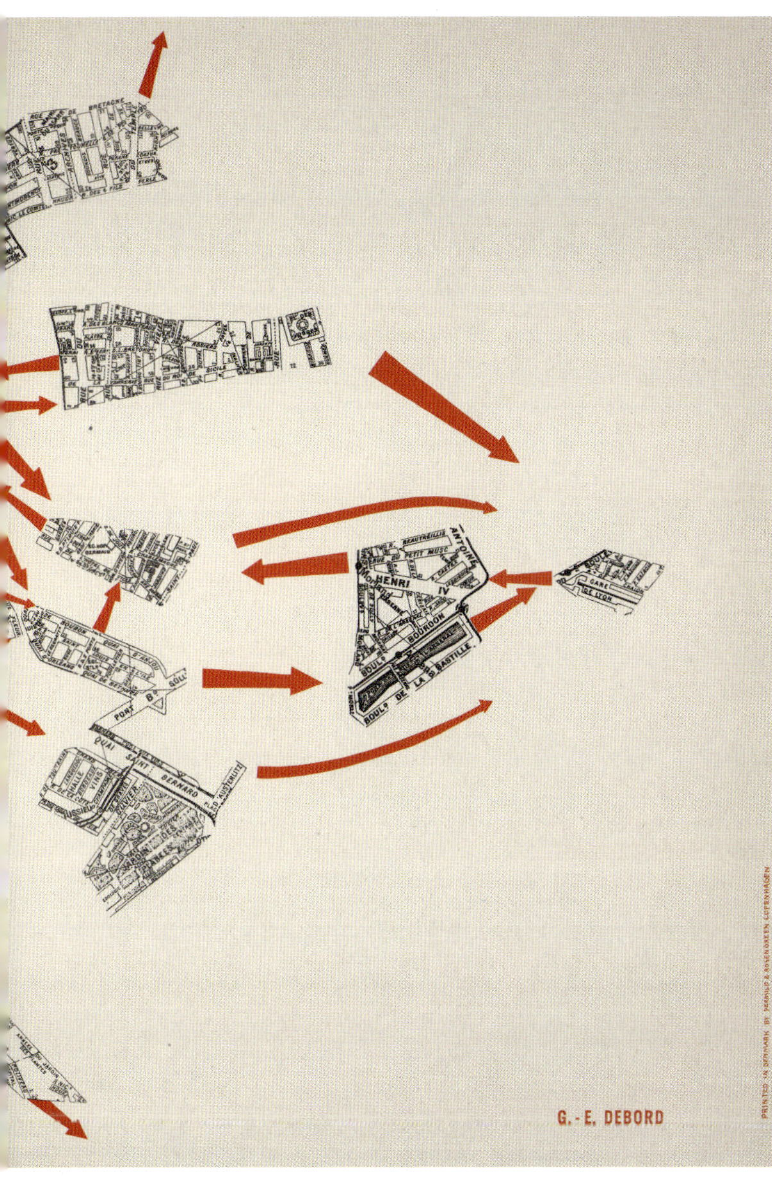

Guy E. Debord and Asger Jorn, *The Naked City*, 1957

relations to reveal where its true self lies. But if one looks closely at the maps, the exposed flesh of Paris turns out not to be so shocking after all. It beckons seductively from the Luxembourg Gardens, the rue de Seine, the boulevard Saint-Germain, and other walk-friendly sites, places perennially haunted by locals and tourists alike.

169

A Downward Spiral

It's a walk like no other in a space like no other, in a building expressly designed for the purpose. Standing out against the rectilinear constructions that surround it, the curved forms of the Solomon R. Guggenheim Museum in New York seem to have emerged from the organic wonders across the street in Central Park. Once inside, visitors cross a ninety-six-foot-high atrium beneath a glass dome to take an elevator to the sixth-story level. Then they slowly descend a continuous, gently sloping quarter-mile-long ramp, one "floor" flowing into the next, admiring master-pieces of abstract art along the way.

Imagined as a "Temple of Spirit" by its first director, Hilla von Rebay, the Guggenheim changed the concept of museums forever when it opened in 1959. Henceforth they would aspire to become artworks in themselves, engaged in dynamic relation to the objects they housed. Asking America's foremost architect to design a home for what was originally the "Museum of Non-Objective Painting," featuring works by Marc Chagall, Wassily Kandinsky, and Piet Mondrian, Rebay told Frank Lloyd Wright that he alone could "test the possibilities" for a new kind of space worthy of these bold creations.

In response, Wright created an "inverted ziggurat." Rather than climb a stepped monument like a Mesopotamian high priest, the museum visitor could worship at the altar of modern art in modern comfort. Wright wanted, he said, to "let the elevator do the lifting so the visitor could do the drifting." But if Wright echoed the Situationist psychogeographers in Paris, his "drift" was tightly scripted by the width of the ramp and the architect's own ideas about how paintings should be experienced. Wright envisioned them not formally mounted but leaning against the outward-tilting wall, to be better lit by natural light from above. For visual variety along the way, visitors could look across the atrium to see both where they had been and where they were going, possibly interacting with people on other levels. Once the downward journey was completed in the lobby, art lovers were now in a position to admire the ultimate oeuvre on display, the building itself. Never one to slight his own accomplishments, Wright claimed that "the building and the painting [are] an uninterrupted, beautiful symphony such as never existed in the World of Art before."

Controversy erupted even before the museum opened. Artists denounced the way works would be displayed, comparing the downward-spiraling ramp to the circles of Dante's Inferno. Cynics saw only utilitarian engineering, designed to move people through as if on a conveyor belt. On the ramp itself, some visitors were discomfited by the absence of any level spot on which to rest their feet or eyes.

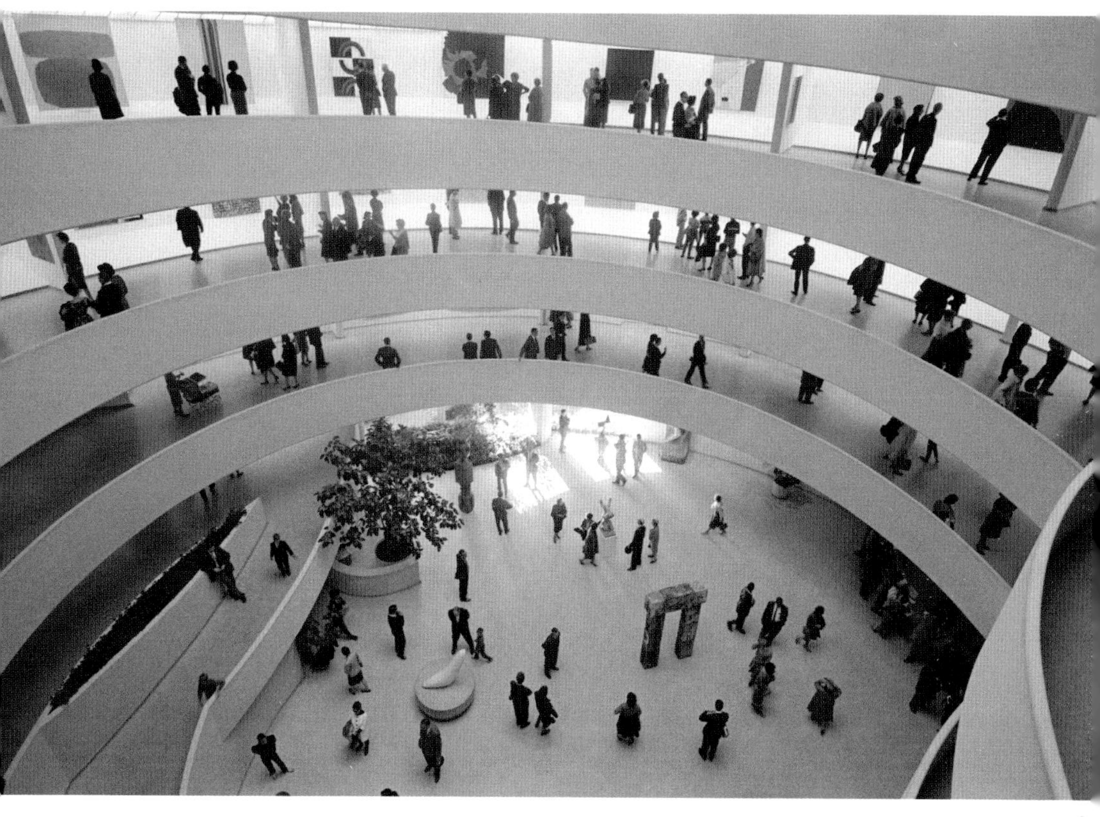

Ernst Hass, *The Spiral Interior of the Solomon R. Guggenheim Museum in New York, Designed by Frank Lloyd Wright*, 1961

Yet on a fundamental pedestrian plane, the building succeeded in its conquest of a pervasive malady, "museum fatigue." First identified more than a century ago by Benjamin Gilman in the *Scientific Monthly*, this peculiar condition saps the mental and physical strength of even the strongest visitor to an exhibition space. Gilman identified poor placement of displays as the major culprit. But Wright blamed the very walls and floors, for forcing visitors to drag themselves back through the entire museum to get out the door. By having visitors to the Guggenheim descend through it, Wright put gravity and the no-detour ramp into the service of his Dantesque mission: spiritual elevation via a circular, guided descent.

The Shopping Mall

Beginning in the 1950s, two very different ideologies pushed back against a common enemy: cars. In semi-socialist Europe, authorities created the pedestrians-only street, reclaiming historic city centers in a way that united tourism and shopping in a strollable environment. The biggest success came in Denmark. In 1962 Copenhagen pedestrianized—a new word—its central shopping street, Strøget, against loud outcries from the commercial and automotive sectors. It was not the first major pedestrian zone in Europe (Lijnbaan in Rotterdam claimed that honor in 1953), but it quickly became the most famous. Attracting tens of thousands of people daily, it spawned imitations across the globe. Britain, for example, boasted over thirteen hundred shopping streets by 1980.

Half-hearted American imitations, however, did not succeed. Although the trend started early (in Kalamazoo, Michigan, in 1959), by the year 2000 about 90 percent of the two hundred converted streets had returned to conventional mixed use. Beyond American car dependency, one key factor doomed the walk-friendly downtown: its mortal enemy, the indoor shopping mall. Downtowns died as free-market capitalism enabled developers to create a privatized version of civic space, a sheltered shopping cluster where the walker's role as consumer would not be disrupted by bad weather, socioeconomic diversity, or political activity.

Although it has become the quintessential image of suburban car culture, the mall was conceived by a transplanted European who loved to walk. In 1956 Austrian immigrant Victor Gruen opened the Southdale Center in Edina, Minnesota. It contained ten acres of shops, the equivalent of seven New York City blocks, nestled in seventy acres of parking. Inspired by the concentration of culture and commerce in downtown Vienna, Gruen did not so much emulate a city center as seek to reseed it in new soil. This early photograph shows the mall functioning as Gruen intended, gathering families and friends for informal socializing amid sculptures, murals, gardens, fountains, and long, open promenades that he hoped would form the basis of new city centers. The promenades would invisibly encourage healthy walking from the distant parking surrounding his indoor mecca.

As malls developed, however, designers found ways to keep people closer to their cars while separating them more efficiently from their money. Artfully located anchor stores enticed shoppers past an array of smaller boutiques, activating what designers ironically called "the Gruen transfer." The sheer dazzle of the mall so disoriented customers that they forgot what they came for; their buying became impulsive. Amassing all the psychogeographical lures a street could offer, mall planners co-opted Guy Debord's anticapitalist "drift." They channeled indoor

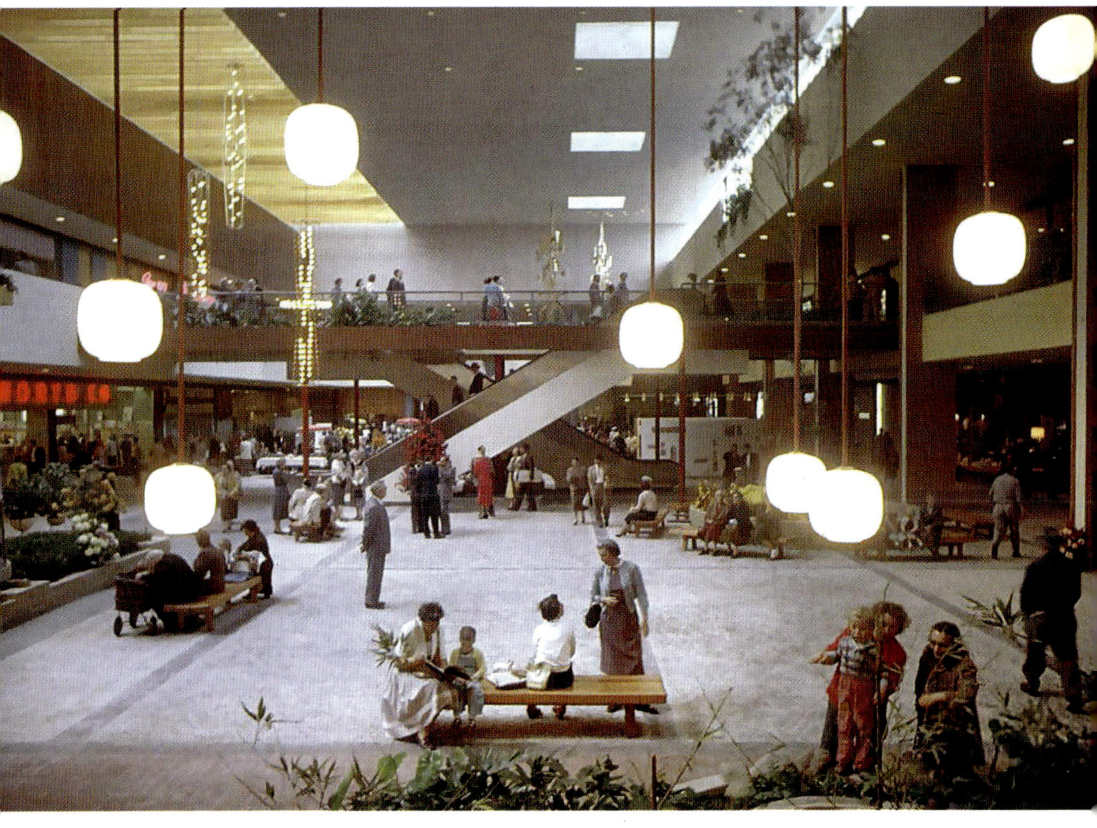

The Southdale Center, Edina, Minnesota, 1956

wanderers toward new forms of reckless consumption, divorced from both need and status.

In a further irony, Gruen's vision of a community-oriented space has been partially realized after all. Overbuilding, recessions, and social changes have added "dead malls" to the American vocabulary, making mixed use essential to malls that want to survive. Enter "mall walkers," who now circulate most mornings, before the stores open, in America's one thousand malls. What but a mall provides a free, safe, flat, climate-controlled space where older people can walk for miles within easy reach of benches and restrooms? Today indoor malls are the second most popular place for Americans to walk, after their own immediate neighborhoods. They come for their health but stay for the company, charting their mileage and spending almost nothing.

Walking on Celluloid

Film captures walking as no other artistic medium can. In an instant a camera can shift from viewing the walker's body moving through space to showing that space as if seen through the walker's eyes. The sight of the walker, in a double sense, offers clues to what the walker thinks, feels, and intends. If a scene employs voice-over, the walk can appear to reveal both mind and body, step by step.

But most films are not documentaries. The walk is never the whole story. It's tied to a plot and to the artistic vision of the director, conveying to the audience how motion in space overlaps with a psychological and narrative journey. When Tony Manero struts down the sidewalks of Brooklyn in time to the Bee Gees' disco music in the opening credits to *Saturday Night Fever* (1977), the shots of his flashy

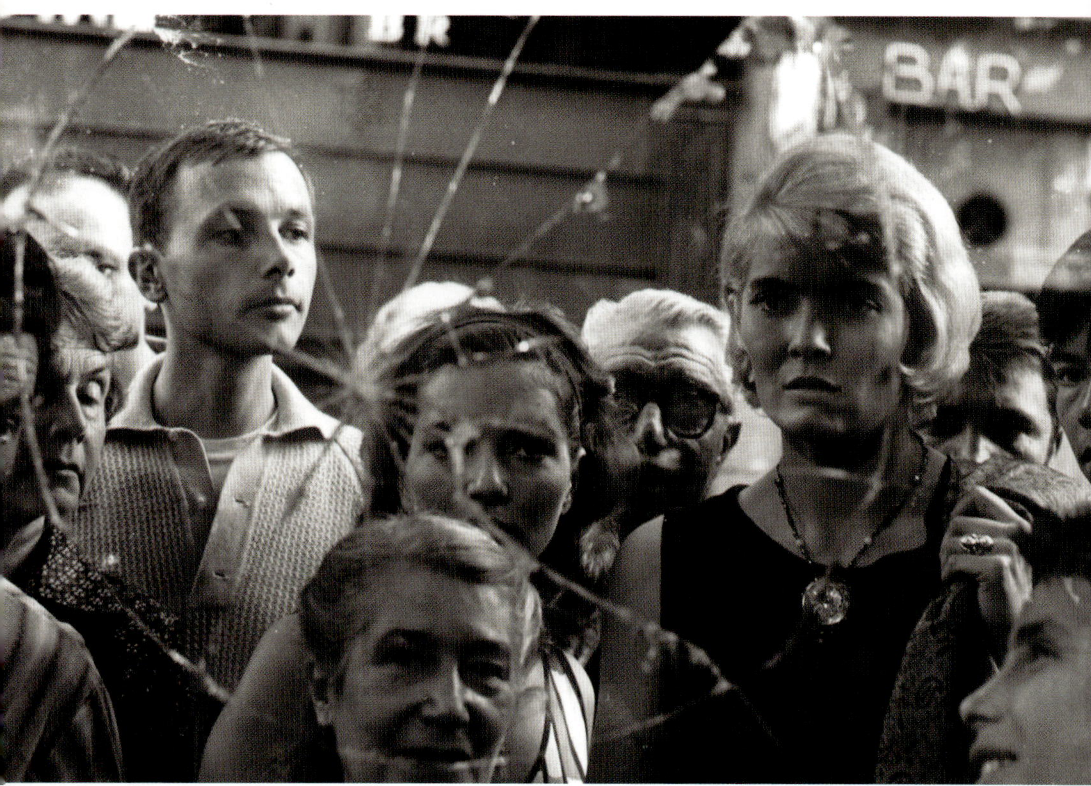

Film still from Agnès Varda, director, *Cléo from 5 to 7*, 1962

shoes and swinging shoulders coincide with the lyrics to spell out his ambition: to strut so that women will notice him. But rapidly the walk reveals the narrative tension driving the action, as it prompts viewers to ask: Where is this person really going? He flirts with sexy women without results; he carries a paint can as part of his dead-end job; he can't yet afford the shirt he wants to wear on Saturday night.

The celebrated ending of *The Third Man* (1949) works the other way around, not opening up possibilities but killing them off. Often called the greatest movie conclusion of all time, it takes place over the course of two long minutes as Anna Schmidt walks from the grave of the title character, her lover Harry Lime. The film uses every trick in the German Expressionist playbook, especially off-kilter Dutch angle shots. But for the final scene director Carol Reed planted the camera squarely in the middle of a leaf-strewn cemetery alley. In an unbroken shot, it records the figure of Anna emerging as a dot on the horizon and walking steadily from the vanishing point. Waiting by the side of the road is the man who unwillingly killed Harry Lime, his former best friend Holly Martins. Martins thinks he can save Anna from herself—and for himself. But he has it all wrong. As she approaches, Anna never looks at him or even slows down. While the zither music twangs regretfully, she walks right past the camera and out of his life.

Most movie walks take place somewhere toward the middle of the film. Typically they advance or frustrate romance, amplify the drama of pursuit or escape, and build tension as opponents march toward confrontation, whether it is a battle for world domination or a showdown at high noon. Exceptionally, however, a walk itself can transform a character. The French New Wave classic *Cléo from 5 to 7* (1962) may well be cinema's most sophisticated presentation of what walking can do psychologically. The director Agnès Varda matches up filmed time and viewing time so closely that each frame becomes a step on Cléo's journey. Cléo is a pop singer, distraught that no one will take her potential cancer diagnosis seriously. At the midpoint in the film, she slips away from her entourage and from then on never stops moving. Prowling the Left Bank, she sheds her own objectified image, yielding to the city's flux. She becomes the camera, seeing herself, seeing for herself, internalizing strange faces, encountering broken mirrors, discovering that she is just one fragment in a city of fragments. By the time she gets her diagnosis at 7:00 p.m. (cancer, maybe curable), she has opened herself to love. She has potentially saved her life by surrendering to a tantalizingly indifferent city, a Paris that welcomes her into its vibrant anonymity.

One Heroic Step

Modern portrayals of children walking often suggest, with humor and affection, the innocent exploration of a wondrous world. From an adult perspective the child's steps convey a joyful sense of discovery that will be hard to recapture in later life. But as the present book shows, an important subset of images depicts children confronting harsh realities that many adults have not experienced. Having no other choice, the children deal with poverty, dangerous labor, crippling disease, the ravages of war, or the hostility of prejudice.

On November 14, 1960, a six-year-old girl named Ruby Bridges was escorted by US marshals past an angry crowd to the William Franz Elementary School in New Orleans, where she would attend first grade. She was one of four African American children who integrated New Orleans schools that day, but the other three—Leona Tate, Tessie Prevost, and Gail Etienne—were conducted together to a school in another part of the city. These perilous walks were a much-delayed response to the 1954 *Brown v. Board of Education* decision declaring that the doctrine of "separate but equal" schools was unconstitutional. Bolstered by the Civil Rights Act of 1960, signed into law a few months earlier, activists now sought desegregation in New Orleans. Keeping her composure in the face of enormous hostility, Bridges, her name unknown at the time, received widespread media attention as the anonymous "little Negro girl" who braved the howling mob outside the school.

Norman Rockwell was an unlikely candidate to produce what would become one of the best-known paintings of the civil rights movement. For decades his covers for the *Saturday Evening Post* had illustrated the homey virtues of the white middle class, a clean-cut vision whose subtle details rarely challenged the overall sentimental effect. But Rockwell was changing with the times. He left the *Post* and joined the politically progressive *Look* magazine, proposing to treat Bridges's courageous walk for his first cover. He chose seven-year-old Lynda Gunn, granddaughter of a Stockbridge friend, as his model. Then he got actual marshals to pose as the escorts, while Gunn put her feet up on blocks to hold the walking pose.

Going to work in his usual painstaking way, Rockwell sought out details that would tell Bridges's story in one concise image. He darkened her skin to match Bridges's and create the strong black/white contrast that anchors the painting. A splattered red tomato evokes the hostile crowd outside the frame, as does the racial slur scrawled on the wall above it. The white of the court order poking out of the foremost marshal's pocket echoes the white of the girl's dress, specially sewn by Gunn's grandmother. Pictured headless, their right fists clenched, the grown men represent the abstract might of federal law, while the little girl with her book and

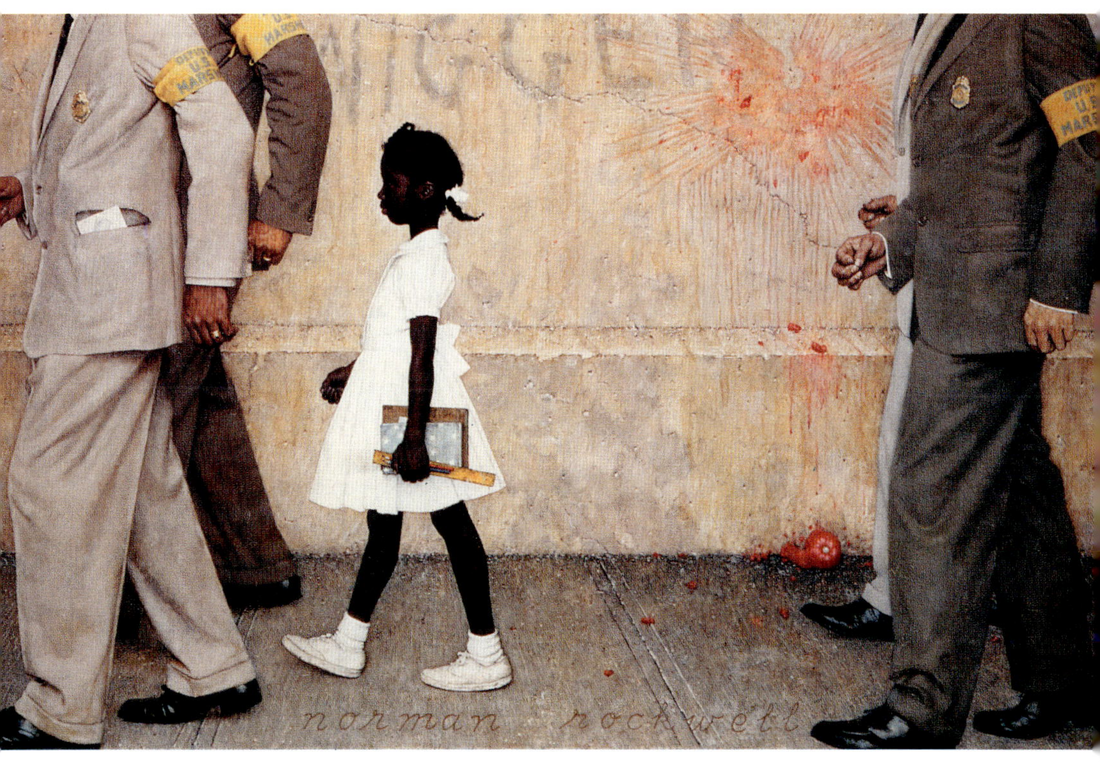

Norman Rockwell, *The Problem We All Live With*, 1963

ruler ("the rule of law") is the particular, carefully individualized person that the law defends. She walks in the "forward" part of the picture, a literal figure of progress. The double line between sections of the sidewalk literalizes the color line, a racial barrier she has just crossed.

Triumphal March

Peaceful, violent, turbulent, triumphant: few social actions in history have accomplished so much as the Selma to Montgomery march. In 1965, protestors led by Dr. Martin Luther King Jr., John Lewis, and other strategists from a coalition of civil rights groups made three attempts to walk the fifty-four miles from Selma, Alabama, to the state capitol at Montgomery. They were demanding voting rights for Black Americans. Despite the passage of the Civil Rights Act the previous year, of the fifteen thousand eligible Black citizens in the county where Selma was located, fewer than two hundred had been able to register to vote. Efforts at registration had been met by physical intimidation, arrests, beatings, and the murder of both Black and white organizers. On "Bloody Sunday," March 7, an unarmed group of five hundred marchers was attacked by club-wielding state police at Edmund Pettus Bridge in Selma. Photographs of the violence, and especially of a local organizer, Amelia Boynton, beaten unconscious, shocked the country and the world.

On March 9, "Turnaround Tuesday," the group, its numbers swelled by clergy of many denominations and religions, succeeded this time in crossing the bridge. But obeying a court order and fearing a police trap, they returned to Selma, where they demanded federal protection. Within two weeks President Lyndon Johnson provided a National Guard escort that enabled the protestors, their numbers now in the thousands, to walk to the state capitol over the course of five days, March 21 to 25. On the final day, twenty-five thousand people arrived at the capitol steps to hear King deliver his "How Long? Not Long!" speech.

King was right: within five months Congress passed the Voting Rights Act, which the president had proposed to Congress on national television between the second and third march. Making clear the link between the quest for justice and the spiritual force that propels pilgrimages, Rabbi Abraham Joshua Heschel said: "For many of us the march from Selma to Montgomery was about protest and prayer. Legs are not lips and walking is not kneeling. And yet our legs uttered songs. Even without words, our march was worship. I felt my legs were praying."

James Karales, on assignment from *Look* magazine, took this now-classic photo on the third march, capturing a triple momentum. The figures at the forefront, three of them stepping in perfect unison, dynamically convey the resolution of the marchers. The surging wedge shape of the mixed-race crowd, stretching off into the far distance, shows how the movement had grown in the face of formidable obstacles. And the way the protesters charge forward between the threatening clouds overhead and the dark earth below, American flag waving under the darkest cloud, tells the viewer that history is being made here. The abstract quality of future freedom has been made actual beneath this gathering storm, a storm of

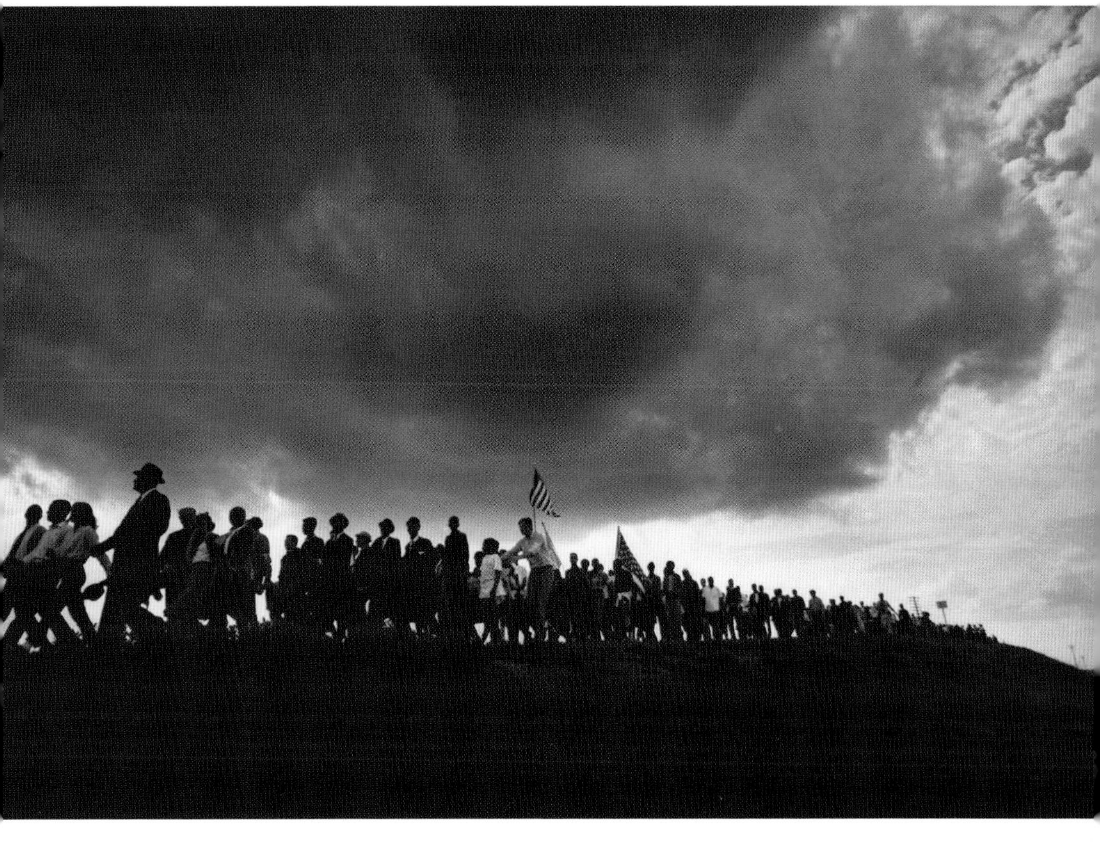

James Karales, *Selma to Montgomery March, Alabama*, 1965

protest undaunted by physical peril and driven by the belief in rights that must not be denied. The low camera angle that Karales chose emphasizes the heroic quality of the marchers' quest. Their itinerary was later designated a National Historic Trail, but the photo enshrined them first. Viewers look up to them as if they were already mounted on the pedestal that future generations would grant them, already a monument to their own monumental struggle.

Walking into Art

Can a walk be a work of art? In the 1960s a confluence of developments in sculpture, Land Art, performance art, and conceptual art culminated in this provocative idea. Antecedents can be found in the Surrealist excursions of the 1920s or the Situationist drifts of the 1950s, or even, stretching it a bit, in the *flânerie* of nineteenth-century Parisians. But in declaring that the walk itself was an artistic act, a new generation of creative walkers found meaning in evanescent gestures that sought to rewrite the very definition of art. The first steps were taken in Japan by Akira Kanayama. His work *Ashiato*, or "Footsteps" (1956), placed stenciled footprints on long pieces of paper that stretched for yards over the ground, as well as up trees and walls. In 1960 the Dutch conceptual artist Stanley Brouwn declared that all shoe shops in Amsterdam constituted an exhibition of his work, while in a group of works two years later he simply named actions: "a walk through a grass field" or "a walk from a to b." Moving toward performance, Yoko Ono gave instructions in her *City Piece* (1961): "Walk all over the city with an empty baby carriage." The sculptor Carl Andre was another pioneer, dispensing with pedestals and setting his materials flat on the ground, requiring the viewer to move along the path they made. "My idea of a piece of sculpture is a road," he said. "We don't have a single point of view for a road at all, except a moving one, moving along it."

The simmering interest in walking coalesced in 1967 around one dramatically simple work, represented by a single black-and-white photograph: Richard Long's *A Line Made by Walking*. Following the logic of Marcel Duchamp's Readymades—it's art because I say so—Long walked, unwitnessed, across a grassy field in southern England, bending the vegetation enough to "draw" a line or path in it. Unlike most people who have done something similar, Long photographed his creation and declared it a work of art. Transforming conceptual art into a physical action that only briefly reshaped the natural world, Long subverted the immense, ecologically insensitive scale of American Land Art, in which artists like Robert Smithson and Michael Heizer used huge machines to move tons of stone to permanently alter the landscape.

Long's modest gesture proved monumental in a different sense. He refused to accept that art required making a tangible object—or even a visible action, since no one watched the walk that made the line. While the meaning of Long's work might be "traditional" in that it represents the human passage through the world, the implications of the gesture are far-reaching. The following year, in *A Ten Mile Walk, England* (1968), Long walked in a straight line across rugged, trackless terrain on Exmoor. He discovered that he could dematerialize sculpture while at the same time extending its scale, according to the length of the walk he took.

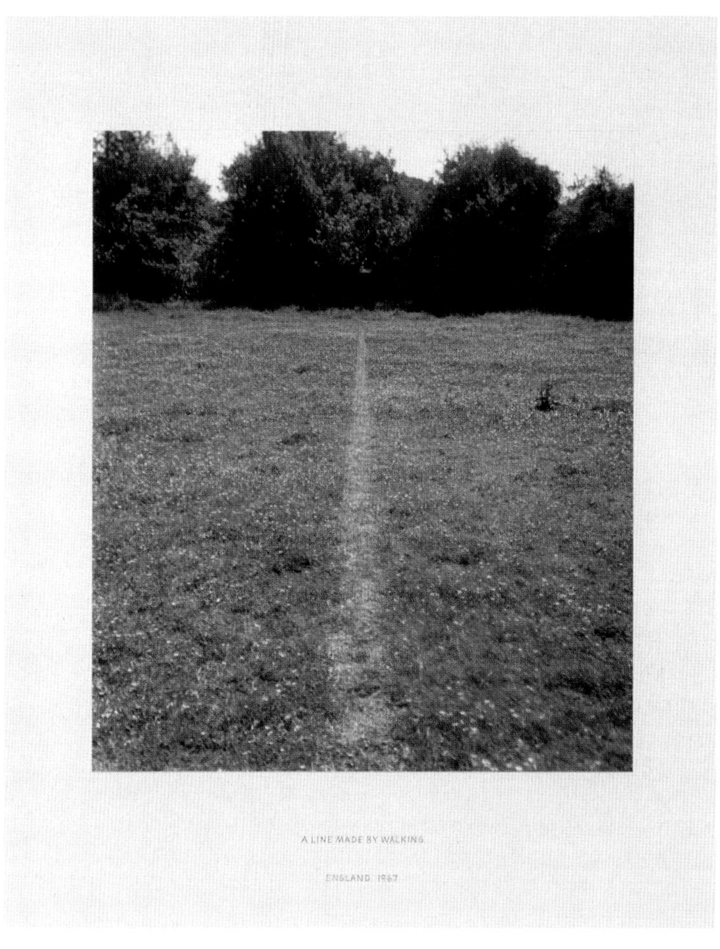

Richard Long, *A Line Made by Walking*, 1967

Where exactly is the art? Perhaps in the prior intention (since each walk is concept-driven); in the walk itself (rarely witnessed by anyone); in the material effect produced by the walk on the landscape; in the photograph of that effect; or maybe in all of the above. Does the document or relic of a walk (a title, a map, a "text-work") constitute necessary proof of an experience inaccessible to a subsequent audience? Or is the unwitnessed act sufficient? Long's friend and fellow walking artist Hamish Fulton insists on the primal value of the action, claiming "no walk, no work." For Fulton, "an object cannot compete with an experience." But Long is more evasive, pacing out lines of thought that become objects of profound contemplation. "My intention was to make a new art which was also a new way of walking: walking as art."

Silly Walks

Anyone who has hiked a trail has followed—and helped to construct—"a line made by walking." This fundamental fact is one of the things that makes Richard Long's work so accessibly profound. But in the later 1960s, the performance aspect of art walking also came to the fore. Strenuous, bizarre, violent, comic, or curious, performed art walks drew attention to the way in which an everyday action could be defamiliarized, reshaped, and proposed to the public as an activity with symbolic resonance, an art based on process rather than product. Bruce Nauman led the way with works both minimalist and gymnastic. He pushed the language of walking into new paths, in hour-long, convention-breaking videos that had no narrative, only a subject: himself. He realized, he said, that "if I was an artist and I was in the studio, then whatever I was doing in the studio must be art. At this point art became more of an activity and less of a product." For the restless artist, the most basic activity would suffice: "pacing around, for example."

Nauman performed *Slow Angle Walk (Beckett Walk)* in front of a camera set on its side, so that his horizontal and vertical postures were reversed. He moved in a slow, demanding, ultimately mesmerizing manner, with his hands clasped behind his back. Evoking the absurd motions of Samuel Beckett's title character from *Molloy* (1951), he lifted a leg forward at a right angle to the ground and held the pose for up to ten seconds. Then he pivoted forty-five degrees and plunged forward, coming to rest standing on that leg. The other leg extended back behind him at a new right angle, for another ten seconds. Finally, he brought the rear leg forward and repeated the whole process. Depending on where his body moved, film viewers saw him at a distance, close up, whole, piecemeal, or completely absent from the frame while his footsteps echoed.

Not long afterward, John Cleese of *Monty Python's Flying Circus* transferred the outlandish deadpan futility of Nauman's studio work into the public sphere, in his "Ministry of Silly Walks" sketch. Comic walking has enlivened dramatic art since ancient times, but Cleese and his troupe made it the central element of their satire, using exaggerated steps and wiggles of the feet to mock British nationalism, government waste, and compulsive international competition. Cleese's walk, his legs alternately kicked high and corkscrewing while he rigidly controlled his briefcase and civil-servant demeanor, quickly acquired the status of a national icon.

Today as thoroughly identified with the British government as John Bull, Cleese's bowler-hatted bureaucrat was depicted walking stiff-legged off a cliff in the wake of the Brexit vote in 2016. In recent years fans have created "silly walks" zones, often with video cameras to record the contortions, on sidewalks and street

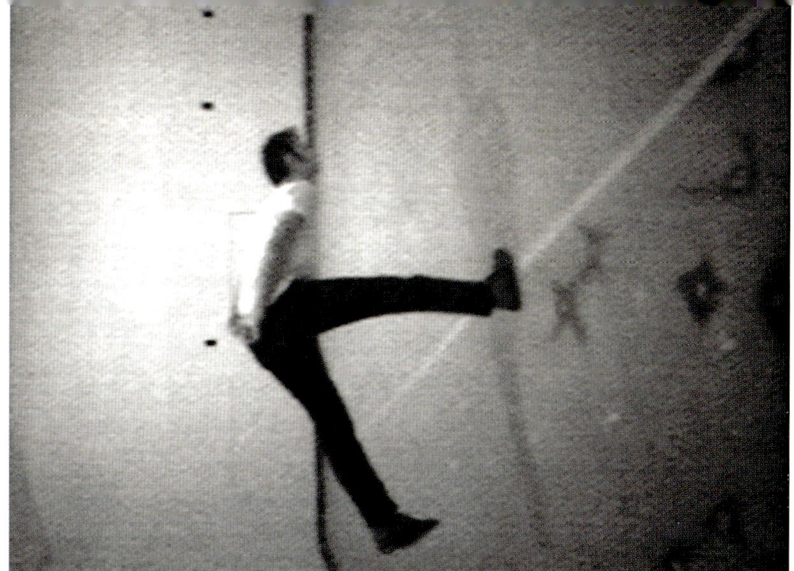

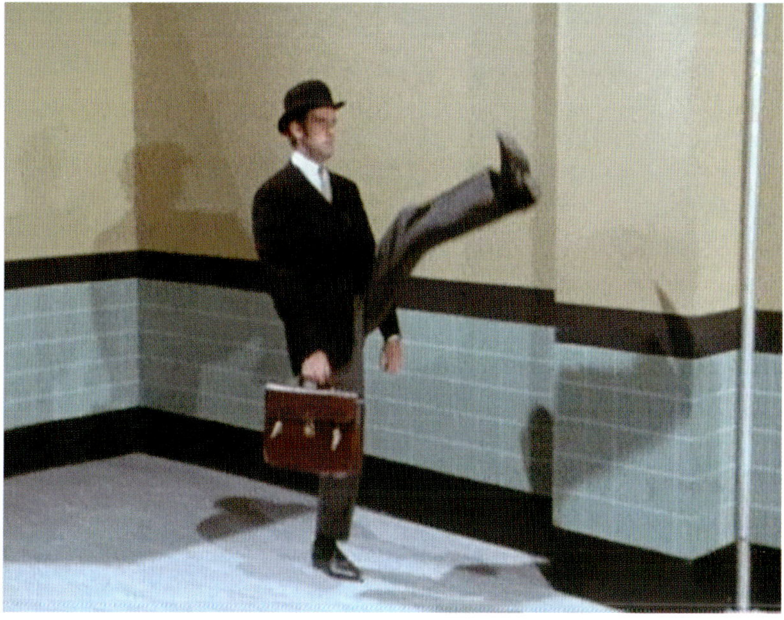

Bruce Nauman, *Slow Angle Walk (Beckett Walk)*, 1968

John Cleese, "The Ministry of Silly Walks," *Monty Python's Flying Circus*, 1970

crossings all over Europe and North America. Is a filmed, serious-looking art-walk different in essence from a filmed, straight-faced comic walk? The answer may depend on how much time a viewer is willing to spend analyzing it, enjoying it, or imitating it.

One Small Step for a Man

Probably the most famous footstep in human history took place on July 20, 1969—although not on Earth. Commander Neil Armstrong descended the ladder of the Apollo 11 lunar module, the *Eagle*, and as his boot touched the powdery lunar surface, he said, "That's one small step for [a] man, one giant leap for mankind." The photo opposite, taken by Armstrong, shows *Eagle* pilot Buzz Aldrin descending to the lunar surface eighteen minutes later, his worldly legs as alien to this landscape as the landing craft he will step away from. His cumbersome white spacesuit and oxygen pack stand out against the black of the airless sky and the gold thermal foil on the descent stage of the module. As if to symbolize this dangerous journey into the unknown, he steps down into the dark shadow cast by the lander. Yet what may be most remarkable about the moment is that there is already a human there to greet him.

That day, Armstrong and Aldrin spent two hours moving across the moon's Sea of Tranquility, a dusty plain pockmarked by eons of meteorite impacts. "Magnificent desolation," Aldrin called it. Bounding, loping, hopping, and mostly walking in one-sixth of the earth's gravity, they had little trouble maintaining balance, although they did have to plan several steps ahead just where they would stop. They took pictures, set up an American flag, and roamed around collecting rock samples. At the farthest point in their exploration, Armstrong traveled about two hundred feet from the lander to inspect a crater.

Together they walked over three thousand feet, collecting forty-seven pounds of rock, soil, and dust. Prepared by years of training and protected by equipment affording warmth and oxygen, they demonstrated that the bipedal form of locomotion that had evolved on Earth over millions of years could be effectively adapted to activity on another celestial body. Humans had already "walked" in space during the 1960s, but the much-repeated phrase, "first to *walk* on the moon," shows how crucial to the achievement is the underlying idea that humans make a place their own though the simple act of pacing across it.

Unlike conscientious hikers, the astronauts left behind more than footprints. They tossed overboard a camera, their life-support backpacks, and almost a hundred other items, to lighten their load for takeoff. But it would be the footprints rather than the litter that prompted questions back on Earth.

In the 1970s, conspiracy theorists began to claim that the moon landings (six in total, from 1969 to 1972) were a hoax, filmed in a secret movie studio by Stanley Kubrick as part of an American government propaganda program. The Armstrong/Aldrin moonwalk photos seemed to contain inconsistencies, starting with the question of who was on the moon to film Armstrong's historic step? (It was an external

TV camera, mounted on the landing craft by Armstrong himself before descending, that sent out the images watched by 600 million people.) Why do the lunar footprints have treads, while Armstrong's spacesuit preserved at the Smithsonian Air and Space Museum features smooth shoes? (He wore treaded overshoes during his walk and left them behind on the moon). How could Armstrong take a picture of his footprint before he had made it? (It was Aldrin's footprint, captured at a later moment). Many people worldwide believe the hoax theory is credible, indicating that fifty years on, the moon walks are still testaments to human ingenuity.

With the confirmation in 2020 that water exists on the moon, the science-fiction dream of establishing a lunar base now seems plausible. And if future colonists find themselves in need of some healthy diversion, a classic recreation awaits. "It's absolutely no trouble to walk around," Armstrong reported. "It's an interesting place to be. I recommend it."

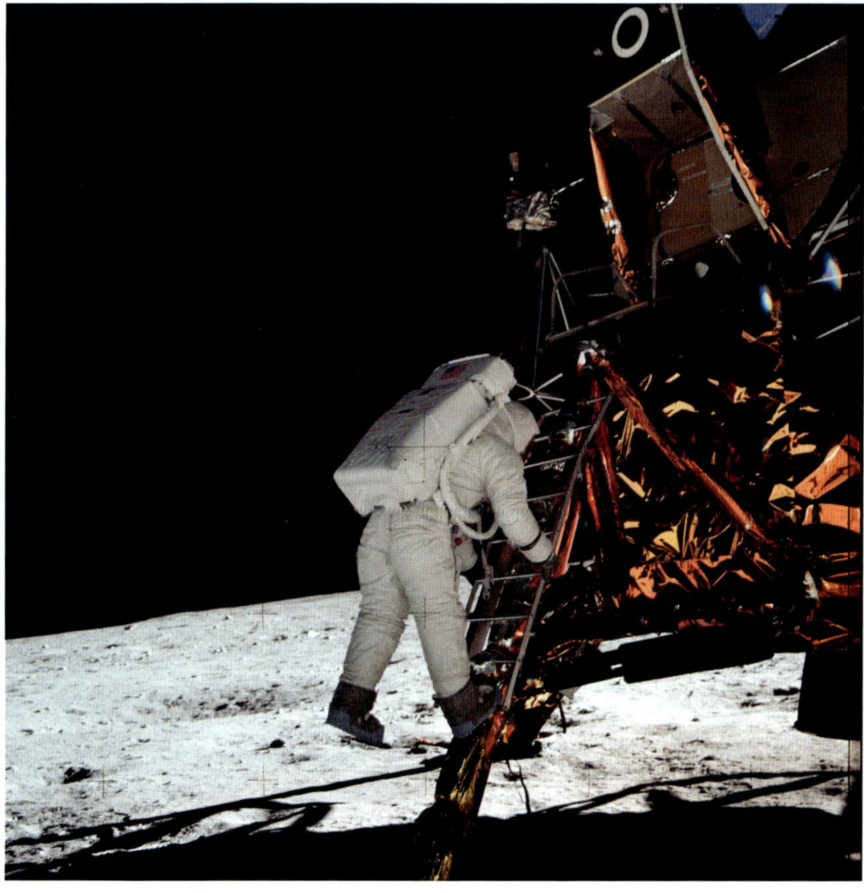

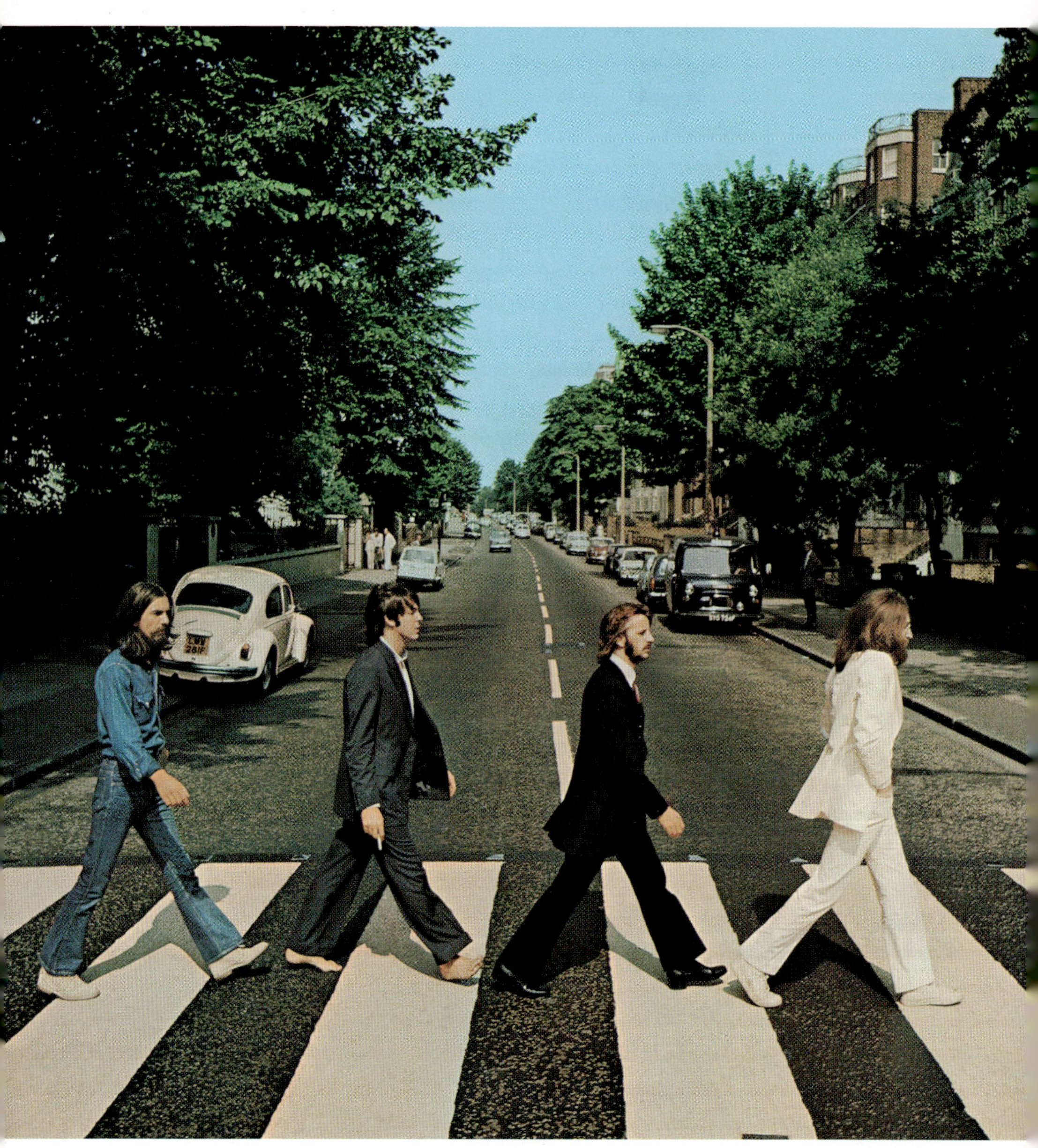

Iain Macmillan, album cover photo for the Beatles' *Abbey Road*, 1969

Crossing into History

With the exception of the travelers on the Yellow Brick Road, no group of walkers has achieved the pictorial fame of the Beatles crossing Abbey Road. The idea was Paul McCartney's, including the walking sequence: John, Ringo, Paul, and George. On August 8, 1969, around 11:30 in the morning, a policeman held up traffic outside the EMI studios in London, where the Fab Four were recording. The Scottish photographer Iain Macmillan mounted a stepladder and gave the signal. It took three back-and-forth traverses to get all the Beatles in full stride, perfectly centered, and without distracting traffic in the background. All but George (in denim) wear suits designed by the Savile Row tailor Tommy Nutter. McCartney selected Macmillan's fifth shot to be the cover for the album *Abbey Road*, the title appearing only in Macmillan's later photograph of the street sign itself. The album bore no band name. Given that the Beatles were, in John Lennon's notorious estimate, "more popular than Jesus," it seemed unnecessary.

The album slowly gained recognition as one of the greatest ever made, but the cover became instantly famous. Not only was the setup endlessly copied and parodied, but elements within the photo were minutely scrutinized, thanks to the "Paul is dead" rumor that began to circulate when the album was released. Supposedly, George was dressed as a gravedigger; Paul, barefoot and out of step, was the corpse; Ringo in black was the undertaker; and John in white represented either religion or death. The Volkswagen behind George bears an intriguing "28IF" license plate (Paul would have been 28 if he had lived, according to the theory). The car now graces a museum in Germany, while in 2010 the crossing itself gained English Heritage status as a site of historical importance.

Why is the image so catchy? Unlike other rock albums of the era, *Abbey Road* depicts the musicians actively doing something prosaic yet symbolic. On a visual level, the energetic horizontal motion of four of the most famous people in the world, "on the move" to further greatness, is played against the strong perspective lines of roadside curbs, street markings, parked cars, and trees as they recede toward a central vanishing point. The perspective is further reinforced by the thick white dashes of the zebra crossing, a pedestrian safety feature that many non-British Beatles fans saw for the first time here. Introduced in 1951, the distinctive black-and-white pavement markings (echoed in the photo by the Beatles' suits) require motorists to give way to pedestrians. On this crossing, one cannot see where the Beatles are coming from or going to, but the viewer is obliged to stop and take notice. Only two weeks later, the Beatles recorded together for the last time, in the studio behind them on the cover. They would not pass this way again.

Walking on Air

Few walks have been as daringly conceived as Philippe Petit's audacious tightrope stroll between the Twin Towers of New York's World Trade Center. At seven in the morning of August 7, 1974, denizens of lower Manhattan looked up to see a miniscule Petit step out onto a two-hundred-foot cable, suspended a quarter mile above their heads. For the next forty-five minutes Petit paraded back and forth, crossing the 138-foot void eight times. Carrying a specially designed pole to help him balance, he walked, danced, knelt, and even lay down on the wire, teasing the police who soon gathered at either end of his path. Alan Welner's photograph catches a moment when Petit seems to bestride the spire of 70 Pine Street, once the world's third-tallest building, but now, at a mere 67 stories, dwarfed by the 110-story Twin Towers.

Petit was just twenty-three when he took his walk, but he had been eyeing the site for six years, since he had first seen architectural models in a magazine. "They called me," he later said of the towers; "I didn't choose them." Painstakingly training himself for what has been called "the artistic crime of the century," in June 1971 Petit promenaded across a wire strung between the two towers of Notre Dame Cathedral in Paris, juggling as he went. In 1973 he walked a cable stretched between the north pylons of the Sydney Harbour Bridge in Australia.

Recognizing the huge technical challenge he had set himself, Petit visited New York repeatedly, scrutinizing every aspect of the buildings. He flew over the towers in a helicopter and studied how they swayed in different weathers. He made scale models to practice his moves. Since the towers were still unfinished, he and his helpers posed as construction workers to gain access to the site, to find anchor points for the tightrope, and to secretly stow their gear just a few steps beneath the 110th floor. Pretending to be a journalist, Petit interviewed actual workers on the roof in order to make final observations. On the night of August 6, Petit and friends used a bow and arrow to send an initial line from the South Tower to the North Tower, where other associates were waiting to haul progressively thicker lines across. The task took most of the night and culminated in the installation of a 450-pound steel cable that Petit would trust with his life.

The awe-inspiring performance sold skeptical New Yorkers on the contribution the Twin Towers made to the skyline, creating in an hour a popularity that civic and financial backers had been unable to produce in a decade. Charges against Petit for trespassing were dropped in exchange for his performing a less risky high-wire act for children in Central Park. To many, the quixotic feat seemed as admirable as the recent moon walk. Petit's motives were purely personal, but his boldness and skill,

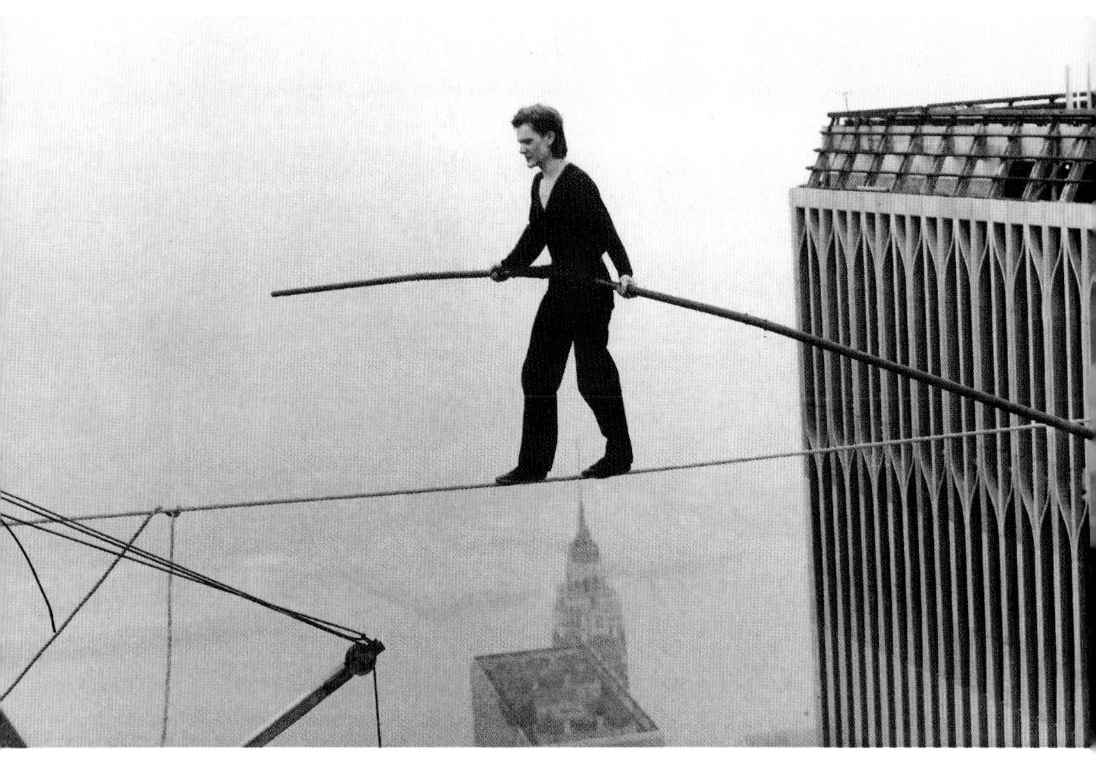

Alan Welner, *Philippe Petit Walking between World Trade Center Towers*, 1974

innocent of any imperialistic designs, won admiration on a universal level. Since 1969 people have looked up at the moon and said in wonder, "Humans have walked there." Petit's feat carries its own enduring capacity to astonish, especially now that it is unrepeatable. Usually, walks are the very definition of ephemerality. Not in this case. The towers are gone, but, captured on film, the walk remains.

Take Back the Night

"Women Unite; Take Back the Night!" Since the 1970s, women fighting sexual violence have taken to the streets after dark to assert their right to walk safely there, no matter the hour. In clamorous processions and solemn candlelight vigils they bear witness to the terrible toll of sexual aggression, while simultaneously refusing to cower out of sight when night falls. As this photo shows, early marches stressed female camaraderie and solidarity. They excluded men and centered on women's rights and safety, only gradually opening in the twenty-first century to a rainbow assembly of all sexual orientations. Assault, rape, pornography, domestic violence, and sexual harassment have been some of the principal targets. But challenging the notion that the nighttime is safe for predators alone has led activists to scrutinize the entire social order, from police methods and criminal law to media representations and childhood education. While there is as yet no universally accepted right to safe passage through the darkness, citizens and governments alike have begun to recognize their responsibility not to abandon half of humanity when the sun goes down.

The first Take Back the Night demonstration in the United States arose spontaneously in October 1975 in Philadelphia, when women marched in anger over the murder of microbiologist Susan Alexander Speeth, stabbed to death a block from her house as she walked home from work one night. As a phrase and rallying cry, "Take back the night" gained prominence after its use in 1977 by National Organization of Women activist Anne Pride at an antiviolence demonstration in Pittsburgh. In the 1980s rising awareness of feminist issues and of violence against women—affecting about one-third of women worldwide—soon made the marches regular events in North America, especially on college campuses.

Meanwhile in Europe the Reclaim the Night movement pursued similar goals, starting with events in Brussels and Rome in 1976. Over the past fifty years, marches demanding nocturnal safety have been staged in almost every country. Related to this effort, the Women's March of January 21, 2017, not only produced the largest single-day protest in US history but engaged over seven million women worldwide, all insisting on a fundamental point: "Women's rights are human rights."

Perhaps the most striking recent tactic in the on-street battle against sexual violence has been the SlutWalk. The first such march occurred in Toronto, Canada, on April 3, 2011, in response to a police officer declaring that "women should avoid dressing like sluts in order not to be victimized." Over three thousand women marched to the Toronto Police Headquarters, dressed in short skirts, black stockings, revealing tops, and other clothing said to suggest promiscuity. Decrying the

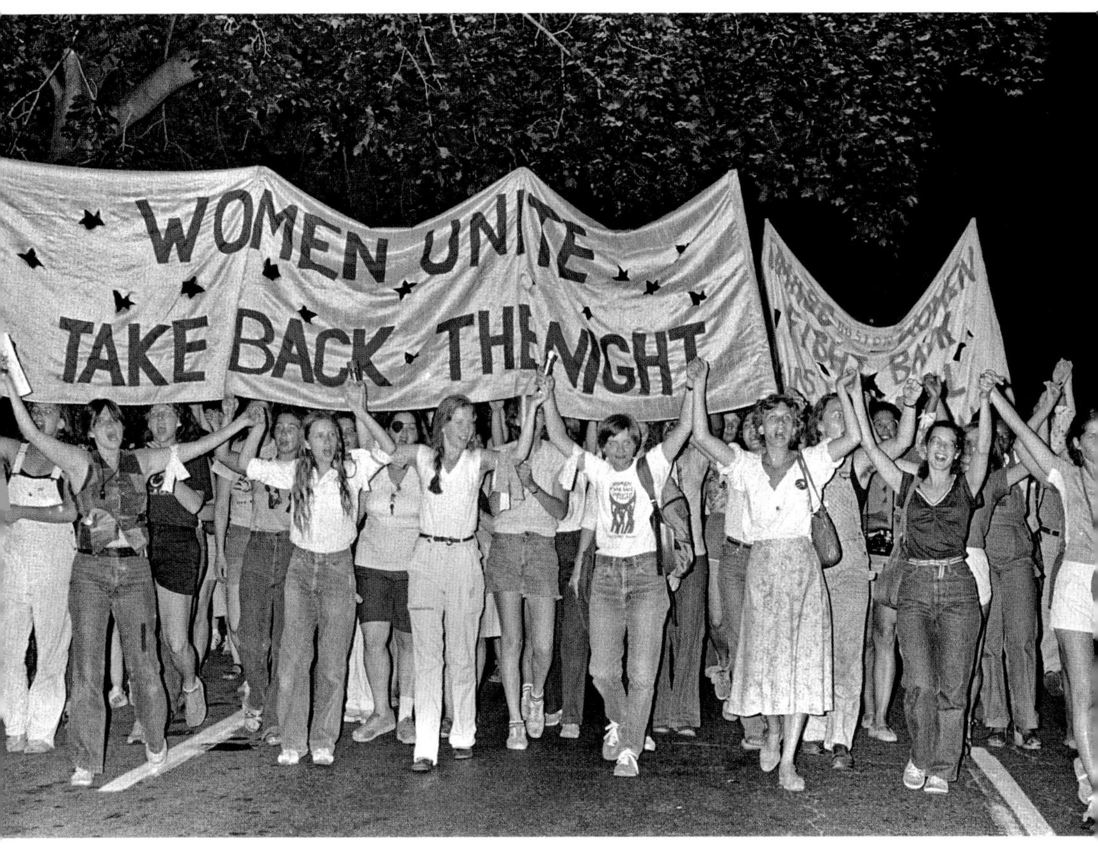

Spencer Grant, "Women Unite, Take Back the Night," Boston, 1979

myth that women are raped because they are "asking for it," the demonstrators proclaimed their right to go wherever they pleased, dressed just as they pleased. "We want Police Services to truly get behind the idea that victim-blaming, slut-shaming, and sexual profiling are never acceptable," said organizer Sonya Barnett. Although the defiant use of the word *slut* has caused controversy, SlutWalks rapidly became a global phenomenon. Within a year the marches had spread to Argentina and Australia, India and Iceland, Singapore and Switzerland. A popular chant expresses the marchers' point succinctly: "Whatever we wear, wherever we go, yes means yes and no means no!"

Portable Sound

Sound can carry, but what does it mean to carry sound? In one of Sony's earliest ads for a Walkman, no one can tell what the businessman is listening to as he swings his briefcase. But the "revolution in the streets" he causes is not much of an overstatement. His jaunty step signals nothing less than the personalized privatization of public space. Already encased in their own music, all the heads around him turn to admire how successfully he has made his own the sidewalk airwaves they used to share.

It was only a few years earlier, in the mid-1950s, that the human race suddenly found itself capable of strolling over hill and dale with a device that allowed words and music from a distant source to emerge from a small box made of metal or plastic. The device was a battery-powered transistor radio. It soon found a mass market with baby boomers eager for popular music, especially the new variety called rock 'n' roll. From the 1950s into the 1970s, hundreds of millions of transistor radios, marketed with convenient handles and carrying cases, traveled everywhere that

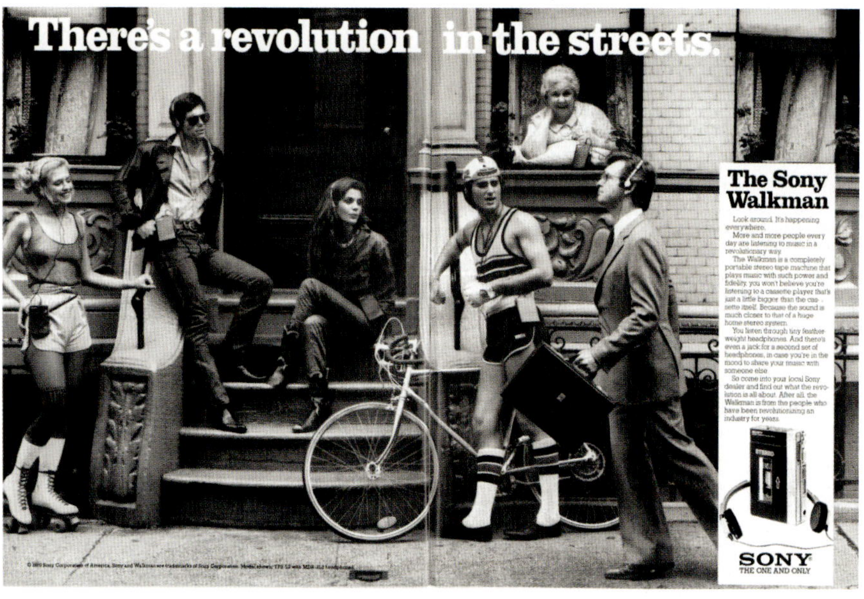

Peter Hoffman, designer, "There's a Revolution in the Streets," advertisement for Sony Walkman, 1980

people or cars could reach. In the 1980s, all-in-one technology produced the boom box, sporting cassette-tape player/recorders and high-volume loudspeakers, in addition to an AM-FM tuner. Especially popular in urban areas among young Black and Latino populations, boom boxes evolved to feature ever-more-powerful bass speakers suited to impromptu parties and the sonic demands of hip-hop music. Individuals who swaggered down the street with twenty-five-pound radios blaring from their shoulders added a distinctive new character to the gallery of athletic walkers.

In the long run, however, neither the transistor nor the boom box possessed the transformative energy of the Sony Walkman, introduced in 1979. While portable radios added mobility to sound, they did not change the listener's age-old, fundamentally public relationship to music. The speakerless Walkman did nothing except play cassette tapes for a private audience of one, but that modest goal ushered in the era of the customized experience that flourishes today, enabling individuals to live in sonic enclaves of their own design.

The catalyst was headphones. While rudimentary earphones were available with some transistor radios, the tinny sound bore no relation to the consciousness-altering environment that a Walkman offered in a portable package. What followed were two culture-bending results: the Walkman, with its compact design, became the first device one could exercise with, and movement could be accompanied by music that the user alone wanted to hear. In the 1980s and 1990s, as the vogue for aerobic exercise helped Walkman sales rise toward two billion, people all over the world moved to individualized soundtracks, marching to the beat of a million different drummers, starring in imagined films of their own lives. Often impervious to aural signals around them, earphoned users enjoyed the defensive cocoon that being visibly "elsewhere" provided them at home or in crowds.

Almost immediately, civic authorities warned of an increase in pedestrian accidents, since the music's protective bubble failed to ward off cars and lampposts. Critics also denounced the antisocial behavior of wearing earphones in public, breaking time-honored norms about the auditory communality of social space. Meanwhile, recording companies and museums quickly exploited personal listening devices to sell music and to program audio tours. From the start consumers realized that they were buying not just physical but emotional freedom, including the freedom to close out others—a sensation now known as "the Walkman effect." The Walkman offered people a way to control space and traverse it in style, to feel confident that they were taking life's journey on their own terms.

A Walk to Remember

Visitors walk slowly, looking for a small part of a very large object. As they search, they encounter the size and extent of the object, made of polished black granite. They see it rise as they descend; they experience its peak and duration; they follow its slow diminution as it tapers off to become part of the earth from which it surged. A walk is not a war, but Maya Lin's Vietnam Veterans Memorial in Washington, DC, uses the temporality of human steps to take individuals through an emotional journey of war's devastating effects. Symbolically, the Wall, as it has come to be called, asks walkers to confront the appalling scale of war, to allow themselves to be caught up in its dark, inexorable power. Just as compellingly, the experience of walking the Wall embodies the aftermath of war: the enormity of grief, the weight of remembrance. The fifty-eight thousand names of the fallen, each carved deep in the granite, tell the searchers for one beloved name that the person they came to honor was not alone. Each was in fact part of a terribly large catastrophe that carried the bearers of all these names, their hopes, lives, and dreams, to the underworld.

Alluding to that classical journey, Lin's half-buried structure guides sorrowing visitors down a ramp, below ground level, so that the reflective black wall looms over them. Having made contact with the dead not only in thought but through the tracing of chiseled letters, they mount the opposite ramp and return to the upper world, renewed by this solemn detour from the walk of life. "I imagined taking a knife and cutting into the earth," said Lin, "opening it up, and with the passage of time, that initial violence and pain would heal."

Sometimes indeed called "the wall that heals," the memorial has since its dedication in 1982 gathered up the conflicted emotions of a nation and helped it mourn the losses of a war it could not win. The abstract, nonfigurative nature of the design caused controversy when first unveiled, but the way the Wall opens itself to the engagement of visitors, who trace the names and leave flowers or mementos beneath them, rapidly won converts. The Wall is now regularly cited as one of the most admired architectural works in the United States. Several scaled-down replicas, "moving walls," have traveled the country so that citizens everywhere can share in the experience. Seen from above, the two 246-foot sections on the Washington Mall form a simple inverted V, the inside of which bears the names, as if Mother Earth were gathering them into her fold.

The inspiring story of Lin's winning the commission for the monument when she was a twenty-one-year-old college student has justly become part of the Wall's meaning, since Lin's design emerged out of a deep concern for the environment and its vulnerability. She wed the Land Art movement's bold reshaping of the landscape to an ecological sensitivity born partially from her own precarious situation as an

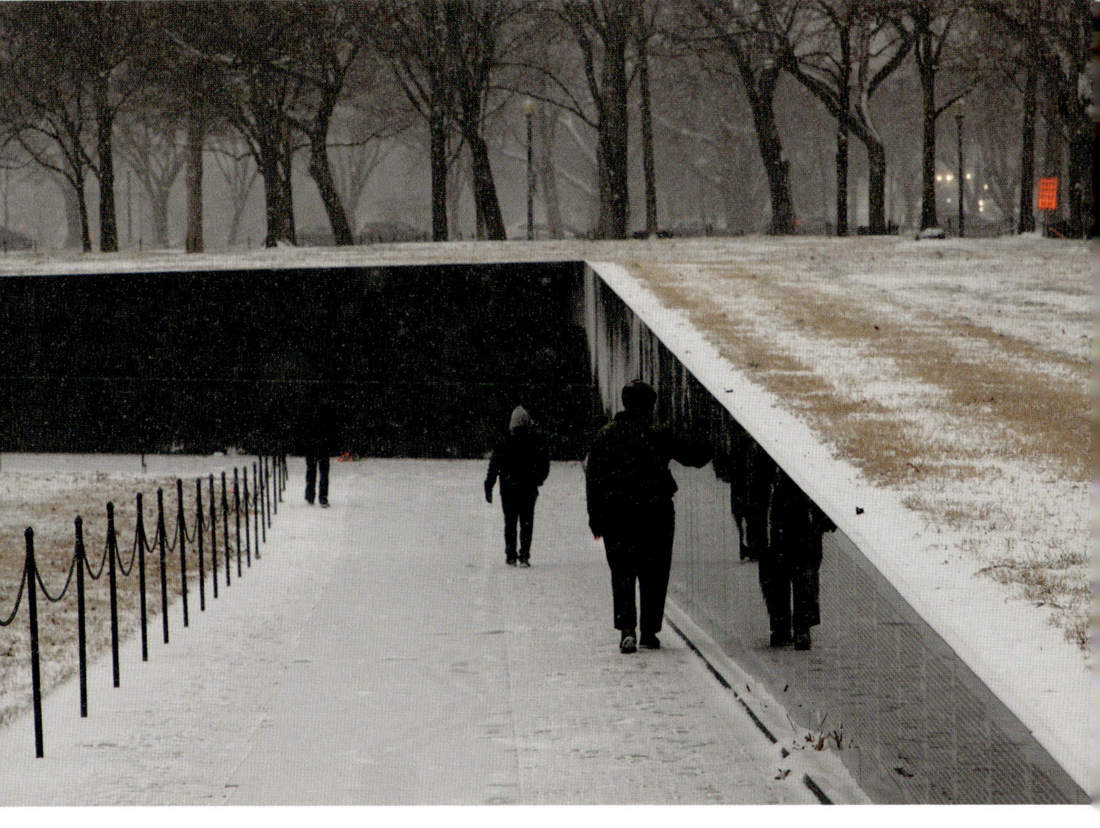

Maya Lin, Vietnam Veterans Memorial, 1982

Asian American woman. Acknowledging human and natural vulnerabilities, the Wall balances earth engineering with a nuanced sense of how sculpture can communicate on a person-to-person level.

Early in the 1960s, the sculptor Carl Andre dispensed with pedestals and set his materials flat on the ground, requiring the viewer to move along the path they made. Using that technique to create a deceptively simple path for emotional and spiritual connection, Lin opened the length of the wall as a pilgrimage site: a journey, arrival, and redeparture contained in 592 feet of intense walking. "The veterans were asking me, 'What do you think people are going to do when they first come here?' " she recalled. "And I wanted to say, 'They're going to cry.' "

Migration

In 2020 nearly eighty million people worldwide found themselves on the road, forced to flee their homes because of war, famine, persecution, climate change, and denial of human rights. According to the United Nations, 40 percent of displaced persons are children. Twenty-first-century migrants travel by boat, train, truck, bus, plane, and, mostly, on foot. They move within countries and across seas, but most visibly and controversially they attempt to cross borders between one country and another.

For desperate, driven people living in Latin America, the border between the United States and Mexico functions as a beacon and a barrier, offering a small chance for those who feel they have none left at home. In the 2010s caravans composed of thousands of political and economic refugees moved northward from Central America, seeking a precarious safety in numbers. A Honduran politician commented that the migrants "do not run after the American dream, they flee the Honduran nightmare." Whether running from or rushing toward, would-be immigrants—individuals, families, sometimes children journeying alone—have piled up for decades at US ports of entry along its Mexican border. Facing detention, crime, disease, rejection, or endless delays, many approach the border outside official channels. On the other side, a promised land may await, but rivers, deserts, and border guards stand in the way, along with a network of barricades and walls.

Luis A. Jiménez Jr., an American artist of Mexican descent, confronts the dilemma of the refugee in his larger-than-life polychrome fiberglass sculpture *Border Crossing*, depicting a man carrying a woman and child on his shoulders. It's based on the experience of Jiménez's grandparents, who crossed the Rio Grande (called the Rio Bravo in Mexico) river border in 1924. The ten-foot-tall work asks its viewers to look up in a literal way to this resolute family group, to consider the physical and emotional burden of a shawl-wrapped baby and its fiercely protective mother. "I had wanted to make a piece that was dealing with the issue of the illegal alien," said Jiménez. "People talked about aliens as if they landed from outer space, as if they weren't really people. I wanted to put a face on them: I wanted to humanize them."

Possibly breaking the law, are these sculpted travelers criminals or saints? The mother and child, symbolizing hope for the future, echo the Madonna-and-Christ-child statues frequently seen in Catholic churches. The man may be crossing the prosaic Rio Grande with his family, but his bent form, bare feet, and rolled-up trousers recall Saint Christopher, who legendarily carried the boy Jesus across a dangerous river. The sparkling acrylic urethane surface of the sculpture gleams in the sun, as if the figures were dripping wet from a river passage that is also a

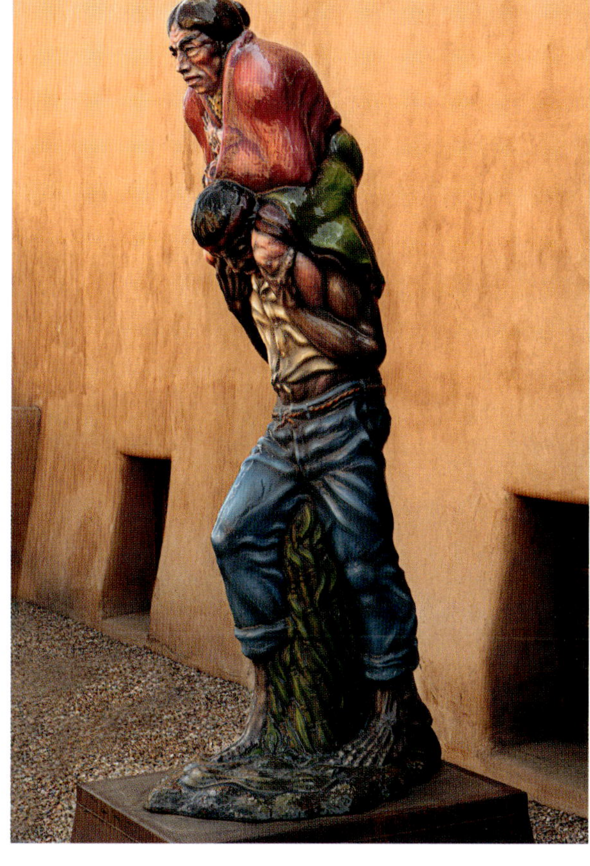

Luis A. Jiménez Jr., *Border Crossing*, 1989

form of baptism. As a work of public sculpture, the piece crosses a figurative border, memorializing those who breach boundaries in pursuit of the happiness that Americans have declared an inalienable right—even for "aliens." With copies located in museums in several states (Iowa, California, New Mexico, and Texas among them), the sculpture celebrates the heroism of ordinary families who build countries as well as enter them. Reaching back in another direction, the work evokes Aeneas carrying his father Anchises from the flames of Troy, beginning the journey of the classical world's most famous displaced people, the Trojans, whose migration ended in the founding of Rome.

Border Crossing recognizes that even if they are as empty-handed as Adam and Eve, all displaced walkers carry burdens: the memory of what they leave behind, the hope of completing the journey, the dream of locating a more secure future for their families. The man lifts his foot, trying, like Bunyan's Pilgrim, to make progress toward a new life. Caught in mid-step, Jiménez's border crossers are poised between two worlds, prompting those who witness the action to reflect on what drives them forward, and what kind of welcome they will receive in the promised land.

Crawling While Black

Disability art asks its audience to encounter the world in a differently abled way, to consider obstacles and insights that the unimpaired body is unlikely to experience. Practitioners of performance art and walking art have found common ground in presenting to the public moments in which walking meets its Other, moments in which a simple walk is neither. In 1972, Hiroshi Yokota left his wheelchair at a pedestrian crossing and crawled across a Tokyo intersection on his hands and knees. Kazuo Hara shocked audiences by recording the action in his film *Goodbye CP* (1972), revealing how people with cerebral palsy had to fend for themselves in Japanese society. A more recent film, *One Morning in May* (2012), follows British artist Noëmi Lakmaier as she wriggles from her wheelchair to crawl, dressed in a business suit, from the domestic space of Tower Hamlets towards the financial district in London, a mile away. Battered, exhausted, her clothes in tatters, she abandons the quest after a day-long struggle, asking, "Can I see the map; I want to see how much I didn't do."

A standout piece of American walking art takes the provocative act of crawling one step further, adding racial discrimination to the discussion of disability. If the phrase "walking while Black" has come to stand for the harassment that African Americans face daily, "crawling while Black" brings into vivid relief the slow pace of progress toward racial equality. Physically unimpaired in a conventional sense, Black artist Pope.L brings the socially constructed nature of disability to a powerful metaphoric realization in *The Great White Way, 22 Miles, 9 Years, 1 Street* (2001–9). Over a period of several years the artist painfully crawled the full length of New York City's longest street, Broadway. The street's nickname, the Great White Way, stems from its bright lights, which have done little to illuminate the dark legacy of slavery. Dragging a black body dressed in a Superman costume through "the great white way" of American culture, Pope.L's work makes visual in an indelible fashion the "out-of-placeness" and paradoxical invisibility of Black people in America. He remarks that "costumes are a way to project yourself into the world and at the same time conceal yourself. And I think that's necessary for the performances I'm trying to do." Over the course of his outings, Pope.L materialized the message of Ralph Ellison's classic novel *Invisible Man* (1952). He crawled with a skateboard strapped to his back to avoid being run over if he took too long to cross an intersection. When he needed to hurry, he flipped over and rolled rapidly to safety. Confronting the ideologically inflicted disability of racism, Pope.L demonstrates the superhuman qualities required for the Black body to navigate the "mainstream" walk of life in America.

The artist is all too aware that mere pictures can never reach the heart of what he feels inside as he fights his way towards a goal. Pope.L comments that "time-based endurance performances like my crawl works . . . have this marvelous creamy nougat center operating inside the performer, and this space is unfortunately not available in the images. . . . So, typically, the surface of the work becomes the life of the work." Yet that surface has an undeniable depth, as the performer confronts the brutal friction of urban surfaces. What humans watch intently, they can feel in their own bodies. Anyone who doubts the reality of kinesthetic empathy has only to watch Yokota or Lakmaier or Pope.L dragging themselves along a sidewalk while other people stride by. Making the wincing viewer want to turn away, these wrenching efforts reach past the intellect into the skin and bone of the onlooker. Part performance, part protest march, and wholly embodied, crawl works scrape their distressing way into "normal" walking. Having witnessed the crawl, one cannot saunter so blithely afterward.

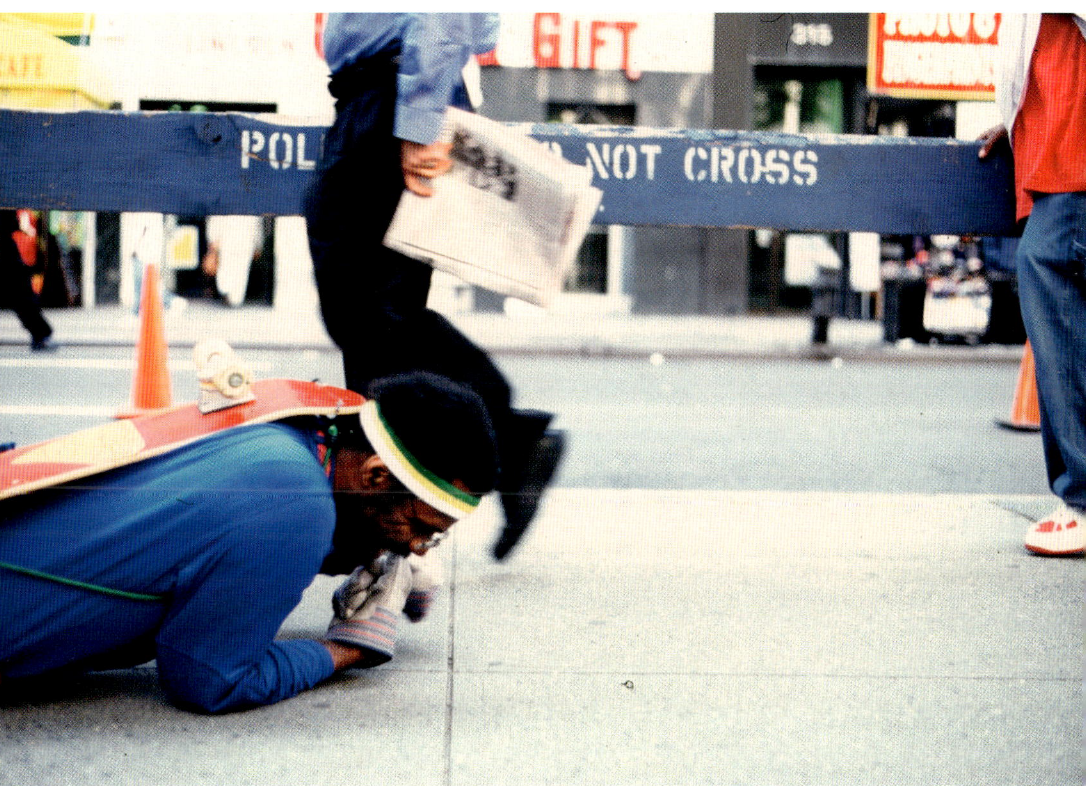

Pope.L, *The Great White Way*, 2001–9

Walking High

Not since eighteenth-century kings turned bulwarks into boulevards has a walking amenity attracted so much acclaim. Recognizing that people will flock to attractive promenades with great views, the creators of New York's High Line struggled for two decades to convert an abandoned railroad line into an elevated green pedestrian avenue, almost two miles long, on the west side of Manhattan. After extensive negotiations between the city, the railroad owner, and the community groups that first sponsored the idea, the High Line opened in several phases between 2009 and 2019. Over eight million visitors a year now stroll and take selfies among meadow plants and artworks seeded along a former eyesore that was nearly demolished in 2001. See and be seen: instead of looking out toward the countryside from an old city wall, contemporary crowds people-watch and peer into the high-rent apartments they pass on the "pry line." But they also marvel at sweeping views of Manhattan, the Hudson River, and the ever-more-congested ridges of the New Jersey shore. The experience is so popular that timed entry tickets became necessary to avoid overcrowding during the COVID pandemic.

Designed by James Corner's Field Operations and by the architects Diller Scofidio + Renfro, the green space features plantings selected by Piet Oudolf, a Dutch landscaper who incorporated native species that had already sprouted between the old rails, left unused for twenty-five years. The inspiration for the High Line came from the Promenade Plantée ("Planted Promenade") in Paris, forerunner of the "Green Streams" of walkable garden corridors now emerging all over Europe. The Promenade Plantée opened in 1993 along the route of a steam train that once linked the area of the Paris Opera to the suburb of Vincennes and its renowned park. Today Parisians can make that same journey on foot, strolling along three miles of greenway, sometimes thirty feet above the city streets, passing through gardens, residential areas, and even between the halves of an apartment building constructed around the path.

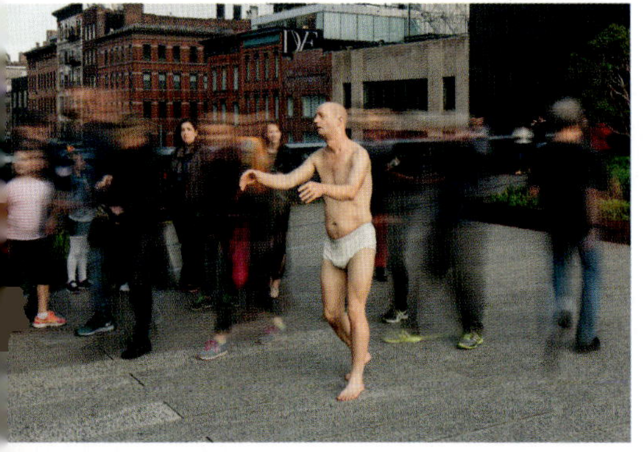

No less enticing than its Manhattan offspring, the Promenade Plantée sits in its shadow in terms of renown. The reason lies in New York's superheated real estate market. With the Whitney Museum of American Art at one terminus and the new Hudson Yards complex at the other end, the High Line has proved a magnet for developers and investors. They rapidly transformed the area along the route with upscale shops,

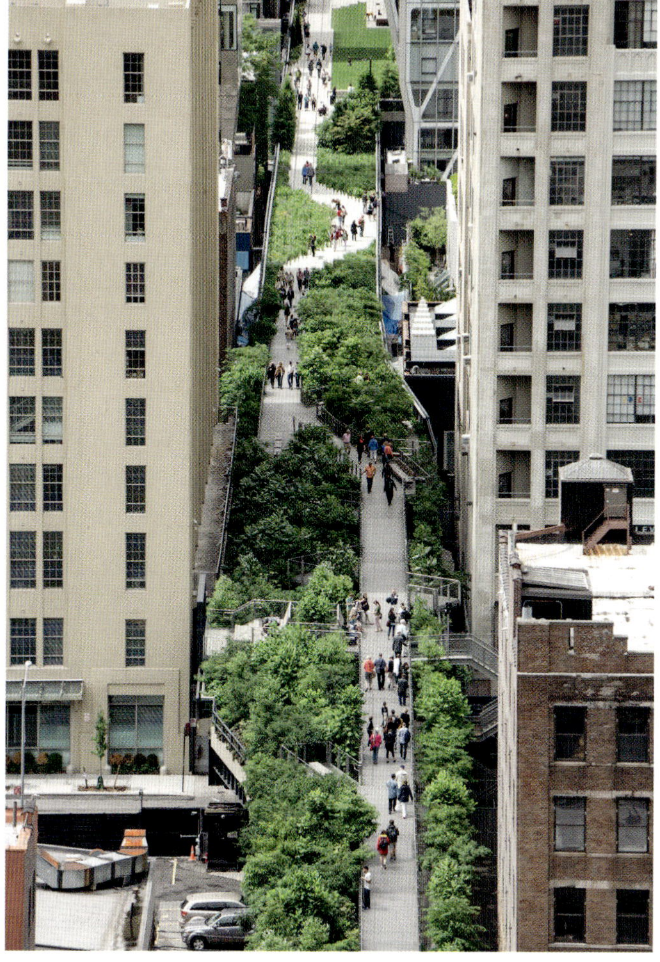

▸ James Corner Field Operations, Diller Scofidio + Renfro, and Piet Oudolf,
the High Line, New York, 2009–19

◂ Strollers on the High Line pass Tony Matelli's *Sleepwalker*, 2016

restaurants, and housing. Rents and prices soared, poorer locals fled, and by 2017 one of the High Line's originators lamented that he had failed the community that his group, the Friends of the High Line, had hoped to serve.

Now hugely influential on the urban planning front (with Chicago, Atlanta, and Philadelphia following suit), the High Line has become both a success story and a cautionary tale. What started as a brilliant concept has been called a tourist-clogged "cattle chute." In 2016 Tony Matelli's lifelike, life-size statue *Sleepwalker* (2014) was displayed on the High Line, entrancing passersby who frequently posed with him. His eyes closed, his hands outstretched, an image of human ignorance or hope, the underpants-clad man cannot see where he is going, even if he has a walk-worthy dream leading him forward.

Re-Viewing the Walking Tour

It is as though the practices organizing a bustling city were characterized by their blindness.
—*Michel de Certeau, "Walking in the City" (1980)*

In the thick of it, you can't see it. The sociologist Michel de Certeau famously declared that walkers in the city are blind wanderers unable to read the script of their own steps. But perhaps there is something unperceptive about the metaphor of blindness itself, something obtuse about always subscribing to the primacy of sight. It is true that few walkers are more visible, and more visibly challenged, than sightless people who navigate crowded city streets. Aided by sound, touch, smell, and memory, they stand out due to the physical guidance of a sighted helper, a dog, or a cane. The obstacles they face seem to offer a metaphor for how human understanding advances uncertainly, "in the dark" about so many of the phenomena around it. And yet there is so much about unsighted experience that the general public does not see.

Foregrounding his own experience as a self-declared "non-visual learner," the Canadian artist Carmen Papalia challenges the notion that blindness means ignorance. Beginning in 2010, Papalia says, he made "an effort to distance myself from marginalizing language like 'blind' and 'visually impaired.'" Instead, he focused on "the position that I occupied as a liberatory space." In *Mobility Device* (2013) and *Long Cane* (2009–11), Papalia decided to make himself extra-visible, examining his own conflicted feelings about the tools he uses to navigate the world. In the first work, he enlisted the aid of a marching band to send aural signals to tell him which way to turn or when to cross a street. In the second performance, he used an outsize white cane, twelve feet long, to sweep the path in front of him: "On one hand, it was a tool that promoted my access and mobility," he remarked. "It showed me things and made my map a whole lot bigger. On the other hand, it institutionalized me."

Opening up this performed visibility to other participants, Papalia invited sighted people to explore the nonvisual world in his company. In the work *Blind Field Shuttle* (2010–ongoing), the artist leads a long "accordion" of up to ninety sighted people through town and country. Papalia's title comes from philosopher Henri Lefebvre, who called the contemporary urban condition a "blind field" that preconceived ideas prevent observers from studying effectively. While participants, eyes closed, "blindly" follow the person in front of them by putting their hands on their shoulders, Papalia metaphorically opens their eyes to new perceptions. He leads them on an hour-long walking tour, sometimes including dense urban itineraries such as New York's High Line, offering insights as he goes. In part,

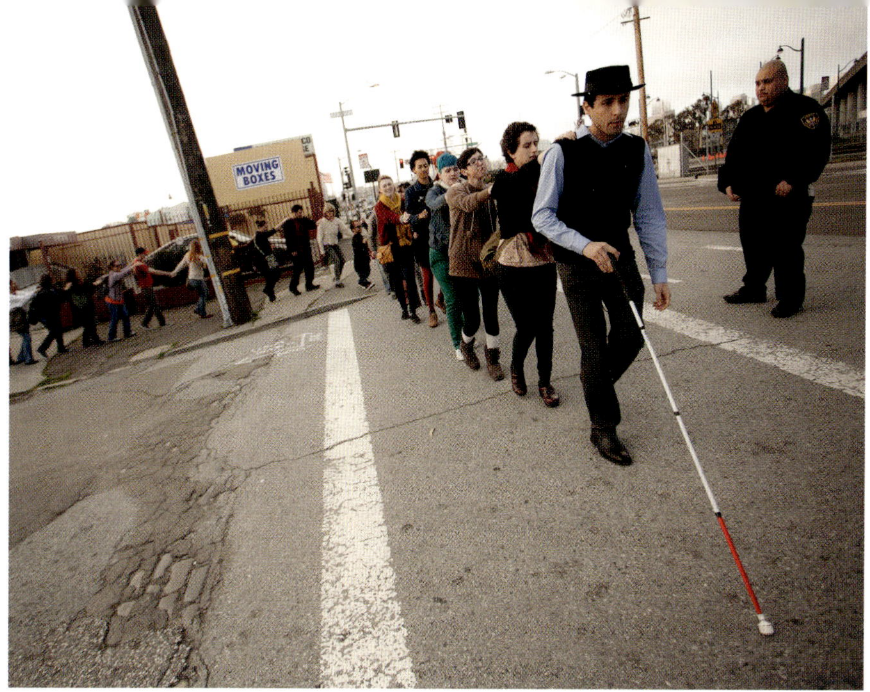

Carmen Papalia, *Blind Field Shuttle*, 2010

the artist reroutes the convention of the museum-based audio guide (in 2013 he led a "touch tour" at the Guggenheim Museum in New York). He also adds his own real-time perspective to one of the most significant developments in walking-based art, the scripted, often prerecorded "sound-walk," in which participants listen to narrative and sonic effects that have been created by an absent artist. Unseeing, in literal touch with each other, Papalia's followers encounter sound—and the sound of his voice—with startling intensity.

Instead of the blind leading the blind to disaster, as in the famous Brueghel painting of 1568, a differently-directed man leads the sighted to discover a fully engaged, other-sensed way of moving through the world. And instead of emulating the tragic procession in John Singer Sargent's *Gassed*, Papalia's shoulder-holding walkers willingly join his association of nonvisual learners. Inviting audiences to inhabit the mobile reality of the artist, Papalia underlines a larger point of disability art: sometimes to move toward the Other in understanding, one must move *as* the Other in practice. At the conclusion, participants chart their progress by making sensory maps of their experience. The work, Papalia says, "helped me exercise my nonvisual senses and find a community with whom I could develop a critical methodology for engaging nonvisual space." Performed in many locales across the United States and Canada, as well as in European countries, *Blind Field Shuttle* aims at nothing less than uncovering unseen vistas of knowledge that blindness about blindness obscures.

Street-Smart *Phoneur* or Smartphone Zombie?

Currently one out of every two people on earth has a smartphone, fundamentally changing how humans walk through the world. Untethered from wires, books, places, persons, and physical sources of information or entertainment, mobile phone users command the full spectrum of human knowledge. As they move, they can summon the sight or sound of almost everything on the planet. Interactive technology grants them immense powers to send and receive ideas and instructions, to register, evaluate, and even shape the environment they traverse.

The phone users' dominance of the world's walkways makes it clear that in the past few decades, connectivity has replaced spatial proximity as the driving force in human activity. Mobile phones and their wireless networks spread rapidly when commercial models became available in 1983. Today almost no sight is more common than that of people bent over their phones as their legs take them forward on autopilot, whether they are pushing strollers, walking dogs, lugging groceries, or simply strolling along, alone or in company.

Idle as they were, nineteenth-century flâneurs were above all observant, acutely registering the spontaneous events and peculiar details that made modern urban life so stimulating. In the twenty-first century, those who might be called *phoneurs* prowl the city with a similar curiosity, even as they confound distance and proximity. They process information from afar to find a restaurant around the corner, and send a snapshot of a shop window to a friend on another continent. They move confidently in places whose sensory input they often ignore. Supplementing and even superseding their five senses, their phones act as navigation systems, recording devices, and trackers-down of amusement.

But as they gather information and send messages, many *phoneurs* intermittently become "smartphone zombies." They disconnect themselves from the immediate vicinity of the world they bestride. On city streets or rural paths, preoccupied individuals stumble and stray, heedless of their surroundings while deeply attentive to voices a thousand miles away. Addictive applications turn their liberation from physical places into a new form of bondage that erodes their privacy and dulls their senses. They look helplessly to a screen to decide whether to turn right or left. Texting with friends, remotely handling a crisis at work, or talking through a family emergency, they find themselves vulnerable to dangers they could easily have avoided, from lampposts and potholes to reckless bicycles and speeding cars.

Across the world, new forms of infrastructure have sprung up to protect both zombies and those in their path. Privately made street signs in Stockholm, created by designers Jacob Sempler and Emil Tiismann, warn drivers about distracted walkers. "One day on my way to work I was almost run over because I was staring

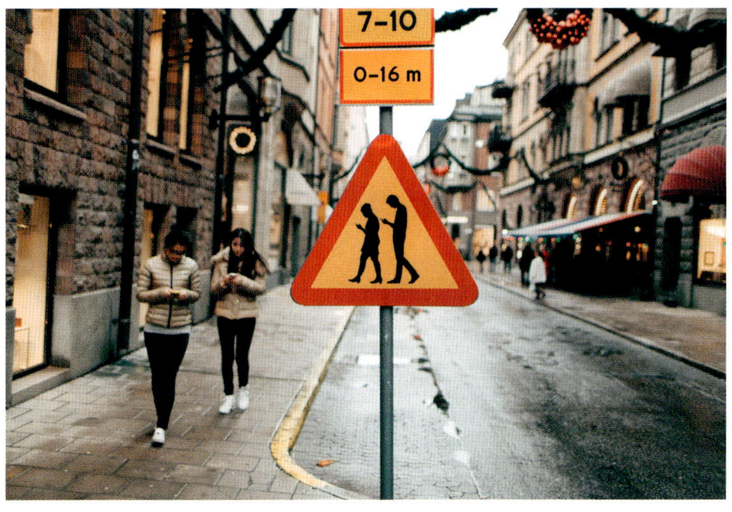

Jacob Sempler and Emil Tiismann, artist-installed traffic signs warning motorists to watch out for cell phone users, Stockholm, 2015

at my phone like a sick person," Sempler explained. "It hit me then that I'm not the only one with this behavior and that it ought to be addressed somehow." While Sempler concedes that most phone users, such as those seen here approaching his sign, will probably not look up long enough to take in the message, authorities in other cities are forcing inattentive pedestrians to walk more responsibly. Antwerp, Belgium, and Chongqing, China, have designated special smartphone lanes on sidewalks. Several German cities have installed curbside lights to warn "the head-down tribe" (as phone users are called in Hong Kong) that they are approaching traffic. Concerned that the out-of-body walker is disrupting the rhythms of modern urban life, Japanese researchers have studied disrupted pedestrian flows as a prelude to new forms of city planning.

Cinematic zombies lumber along in a trance because more powerful forces have taken over their bodies. Zombified phone users, in quiet moments when they are free from such forces, must balance the benefits of instantaneous communication against the ever-growing threat that political and commercial interests will turn that information against them. Not only does the ubiquity of smartphones erode the restorative division between personal and working life, or between living and consuming, but it also permits governments and corporations to track where people go and what they do, say, or buy. The first handheld walkie-talkies helped rifle companies and paratroopers maintain contact as they fanned out behind enemy lines during World War II. Entangled in the virtual as they navigate the real, *phoneurs* and zombies alike may be less certain than GIs about when they have crossed into "enemy" territory—tracked by those who find it valuable to know their every move.

Body as Stylus

A footprint, a stick figure, an oil painting, or semiopaque tones caught on a piece of celluloid film: the look of a walk changed yet again with the arrival of digital images and tracking technology. The twenty-first century represents a new period in walking history. People now have the ability to record every step as it happens—the selfie walk, the social media walk, the livestreamed look-at-me walk, the crime-in-progress walk. In the realm of mere data, microaccelerometers allow a Fitbit or smartphone to register the day's ambulation in the form of steps, stairways climbed, or miles traversed. More visually engrossing, software programs use global positioning systems to trace a device wearer's movements as a line on a map on a screen. When Bauhaus artist Paul Klee famously described drawing as "taking a line for a walk," he could not have anticipated how literally true this action would become. A growing number of walkers and joggers routinely "draw" hearts and flowers, faces and phrases, in the course of their outings. The interaction of the walker with the walk, on the ground level, becomes less important than the panoptic view of a moving bit of gadgetry, electronically displayed.

Engaging in a form of autosurveillance that may be the latest version of the self-portrait, art makers have not been slow to learn how to draw with their feet. Working at the intersection of mapping and performance, they demonstrate just how inventively the walking body can be used as a stylus. In *Running Stitch* (2006), Jen Southern and Jen Hamilton connected mapped walking to a history of tapestry making that goes back to antiquity and Greek mythology. Participants in southern England carried GPS tracking devices that the artists turned into sewn lines on fabric, tracing the intermeshed routes on a material rather than a digital screen. *Matrix of Movement* (2016–18) by Tracy Claire Hill translates data from portable surveying scanners to create printed and hand-drawn landscapes of "waste" areas, revealing the mysteriously dynamic beauty encountered in remote wetlands. In such works, the walker becomes a mark maker, a stylus, a stitch, a line physically distanced from the document or recording medium that accretes signals and eventually represents the scope of a walk. The sight of the walker, whether in motion or at rest, is not located in a shared space. One of the contradictions of distance-collapsing technologies is that viewers of the artwork do not see the body that limns the walk.

Connected to tireless feet, electronic tracing can produce an engrossing visual and conceptual effect: the walk *is* the map. Reconceiving the metaphor of life as a journey, artist Jeremy Wood picked up a GPS device in the year 2000 and wore it constantly for well over a decade, turning his body, he said, into a "geodetic pencil." The result, *My Ghost (Sixteen Years of Mapping My Life in London with GPS),*

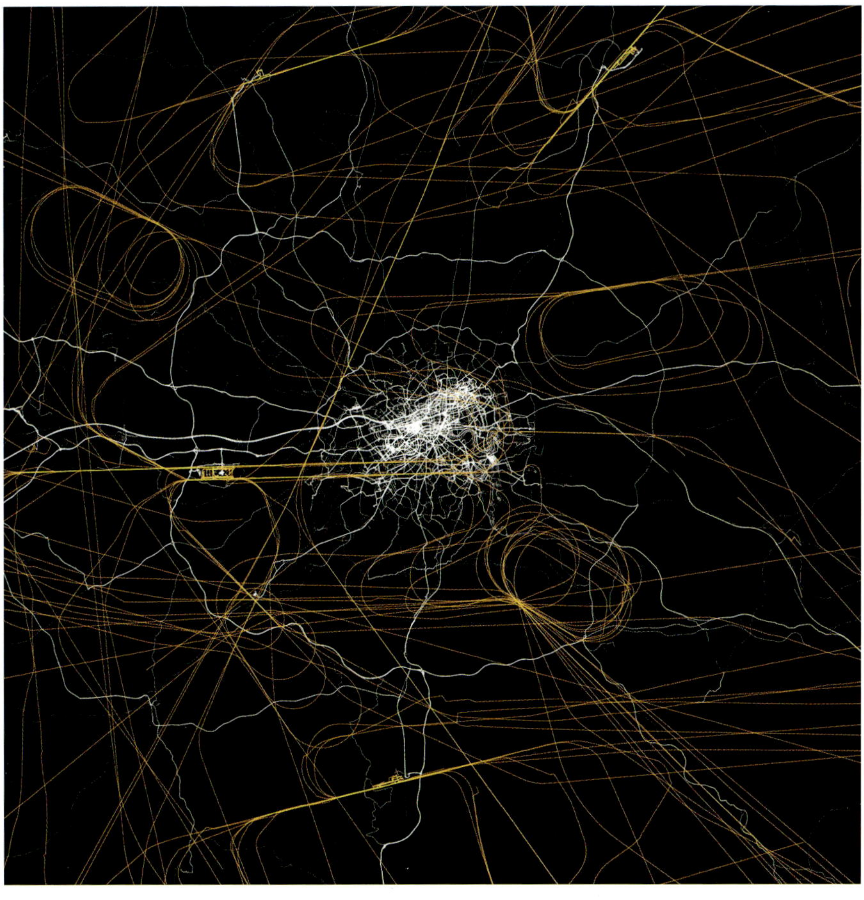

charts his life as an animated tangle of light that, projected on a black background, is recognizably London as a cartographer would see it. This ever-more convoluted "line made by walking" tightens into a Gordian knot in central London and then stretches out around its edges like Ariadne's thread. White lines, glowing incandescently from re-pacing at the center, trace his path on the ground, while yellow lines describe his airborne passages and holding patterns around Heathrow and Gatwick airports. "Among the intricacies in the line qualities," Wood says, "I can read my routes and ruts, and recall my dithering and my adventures. They are of my ghost, captured in places of a different time." The haunting effect of seeing part of a lifetime spatially described lends Wood's map-ghost an uncanny power. Ghosts walk because they have unfinished business with the living. The more vividly they loom, the more the traces of our past steps seem to demand a role in shaping the steps to come.

The Watched Walker

Today, almost no walk goes unnoticed. "When the Government tracks the location of a cell phone it achieves near perfect surveillance, as if it had attached an ankle monitor to the phone's user." So declared the US Supreme Court in a 2018 ruling telling police that they could not search phone location data without a warrant. Police, in return, might argue that they are following a divine precedent. The first watched walkers were Adam and Eve, hounded from Eden by an angel with a flaming sword. Ever since, walkers have been eyed suspiciously and often punished for walking in the purportedly wrong places, at the wrong times, with the wrong clothing; for being the wrong color or gender or ethnicity or sexual orientation; for moving too fast, too slow, too far to the left or right—an endlessly inventive array of interdictions. If they had forgotten their fig leaves, Adam and Eve could have been picked up under a 2014 European Court of Human Rights decision declaring that Stephen Gough, "the naked rambler," did not have the right to walk nude in public or to repeat his notorious in-the-buff hike from Land's End to John O'Groats in 2004.

The anonymous walkers of centuries past have disappeared, replaced by digital footprints, ranked by the perceived threat that they may pose to public safety. Omnivorous cameras consume human motion with no aesthetic or documentary intent. People increase in visibility when their features or movements trigger other bits of data in facial recognition systems. Arrests may be made before the predicted crime is committed. In New York City, the Domain Awareness System conducts "pre-crime screening" of suspicious behavior through a network of over eighteen thousand private and public CCTV cameras. Rights groups have resisted, but while waiting for legal protections to take effect, activists attempt to foil technology with AI-confounding clothing or pixel-puzzling masks, makeup, and sunglasses.

Yet what if the walk itself gives a person away? Gait recognition systems make walking itself a vulnerability, because everyone walks differently. Monitoring devices match walkers against databases to identify anyone in sight as friend or foe. Some security systems focus on silhouette extraction or step patterns on sensitized walkways, while others analyze the shifting relations between dozens of body parts in the course of a stride. Already in use in Beijing and Shanghai to catch jaywalkers, the technology has broad corporate and government appeal, says a manufacturer, because "you don't need people's cooperation for us to be able to recognize their identity."

Dehumanized by the data they generate, humans turn into zombie Others, the sort of walkers that need to be tracked and "dealt with" for the common good. Performance works by artists such as Vito Acconci (*Following Piece*, 1969), Sophie

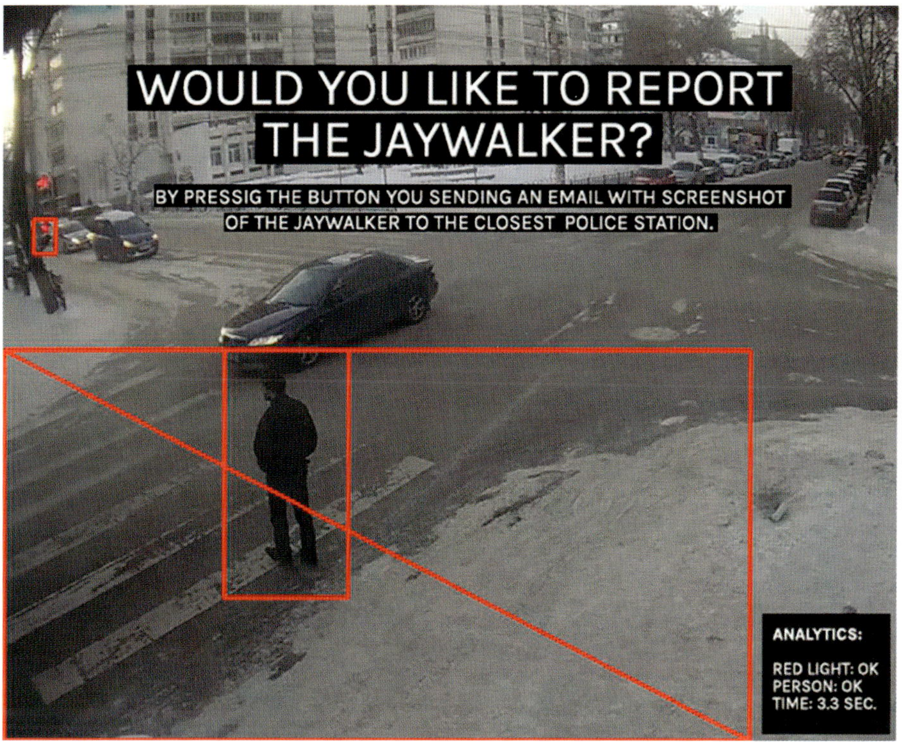

Dries Depoorter, *Jaywalking*, 2015–ongoing

Calle (*Venetian Suite*, 1979), and Jill Magid (*Trust*, 2004) have raised awareness about public surveillance. But maybe it takes being put on the spot as a watched walker, or a walker-watcher, to realize the implications of citizen surveillance, now a growing concern as consumers acquire their own spyware.

In *Jaywalking* (2015–ongoing), the Belgian artist Dries Depoorter exploits open links to CCTV cameras across the globe, confronting gallery visitors with surveillance evidence. "Would you like to report the jaywalker?" reads the headline on a screen. "By pressing the button you are sending a report of the jaywalker to the closest police station." Asking the public to reflect on its own relationship to law and order, to walking and watching, Depoorter pushes the psychological buttons of a society often told that walking itself implies a crime.

Walking on Water, Again

It was a miracle. In a *Wizard of Oz*-meets-the-Gospels scenario, over a million people who had faith in art walked on water at Lake Iseo in northern Italy, in July 2016. Reimagining the footsteps of Jesus and Peter, Dorothy and Toto, they strolled for almost two miles on a fifty-foot-wide strip of golden fabric, set atop two hundred thousand polyethylene cubes anchored to the lake floor in depths up to three hundred feet. The dramatic vectors of the shimmering pathway took them from the towns of Sulzano and Monte Isola out onto the lake, around the island of San Paolo, and back to shore. The temporary artwork, offered free to the public at a cost of $17 million to the artist, continued the wonder-walking experiment that Christo and Jeanne-Claude began with their monumental *The Gates* (2005). That project transformed New York's Central Park, drawing four million people to pass

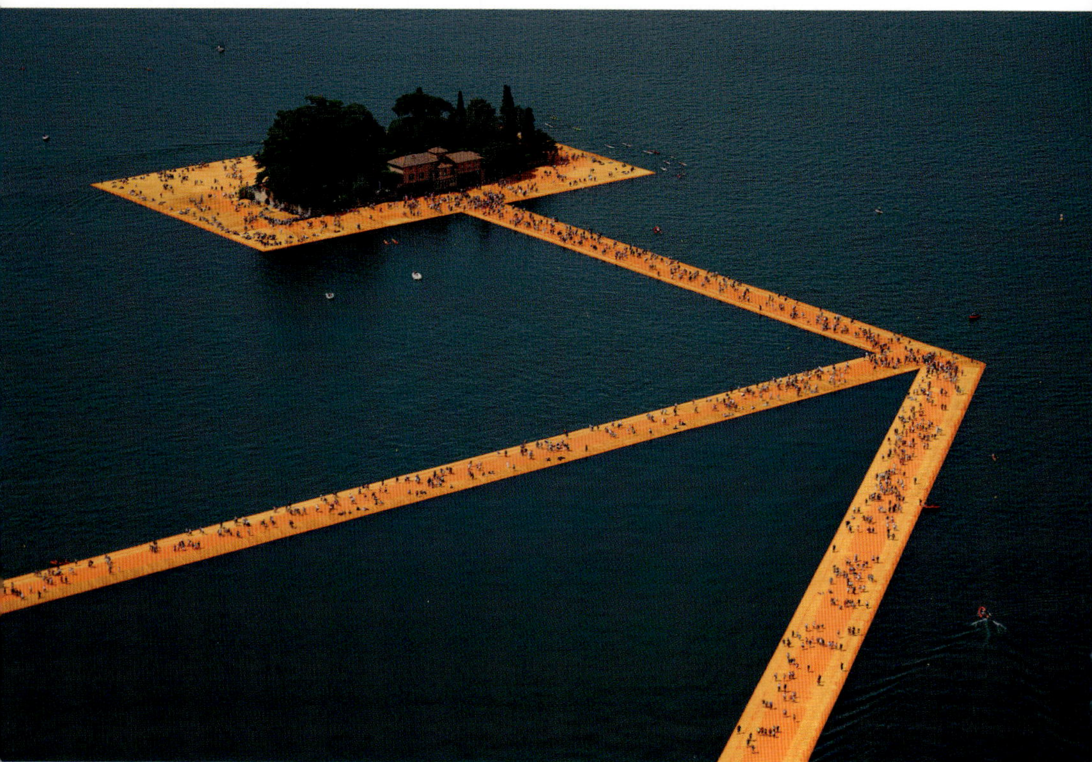

Christo and Jeanne-Claude, *The Floating Piers, Lake Iseo, Italy, 2014–16*

through some of the 7,503 portals set along twenty-three miles of pathways. Each gate was made from vinyl with free-hanging saffron-hued fabric panels. The couple conceived *Floating Piers* in 1970, but the long gestation meant that it was the first large-scale artwork for Christo to finish alone after Jeanne-Claude's death in 2009.

At Lake Iseo, *Floating Piers* found an ideal location. The walkway interacted spectacularly with the surrounding human and natural topography. Christo explained: "The art is not just the pier or the color or the fabric, but is the lake and the mountains. The whole landscape is the work of art. It's all about you having a personal relationship with it." The color combinations of land, water, sky, and pathway connected to the tactile experience of navigating the undulating, receptive surface of the rippled cloth and the aural impressions of wind, wave, and polyglot fellow wanderers. For many visitors, the social dimension of shared delight matched their wonder at the engineering needed to make the miracle happen. Others compared the once-in-a-lifetime promenade to a joyful pilgrimage in which the walk itself was the destination.

Ever since the Tower of Babel fell, dreams of a stairway to heaven have been plentiful. What Christo and Jeanne-Claude accomplished was something equally daring, all the more so because it was not only down-to-earth but precariously laid on water. The transcendent walking of *Floating Piers* was the product of human ingenuity, the concerted effort to bring, the artists said, "joy and beauty" to as many people as possible. They showed how a simple walk, taken under hitherto unimagined circumstances, could generate awe and enlarge physically and emotionally the relationship of walker and world.

Yet for all the splendor of *Floating Piers*, the ability to see the world Oz-like, with or without a yellow "road," is a transferable skill. It's accessible to everyone lucky enough to find the right circumstances, when a bright day and good footing make life seem miraculous. More than a century ago, putting succinctly what dedicated walkers have always known, Charles Dickens said: "The sum of the whole is this. Walk and be healthy, walk and be happy."

The Walking Wed

For many people, "the walk down the aisle" is the most significant walk of their lives. Yet historically, European or North American wedding ceremonies rarely involved a procession. Christian couples went into a church and up to the altar with a minimum of fuss. It was before and after the event that celebratory walks took place: friends, relatives, and even a whole village might accompany the bride and groom to the church and then to the threshold of a new life together. Amid the festivities, the community looked forward to its own rebirth, as the next generation prepared for parenthood.

It was not until the nineteenth century, thanks to the British royal family's love of pageantry, that a choreographed bridal walk down the aisle became fashionable. The trend began in 1840 with the marriage of Queen Victoria to Prince Albert of Saxe-Coburg. The couple's clear affection for each other brought romantic love, along with a white wedding dress and long train, to the fore.

Then when Victoria's daughter "Vicky" married Prince Frederick William of Prussia in 1858, another feature was added. Vicky selected two of her favorite pieces of music to accompany her carefully staged entrance and exit. She entered the Chapel Royal to the strains of Richard Wagner's "Bridal Chorus" from *Lohengrin* (1850), better known today as "Here Comes the Bride." After a service in which the archbishop of Canterbury skipped several parts because he was so nervous, Vicky and her new husband swept out to the sound of Felix Mendelssohn's "Wedding March" from his *Midsummer's Night's Dream* (1842). By linking specific, stately music to the bride's arrival and departure, this wedding formalized both. The fame of the wedding made the idea of a church procession, hitherto reserved for royalty, attractive to ordinary people, who soon began to imitate it.

Royal tradition met the commoner's search for self-expression when Meghan Markle walked alone down the aisle of St. George's Chapel at Windsor Castle in 2018 to marry Prince Harry. Given the couple's later break from the royal family, it is hard not to read volumes into the dark shadows that surrounded the bride on her entrance. But her solitary progress was intended to demonstrate a modern bride's independence. Rejecting the idea that a woman should be escorted by a man who will "give her away" in the rites that follow, Meghan Markle joined the thousands of women who began reconfiguring the practice in the later twentieth century. The legalization of gay marriage in the twenty-first century further challenged norms. Many couples now enter side by side, hand in hand.

Regal or relaxed, this is one fairy-tale walk that looms large in the Western vocabulary of life-shaping events. Whether they navigate a church aisle or an out-

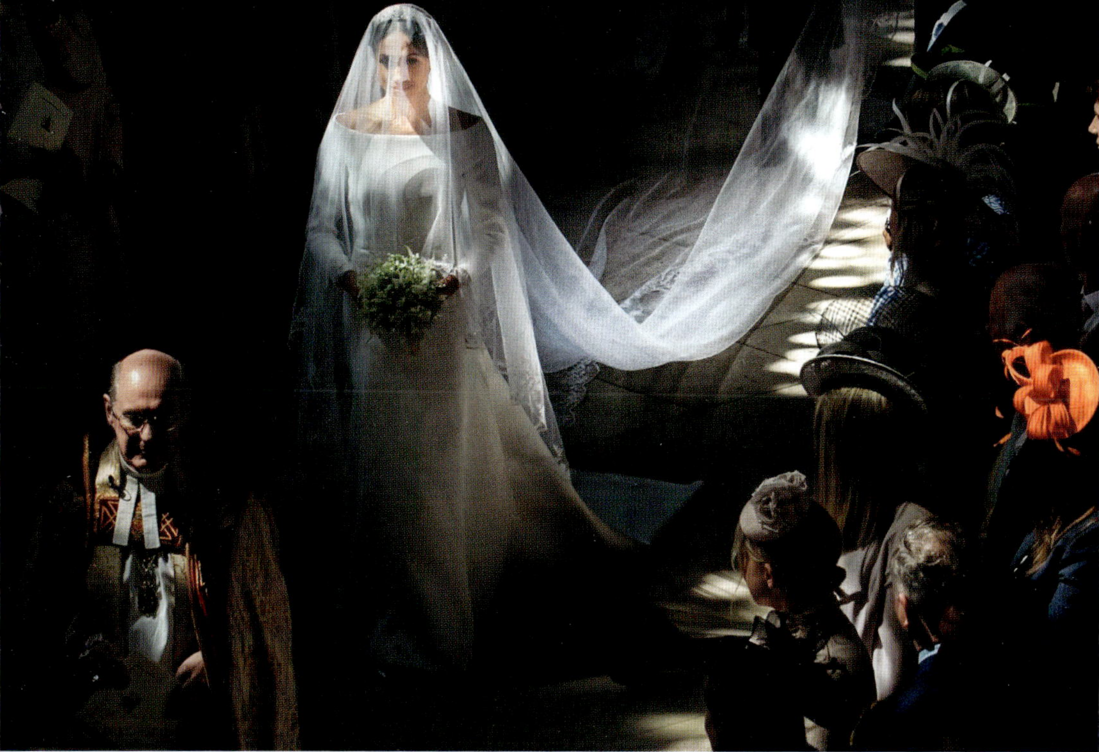

Danny Lawson, Meghan Markle walks alone down the aisle, St. George's Chapel, Windsor Castle, May 19, 2018

door path, the bridal party is often coached to adopt a "hesitation step" to make their entry more majestic, as music plays and handkerchiefs come out. It's all a way for the couple involved to say, "This walk is as consequential as anything a king or queen can do; this is my own royal wedding."

Pandemic Walking

In February and March 2020, human walking took one of the most surprising turns in its long evolution. As the coronavirus spread around the world, governments began to limit the movements of their citizens, in some places putting them under virtual house arrest. Curfews, special paperwork, police checkpoints, and restrictions on when, how long, or how far one might walk all came into play. Some of the ordinances recalled the pre-gaslight policing of nocturnal streets, while others evoked wartime occupation by enemy troops. New, however, was the skittishness about human contact. Maintaining "social distance" became an unprecedented self-inhibition, a novel set of measured steps aimed at shielding the human body from an invisible foe. People crossed streets to avoid brushing past fellow pedestrians; shoppers strained to keep six-foot distances indoors; wariness about the slightest personal interaction became ingrained.

As usual, walkers adapted. Confirmed ramblers redoubled their efforts to get out and away from crowds, while the very thought of being confined suddenly converted thousands to the secular religion of Rousseau and Wordsworth. Whole swaths of the population discovered their inner Romantic walker, realizing for the first time how much a simple walk could contribute to health or sanity. Many of those dubbed "essential workers" walked miles to avoid the close quarters of mass transit. Sales of treadmills soared, as did purchases of dogs, who provided legitimate cover for strolls at all hours. In Paris, a group of neighbors were caught using the same dog for a dozen walks a day. A woman in Quebec walked her husband on a leash, in a declaration of defiance.

When restrictions eased in the summer of 2020, people flooded the countryside, clogging the hiking trails. As cases soared in Europe, police used drones, informants, and cell-phone tracking to clear the landscape. In crowded areas of Britain the law-abiding citizenry turned a normally stress-relieving activity into a stress-inducing one, as exercisers turned against one another for perceived infractions, such as being too far from home. Mindful of such difficulties, the worldwide community of walking artists organized hundreds of solitary but synchronized virtual walks. Some used mobile phones to connect walkers separately "drifting" through far-flung or even imaginary locales. At the same time, slowed-down cities across the world were discovering the benefits of reduced traffic and cleaner air. Walk-friendly areas expanded; emptied avenues became promenades. Yet the effect was only temporary; aggressive driving caused pedestrian fatalities to soar by the end of 2020 and worsen further in 2021 and 2022.

In March 2020, when lockdowns limited mobility all over Europe, an anonymous internet artist updated Caspar David Friedrich's *Wanderer above the Sea of*

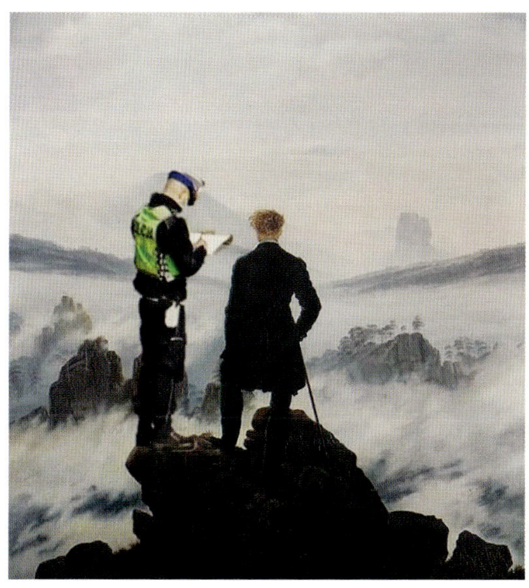

Unknown creator, Internet meme, "Pandemic Walking,"
March 2020, based on Caspar David Friedrich, *The
Wanderer above the Sea of Fog*, 1818

Fog (1818). The classic painting of Romantic walking became an apt emblem for the restrictions of pandemic life: a masked policeman issues a summons to the Wanderer, presumably for exceeding his daily allotment of steps. Friedrich had helped to advertise the rapturous rewards of walking alone in nature. But COVID-19 made the walker's very desire to roam suspect. Governmental efforts to halt the spread of the disease ran headlong into the need of the populace to exercise a hitherto unrecognized human right. Even if they accepted restrictions on social and economic activity, people clamored for the chance to get out and walk—to be restored, refreshed, or simply distracted by setting their feet in motion.

Standing out above a foggy sea of regulations, the Wanderer becomes a target. His morals, motives, and potentially disease-bearing microbes demand scrutiny. In the era of watched walkers, those who wander must be policed to be protected, and if necessary, confined to be cured. The walk that made humans human has become a threat to all humanity.

Conclusion

No walk lasts forever. All the parts of Christo's magnificent *Floating Piers* were recycled within months of the golden path's opening. Christo insisted on this impermanence, remarking that "the disappearance of the artworks is a part of the aesthetic concept. That makes them deeply rooted into freedom." Built to provide an ephemeral, magical experience, the water walkway came and went like the people it supported, leaving only footprints in water, erased in all but memory (and millions of digital images).

For thousands of years art has provided exceptional experiences, made repeatable through the preservation of carefully crafted objects. In the past hundred years, art-as-object has been increasingly supplemented by art-as-ephemeral-encounter. Like a walk in a now-altered landscape, the site-specific, temporary event can be recalled but not repeated. In the past fifty years, as walking has become an integral, intensively explored part of artistic practice, the once disparate categories of life, art, and walking have drawn closer together. Life has always been an extended form of walking, and now art-making and walk-taking intertwine with ever greater frequency.

What happens to a walk once it is completed? The walk is gone, but million-year-old footprints still have stories to tell. So do living bodies and the ever-thickening archaeological layers of artworks, keepsakes, and castoffs that document the passage of humans marching through time. We cannot think of walking without picturing it. What does a walk look like, on a surface or in the memory? These pages have proposed some partial answers: a footstep, a pilgrim, a procession, a garden path, a yellow brick road, a protest march, an urban drift, a line on a screen, or even a golden arrow along which a thousand people at a time can saunter on the waves.

In the end, a visual history of walking may be as evanescent as the activity that it sketches but can never fully describe. Thought lines made by walking in the dawn will change and fade as the sun rises higher over new paths only beginning to form. The poet Wallace Stevens imagined the first humans awakening not just to the consciousness of their immense possibilities but also to the knowledge of how astonishingly transitory their steps would be:

> *And whence they came and whither they shall go*
> *The dew upon their feet shall manifest.*

Notes and Credits

Introduction

"Darwin's bulldog": Thomas Henry Huxley, *Evidence as to Man's Place in Nature* (London: Williams and Norgate, 1863), frontispiece.

"The Road to Homo Sapiens": Zallinger's full illustration shows fifteen figures; the folded version pictured here condenses the sequence into six figures, three of the earliest plus the three latest in the evolutionary schema. Surrounding captions explained that this evolution was not linear or progressive, but Zallinger's visual image overwhelmed the text. Hence, the image's popular nickname, "The March of Progress." Rudolph Franz Zallinger, "The Road to Homo Sapiens," 1965, illustration in F. Clark Howell, *Early Man* (New York: Time-Life, 1965), 41–45.

"worded walking": As a narrative device, walking is central to the Western tradition, from Dante's *Inferno* (1320) and Joyce's *Ulysses* (1922) to Tolkien's *Lord of the Rings* (1954–55) and Cormac McCarthy's *The Road* (2006). The "walk poem," from Wordsworth's autobiographical epic *The Prelude* (1850) to T. S. Eliot's meandering "Love Song of J. Alfred Prufrock" (1915) to Frank O'Hara's casually profound "A Step Away from Them" (1956), plays an equally vital role in modern poetics. Popular anthologies of writing about walking include Ronald Strickland, *Shank's Mare: A Compendium of Remarkable Walks* (New York: Paragon House, 1988); and Duncan Minshull, *While Wandering: A Walking Companion* (New York: Random House, 2014). Most writing about walking comes from a male perspective; for feminine/feminist perspectives, see Kerri Andrews, *Wanderers: A History of Women Walking* (London: Reaktion Books, 2020).

the Romantic walker: See Rebecca Solnit, *Wanderlust: A History of Walking* (New York: Penguin, 2000), esp. 14–29 and 81–132. This may be the best book ever written on walking, combining on-the-trail experiences with cultural history and deep critical insight. See also Morris Marples, *Shank's Pony: A Study of Walking* (London: Country Book Club, 1960); and Joseph A. Amato, *On Foot: A History of Walking* (New York: New York University Press, 2004). On walking in modern culture, see Klaus Benesch and François Specq, eds., *Walking and the Aesthetics of Modernity: Pedestrian Mobility in Literature and the Arts* (New York: Palgrave Macmillan, 2016); and Matthew Beaumont, *The Walker: On Losing and Finding Yourself in the Modern City* (London: Verso, 2020). On walking as a social practice and artistic medium, see C. Hall, Y. Ra, and N. Shoval, eds., *The Routledge International Handbook of Walking* (New York: Routledge, 2018); and Helen Billinghurst, Claire Hind, and Phil Smith, eds., *Walking Bodies: Papers, Provocations, Actions* (Axminster, UK: Triarchy, 2020).

the broader historical terrain: On walking in twentieth-century art, see Maurice Frechuret, ed., *Un siècle d'arpenteurs: Les figures de la marche* (Antibes: Musée Picasso; Paris: Réunion des Musées Nationaux, 2000), containing substantial essays by Daniel Arasse, Thierry Davila, and Patricia Falguières, among others. Arasse's essay in that volume, "La meilleure façon de marcher: Introduction à une histoire de la marche," 35–62, is the best survey to date of the walking motif in European painting. On nineteenth-century walking, see Birgit Verwiebe and Gabriel Montua, eds., *Wanderlust: Von Caspar David Friedrich bis Auguste Renoir* (Munich: Hirmer, 2018). Karin Sagner, *Women Walking: Freedom, Adventure, Independence*, trans. Russell Stockman (2016; New York: Abbeville, 2017), offers brief commentaries on nineteenth-century images. Cultural histories converge on nineteenth-century Paris as central to the meaning of modern walking, and classic studies of Parisian art by T. J. Clark, Hollis Clayson, Robert Herbert, and Theodore Reff, while not singling out walking per se, give rich accounts of how the life of the streets impacts modern art. For a specific treatment, see Nancy Forgione, "Everyday Life in Motion: The Art of Walking in Late 19th-Century Paris," *Art Bulletin* 87, no. 4 (2005): 664–87. On Parisian street sights, see Patrice de Moncan, *La rue parisienne* (Paris: Mécène, 2012).

literary histories of walking: See for example Solnit, *Wanderlust*; Geoff Nicholson, *The Lost Art of Walking: The History, Science, and Literature of Pedestrianism* (New York: Riverhead, 2009); and Merlin Coverley, *The Art of Wandering: The Writer as Walker* (Harpenden, UK: Oldcastle, 2012).

"the march of modern history": Karl Marx, *The Communist Manifesto*, ed. Samuel H. Beer (1848; New York: Appleton Century Crofts, 1955), 33.

works of art themselves: Since its emergence in the 1960s, walking as an artistic practice has been extensively studied, even while remaining little known to the general public. Monographs abound on individual artists, such as Richard Long, Hamish Fulton, and Marina Abramović. For overviews, see Thierry Davila, *Marcher, Créer: Déplacements, flâneries, dérives dans l'art de la fin du XXe siècle* (Paris: Le Regard, 2002); Karen O'Rourke, *Walking and Mapping: Artists as Cartographers* (Cambridge, MA: MIT Press, 2013); David Evans, *The Art of Walking: A Field Guide* (London: Black Dog, 2013); Cynthia Morrison-Bell, *Walk On: 40 Years of Art Walking: From Richard Long to Janet Cardiff* (Sunderland, UK: Art Editions North, 2013); Lexi Lee Sullivan, *Walking Sculpture, 1967–2015* (New Haven: Yale University Press, 2015); and Francesco Careri, *Walkscapes: Walking as an Aesthetic Practice* (2002; Ames, IA: Culicidae, 2017). Revisiting art walking from a feminist perspective, one essay has had particular influence: Deirdre Heddon and Cathy Turner, "Walking Women: Shifting the Tales and Scales of Mobility," *Contemporary Theatre Review* 22, no. 2 (2012): 224–36.

A partial list of exhibitions on walking art include: *Walking and Thinking and Walking*, curated by Bruce Ferguson, Louisiana Museum of Modern Art, Humlebæk, Denmark, 1996; *Walk Ways*, curated by Stuart Horodner, Portland Institute of Contemporary Art, Portland, Washington, and other locations, 2002–4; *Of Walking*, Museum of Contemporary Photography, Columbia College, Chicago, 2013; *Artists' Walks: The Persistence of Peripateticism*, Dorsky Curatorial Projects, New York, 2013; *Walking Sculpture, 1967–2015*, deCordova Sculpture Park and Museum, Lincoln, MA, 2015; *Walking Women*, Somerset House, London; Drill Hall, Forest Fringe, Edinburgh, 2016; and *Walk!*, Schirn Kunsthalle Frankfurt, 2022.

"in walking one escapes even the idea of identity": Frédéric Gros, *Marcher: Une philosophie* (Paris: Flammarion, 2011), 15.

"watched walker": On pedestrian surveillance, see Kashmir Hill, "Your Face Is Not Your Own," *New York Times*, March 19, 2021.

represented in every medium: Unavoidably, a picture book must focus on the nonmoving image, its peculiar power to suggest motion from a position of silence and stasis. Limited though they seem, still images admit what films cover up, the insufficiency of any attempt to portray a walk. By their very absences, frozen steps evoke moments gone before and yet to go.

"Flâner, c'est vivre": Honoré de Balzac, *Physiologie du Mariage* (1829), vol. 16 of *Œuvres complètes de H. de Balzac* (Paris: A. Houssiaux, 1855), 361.

Walking made us human: See Mary Leakey, *National Geographic*, April 1979, 453, cited in Solnit, *Wanderlust*, 41: "This new freedom of forelimbs posed a challenge. The brain expanded to meet it. And mankind was formed."

Image: Rudolph Franz Zallinger, "The Road to Homo Sapiens," 1965. Illustration in F. Clark Howell, *Early Man* (New York: Time-Life, 1965), 41–45.

First Steps

"bipedalism in hominid development": Mary Leakey, *National Geographic*, April 1979, 453.

Why stand up in the first place?: For theories, see Rebecca Solnit, *Wanderlust: A History of Walking* (New York: Penguin, 2000), 30–44. On the evolution and physiology of bipedal motion, see Shane O'Mara, *In Praise of Walking: A New Scientific Exploration* (New York: Random House, 2020), 29–54; and Jeremy DeSilva, *First Steps: How Upright Walking Made Us Human* (New York: Harper, 2021). DeSilva discusses the Laetoli footprints, 89–112, and sums up walking's importance to our species: "Bipedalism set in motion all of the major evolutionary events in the human lineage, from tool use and cooperative parenting to trade networks and language, eventually allowing us, a once humble ape standing in the Miocene forests, to populate the globe" (253).

"Eve's footprints": Lee R. Berger with Brett Hilton-Barber, *In the Footsteps of Eve: The Mystery of Human Origins* (Washington, DC: National Geographic Society, 2000); and Erin Wayman, "Becoming Human: The Evolution of Walking Upright," *Smithsonian Magazine*, August 6, 2012. See also "Earliest 'Human Footprints' Found," BBC News, February 26, 2009, http://news.bbc.co.uk/2 /hi/science/nature/7913375.stm; and Maya Wei-Haas, "Oldest Footprints in Saudi Arabia Reveal Intriguing Step in Early Human Migration," *National Geographic*, September 17, 2020.

Image: Trail of Laetoli footprints, Tanzania, 3.66 million years old. Photo: John Reader / Science Photo Library.

Walking on the Wall

behavioral modernity: For an overview of the debates on this concept, see https://en.wikipedia .org/wiki/Behavioral_modernity. See also Jared Diamond, *The Third Chimpanzee: The Evolution and Future of the Human Animal* (New York: Harper, 2006).

Cave of Swimmers: László Almásy, *The Unknown Sahara*, trans. Andras Zboray (1934; Newbury, UK: Fliegel Jezerniczky Expeditions, 2002).

Cave of Beasts: Rudolph Kuper, *Wadi Sura: The Cave of Beasts* (Cologne: Africa Praehistorica, 2013).

Image: Wall painting, Cave of Beasts, Gilf Kebir, Western Sahara, Egypt, c. 5000 BCE. Photo: John Zada / Alamy Stock Photo.

The First Shoes

Big toes provide stability: Matthew Beaumont, *The Walker: On Losing and Finding Yourself in the Modern City* (London: Verso, 2020), 187–210.

The world's oldest known leather shoe: Kate Ravilious, "World's Oldest Leather Shoe Found— Stunningly Preserved," *National Geographic News*, June 11, 2010, https://www.nationalgeographic .com/news/2010/6/100609-worlds-oldest-leather-shoe-armenia-science/.

all but the poorest Romans wore shoes: On Roman customs, see Harold Whetstone Johnston and Mary Johnston, *The Private Life of the Romans* (Chicago: Scott, Foresman, 1932), sections 250–51, https://www.forumromanum.org/life/johnston_7.html#250. See also T. M. O'Sullivan, *Walking in Roman Culture* (Cambridge, UK: Cambridge University Press, 2011).

Otzi the Iceman: Pam Belluck, "This Shoe Had Prada Beat by 5,500 Years," *New York Times*, June 9, 2010; and Norman Hammond, "Iceman Was Wearing 'Earliest Snowshoes,'" *Times Online*, February 21, 2005, https://www.stonepages.com/news/archives/001167.html.

Image: Prehistoric shoe, Areni-1 Cave, Armenia, c. 3500 BCE. Photo source: R. Pinhasi, B. Gasparian, G. Areshian, D. Zardaryan, A. Smith et al., "First Direct Evidence of Chalcolithic Footwear from the Near Eastern Highlands," *PLoS One* 5, no. 6 (2010): e10984, doi:10.1371/journal.pone.0010984.

A Royal Procession

"first historical document in the world": Bob Brier and Hoyt Hobbs, *Daily Life of the Ancient Egyptians* (Westport, CT: Greenwood, 1999), 202. See also Jacques Kinnaer, "What Is Really Known about the Narmer Palette?" *KMT: A Modern Journal of Ancient Egypt* (Spring 2004): 48–54; and Robert J. Wenke, *The Ancient Egyptian State: The Origins of Egyptian Culture, c. 8000–2000 BC* (Cambridge, UK: Cambridge University Press, 2009).

Image: Narmer Palette, c. 3000 BCE. Siltstone, c. 25³⁄₁₆ × 16⁹⁄₁₆ in. (c. 64 × 42 cm). Egyptian Museum, Cairo [CG 14716].

Walking and Working with Animals

agricultural laborers of the Neolithic period: Peter Bellwood, *First Farmers: The Origins of Agricultural Societies* (Hoboken, NJ: Wiley-Blackwell, 2004).

groups moved just a few miles each day: Shane O'Mara, *In Praise of Walking: A New Scientific Exploration* (New York: Norton, 2019), 42–43.

"burial equipment": Dorothea Arnold, "An Egyptian Bestiary," *Metropolitan Museum of Art Bulletin* 52, no. 4 (Spring 1995): 1, 7–64; and John Taylor, *Death and the Afterlife in Ancient Egypt* (Chicago: University of Chicago Press, 2001).

Image: Model of a man plowing, burial equipment, c. 1981–1885 BCE. Painted wood, 7⁷⁄₈ × 19⁵⁄₈ × 7⁵⁄₈ in. (20 × 49.8 × 19.4 cm). Metropolitan Museum of Art, New York, Gift of Valdemar Hammer Jr., in memory of his father, 1936 [36.5].

Marching into Battle

The Chigi Vase: Jeffrey M. Hurwit, "Reading the Chigi Vase," *Hesperia* 71, no. 1 (January–March 2002): 1–22.

"Nor is anything of more consequence": Vegetius, *Military Institutions of the Romans*, trans. John Clarke (1767; repr., Los Angeles: Enhanced Media, 2017), 12.

"should march with the common military step": Vegetius, *Military Institutions*, 12.

Image: Hoplites marching, Chigi Vase, c. 650 BCE. Polychrome pottery, height 10¼ in. (26 cm). National Etruscan Museum, Villa Giulia, Rome [22679].

A Beautiful Step

kouroi: On *kouroi* and the evolution of Greek statuary, see John Boardman, *Greek Sculpture: The Archaic Period, a Handbook* (London: Thames & Hudson, 1991). Translated, an inscription on the base of the Kroisos Kouros reads: "Stop and show pity beside the marker of Kroisos, dead, whom, when he was in the front ranks, raging Ares destroyed." David M. Robinson, Gorham Phillips Stevens, and Eugene Vanderpool, "An Inscribed Kouros Base," *Hesperia Supplements* 8 (1949): 361–484.

contrapposto: Jason Daley, "Why Viewers Are Drawn to Renaissance Artists' Go-To Pose," *Smithsonian Magazine,* October 28, 2019, https://www.smithsonianmag.com/smart-news/why-pose -preferred-renaissance-artists-so-appealing-180973417/.

Images: Kroisos Kouros, c. 530 BCE. Parian marble, height 74^{13}/$_{16}$ in. (190 cm). National Archaeological Museum of Athens [3851]. Photo: akg-images / De Agostini Picture Lib. / G. Dagli Orti.

    Polykleitos, *Doryphoros*, c. 450 BCE. Marble Roman copy after a lost bronze original, height 78^{11}/$_{16}$ in. (200 cm). Naples National Archeological Museum. Photo: dea / g. nimatallah, Getty Images.

She Who Steps

korai: On *kore* statuary, see John Boardman, *Greek Art*, 5th ed. (London: Thames & Hudson, 2016).

Gradiva: A Pompeian Fantasy: Both Jensen's novella and Freud's interpretation can be found in Helen M. Downey, trans. and ed., *Delusion and Dream* (New York: Moffat, Yard, 1922), available at https://www.gutenberg.org/files/44917/44917-h/44917-h.htm.

"by her gait the true goddess is known": Virgil, *Aeneid* 1.405 ("vera incessu patuit dea").

unlock the Unconscious: Andreas Mayer, "Gradiva's Gait: Tracing the Figure of a Walking Woman," *Critical Inquiry* 38, no. 3 (2012): 554–78.

Image: "Gradiva," Neo-Attic Roman bas-relief, c. 2nd century CE, probably a copy of a Greek original, 4th century BCE. Marble, height 28^{15}/$_{16}$ in. (73.5 cm). Chiaramonte Museum, Vatican, Rome [1284].

Walking on Stone

the designer of the bridge: Caius Julius Lacer is buried at one end of the bridge in a small temple whose inscription declares that the bridge will last as long as the earth does. Surprisingly, given the impressive stonework that greets travelers, the longevity of the bridge owes much to its concealed concrete core, a building method the Romans used extensively from 150 BCE but that no other society attempted until the Industrial Revolution. While the mighty arches have been largely impervious to weather and the passage of time, they were partially destroyed four times from 1214 to 1836, to prevent enemy troops and supplies from crossing.

the first paved roads: Whatever the location and motivation for a road, it would have been used mainly by walkers until the twentieth century. Drivers of carts and wagons routinely led their horses, donkeys, or oxen on foot. Passengers got out of a coach to walk up a steep hill or to push if the coach got stuck in snow or mud. And poorer people had no choice but to walk. Even in modern times, photographs of major cities show crowds of pedestrians cutting every which way across streets, competing with buses, streetcars, and automobiles, trying to take the most direct line to their destinations.

the walker's perennial desire: Gretchen Reynolds, "Born to Be Lazy? What Bears Can Teach Us about Our Exercise Habits," *New York Times*, April 13, 2021.

A trail is encoded information: Robert Moor, *On Trails: An Exploration* (New York: Simon & Schuster, 2016), 24–27, 254.

Image: Trajan's Bridge at Alcántara, Spain, 104–6. Photo: Dantla, Wikimedia.

A Cross to Bear

a carved ivory casket: British Museum catalogue information at https://www.britishmuseum.org/collection/object/H_1856-0623-4. See also Jeffrey Spier, ed., *Picturing the Bible: The Earliest Christian Art* (New Haven, CT: Yale University Press, 2007).

Via Dolorosa: Herbert Thurston, *The Stations of the Cross* (London: Burns & Oates, 1906); "Via Dolorosa," https://en.wikipedia.org/wiki/Via_Dolorosa; and George Cyprian Alston, "Way of the Cross," *The Catholic Encyclopedia*, vol. 15 (New York: Robert Appleton, 1912), http://www.newadvent.org/cathen/15569a.htm.

Image: Panel from a casket, Late Roman, 420–30. Ivory, $2^{15}/_{16} \times 3^{7}/_{8}$ in. (7.5 × 9.8 cm). British Museum [1856,0623.4].

Walking Impaired

"Grace is poured": Psalms 45.2 (AV), "Grace is poured into thy lips: therefore God hath blessed thee for ever." (Latin Vulgate: "Diffusa est gratia in labiis tuis; propterea benedixit te Deus in aeternum.")

"What goes on four feet at dawn": The riddle of the Sphinx was widely known in the ancient world and alluded to in Sophocles's *Oedipus the King*, first performed 429 BCE.

an aged nun: For context see Philippe Hernigou, "Crutch Art Painting in the Middle Age as Orthopaedic Heritage, Part I: The Lepers, the Poliomyelitis, the Cripples," *International Orthopaedics* 38, no. 6 (2014): 1329–35, https://doi.org/10.1007/s00264-013-2266-x.

Images: Allegorical figure on crutches embodying Vieillesse (Old Age), c. 1490–1500, in *The Romance of the Rose*, from the Netherlands (Bruges). British Library [Harley Ms. 4425, f. 10v]. Photo: © British Library Board. All Rights Reserved / Bridgeman Images.

Decorated initial D, c. 1260–70. Music manuscript, France or Flanders. Leaf: $18^{15}/_{16} \times 13^{3}/_{4}$ in. (48.1 × 34.9 cm). J. Paul Getty Museum, Los Angeles [Ms. 44 / Ludwig VI 5 (92.MH.22), p. 202].

Pilgrimage

pilgrimage to a sacred site: On pilgrimage as a concept, see Rebecca Solnit, *Wanderlust: A History of Walking* (New York: Penguin, 2000), 45–63.

the earliest account of a Christian pilgrimage: See John Wilkinson, *Egeria's Travels* (Oxford, UK: Aris & Phillips, 2006).

Masters of the Gold Scrolls: These were illuminators from the Netherlands, especially Bruges. Active in the early fifteenth century, they take their name from a characteristic use of gold foliated decoration in their backgrounds.

Image: Masters of the Gold Scrolls, *Pilgrim on the Road to the Shrine of Saint James*, from a Book of Hours, Belgium, perhaps Bruges, c. 1440. Vellum, 8⅞ × 6⁵⁄₁₆ in. (22.5 × 16.1 cm). Morgan Library & Museum, New York [MS M.19 fol. 165v]. Purchased by J. Pierpont Morgan (1837–1913) in 1900. Photo: The Morgan Library & Museum, New York.

Converging on the Cathedral

Chartres: See Malcolm Miller, *Chartres Cathedral* (New York: Riverside, 1997).

Good Samaritan window: See Jean-Paul Deremble and Colette Manhes, *Le vitrail du Bon Samaritain: Chartres, Sens, Bourges* (Paris: Le Centurion, 1987); and "The Good Samaritan Window, Chartres Cathedral," https://en.wikipedia.org/wiki/The_Good_Samaritan_Window,_Chartres_Cathedral.

Image: Good Samaritan Window, panel 7, Chartres Cathedral, 13th century. Photo © Jill K H Geoffrion, jillgeoffrion.com.

Covered Walking

the people of Bologna built sheltering arches: Francesca Bocchi, *I portici di Bologna e l'edilizia civile medievale* (Bologna: Grafis Edizioni, 1990); "I Portici di Bologna," http://comune.bologna.it /portici/en/porticoes-world; and the UNESCO list of World Heritage Sites, https://whc.unesco.org /en/list/.

Image: Arcades, Bologna, Italy, 11th century onward. Photo: Nacchio Brothers.

Out of Eden

Masaccio's *Expulsion from the Garden of Eden*: On the *Expulsion* and the Brancacci Chapel paintings, see John T. Spike, *Masaccio* (New York: Abbeville, 1996); and Diane Cole Ahl, "The Brancacci Chapel," in *The Cambridge Companion to Masaccio*, ed. Diane Cole Ahl (Cambridge, UK: Cambridge University Press, 2002), 138–57.

Image: Masaccio, *Expulsion from the Garden of Eden*, 1425. Fresco, 81⅞ × 34⅝ in. (208 × 88 cm). Brancacci Chapel, Florence.

Walking on Water

an actual landscape: Till-Holger Borchert, "Konrad Witz: Basel," *Burlington Magazine* 153 (July 2011): 497–99.

Image: Konrad Witz, *The Miraculous Draft of the Fishes*, 1444. Oil on panel, 52 × 59¹³⁄₁₆ in. (132 × 154 cm). Musée d'Art et d'Histoire, Geneva.

Wandering Jews

Washington Haggadah: For the fuller context of this image, see Joel ben Simeon, *The Washington Haggadah: A Fifteenth-Century Manuscript from the Library of Congress*, essays by David Stern and

Katrin Kogman-Appel (Washington, DC: Library of Congress, 2011). On Ben Simeon's travels, see Sandra Hindman, "I Am the Scribe, Joel Ben Simeon," *Les Enluminures*, January 19, 2021, https://www.textmanuscripts.com/blog/entry/01-21-joel-ben-simeon.

the walker blithely ignores European regulations: Anti-Semitic legislation snowballed in Europe starting in the thirteenth century, after the Lateran Council of 1215 decreed that Jews living in Christian lands had to dress in a way that marked their difference.

"I shall stand and rest": The earliest source is Roger of Wendover's Latin chronicle *Flores Historiarum*, year 1228 (recorded c. 1235). See J. A. Giles, *Roger of Wendover's Flowers of History* (London: Bohn, 1849), 2:513.

the endless struggles of the working class: Daniel Arasse, "La meilleure façon de marcher: Introduction à une histoire de la marche," in *Un siècle d'arpenteurs: Les figures de la marche*, ed. Maurice Frechuret (Paris: Réunion des Musées Nationaux, 2000), 54–59. See also Linda Nochlin, "Gustave Courbet's *Meeting*: A Portrait of the Artist as a Wandering Jew," *Art Bulletin* 49 (1967): 209–22. The Wandering Jew's perceived connection to the "march of history" motif was summed up in the title of a French magazine in 1834: *The Wandering Jew: Monthly Review of Progress*.

the weary wanderer has appeared: On further images of the Wandering Jew motif, see Richard I. Cohen, "The 'Wandering Jew' from Medieval Legend to Modern Metaphor," in *The Art of Being Jewish in Modern Times*, ed. Barbara Kirsheblatt Gimblett and Jonathan Karp (Philadelphia: University of Pennsylvania Press, 2007), 147–75; and Joanna L. Brichetto, "The Wandering Image: Converting the Wandering Jew" (master's thesis, Graduate School of Vanderbilt University, 2006), https://core.ac.uk/download/pdf/46926339.pdf. Claims of actual sightings of the Wandering Jew have also kept the legend alive. A partial list of encounters includes Hamburg in 1547, Vienna in 1599, Prague in 1602, Brussels in 1640, Leipzig in 1642, Paris in 1644, Munich in 1721; Brussels in 1774, and Newcastle in 1790. Perhaps passing the torch of peripatetic religion, the Wandering Jew was last claimed to be seen by a Mormon, in Utah in 1868.

Images: Marc Chagall, *The Wandering Jew*, 1923–25. Oil on canvas, 28 ⅓ × 22½ in. (72 × 57 cm). Musée d'Art Moderne et Contemporain (MAMCO), Geneva, Switzerland.

Joel ben Simeon, traveling figure, Washington Haggadah (detail), Germany, 1478. F. 34v, MS Heb. 1. Parchment, page 8⅞ × 6⅛ in. (22.5 × 15.5 cm). Library of Congress, African and Middle Eastern Division, Washington, DC [2018757799].

A Hell of a Walk

a revolutionary book design: Barbara J. Watts, "Sandro Botticelli's Drawings for Dante's 'Inferno': Narrative Structure, Topography, and Manuscript Design," *Artibus et Historiae* 16, no. 32 (1995): 163–201; and Heinrich-Thomas Schulze Altcappenberg, *Sandro Botticelli: The Drawings for Dante's Divine Comedy* (New York: Harry N. Abrams, 2000).

Image: Sandro Botticelli, *Divine Comedy*, canto 18, c. 1490. Parchment, 12⅝ × 18½ in. (32 × 47 cm), projected page size 25³⁄₁₆ × 18½ in. (64 × 47 cm). Berlin Museum [MS Ham. 31, Cim. 33].

A Miraculous Procession

the Scuola decided to commission nine paintings: For the context of the painting, see "Bellini, Gentile: Miracle of the Cross at the Bridge of San Lorenzo," Web Gallery of Art, https://www.wga.hu/frames-e.html?/html/b/bellini/gentile/miracl2.html.

official painter for the Doges of Venice: On Bellini in Venice, see Hugh Honour, *The Companion Guide to Venice* (Englewood Cliffs, NJ: Prentice-Hall, 1983).

Image: Gentile Bellini, *The Miracle of the Cross at the Bridge of S. Lorenzo,* 1500. Oil on canvas, 10 ft. 7³⁄₁₆ in. × 14 ft. ⁵⁄₁₆ in. (323 × 430 cm). Gallerie dell'Accademia, Venice.

Peripatetic Philosophy

modern scientific study confirms it: Ferris Jabr, "Why Walking Helps Us Think," *New Yorker,* September 3, 2014, https://www.newyorker.com/tech/annals-of-technology/walking-helps-us -think; and May Wong, "Stanford Study Finds Walking Improves Creativity," *Stanford News,* April 24, 2014, https://news.stanford.edu/2014/04/24/walking-vs-sitting-042414/.

Using the school as a focal point: Giorgio Vasari, "Raphael of Urbino," in *Lives of the Artists,* trans. Julia Conaway Bondanella and Peter Bondanella (Oxford, UK: Oxford University Press, 1991), 314–17.

connecting the vaulted space: Heinrich Wölfflin, *Classic Art: An Introduction to the Italian Renaissance,* 2nd ed. (London: Phaidon, 1953), 94.

"If we observe very carefully someone who is walking": Thomas Bernhard, *Walking: A Novella,* trans. Kenneth J. Northcott (1971; repr., Chicago: University of Chicago Press, 2015), 73.

Images: Raphael, *The School of Athens,* 1509–11. Fresco, 18 ft. ⁹⁄₁₆ in. × 25 ft. 3 in. (550 × 770 cm). Pinacoteca Ambrosiana, Vatican Museums.

Raphael, Plato and Aristotle walking and disputing, *The School of Athens* (detail), 1509–11. Fresco. Pinacoteca Ambrosiana, Vatican Museums. Photo: Eric Vandeville / akg-images.

Vagrants, Vagabonds, and Beggars

"sturdy beggar," "whipped until the blood streams from their bodies," "if it happens that a vagabond has been idling," "rogues": Quotations and information from Karl Marx, "Bloody Legislation against the Expropriated, from the End of the 15th Century: Forcing Down of Wages by Acts of Parliament," chap. 28 in *Capital: A Critique of Political Economy,* vol. 1, ed. Friedrich Engels, trans. Samuel Moore and Edward Aveling (Moscow: Progress, 1887), 522–27.

Image: Heinrich Aldegrever, after Cornelis Anthonisz., allegorical figure of Poverty as a wandering vagabond, 1549. Engraving, 2³⁄₄ × 2 in. (7 × 5 cm). Rijksmuseum, Amsterdam [RP-P-OB-2730].

Walking Blind

medical conditions specific enough: Zeynel A. Karcioglu, "Ocular Pathology in *The Parable of the Blind Leading the Blind* and Other Paintings by Pieter Bruegel," *Survey of Ophthalmology* 47, no. 1 (2002): 55–62, doi:10.1016/S0039-6257(01)00290-9.

Brueghel interposes an actual landscape: Andre de Vries, *Flanders: A Cultural History* (New York: Oxford University Press, 2007), 232.

Image: Pieter Brueghel the Elder, *The Blind Leading the Blind,* 1568. Distemper on linen, 33⁷⁄₈ × 60⁵⁄₈ in. (86 × 154 cm). Museo e Real Bosco di Capodimonte, Naples.

High Heels Arrive

elaborately decorated cork-soled platform shoes: Hunter Oatman-Stanford, "These Chopines Weren't Made for Walking: Precarious Platforms for Aristocratic Feet," *Collectors Weekly*, April 17, 2014, https://www.collectorsweekly.com/articles/these-chopines-werent-made-for-walking/.

lift-the-flap format: Many students learned anatomy through lifting layers of illustrations that followed the order of a dissection, as in *De Humani Corporis Fabrica Librorum Epitome*, printed by Andreas Vesalius in 1543 in Basel. On Bertelli's context and other projects, see Suzanne Karr Schmidt, "Interactive and Sculptural Printmaking in the Renaissance" (PhD diss., Yale University, 2006), chap. 12, doi: 10.1163/9789004354135_014.

"this extension keeps her body attractive and erect": Fabritio Caroso, in *Nobilità di dame* (1600), translated as *Courtly Dance of the Renaissance* by Julia Sutton (New York: Dover, 1995), 141.

Images: Pietro Bertelli, publisher, *Courtesan and Blind Cupid*, c. 1588. Engraving with skirt flap (shown flat and lifted), 5½ × 7⁷⁄₁₆ in. (14 × 18.9 cm). Metropolitan Museum of Art, New York, Elisha Whittelsey Collection, The Elisha Whittelsey Fund, 1955 [55.503.30]. The large Bertelli family was active in publishing in Venice in the second half of the sixteenth century; the attribution and dating provided here are based on similarities to works in the New York Public Library (mem b537v) and British Museum (1880,0710.842 and 1880,0710.854).

The Pilgrim's Progress

first novel in English: One of the earliest claims was made by J. Chapman in *Westminster Review* 138 (1892): 610.

Over twenty places near Bunyan's Bedfordshire home: Vera Brittain, *In the Steps of John Bunyan* (London: Rich & Cowan, 1949).

the most reprinted book: John Bunyan, *The Pilgrim's Progress*, ed. W. R. Owens, Oxford World's Classics (Oxford, UK: Oxford University Press, 2003), xiii.

Image: John Bunyan, *The Pilgrim's Progress*, frontispiece and title page (London: Nathaniel Ponder, 1679). Photo: Beinecke Rare Book and Manuscript Library, Yale University.

Walking with the Sun King

The nobility took the first step: Rebecca Solnit, *Wanderlust: A History of Walking* (New York: Penguin, 2000), 86–87.

a larger group of the wealthy: Philippe Prévôt, *Histoire des jardins* (Bordeaux, France: Éditions Sud Ouest, 2006), 133–34.

Standing at the center of European fashion: Ian Thompson, *The Sun King's Garden: Louis XIV, André Le Nôtre and the Creation of the Gardens of Versailles* (London: Bloomsbury, 2006).

"the most public palace in Europe": Daniëlle O. Kisluk-Grosheide and Bertrand Rondot, eds., *Visitors to Versailles: From Louis XIV to the French Revolution* (New York: Metropolitan Museum of Art, 2018), 2.

The king himself enjoyed conducting: Kisluk-Grosheide and Rondot, *Visitors to Versailles*, 15.

Image: Étienne Allegrain, *Louis XIV Taking a Walk, Seen from the North Parterre of the Gardens of Versailles* (detail), 1688. Oil on canvas, 7 ft. 6⅛ in. × 9 ft. 8¾ in. (234 × 296.5 cm). Musée National des Châteaux de Versailles et de Trianon [MV 752].

A Good Walk Spoiled

"A good walk spoiled": Popularly attributed to Mark Twain, the saying appears to date to 1903. "Golf Is a Good Walk Spoiled," May 28, 2010, https://quoteinvestigator.com/2010/05/28/golf-good-walk/.

The US Supreme Court ruled: Dave Anderson, "The Cart Doesn't Hit the Ball," *New York Times*, May 30, 2001.

Image: Unknown artist (attributed to William Mosman), *Sir James MacDonald, 1741–1766, and Sir Alexander MacDonald, 1744/45–1795* (*The MacDonald Boys Playing Golf*), c. 1749. Oil on canvas, 69½ × 58 in. (176.5 × 147.3 cm). National Galleries of Scotland, Edinburgh [PG 2127].

Picture Perfect

"Pictures to walk into": Martin Warnke, *Political Landscape: The Art History of Nature* (London: Reaktion, 1994), 80. In 1752 "garden designer Joseph Spence defined the garden as a picture gallery under the open sky," 81.

"All gardening is landscape painting": Alexander Pope, cited in Joseph Spence, *Observations, Anecdotes, and Characters of Books and Men Collected from Conversation*, ed. James M. Osborn, 2 vols. (Oxford: Clarendon, 1966), Anecdote 606.

"Kent leaped the fence": Horace Walpole, "On Modern Gardening," in *Anecdotes of Painting in England*, 4th ed. (London: 1796), 4:289.

Image: Jean Baptiste Claude Chatelain, artist; George Bickham, engraver, *A View to the Grotto of the Serpentine River in the Alder Grove in the Gardens of Earl Temple at Stow, in Buckinghamshire*, 1753. Hand-colored engraving on wove paper, 9¹³⁄₁₆ × 15³⁄₁₆ in. (25 × 38.5 cm). Yale Center for British Art, Paul Mellon Collection [B1995.13.172].

Public Parks

Gabriel de Saint-Aubin specialized in painting: Ken Johnson, "Forever Drawing the World in All Its Minuscule Detail," *New York Times*, November 2, 2007.

a new form, the "public" park: On the historical interplay between park and garden, see Colta Ives, *Public Parks, Private Gardens: Paris to Provence* (New York: Metropolitan Museum of Art, 2018).

"To walk abroad and recreate yourselves": William Shakespeare, *Julius Caesar*, act 3, scene 2, lines 261–65.

"everyone he sees serves as a book": François de Grenaille, *Les plaisirs des dames* (1641), cited in Laurent Turcot, *Le promeneur à Paris au XVIIIe siècle* (Paris: Gallimard, 2007), 42 (my translation).

Image: Gabriel de Saint-Aubin, *Society Taking a Promenade*, c. 1761. Pen, ink, and some watercolor, 12⅜ × 10³⁄₁₆ in. (31.4 × 25.8 cm). Hermitage Museum, St. Petersburg.

The Walk of Self-Discovery

"the pleasures of going one knows not where": Jean-Jacques Rousseau, *Confessions*, trans. J. M. Cohen (Harmondsworth: Penguin, 1953), 124.

"I can only meditate when I am walking . . . my mind only works with my legs": Rousseau, *Confessions*, 382.

"Never did I think so much, exist so vividly": Rousseau, *Confessions*, 158.

"Brightly colored flowers": Jean-Jacques Rousseau, *Reveries of a Solitary Walker* (1782), trans. Russell Goulbourne (New York: Oxford University Press, 2011), 77.

Image: Jean Charles Thévenin, engraver, *Jean Jacques Rousseau*, 1840. Steel engraving with later coloring after a design by Charles Gleyre (1806–1874), after the 1764 pastel bust portrait of Rousseau by Quentin de La Tour. Published in *Le Plutarque français*, vol. 5 (Paris: Langlois et Leclercq, 1846), 271. Photo: Paul D. Stewart / Science Photo Library.

Night Walks

"What things to see when all eyes are closed!": Nicolas Edme Restif de La Bretonne, *Les nuits de Paris, ou Le spectateur-nocturne* (Paris, 1788), 3–4 (my translation). Original text available at https://gallica.bnf.fr/ark:/12148/bpt6k6423512k.

"Rousseau of the gutter": This assessment came from a contemporary, the playwright Jean-François de La Harpe. See G. Peignot, *Recherches historiques, bibliographiques et littéraires sur La Harpe* (Paris, 1820), 41.

"I exposed my health, my life, my honor, my virtue": Restif de La Bretonne, *Les nuits de Paris*, 5 (my translation).

"Prepare for Death, if here at Night you roam": Samuel Johnson, "London" (1738). Yale digital edition of the *Works of Samuel Johnson*, 59, http://www.yalejohnson.com/frontend/sda_viewer?n=107785. On the challenges of walking London by night, see Matthew Beaumont, *Nightwalking: A Nocturnal History of London* (London: Verso, 2015).

"on their new-found lantern": George Gordon, Lord Byron, *Don Juan*, canto 11, stanza 26.

Image: Jean-Michel Moreau, known as Moreau le Jeune, "The Owl-Spectator, Walking at Night in the Streets of the Capital," engraving, frontispiece for Nicolas Edme Restif de La Bretonne, *Les nuits de Paris* (Paris, 1788). 6⅞ × 4¹⁄₁₆ in. (17.5 × 10.3 cm). Bibliothèque Nationale / Gallica, Paris.

The Women's March to Versailles

recording history as it happened: Claudette Hould, *La révolution par l'écriture: Les tableaux historiques de la Révolution française, une entreprise éditorial d'information, 1791–1817* (Paris: Vizille, 2005).

"Here is the baker, the baker's wife, and the baker's little boy": "The Women of Paris March on Versailles," Joseph Weber et al. (1789) in E. L. Higgins, *The French Revolution As Told by Contemporaries* (Boston: Houghton Mifflin, 1938), 131.

Image: Unknown artist, "To Versailles, to Versailles," c. 1792. Hand-colored engraving, folio size, $12^5/_8 \times 19^1/_{16}$ in. (32 × 48.5 cm). Published in *Tableaux historiques de la Révolution française*, no. 31 (Paris: Pierre Didot, 1791–96).

Walking Tours

"rough fragments of ruin": William Gilpin, *Observations on the River Wye: And Several Parts of South Wales, & c. Relative Chiefly to Picturesque Beauty; Made in the Summer of the Year 1770* London: R. Blamire, 1789), 50.

"There is a joy in every spot made known by times of old": John Keats, July 19, 1818, "Lines Written in the Highlands after a Visit to Burns's Country," in *The Poems of John Keats*, ed. E. de Selincourt (New York: Dodd, Mead, 1905), 358.

"to make a sort of Prologue to the Life I intend to pursue": John Keats to Benjamin Haydon, April 8, 1814, *The Letters of John Keats, 1814–1821*, 2 vols., ed. Hyder Edward Rollins (Cambridge, MA: Harvard University Press, 1958), 2:264.

"Life to him would be death to me": John Keats to his brother George, September 17, 1819, *Letters of John Keats*, 2:212.

Image: J. M. W. Turner, *Tintern Abbey: The Crossing and Chancel, Looking towards the East Window*, 1794. Graphite and watercolor on paper, $14^1/_8 \times 9^{13}/_{16}$ in. (35.9 × 25 cm). Tate Gallery, London [D00374 Turner Bequest].

The Romantic Walker

"The artist should paint not only what he sees before him": Helmust Börsch-Supan, *Caspar David Friedrich*, trans. Sarah Twohig (New York: George Braziller, 1974), 7–8.

"figures seen from behind": On Friedrich's figures in the landscape, see Joseph Leo Koerner, *Caspar David Friedrich and the Subject of Landscape* (New Haven, CT: Yale University Press, 1995).

"They gaily ascended the downs": Jane Austen, *Sense and Sensibility* (1811; Harmondsworth, UK: Penguin, 1969), 74 (chap. 9).

"Walked I know not where": Dorothy Wordsworth, Alfoxden Journal (March 30, 1798), in *Journals of Dorothy Wordsworth*, ed. William Knight (London: Macmillan, 1897), 1:30.

"I only went out for a walk": John Muir, *John of the Mountains: The Unpublished Journals of John Muir*, ed. Linnie Marsh Wolfe (Boston: Houghton Mifflin, 1938), 471.

Image: Caspar David Friedrich, *Chalk Cliffs on Rügen*, 1818. Oil on canvas, $35^5/_8 \times 27^{15}/_{16}$ in. (90.5 × 71 cm). Kunst Museum, Winterthur, Switzerland.

Crossing the Street

"One need only push some criminal or godless debtor gently through the garden gate": Ludwig

Tieck, cited in Martin Warnke, *The Political Landscape: The Art History of Nature* (London: Reaktion, 1994), 82.

"The human species . . . walks with a firm and sure step on the path of the truth": Marquis de Condorcet, *Esquisse d'un tableau historique des progrès de l'esprit humain*, 1795 (Paris: Editions Sociales, 1971), 284 (my translation).

Image: Louis-Léopold Boilly, *Pay to Pass (Passez-Payez)*, also known as *L'averse* ("The Shower"), c. 1803. Oil on canvas, $12^{13}/_{16} \times 15^{15}/_{16}$ in. (32.5 × 40.5 cm). Louvre Museum, Paris.

Arcades

The Palais Royal and its successors: Long passageways of sheltered shops became not only commercial centers but tourist attractions in their own right. In Paris the well-to-do flocked to the Passage des Panoramas (1800) and the elegant Galerie Vivienne (1823); London sported the Burlington Arcade (1819); the Galeries Royales Saint-Hubert (1846–47) dazzled Brussels; and the imposing Galleria Vittorio Emanuele (1878) in Milan still draws crowds today. See Bertrand Lemoine, *Les passages couverts* (Paris: Délégation à l'Action Artistique de la Ville de Paris [AAVP], 1990); and Andrew Ayers, *The Architecture of Paris* (Stuttgart: Axel Menges, 2004), 47–49.

Image: Georg Emanuel Opiz, *Palais Royal*, 1815. Pen and ink with watercolor, $13^{11}/_{16} \times 10^{9}/_{16}$ in. (34.7 × 26.8 cm). Bibliothèque Nationale, Paris [ark:/12148/btv1b10303273h].

London Flamboyance

Hyde Park and its tony thoroughfare: Roy Porter, *London: A Social History* (London: Penguin UK, 2000); and Paul Rabbitts, *Hyde Park: The People's Park* (Stroud, UK: Amberley, 2015).

the first unclothed statue: The Wellington monument was reviewed in *Gentleman's Magazine* 92, part 2 (1822): 70–71.

satirized the statue in another drawing: George Cruikshank, "Backside & front view of the ladies fancy-man, Paddy Carey O'Killus Esqr." (1822), https://www.britishmuseum.org/collection /object/P_1865-1111-2120.

Image: George Cruikshank, *Monstrosities of 1822*, 1822. Hand-colored etching, $10^{3}/_{16} \times 14^{3}/_{16}$ in. (25.8 × 36.1 cm). Library of Congress [PC 1–14438].

The Underground Railroad

"When her master saw her": *The Narrative of Sojourner Truth*, ed. Olive Gilbert (Boston: Printed for the Author, 1850), 43, https://digital.library.upenn.edu/women/truth/1850/1850.html.

"they who took passage": Andrew Ritchie, *The Soldier, the Battle, and the Victory: Being a Brief Account of the Work of Rev. John Rankin in the Anti-Slavery Cause* (Cincinnati: Western Tract and Book Society, 1870), 96–97.

an estimated hundred thousand people: James A. Banks, and Cherry A. Banks, *March toward Freedom: A History of Black Americans* (Belmont, CA: Fearon, 1974); and David W. Blight, ed., *Passages to Freedom: The Underground Railroad in History and Memory* (Washington, DC: Smithsonian, 2004).

"I never ran my train off the track": Quoted in Catherine Clinton, *Harriet Tubman: The Road to Freedom* (New York: Little, Brown, 2004), 192.

Image: Unknown artist, "The Runaway," 1837, in *The Anti-Slavery Record* 3 (July 1837): 1. Rare Book & Manuscript Library, Columbia University.

The Self-Guided Walk

"the tableau of nature's grandeur": Claude-François Denecourt, *Guide du voyageur dans la forêt de Fontainebleau* (Paris: Delaunay, 1839), 2, http://www.fontainebleau-foret.fr/SiteEncyclo/pdf/denecourt.pdf (my translation).

an artistic sense of his own: On the artistic exploration of the forest, see Kimberly A. Jones, ed., *In the Forest of Fontainebleau: Painters and Photographers from Corot to Monet* (New Haven, CT: Yale University Press, 2008).

"The seven- or eight-hundred-year-old oaks": "Claude-François Denecourt, le sylvain de la forêt," *Le guide Denecourt*, 1847, http://www.fontainebleau-photo.fr/2011/01/claude-francois-denecourt_30 (my translation).

"pictures to walk into": Martin Warnke, *Political Landscape: The Art History of Nature* (London: Reaktion, 1994), 80.

the world's first national park: "Forêt de Fontainebleau," https://fr.wikipedia.org/wiki/For%C3%AAt_de_Fontainebleau.

Image: Edme Blondeau, engraver, *Map Indicating the Notable Sites and Viewpoints in the Forest of Fontainebleau, 1839.* 12 $\frac{1}{8}$ × 16 in. (30.8 × 40.6 cm). Château de Fontainebleau, Photo © RMN-Grand Palais (Château de Fontainebleau) / Gérard Blot.

The Flâneur

"The observer at rest is only half an observer": Auguste de Lacroix, "Le Flâneur," in *Les français peints par eux-memes*, vol. 3 (1841; Paris: Philippart, 1876), 26 (my translation). Gavarni's drawing accompanied this article.

"We do not admit even the existence of a flâneur anywhere but Paris": Lacroix, 26. On the larger social context, see Priscilla Parkhurst Fergusson, *Paris as Revolution: Writing the Nineteenth-Century City* (Berkeley: University of California Press, 1997).

"What separates the Man from the brute": Louis Huart, *Physiologie du flâneur* (Paris: Aubert, 1841), 7, https://gallica.bnf.fr/ark:/12148/bpt6k62352r (my translation). Adapting Plato's famous definition of a human, Huart concludes, man is "a featherless biped in a double-breasted overcoat, who smokes as he strolls," 8.

"For the perfect *flâneur*": Charles Baudelaire, *The Painter of Modern Life* (1863), trans. Jonathan Mayne (New York: Da Capo, 1964), 9.

the Marxist critic Walter Benjamin: Walter Benjamin, "On Some Motifs in Baudelaire" (1939), in *Illuminations: Essays and Reflections*, ed. Hannah Arendt, trans. Harry Zohn (New York: Schocken, 1968), 155–200.

"invisible flâneuse": See Aruna D'Souza and Tom McDonough, eds., *The Invisible Flaneuse?: Gender, Public Space and Visual Culture in Nineteenth Century Paris* (Manchester, UK: Manchester University Press, 2006); and Lauren Elkin, *Flâneuse: Women Walk the City in Paris, New York, Tokyo, Venice, and London* (New York: FSG, 2017).

"to see the world": Baudelaire, *Painter of Modern Life*, 9.

by way of Virginia Woolf: Her classic essay is "Street Haunting: A London Adventure" (1927), in *The Death of the Moth and Other Essays* (London: Hogarth, 1948).

"No one paid any attention to me": George Sand, cited in Anke Gleber, *The Art of Taking a Walk* (Princeton, NJ: Princeton University Press, 1999), 173.

Image: Paul Gavarni (Sulpice Guillaume Chevalier), "The Flâneur," in *Les français peints par eux-mêmes*, 1841. Hand-colored print, engraved by Aristide Louis, 10½ × 5¹³⁄₁₆ in. (26.7 × 14.8 cm). From the article "Le Flâneur" by Auguste de Lacroix, vol. 3. Slovak National Library.

Walking Work

"My dream is to characterize the type": Quoted in Estelle M. Hurll, *Jean Francois Millet* (Frankfurt: Outlook, 2000), 4. On the heroism of the walking laborer, see Daniel Arasse, "La meilleure façon de marcher: Introduction à une histoire de la marche," in *Les figures de la marche: Un siècle d'arpenteurs*, ed. Maurice Frechuret (Paris: Réunion des musées nationaux, 2000), 55–59.

the muddy nobility of agriculture: Walt Whitman lauded Millet's "sublime murkiness and original pent fury." See "Jean-François Millet," The Art Story, https://www.theartstory.org/artist/millet-jean-francois/artworks/.

Images: Jean-François Millet, *The Sower*, 1850. Oil on canvas, 40 × 32½ in. (101.6 × 82.6 cm). Museum of Fine Arts, Boston. Gift of Quincy Adams Shaw through Quincy Adams Shaw, Jr., and Mrs. Marian Shaw Haughton [17.1485]. Photo: © 2023 Museum of Fine Arts Boston.

Honoré Daumier, *The Laundress*, c. 1863. Oil on panel, 19 × 13³⁄₁₆ in. (49 × 33.5 cm). Musée d'Orsay, Paris.

A Walk Captured

one of the earliest depictions of people in motion: Ian Jeffrey, *The Photography Book*, 2nd ed. (London: Phaidon, 2000), 343.

the faster, more flexible calotype process: Roger Taylor with Larry J. Schaaf, *Impressed by Light: British Photographs from Paper Negatives, 1840–1860* (New York: Metropolitan Museum of Art, 2007).

"painters of modern life": From the title of Charles Baudelaire's essay "Le peintre de la vie moderne," 1863, translated by Jonathan Mayne as *The Painter of Modern Life* (New York: Da Capo, 1964).

Image: Charles Nègre, *Chimney Sweeps Walking*, December 1851. Salted paper print, 6 × 7¹³⁄₁₆ in. (15.2 × 19.8 cm). National Gallery of Canada, Ottawa [1968-32485]. Photo: NGC.

Freedom Dress

"I can't express the pleasure my boots gave me": Anke Gleber, *The Art of Taking a Walk* (Princeton, NJ: Princeton University Press, 1999, 173.

Bloomers got their start in 1849: *Water-Cure Journal*, October 1849. See Catherine Smith and Cynthia Greig, *Women in Pants: Manly Maidens, Cowgirls, and Other Renegades* (New York: Abrams, 2003), 28.

"Bloomerism in Edinburgh": *Times* of London, August 28, 1851, 7, http://www.victoriancyclist.com/bloomerism-in-edinburgh-1851/.

"Let men be compelled to wear our dress": Amelia Bloomer, *Lily* 3, no. 3 (March 1851): 21.

Image: Unknown artist, "Bloomerism—An American Custom," cartoon, in *Punch* 21, September 27, 1851.

Caught in the Act

"We never understood it thoroughly": Oliver Wendell Holmes, "The Physiology of Walking" (1859), in *Pages from an Old Drawing of Life* (Boston: Houghton Mifflin, 1892), 127–28.

"balanced vertical projection": Oliver Wendell Holmes, "The Human Wheel," in *Soundings from the Atlantic* (Boston: Ticknor & Fields, 1864), 286.

"a perpetual falling with a perpetual self-recovery": Holmes, "Physiology of Walking," 127.

"no artist would have dared": Holmes, "Physiology of Walking," 127.

"Instantaneous" snapshots: On the evolution and blurry definition of instantaneous photography, see Phillip Prodger, *Time Stands Still: Muybridge and the Instantaneous Photography Movement* (New York: Oxford University Press, 2003). See also Brooke Belisle, "The Dimensional Image: Overlaps in Stereoscopic, Cinematic, and Digital Depth," *Film Criticism* 37, no. 3 (2013): 117–37, https://www.jstor.org/stable/24777979.

"Every foot is caught in its movement": Holmes, "Sun-Painting and Sun-Sculpture," in *Soundings from the Atlantic*, 184.

Images: F. O. C. Darley, "Walker Drawn from Stereoscopic View," illustration for Oliver Wendell Holmes, "The Physiology of Walking" (1859), in *Pages from an Old Volume of Life: A Collection of Essays, 1857–1881*, 7th ed. (Boston: Houghton, Mifflin, 1887), 125.

Edward Anthony, *Broadway on a Rainy Day*, stereoscopic view, 1859. Albumen silver print, $3\frac{1}{4} \times 6\frac{3}{16}$ in. (8.3 × 15.7 cm). Metropolitan Museum of Art, New York, Warner Communications Inc. Purchase Fund, 1980 [1980.1056.1].

The Long Walk

"the defense of the indefensible": George Orwell, "Politics and the English Language" (1946), in *Princeton Readings in Political Thought: Essential Texts from Plato to Populism*, ed. Mitchell Cohen (Princeton: Princeton University Press, 2018), 588.

"Indian Removal Act": Gary C. Anderson, *Ethnic Cleansing and the Indian: The Crime that Should Haunt America* (Oklahoma City: University of Oklahoma Press, 2014).

treated cruelly and left to die: Ruth Roessel, ed., *Navajo Stories of the Long Walk Period* (Tsaile, AZ: Navajo Community College Press, 1973).

the poorly chosen site: Gerald Thompson, *The Army and the Navajo: The Bosque Redondo Reservation Experiment, 1863–1868* (Tucson: University of Arizona Press, 1976).

photography is the imperialist tool: Cf. Roland Barthes, *Camera Lucida*, trans. Richard Howard (New York: FSG, 1981), 13: "Photography transformed subject into object, and even, one might say, into a museum object."

Image: Unknown photographer, Navajos under guard after a forced march to Fort Sumner, New Mexico, c. 1864. Original caption: "Fort Sumner, New Mexico. Guadeloupe County at the Bosque Redondo on Pecos River. Counting Indians." Photographic print, Department of Defense, Department of the Army, Office of the Deputy Chief of Staff for Operations, US Army Audiovisual Center, c. 1974–5/15/1984. Retrieved from the Digital Public Library of America, http://catalog.archives .gov/id/142663619. Reference number 87964 written on photo.

Terrific Apparition

"with due regard to the safety of Foot Passengers": Metropolitan Police handbill, 1868. Reproduced at https://en.wikipedia.org/wiki/File:Police_crossing_notice_1868.png.

"similar structures will no doubt be speedily erected": *South London Chronicle*, cited in Lorraine Boissoneault, "When the Street Light First Came to London, Disaster Ensued," *SmithsonianMag .com*, December 6, 2018, https://www.smithsonianmag.com/history/when-street-light-first-came -london-disaster-ensued-180970965/.

Images: Unknown artist, "The New Street Semaphore at Westminster," *Illustrated Times*, January 16, 1869. © The British Library Board. All Rights Reserved. With Thanks to The British Newspaper Archive (www.britishnewspaperarchive.co.uk)

Unknown artist ("L. T."), "Terrific Apparition—Seen during the Recent Fog at Westminster," *Punch*, March 20, 1869. Chronicle / Alamy Stock Photo.

A Sunday Walk with Madame Monet

painted outdoors: National Gallery of Art, "Woman with a Parasol—Madame Monet and Her Son, 1875," https://www.nga.gov/collection/art-object-page.61379.html.

"the heroism of modern life": Charles Baudelaire, "The Salon of 1846: On the Heroism of Modern Life," in *Modern Art and Modernism: A Critical Anthology*, ed. Francis Frascina and Charles Harrison (New York: Harper & Row, 1982), 17.

Image: Claude Monet, *Woman with a Parasol: Madame Monet and Her Son*, 1875. Oil on canvas, $39\frac{3}{8} \times 31\frac{7}{8}$ in. (100 × 81 cm). National Gallery of Art, Washington, DC, Collection of Mr. and Mrs. Paul Mellon [1983.1.29].

A Walk in the Rain

"Old Paris is no longer": Charles Baudelaire, "Le Cygne" (1861), in Baudelaire, *Les Fleurs du Mal, Œuvres Complètes*, ed. Claude Pichois (Paris: Gallimard 1961), 1:85 (my translation).

Caillebotte took stock: On Caillebotte's urban milieu, see Michael Marinnan, *Gustave Caillebotte: Painting the Paris of Naturalism, 1872–1887* (Los Angeles: Getty Research Institute, 2017); Kirk Vardenoe, *Gustave Caillebotte* (New Haven, CT: Yale University Press, 2000); and Hollis Clayson, *Illuminated Paris* (Chicago: University of Chicago Press, 2019).

Image: Gustave Caillebotte, *Paris Street; Rainy Day*, 1877. Oil on canvas, 83$\frac{9}{16}$ × 108$\frac{3}{4}$ in. (212.2 × 276.2 cm). Art Institute of Chicago, Charles H. and Mary F. S. Worcester Collection, [1964.336].

Women in the Mountains

"the free use of all the people": *Annual Report of the Forest Commission of the State of New York, 1892* (Albany: James Lyon, 1892), 22.

"It is of great merit that you climbed Mont Blanc": *Annuaire, Club Alpin Français 1894*, 20 (Paris: Hachette, 1894), 419 (my translation).

Image: Winslow Homer, *In the Mountains*, 1877. Oil on canvas, 23$\frac{7}{8}$ × 38 in. (60.6 × 96.6 cm). Brooklyn Museum, Dick S. Ramsay Fund [32.1648]. Photo: Wikimedia Commons.

Pedestrianism

Weston did more than anyone to bring pedestrianism to the masses: Matthew Algeo, *Pedestrianism: When Watching People Walk Was America's Favorite Spectator Sport* (Chicago: Chicago Review Press, 2014). See also Brian Phillips, "Pedestrian Mania: How Edward Payson Weston Became the Most Well-known Athlete in the World . . . in the 1870s," September 7, 2012, http://grantland .com/features/brian-phillips-edward-payson-weston/.

Image: Montague Chatterton and Co., advertisement for Astley Belt Competition, 1879. Photo: Islington Local History Centre.

The Shrouded Stride of Liberty

Bartholdi's aim was to signify: Behind Liberty's colossal form lurks the sculptor's earlier idea for a monumental statue of an Egyptian peasant woman, standing at the entrance to the Suez Canal, representing "Egypt Bringing Light to Asia."

Édouard René de Laboulaye, president of the French Anti-Slavery Society: Yasmin Sabina Khan, *Enlightening the World: The Creation of the Statue of Liberty* (Ithaca, NY: Cornell University Press, 2010), 40.

"Give me your tired, your poor": Emma Lazarus, "To the New Colossus" (1883), in *The Oxford Book of American Poetry*, ed. David Lehman (New York: Oxford University Press, 2006), 184.

Images: Frédéric Auguste Bartholdi, *Liberty Enlightening the World*, 1886. Photo: Pablo Costa Tirado, 2009, Wikimedia Commons.

Eugène Delacroix, *Liberty Leading the People*, 1830. Oil on canvas, 102⅜ × 128 in. (260 × 325 cm). Louvre, Paris.

Portrait in Shoe Leather

"In the stiffly rugged heaviness of the shoes": Martin Heidegger, "The Origin of the Work of Art" (1960), in *Off the Beaten Track*, ed. and trans. Julian Young and Kenneth Haynes (Cambridge, UK: Cambridge University Press, 2002), 14.

"veridical portraits of aging shoes": Meyer Schapiro, "The Still Life as a Personal Object—A Note on Heidegger and van Gogh" (1968), in *The Art of Art History: A Critical Anthology*, ed. Donald Preziosi (New York: Oxford University Press, 2009), 299.

Millet's drawing of a peasant child: Millet's monochrome drawing *First Steps* (*Les premiers pas*; c. 1858) was copied and colored by Van Gogh in January 1890.

Image: Vincent van Gogh, *Shoes*, 1886. Oil on canvas, 15 × 17¹³⁄₁₆ in. (38.1 × 45.3 cm). Van Gogh Museum, Amsterdam (Vincent Van Gogh Foundation) [s0011V1962]. Photo: Peter Barritt / Alamy Stock Photo.

Disembodied Motion

Marey had pictured motion without a body: Philippe-Alain Michaud, "Etienne-Jules Marey et la question des mobiles," *Cinémathèque* 10 (Autumn 1996), 113. On the larger context of Marey's work, see Andreas Mayer, *The Science of Walking: Investigations into Locomotion in the Long Nineteenth Century* (Chicago: University of Chicago Press, 2020).

There is a short line to be drawn: Richard Baker, "The History of Gait Analysis Before the Advent of Modern Computers," *Gait & Posture* 26, no. 3 (2007): 331–42.

"a luminous trace . . . at once multiple and unique": Jules Marey, *La chronophotographie* (Paris: Gautier-Villards, 1884), 11 (my translation).

Image: Étienne-Jules Marey, *Walking Man*, 1884. Photograph. Collège de France. Archives. Fonds Marey (3 PV 65).

The Walk Stripped Bare

Muybridge's eureka moment came: Gordon Hendricks, *Eadweard Muybridge: The Father of the Motion Picture* (New York: Dover, 2001); and Brian Clegg, *The Man Who Stopped Time: The Illuminating Story of Eadweard Muybridge, Pioneer Photographer, Father of the Motion Picture, Murderer* (Washington, DC: Joseph Henry Press, 2007).

Image: Eadweard Muybridge, nude man walking, in *Animal Locomotion: An Electro-Photographic Investigation of Connective Phases of Animal Movements* (Philadelphia: University of Pennsylvania / The Photo-gravure Company, 1887), plate 1.

The Gates Open

They experimented with movies for little more than a decade: Bernard Chardère, *Les images des Lumière* (Paris: Gallimard, 1995); and David Cook, *A History of Narrative Film*, 4th ed. (New York: W. W. Norton, 2004). The Lumière brothers believed that another of their inventions, color film, had more promise than motion pictures. See Bertrand Lavédrine and Jean-Paul Gandolfo, *The Lumière Autochrome: History, Technology, and Preservation* (Los Angeles: Getty, 2013).

Image: Lumière brothers, *Workers Leaving the Lumière Factory*, 1895. Still, 35mm film.

What the Walker Heard

"One evening I was walking along a path": Edvard Munch, diary entry, Nice, January 22, 1892, quoted in Zuzanna Stanska, "The Mysterious Road from Edvard Munch's *The Scream*," *Daily Art Magazine*, December 12, 2016, https://www.dailyartmagazine.com/the-mysterious-road-of-the -scream-by-edvard-munch/.

the bloodred sky originated: Fred Prata, Alan Robock, and Richard Hamblyn, "The Sky in Edvard Munch's *The Scream*," *Bulletin of the American Meteorological Society* 99, no. 7 (2018): 1377–90.

"You know my picture, 'The Scream?'": Quoted in Sue Prideaux, *Edvard Munch: Behind the Scream* (New Haven, CT: Yale University Press, 2005), 152.

"I was walking along the road with two friends": Quoted in Stanska, "Mysterious Road."

Image: Edvard Munch, *The Scream*, 1893. Oil, tempera, pastel and crayon on cardboard, $36 \times 28\,^{15}/_{16}$ in. (91 × 73.5 cm). National Gallery and Munch Museum, Oslo, Norway [NG.M.00939].

Walking in Love

An irony of copyright: "Jane Austen Illustrated," *Peter Harrington Journal* (blog), January 15, 2019, https://www.peterharrington.co.uk/blog/jane-austen-illustrated/.

Image: Charles Edmund Brock, "Most Beloved Emma—tell me at once!" Color lithograph from pen and ink drawing tinted in watercolor, in Jane Austen, *Emma* (London: Dent, 1898). Photo: © Look and Learn / Bridgeman Images.

The March of History

"The march of modern history": Karl Marx, *The Communist Manifesto*, ed. Samuel H. Beer (1848; New York: Appleton Century Crofts, 1955), 33.

the democratizing trend of the nineteenth century: Daniel Arasse, "La meilleure façon de marcher: Introduction à une histoire de la marche," in *Un siècle d'arpenteurs: Les figures de la marche*, ed. Maurice Frechuret (Paris: Réunion des Musées Nationaux, 2000), 35–62.

Anarchists, Communists, socialists: On the political side of Divisionist technique, see Dario del Puppo, "Il Quarto Stato," *Science & Society* 58, no. 2 (Summer 1994): 136–62.

an inevitable class struggle: Director Bernardo Bertolucci used *The Fourth Estate* in the opening credits of his 1976 film *Novecento*, to set the scene for his epic of class conflict in twentieth-century Italy.

"true strength is found in good, intelligent workers": Giuseppe Pellizza da Volpedo, cited in Arasse, "Meilleure façon de marcher," 60 (my translation).

Image: Giuseppe Pellizza da Volpedo, *The Fourth Estate/The Path of Workers*, 1899–1901. Oil on canvas, 9 ft. 7 in. × 17 ft. 11 in. (293 × 545 cm). Museo del Novecento, Milan.

Women Walk for Themselves

"awake at last": Emmeline Pankhurst, *My Own Story* (London: Eveleigh Nash, 1914), 38.

"the baby suffragette": "Infant Agitators," *Times* of London, March 22, 1907, "The Baby Suffragette," *Sheffield Daily Telegraph*, March 28, 1907, and "Baby Suffragette," *Leeds Mercury*, March 27, 1907; "You are only a child. You ought to be in school": *Sheffield Daily Telegraph*, March 28, 1907; "I don't wish to go back, sir": *Hull Daily Mail*, March 25, 1907. All are quoted in McKenzi Christensen, " 'Baby Suffragettes': Girls in the Women's Suffrage Movement across the Atlantic," *Thetean: A Student Journal for Scholarly Historical Writing* 48, no. 1 (2019): 85, https://scholarsarchive.byu.edu/thetean/vol48/iss1/7.

"We find ourselves in agreement with his Honour": *Sheffield Daily Telegraph*, March 28, 1907, quoted in Christensen, " 'Baby Suffragettes,' " 83.

"Now the hike along the Hudson seemed a foolish trip and vain": *Woman's Journal*, March 5, 1913; quoted in Jaime Schultz, "The Physical Is Political: Women's Suffrage, Pilgrim Hikes and the Public Sphere," in *Women, Sport, and Society*, ed. Roberta J. Park and Patricia Vertinsky (New York: Routledge, 2011), 29.

Image: Dora Thewlis being taken into custody, photo illustration in "Suffragettes Storm the House—Desperate Encounter with the Police—Wholesale Arrests," *Daily Mirror*, March 21, 1907. History and Art Collection / Alamy Stock Photo.

Sculpted Motion

"to contemplate it, to see it live, I don't need the fingers": Auguste Rodin, "La tête Warren," *Le Musée*, November–December, 1904, 298–301 (my translation).

Image: Auguste Rodin, *Walking Man*, 1907. Plaster model, large version, 84¼ × 64⁹⁄₁₆ × 27⁹⁄₁₆ in. (214 × 164 × 70 cm). Musée Rodin, Meudon. Photo: Adam Rzepka.

A Walk Goes to Pieces

"an explosion in a shingle factory": Julian Street, "Why I Became a Cubist," *Everybody's Magazine* 28 (June 1913), https://blackbird.vcu.edu/v12n2/gallery/street_j/cubist_page.shtml.

"The fact that I had seen chronophotographs": Marcel Duchamp, interview by Katherine Kuh, BBC, March 29, 1961, published in *The Artist's Voice: Talks with Seventeen Artists*, ed. Katherine Kuh (New York: Harper & Row, 1962), 103.

Echoing a twelve-frame sequence: Eadweard Muybridge, "Descending stairs and turning around" (1887), plate 137 of *Animal Locomotion: An Electro-Photographic Investigation of Consecutive Phases of Animal Movements*, National Gallery of Art website, https://www.nga.gov/collection/art-object-page.166637.html.

"Movement is an abstraction": Quoted in Pierre Cabanne, *Dialogues with Marcel Duchamp*, trans. Ron Padgett (Cambridge, MA: Da Capo, 1987), 30.

"one just doesn't do a nude woman coming down the stairs": Quoted in Cabanne, *Dialogues*, 44.

Newspapers mocked: J. F. Griswold, "Seeing New York with a Cubist: The Rude Descending a Staircase (Rush-Hour at the Subway)," *New York Evening Sun*, March 20, 1913.

"Fundamentally, movement is in the eye of the spectator": Quoted in Cabanne, *Dialogues*, 30.

Image: Marcel Duchamp, *Nude Descending a Staircase (No. 2)*, 1912. Oil on canvas, 57⅞ × 35⅛ in. (147 × 89.2 cm). Philadelphia Museum of Art. © Association Marcel Duchamp / ADAGP, Paris / Artists Rights Society (ARS), New York 2022.

In the Canyon

The photo has become an icon of American modernity: On Strand and "straight" photography, see Holland Cotter, "Young Paul Strand: Impressionable, Experimental," *New York Times*, March 20, 1998; and Peter Barberie and Amanda N. Bock, eds., *Paul Strand: Master of Modern Photography* (New Haven: Yale University Press, 2014).

Image: Paul Strand, *Wall Street*, 1915. Photograph.

The Tramp

"I wanted everything a contradiction"; "made me feel the person he was": Charles Chaplin, *My Autobiography* (1964; London: Penguin Classics, 2003), 145.

"He actually became a man with a soul": Charlie Chaplin, "A Comedian Sees the World," *Woman's Home Companion*, November 1933, quoted in https://en.wikipedia.org/wiki/The_Tramp.

"The Chivalric and heroic spirit": Henry David Thoreau, "Walking," *Atlantic Monthly* 9, no. 56 (June 1862): 658.

Image: Charles Chaplin, director, *The Tramp*, 1915. Film still, Essanay Studios, General Film Company.

From Walk of Life to March of Death

Over two hundred posters like this one: On the British recruitment effort, see Peter Simkins, *Kitchener's Army: The Raising of the New Armies, 1914–1916* (Manchester, UK: Manchester University Press, 1988).

Image: Unknown artist, Parliamentary Recruiting Committee poster, 1915. Library of Congress [cph 3g11013].

Into the Sunset

"a harrowing sight": John Singer Sargent to Evan Charteris, September 11, 1918, in Evan Charteris, *John Sargent* (New York, Scribner, 1927), 214.

"Gassed cases kept coming in": Quoted in Richard Ormond, *John Singer Sargent: Paintings Drawings Watercolours* (London: Phaidon, 1970), 258.

Image: John Singer Sargent, *Gassed*, 1919. Oil on canvas, 7 ft. 7 in. × 20 ft. ½ in. (231 × 611 cm). Imperial War Museum, London.

The Birth of the Long-Distance Trail

"a sanctuary and a refuge from the scramble of every-day worldly commercial life": Benton MacKaye, "An Appalachian Trail: A Project in Regional Planning," *Journal of the American Institute of Architects* 9 (October 1921): 329.

"1. to walk; 2. to see; and 3. to *see* what you see!": Benton MacKaye, 1971 interview, cited in Robert Moor, *On Trails* (New York: Simon & Schuster, 2016), 234.

"The AT as originally conceived": Benton MacKaye, quoted in Moor, *On Trails*, 241.

Image: E. S. Shipp, "Above the clouds on sharp top mountain peaks of Otter Country on the Appalachian Trail, Jefferson National Forest, Virginia," 1925. Forest History Society [FHS6470].

Mass Trespass

"hundreds of young men and women": Marcus Barnett, "The Kinder Scout Mass Trespass," *Jacobin Magazine*, April 21, 2018, https://jacobinmag.com/2018/04/kinder-scout-anniversary-worker -rambling-private-property.

the Countryside and Rights of Way Act 2000: https://www.legislation.gov.uk/ukpga/2000/37 /part/I.

"The law locks up the man or woman": English oral tradition, first known publication, 1800. Ian D. Morris, "Who Steals the Common from the Goose?" March 7, 2018, http://www.iandavidmorris .com/who-steals-the-common-from-the-goose/.

Image: "Peak District Ramblers in Trouble: Walking towards Kinder Scout on the Occasion of Their Battle with the Gamekeepers," photo illustration, *Illustrated London News*, April 25, 1932. © Illustrated London News Ltd. / Mary Evans / Mary Evans Picture Library Ltd. / agefotostock.

Goose-Stepping

"is only possible in countries where the common people dare not laugh": George Orwell, *The Lion and the Unicorn: Socialism and the English Genius* (London: Secker and Warburg, 1941), 21.

"The goose-step": Orwell, *Lion and the Unicorn*, 21.

"Satan couldn't have devised": Frank Capra, *The Name above the Title: An Autobiography* (New York: Macmillan, 1971), 346.

Schichlegruber: This was Hitler's grandmother's family name, and that of her illegitimate son, Hitler's father Alois, until he changed it in 1876 at the age of forty.

"animalistic hopping": Adam Green, "Lambeth Walk—Nazi Style (1942)," Open Knowledge Foundation, June 20, 2012, https://planet.okfn.org/category/charles-a-ridley/.

Image: Unknown photographer, Hitler reviews goose-stepping SS troops in front of the Frauen-kirche, Nuremberg, at a Nazi Party rally, c. 1935–38. Photo: Rue des Archives / granger.

Criminalizing the Walker

"Pedestrians must be educated": George M. Graham, address to the Society of Automotive Engineers, Washington, DC, December 15, 1924, published as "Cause and Prevention of Accidents," *Journal of the Society of Automotive Engineers* 16 (January 1925): 12. Quoted in Peter D. Norton, "Street Rivals: Jaywalking and the Invention of the Motor Age Street," *Technology and Culture* 48, no. 2 (April 2007): 354.

"one who crosses a street without observing the traffic regulations": Clive Thompson, "When Pedestrians Ruled the Streets," *Smithsonian Magazine*, December 2014, 2, https://www .smithsonianmag.com/innovation/when-pedestrians-ruled-streets-180953396/?page=1.

"all persons have an equal right": Miller McClintock for the Chicago Association of Commerce, "Report and Recommendations of the Metropolitan Street Traffic Survey," 133, quoted in Peter Norton, *Fighting Traffic: The Dawn of the Motor Age in the American City* (Cambridge, MA: MIT Press, 2008), 289.

"the slaughter of pedestrians": Quoted in Tom Vanderbilt, "In Defense of Jaywalking," *Slate*, November 2, 2009, https://slate.com/human-interest/2009/11/a-defense-of-jaywalking.html.

"A campaign of ridicule": *Grants Pass (OR) Rogue River Courier*, September 5, 1913, 3, Library of Congress, *Chronicling America: Historic American Newspapers*, https://chroniclingamerica.loc .gov/lccn/sn96088281/1913-09-05/ed-1/seq-3/.

National Automobile Chamber of Commerce falsely claimed: Norton, "Street Rivals," 356.

"DO YOU KNOW YOU ARE GUILTY OF JAYWALKING": Barron Collier, *Stopping Street Accidents: A History of New York City's Bureau of Public Safety* (New York, 1925), 76, quoted in Norton, "Street Rivals," 346.

"Pedestrians Have the Right of Way": For a nonlethal vision of urban design, see Jeff Speck, *Walkable City: How Downtown Can Save America, One Step at a Time* (New York: Farrar, Straus, Giroux, 2012). Nonwhite walkers are more likely to be hit: on racial disparities in pedestrian fatalities, see Angie Schmitt, *Right of Way: Race, Class, and the Silent Epidemic of Pedestrian Deaths in America* (Washington, DC: Island, 2020).

Image: Isadore Posoff, "Don't Jay Walk / Watch Your Step." Woodcut, Works Progress Administration Federal Art Project poster, Pennsylvania, 1937. Library of Congress [98518433]. Photo: Alpha Stock / Alamy Stock Photo.

Follow the Yellow Brick Road

The path stands out clearly, in a golden color: Gerald Clarke, *Get Happy: The Life of Judy Garland* (New York: Random House, 2000), 94. For background on the film, see John Fricke, William Stillman, and Jay Scarfone, *The Wizard of Oz: The Official 50th Anniversary Pictorial History* (New York: Warner, 1989).

Image: MGM studios publicity still for *The Wizard of Oz* depicting Judy Garland, Ray Bolger, Bert Lahr, Jack Haley, 1939. Photo: Photo 12 / Alamy Stock Photo.

Holocaust Death March

Nazi forces moved hundreds of thousands of prisoners: Joseph Freeman and Donald Schwartz, *The Road to Hell: Recollections of the Nazi Death March* (St. Paul, MN: Paragon House, 1998); "Dachau Concentration Camp," https://en.wikipedia.org/wiki/Dachau_concentration_camp#cite_note-Comit%C3%A9-35; and "Death Marches," https://encyclopedia.ushmm.org/content/en/article/death-marches.

reconsideration of the walking memorial: On "stumbling stones," see "Stolperstein," https://en.wikipedia.org/wiki/Stolperstein. On their controversial quality, see Project "Stumbling Blocks," minutes of the Munich, Germany, city council meeting, June 16, 2004, http://alt.stolpersteine-muenchen.de/Archiv/Docu/docu-040616-sitzg.htm.

Image: Fritz Melbach, a column of prisoners being evacuated from the Dachau concentration camp walk along Nördliche Münchner Strasse in Grünwald on a forced march to an unknown destination, April 29, 1945. CBW / Alamy Stock Photo.

The March of Dimes

"a march of dimes": Eddie Cantor, 1938, quoted in Barabara Maranzani, "Franklin Rooevelt's Personal Polio Crusade," August 31, 2018, https://www.history.com/news/franklin-roosevelts-personal-polio-crusade. On the larger organization and the crucial role of its co-founder Basil O'Connor, see David M. Oshinsky, *Polio: An American Story; The Crusade That Mobilized the Nation against the 20th Century's Most Feared Disease* (New York: Oxford University Press, 2005).

"Your dimes did this for me!": March of Dimes poster for year 1946, National Foundation for Infantile Paralysis.

beloved comedian Ramón Rivero: On Rivero's first walkathon, see http://www.diplo.org/_caminata/_esp/caminata_esp.htm.

Walkathons draw on the classic attractions: On charitable walkathons, see Rebecca Solnit, *Wanderlust: A History of Walking* (New York: Penguin, 2000), 59–61.

original walkathons of the Depression era: "The Walkathon of the 1930s," https://ultrarunninghistory.com/the-walkathon-walk-till-you-drop/.

Image: "Look! I Can Walk Again," March of Dimes poster (Linda Brown pictured), 1949. National Foundation for Infantile Paralysis.

Reading the Walker

To some, it is a classic: In an internet forum discussion of the picture in 2021, almost all commenters regarded the photo as depicting street harassment, one person remarking, "I would rather die than be in that woman's shoes. I know it's staged . . . but I can actually feel her terror." https://www.reddit.com/r/HistoryPorn/comments/of3uh7/american_girl_in_italy_1951_photo_by_ruth_orkin/.

"Public admiration . . . shouldn't fluster you": "When You Travel Alone," *Cosmopolitan*, September 1952, quoted in Emanuella Grinberg, "The Real Story behind 'An American Girl in Italy,' " CNN, March 30, 2017, https://www.cnn.com/2017/03/30/europe/tbt-ruth-orkin-american-girl-in-italy.

"I was thrilled": Ninalee Craig, 2017 interview, in Grinberg, "Real Story."

"Here was the perfect setting": Quoted in "Contemporary Photographs Explore Truth and Illusion in Reality Check," Metropolitan Museum of Art Press release, October 30, 2008, 6. Thomas J. Waston Library Digital Collections, https://libmma.contentdm.oclc.org/digital/collection/p16028 coll12/id/15125/.

"Got idea for pic story. Satire on Am. girl alone in Europe": Quoted in David Schonauer, "An Image of Innocence Abroad," *Smithsonian Magazine*, October 2011, https://www.smithsonianmag .com/travel/an-image-of-innocence-abroad-72281195/.

"the men were not arranged": Quoted in Schonauer, "Image of Innocence."

Image: Ruth Orkin, *American Girl in Italy*, 1951. Copyright 1952, 1980 Ruth Orkin. Used with special permission of the Ruth Orkin Photo Archive.

The Catwalk

Advisers to prospective models agree: "How to Walk Like a Catwalk Model," https://www .wikihow.com/Walk-Like-a-Catwalk-Model.

in Paris at the House of Worth: "Charles Frederick Worth (1825–1895) and the House of Worth," https://www.metmuseum.org/toah/hd/wrth/hd_wrth.htm. See also Amanda Fortini, "How the Runway Took Off: A Brief History of the Fashion Show," *Slate Magazine*, February 8, 2006, https://slate .com/culture/2006/02/a-brief-history-of-the-fashion-show.html.

Givenchy's debut show in Paris: "Backstage at Givenchy's First Collection—Spring 1952," May 6, 2016, https://glamourdaze.com/2015/03/backstage-at-givenchys-first-collection-spring -1952.html.

Image: Unknown photographer, Maison de Givenchy fashion show, Ivy Nicholson modeling, Paris, 1952.

Drifting

"The sudden change of ambiance": Guy Debord, "Introduction to a Critique of Urban Geography," trans. Ken Knabb, *Les Lèvres Nues* 6 (September 1955), https://www.cddc.vt.edu/sionline/presitu /geography.html.

"the society of the spectacle": Translation of title of Guy Debord's *La société du spectacle* (Paris: Buchet Chastel, 1967).

"*Psychogeography*": Debord, "Critique of Urban Geography."

"Never work": Graffito painted by Guy Debord on a wall in the rue de Seine, Paris, 1953, "Ne travaillez jamais," https://www.marxists.org/reference/archive/debord/1963/never-work.htm.

"a technique of rapid passage": Guy Debord, "Theory of the Dérive," trans. Ken Knabb, *Les lèvres nues* 9 (November 1956), https://www.cddc.vt.edu/sionline/si/theory.html.

"let themselves be drawn": Debord, "Theory of the Dérive."

Image: Guy E. Debord and Asger Jorn, *The Naked City: Illustration de hypothèse des plaques tournantes en psychogéographique*, 1957. Lithograph, 13 × 18½ in. (33 × 47 cm). Printed in Copenhagen,

May 1957. Reprinted in Asger Jorn, *Pour la Forme* (Paris: Internationale Situationniste, 1958). Reproduction courtesy A. Debord, Bibliothèque Nationale, and Beinecke Rare Book and Manuscript Library, Yale University.

A Downward Spiral

"Temple of Spirit," "test the possibilities": Quoted in *The Guggenheim: Frank Lloyd Wright and the Making of the Modern Museum* (New York: Guggenheim Museum Publications, 2009), 217–18.

"inverted ziggurat": William Allin Storrer, *The Architecture of Frank Lloyd Wright: A Complete Catalogue* (Chicago: University of Chicago Press, 2002), 400.

"let the elevator do the lifting": Quoted in Elyssa Goodman, "A Historical Look at the Solomon R. Guggenheim Museum," October 21, 2009, https://www.crfashionbook.com/culture/a29517903/a-historical-look-at-the-solomon-r-guggenheim-museum/.

"an uninterrupted, beautiful symphony": Frank Lloyd Wright to Harry Guggenheim, July 15, 1958, in *Frank Lloyd Wright: From Within Outward* (New York: Solomon R. Guggenheim Foundation, 2009), 268.

"museum fatigue": Benjamin Ives Gilman, "Museum Fatigue," *Scientific Monthly* 2, no. 1 (January 1916): 62–74.

Image: Ernst Hass, *The Spiral Interior of the Solomon R. Guggenheim Museum in New York, Designed by Frank Lloyd Wright*, 1961. Photo: Getty Images.

The Shopping Mall

"the Gruen transfer": M. Jeffrey Hardwick, *Mall Maker: Victor Gruen, Architect of an American Dream* (Philadelphia: University of Pennsylvania Press, 2015), 2.

Image: The Southdale Center, Edina, Minnesota, 1956. Photo: vint3 / Alamy Stock Photo.

Walking on Celluloid

The celebrated ending: Graham Greene, who wrote both the screenplay and the novella it was based on, imagined a happy ending. "One of the very few major disputes between Carol Reed and myself," Greene recalled, "concerned the ending, and he has been proved triumphantly right." See " 'The Third Man' as a Story and a Film," *New York Times*, March 19, 1950.

a walk itself can transform a character: Janice Mouton, "From Feminine Masquerade to Flâneuse: Agnès Varda's *Cléo in the City*," *Cinema Journal* 40, no. 2 (Winter 2001): 3–16; and Molly Haskell, "*Cléo from 5 to 7*," *Criterion Collection*, May 15, 2000, https://www.criterion.com/current/posts/87-cl-o-from-5-to-7. On cinematic walking, see Asli Özgen-Havekotte, *The Aesthetics and Politics of Cinematic Pedestrianism* (Amsterdam: Amsterdam University Press, 2022) and Thomas Deane Tucker, *The Peripatetic Frame: Images of Walking in Film* (Edinburgh: Edinburgh University Press, 2020).

Image: Agnès Varda, director, *Cléo from 5 to 7*, 1962. Film still, Athos Films.

One Heroic Step

Norman Rockwell was an unlikely candidate: Tom Carson, "The Awakening of Norman Rockwell," *Vox*, February 26, 2020, https://www.vox.com/the-highlight/2020/2/19/21052356/norman-rockwell-the-problem-we-all-live-with-saturday-evening-post.

Image: Norman Rockwell, *The Problem We All Live With*, 1963. Oil on canvas, 36 × 58 in. (91.4 × 147.3 cm). Illustration for *Look* magazine, January 14, 1964. Norman Rockwell Museum Collections. ©Norman Rockwell Family Agency.

Triumphal March

few social actions in history have accomplished so much: Gary May, *Bending Toward Justice: The Voting Rights Act and the Transformation of American Democracy* (New York: Basic Books, 2013); Wally G. Vaughn and Mattie Campbell, eds., *The Selma Campaign, 1963–1965: The Decisive Battle of the Civil Rights Movement* (Dover, MA: Majority Press, 2016); and "Selma to Montgomery Marches," https://en.wikipedia.org/wiki/Selma_to_Montgomery_marches.

"my legs were praying": Susannah Heschel, "Following in my Father's Footsteps: Selma 40 Years Later," https://www.dartmouth.edu/~vox/0405/0404/heschel.html.

Image: James Karales, *Selma to Montgomery March, Alabama*, 1965. Gelatin silver print. Photograph published in *Look* 29, no. 10, May 18, 1965, 32–33. © Estate of James Karales, Courtesy of Howard Greenberg Gallery, New York.

Walking into Art

"a walk through a grass field": Andrew Russeth, "Stanley Brouwn, Whose Works Examine Measurement and Memory, Dies at 81," *ARTnews*, May 22, 2017, https://www.artnews.com/art-news/news/stanley-brouwn-whose-works-examine-measurement-and-memory-dies-at-81-8380/.

"Walk all over the city with an empty baby carriage": Yoko Ono, *City Piece* (1961), in Yoko Ono, *Grapefruit* (1964; repr., New York: Simon & Schuster, 2000), 39.

"My idea of a piece of sculpture is a road": Phyllis Tuchman, "An Interview with Carl Andre," *Artforum* 8, no. 6 (June 1970): 57.

one dramatically simple work: Deiter Roelstraete, *Richard Long: A Line Made by Walking* (London: Afterall Books, 2010).

"no walk, no work": Quoted in "Hamish Fulton: Walking Journey," exhibition at Tate Britain, 2002, https://www.tate.org.uk/whats-on/tate-britain/exhibition/hamish-fulton-walking-journey.

"an object cannot compete with an experience": *Hamish Fulton: An Object Cannot Compete with an Experience*, exh. cat. (Norwich, UK: Sainsbury Centre for the Visual Arts, 2001). The artistic walking experience, often collective, has been traced by Blake Morris in *Walking Networks: The Development of an Artistic Medium* (London: Rowman & Littlefield, 2020).

"My intention was to make a new art": Quoted in Ben Tufnell, ed., *Richard Long: Selected Statements and Interviews* (London: Haunch of Venison, 2007), 39.

Image: Richard Long, *A Line Made by Walking*, 1967. © 2022 Richard Long. All Rights Reserved, DACS, London / ARS, NY. Photo: Tate.

Silly Walks

performed art walks drew attention: Ruth Burgon, "Pacing the Cell: Walking and Productivity in the Work of Bruce Nauman," *Tate Papers*, no. 26 (Autumn 2016), https://www.tate.org.uk/research /publications/tate-papers/26/pacing-the-cell.

"whatever I was doing in the studio must be art": Quoted in Art21.org, http://www.art21.org /artists/bruce-nauman.

"pacing around, for example": Bruce Nauman in Joan Simon, "Breaking the Silence: An Interview with Bruce Nauman," *Art in America* 76, no. 9 (September 1988): 140–48, https://www.artnews .com/art-in-america/features/breaking-silence-interview-bruce-nauman-63570/.

depicted walking stiff-legged off a cliff: Barry Blitt, "Silly Walk off a Cliff," cover illustration, *New Yorker*, July 4, 2016.

Images: Bruce Nauman, *Slow Angle Walk (Beckett Walk)*, 1968. Film still. © 2022 Bruce Nauman / Artists Rights Society (ARS), New York. Photo: Courtesy Electronic Arts Intermix (EAI), New York.
    John Cleese, "The Ministry of Silly Walks" sketch, *Monty Python's Flying Circus*, series 2, episode 1, aired September 15, 1970, BBC, screen capture.

One Small Step for a Man

"That's one small step for [a] man": "Armstrong 'Got Moon Quote Right,' " BBC News 2, October 2006, http://news.bbc.co.uk/2/hi/americas/5398560.stm. Analysis shows that Armstrong did not forget the "a"; it was covered by transmission static.

Yet what may be most remarkable: Rebecca Boyle, "The Most Compelling Photo of the Moon Landing," *Atlantic,* July 19, 2019, https://www.theatlantic.com/science/archive/2019/07/most -compelling-photo-moon-landing/594274/.

"Magnificent desolation": Quoted in Eric M. Jones, ed., "One Small Step," *Apollo 11 Lunar Surface Journal*, NASA, 1995, https://www.hq.nasa.gov/alsj/a11/a11.step.html. See also Buzz Aldrin, *Magnificent Desolation: The Long Journey Home from the Moon* (New York: Harmony, 2009), chap. 2.

"It's absolutely no trouble to walk around": Quoted in Jones, "One Small Step," 1995.

"I recommend it": Quoted in *60 Minutes* interview (2005), https://www.youtube.com/watch?v =iqzbnSymE2w&ab_channel=TheApollo11Channel.

Image: Neil Armstrong, Buzz Aldrin descending ladder, July 20, 1969. Photograph. NASA.

Crossing into History

"more popular than Jesus": John Lennon, quoted in Maureen Cleave, "How Does a Beatle Live? John Lennon Lives Like This," *London Evening Standard*, March 4, 1966. See also Meg Matthias,

"Did the Beatles Really Say They Were More Popular than Jesus?" https://www.britannica.com /story/did-the-beatles-really-say-they-were-more-popular-than-jesus.

Image: Iain Macmillan, album cover photo for the Beatles, *Abbey Road*, 1969. Photo: ©Apple Corps Ltd.

Walking on Air

"They called me": Philippe Petit, cited in "Tightrope Between the Towers," *PBS American Experience,* https://www.pbs.org/wgbh/americanexperience/features/newyork-tightrope.

Image: Alan Welner, *Philippe Petit Walking between World Trade Center Towers*, 1974. Associated Press.

Take Back the Night

As a phrase and rallying cry: The slogan was, however, used as a newspaper headline reporting on the original march in 1975. See Larry Eichel, "W. Phila. Poised to 'Take Back the Night,'" *Philadelphia Inquirer*, October 24, 1975.

largest single-day protest: Matt Broomfield, "Women's March against Donald Trump Is the Largest Day of Protests in US History, Say Political Scientists," *Independent*, January 25, 2017.

"Women's rights are human rights": Alejandra Maria Salazar, "Organizers Hope Women's March on Washington Inspires, Evolves," NPR.org. December 21, 2016. See also "2017 Women's March," https://en.wikipedia.org/wiki/2017_Women%27s_March.

"victim-blaming, slut-shaming, and sexual profiling are never acceptable": Quoted in https:// shamelessmag.com/blog/entry/this-sunday-wear-your-slut-pride-at-slutwalk.

"Whatever we wear": "Slutwalk—Whatever We Wear, Wherever We Go, Yes Means Yes and No Means No," *Cosmopolitan*, June 16, 2011, https://www.cosmopolitan.com/uk/worklife/campus /a12435/slutwalk-report/.

Image: Spencer Grant, "Women Unite, Take Back the Night," march led by the Boston Area Rape Crisis Center, the Fenway, Boston, 1979. Photo: Marmaduke St. John / Alamy Stock Photo.

Portable Sound

Walkman: https://en.wikipedia.org/wiki/Walkman.

"the Walkman effect": The term was introduced in 1984 in Shuei Hosokawa, "The Walkman Effect," *Popular Music* 4 (1984): 165–80. See also Michael Bull, "Investigating the Culture of Mobile Listening: From Walkman to Ipod," *Consuming Music Together: Computer Supported Cooperative Work* 35 (2006): 131–49. doi:10.1007/1-4020-4097-0_7.

Image: Peter Hoffman, designer, "There's a Revolution in the Streets," advertisement for Sony Walkman, 1980. Used by permission of Sony Electronics, Inc. All Rights Reserved.

A Walk to Remember

"I imagined taking a knife and cutting into the earth": Quoted in "The Woman Who Healed America," https://www.theattic.space/home-page-blogs/2019/10/23/the-woman-who-healed-america.

"I wanted to say, 'They're going to cry' ": Quoted in "Here's How a Controversial Work of Art Healed America after Vietnam," *Studio 360*, October 6, 2013, https://theworld.org/stories/2013-10-06/heres -how-controversial-work-art-healed-america-after-vietnam.

Image: Maya Lin, Vietnam Veterans Memorial ("The Wall"), National Mall, Washington, DC, 1982. Two polished granite walls (each comprised of 72 stone panels), 246 ft. 9 in. (75.21 m) in length, ranging from 10 ft. 21/16 in. (3.1 m) to 8 in. (20.3 cm) in height. Photo: National Park Service / Victoria Stauffenberg, 2000.

Migration

"they flee the Honduran nightmare": "Le Honduras, un pays 'pris en étau entre pauvreté extrême et ultraviolence,' " *Le Monde*, October 22, 2018, translated and cited in "Central American Migrant Caravans," https://en.wikipedia.org/wiki/Central_American_migrant_caravans.

"I had wanted to make a piece": Quoted in "Featured Artwork: Luis Jiménez," https://wfma .msutexas.edu/collection/featured-artwork/featured-artwork-luis-jimenez/.

With copies located in museums in several states: The Museum of Contemporary Art San Diego; the Blanton Museum of Art, Austin; the University of Texas at San Antonio; the Museum of Fine Arts, Houston; New Mexico Museum of Art, Santa Fe; and Iowa State University, Ames.

Image: Luis A. Jiménez Jr., *Border Crossing*, 1989. Polychrome fiberglass, 128 × 40 × 55 in. Collection of the New Mexico Museum of Art. Museum purchase with funds from the Los Trigos Fund, Herzstein Family Acquisition Endowment Fund, Friends of Contemporary Art, Margot and Robert Linton and Rosina Yue Smith, 1994 (1994.73.1). © Luis A. Jiménez Jr. Estate. Photo by Cameron Gay.

Crawling While Black

"Can I see the map": *One Morning in May* (2012), http://www.noemilakmaier.co.uk/html/omim .html. On challenges faced by disabled walking artists, see Morag Rose, "Access Denied? Walking Art and Disabled People," in *Walking Bodies: Papers, Provocations, Actions*, ed. Helen Billinghurst, Claire Hind, and Phil Smith (Axminster, UK: Triarchy, 2020), 225–34.

"costumes are a way to project yourself into the world": William Pope.L, Museum of Modern Art, https://www.moma.org/audio/playlist/301/3909.

"time-based endurance performances": William Pope.L, cited in Ross Simonini, "William Pope.L," *Interview Magazine*, January 20, 2013, https://www.interviewmagazine.com/art/william -popel.

the reality of kinesthetic empathy: "As a viewer, my perception of a moving body cannot be usefully separated from my imagining . . . what it might be like for my body to move that way." Katherine Profeta, *Dramaturgy in Motion: At Work on Dance and Movement Performance* (Madison: University of Wisconsin Press, 2015), 147.

Image: Pope.L, *The Great White Way, 22 Miles, 9 Years, 1 Street*, 2001–9, Performance © Pope.L. Photo: Courtesy of the artist and Mitchell-Innes & Nash, New York.

Walking High

"pry line": Annie Karni, "Life on the 'Pry' Line," *New York Post*, July 17, 2011.

lamented that he had failed the community: Laura Bliss, "The High Line's Next Balancing Act," *CityLab*, February 7, 2017, https://www.bloomberg.com/news/articles/2017-02-07/the-high-line -and-equity-in-adaptive-reuse.

"cattle chute": Justin Davidson, "The High Line Has Become a Tunnel Through Glass Towers," *New York Magazine Intelligencer*, January 7, 2019, https://nymag.com/intelligencer/2019/01/the -high-line-has-become-a-tunnel-through-glass-towers.html.

statue *Sleepwalker*: Vulnerable, even cuddly, in urban space, the statue appeared predatory to many in 2014 when situated on the rural campus of Wellesley College, an all-women's institution.

Images: Strollers on the High Line pass Tony Matelli's *Sleepwalker*, 2016. Photo: Li Muzi / Xinhua / Alamy Live News.
James Corner Field Operations, Diller Scofidio + Renfro, and Piet Oudolf, the High Line, New York, 2009–19. Photo: Timothy Schenck, Courtesy of Friends of the High Line, 2013.

Re-Viewing the Walking Tour

"characterized by their blindness": Michel de Certeau, "Walking in the City" (1980), in *The Practice of Everyday Life*, trans. Steven Rendall (Berkeley: University of California Press, 1984), 93.

"non-visual learner," "an effort to distance myself": Carmen Papalia, "Award 2017— Longlisted: *Blind Field Shuttle*," *Visible*, https://www.visibleproject.org/blog/project/blind-field -shuttle/.

"the position that I occupied": Papalia, "Award 2017."

"a tool that promoted my access and mobility": Carmen Papalia, "A New Model for Access in the Museum," *Disability Studies Quarterly* 33, no. 3 (2013), DOI: http://dx.doi.org/10.18061/dsq .v33i3.3757.

"blind field": Henri Lefebvre, *The Urban Revolution*, 1970, trans. Robert Bononno (Minneapolis: University of Minnesota Press, 2003), 29.

the scripted, often prerecorded "sound-walk": "Soundwalks," https://en.wikipedia.org/wiki /Soundwalk; and Lorna Parkes, " 'Sound walks' offer a new way to travel in lockdown," *Guardian*, November 16, 2020, https://www.theguardian.com/travel/2020/nov/16/sound-walks-new-way-to -travel-in-lockdown.

"helped me exercise my nonvisual senses": Papalia, "Award 2017."

Image: Carmen Papalia, *Blind Field Shuttle*, San Francisco, 2010–ongoing. Collaborative performance. Photo: Jordan Reznick, 2010, courtesy of the artist.

Street-Smart *Phoneur* or Smartphone Zombie?

Mobile phones and their wireless networks spread rapidly: The first cell phone call from a hand-held device was made by Motorola engineer Martin Cooper on April 3, 1973, while walking between Fifty-Third and Fifty-Fourth Streets on Sixth Avenue in Manhattan. By the early 2000s voice communication had yielded primacy to information processing. Phones added keyboards and then, with the iPhone in 2007, made widely available the capacitive touch screens that could input, display, alter, send, and receive digital images and data. "Given a choice, people will demand the freedom to communicate wherever they are," Cooper later explained, "unfettered by the infamous copper wire." See "Martin Cooper with Roman Kikta," January 30, 2012, https://mobilityventures.com/martin-cooper-with-roman-kikta-video/.

those who might be called *phoneurs*: On the model of the flâneur, a *phoneur* strolls the city erratically, but less through choice than due to distraction caused by the phone. The term was the result of a discussion on the Walking Artists Network (https://www.walkingartistsnetwork.org/) in October 2017, regarding possible terms for flâneurs who walk and listen.

"smartphone zombies": More used in Europe and Asia than in North America, the term appeared about 2014, describing preoccupied walkers in China, Japan, Hong Kong, Korea, Germany, and Britain. See https://en.wikipedia.org/wiki/Smartphone_zombie.

"One day on my way to work I was almost run over": Quoted in Daniel Uria, "Swedish Artist's Road Signs Warn against Smartphone Usage," November 17, 2015 https://www.upi.com/Odd_News/2015/11/17/Swedish-artists-road-signs-warn-against-smartphone-usage/8051447791990/.

forcing inattentive pedestrians: David Raven, "World's First Mobile Phone Walking Lane for 'Zombie Pedestrians' Addicted to Texting," *Daily Mirror*, September 15, 2014; and Janek Schmidt, "Always Practise Safe Text: The German Traffic Light for Smartphone Zombies," *Guardian*, April 29, 2016.

disrupting the rhythms of modern urban life: Veronique Greenwood, "If You Look at Your Phone While Walking, You're an Agent of Chaos," *New York Times*, March 30, 2021, D2.

walkie-talkies: The first device to be so named was a thirty-five-pound battery-powered backpack called the SCR-300. Made by Motorola for the United States military during World War II, it arrived in time to help the Allies invade Italy in 1943, and then featured in the Normandy invasions.

Image: Jacob Sempler and Emil Tiismann, artist-installed traffic signs warning motorists to watch out for cell phone users, Stockholm, 2015. Photo: Courtesy Jacob Sempler.

Body as Stylus

"taking a line for a walk": Paul Klee, Notebooks 1, *The Thinking Eye*, ed. Jurg Spiller, trans. Ralph Manheim (London: LH, 1961), 105.

***Running Stitch*:** Jen Southern and Jen Hamilton, *Running Stitch*, November 18–December 17, 2006, exhibition archive at https://www.fabrica.org.uk/running-stitch.

***Matrix of Movement*:** Tracy Claire Hill, "Matrix of Movement and Haecceity: Walking in Spatiotemporal Landscapes," *Living Maps Review*, no. 7 (2019), http://clok.uclan.ac.uk/31193/.

"geodetic pencil": Quoted in Simon Ferdinand, "Cartography at Ground Level: Spectrality and Streets in Jeremy Wood's *My Ghost* and *Meridians*," *Mapping beyond Measure: Art, Cartography, and the Space of Global Modernity* (Lincoln: University of Nebraska Press, 2019): 189, 179.

"Among the intricacies in the line qualities": Jeremy Wood, "GPS Tracings—Personal Cartographies," *Cartographic Journal* 46, no. 4 (November 2009): 365.

Image: Jeremy Wood, *My Ghost (Sixteen Years of Mapping My Life in London with GPS)*, 2016. Giclée print, 39⅜ × 39⅜ in. (100 × 100 cm). Photo: Courtesy of the artist.

The Watched Walker

"When the Government tracks the location of a cell phone": Editorial Board, "The Government Uses 'Near Perfect Surveillance' Data on Americans," *New York Times,* February 7, 2020.

"the naked rambler": "Top European Court Tells Nude Activist to Put Some Clothes On," *Time,* October 28, 2014, https://time.com/3543408/europe-court-naked-rambler/.

"you don't need people's cooperation": Huang Yongzhen, the CEO of Watrix, quoted in Dake Kang, "Chinese 'gait recognition' tech IDs people by how they walk," *AP News,* November 6, 2018, https://apnews.com/article/bf75dd1c26c947b7826d270a16e2658a.

"Would you like to report the jaywalker?": Dries Depoorter, *Jaywalking,* in Andy Greenberg, "Turning Live Surveillance Feeds into Unsettling Works of Art," *Wired,* March 25, 2016, https://www.wired.com/2016/03/turning-live-surveillance-feeds-unsettling-works-art/. On the resistance to watched walking, see Melanie Kloetzel and Phil Smith, *Covert: A Handbook* (Axminster, UK: Triarchy Press, 2021).

Image: Dries Depoorter, *Jaywalking,* 2015–ongoing. Gallery installation in Europe and North America. Photo: courtesy of the artist.

Walking on Water, Again

"The art is not just the pier": Jeff MacGregor, "The Inside Story of Christo's Floating Piers," *Smithsonianmag.com,* June 2017, https://www.smithsonianmag.com/arts-culture/inside-story-christo-floating-piers-180959072/.

"joy and beauty": Jeanne-Claude, cited in William Grimes, "Jeanne-Claude, Christo's Collaborator on Environmental Canvas, Is Dead at 74," *The New York Times,* November 19, 2009.

"The sum of the whole is this": Charles Dickens, cited in Maturin M. Ballou, *Treasury of Thought* (Boston: Houghton Mifflin, 1894), 547.

Image: Christo & Jeanne-Claude, *The Floating Piers, Lake Iseo, Italy, 2014–16.* Photo: Wolfgang Volz. © Christo and Jeanne-Claude Foundation. © 2022 Artists Rights Society (ARS), New York / ADAGP, Paris.

The Walking Wed

Richard Wagner's "Bridal Chorus": Elizabeth Hafkin Pleck, *Celebrating the Family: Ethnicity, Consumer Culture, and Family Rituals* (Cambridge, MA: Harvard University Press, 2000), 212.

Felix Mendelssohn's "Wedding March": William Emmett, *The National and Religious Song Reader* (New York: Haworth, 1996), 755.

walked alone down the aisle: On changing norms, see Heather Lee, "The Ultimate Guide to the Wedding Processional Order," September 11, 2020, https://www.brides.com/story/wedding -processional-order-guide; and Danielle Braff, "Walking Down the Aisle Alone," *New York Times*, March 18, 2021, https://www.nytimes.com/2021/03/18/style/walking-down-the-aisle-alone.html.

Image: Danny Lawson, Meghan Markle walks alone down the aisle, St. George's Chapel, Windsor Castle, May 19, 2018. PA Images.

Pandemic Walking

Whole swaths of the population: In the UK, for example, the number of walkers and walks taken both increased by about 25 percent in 2020. John Harris, "Walking Is a Glorious, Primal Pastime– and Far More Radical Than You Think," *Guardian*, December 26, 2021, https://www.theguardian .com/commentisfree/2021/dec/26/walking-glorious-primal-radical-hobby-lifeline/. For a deeper look at pandemic walking in the UK, see Dee Heddon, Morag Rose, Maggie O'Neill, Clare Qualmann, Harry Wilson, and Matthew Law, "These Times Were Made for Walking," in Matthias Ulrich, Fiona Hesse, and Marie Oucherif, eds., *Walk!* (Frankfurt: Schirn Kunsthalle Frankfurt, 2022), 137–43.

walked her husband: "Husband on Leash Breached Quebec's Covid Curfew," *BBC News*, January 12, 2021, https://www.bbc.com/news/world-us-canada-55631198. On other pandemic adaptations, see Sonia Overall, "Walking Together Apart," February 19, 2021, audio blog, http:// www.walkingartistsnetwork.org/2021/02/19/walking-together-apart-sunday-lockdown-walks/. See also Sonia Overall, "Distance Drift," February 3, 2019, in *Walkie Talkies: Christ Church Sport and Active Health*, presented by Paul Carney, podcast, https://anchor.fm/cccu-walkie-talkies; and Sonia Overall, "Walking through the Pandemic," interview by Stephen Donnelly, February 4, 2021, in *Four33: An Improvation Podcast*, hosted by Stephen Donnelly and Karey West, https://www .artseverywhere.ca/four33-episode-4/.

caused pedestrian fatalities to soar: Simon Romero, "Pedestrian Deaths Spike in U.S. as Reckless Driving Surges," *New York Times*, February 15, 2022, https://www.nytimes.com/2022/02/14/us /pedestrian-deaths-pandemic.html.

Image: Unknown creator, Internet meme, "Pandemic Walking," March 2020, based on Caspar David Friedrich, *The Wanderer above the Sea of Fog*, 1818. Oil on canvas, 37⅝ × 29⅞ in. (94.8 cm × 74.8 cm). Hamburger Kunsthalle, Germany.

Conclusion

"the disappearance of the artworks is a part of the aesthetic concept": Quoted in Gaby Reucher, "Why Christo's Floating Piers Had to Be Destroyed," August 5, 2016, https://www.dw.com/en/why -christos-floating-piers-had-to-be-destroyed/a-19450807.

"And whence they came": Wallace Stevens, "Sunday Morning" (1923), *The Collected Poems of Wallace Stevens* (1954; New York: Vintage, 1990), 70.